The
African American
Encyclopedia

Second Edition

The African American Encyclopedia

Second Edition

Volume 4
Fed-Hil

Editor, First Edition
Michael W. Williams

Consulting Editor, Supplement to First Edition
Kibibi Voloria Mack

Advisory Board, Second Edition

Barbara Bair
Duke University

Carl L. Bankston III
Tulane University

David Bradley
City University of New York

Shelley Fisher Fishkin
University of Texas, Austin

Wendy Sacket
Coast College

Managing Editor, Second Edition
R. Kent Rasmussen

Marshall Cavendish
New York • London • Toronto • Sydney

RT

Project Editor: McCrea Adams
Production Editor: Cindy Beres
Assistant Editor: Andrea Miller
Research Supervisor: Jeffry Jensen
Photograph Editor: Philip Bader
Page Layout: William Zimmerman

Marshall Cavendish Corporation
99 White Plains Road
Tarrytown, New York 10591-9001

© 2001 Marshall Cavendish Corporation
Printed in the United States of America
09 08 07 06 05 04 03 02 01   5 4 3 2 1

Library of Congress Cataloging-in-Publication Data

The African American encyclopedia.—2nd ed. / managing editor, R. Kent Rasmussen.
        p. cm.
Includes bibliographical references and index.
1. Afro-Americans—Encyclopedias. I. Rasmussen, R. Kent.
E185 .A253   2001
973'.0496073'003—dc21
ISBN 0-7614-7208-8 (set)   00-031526
ISBN 0-7614-7212-6 (volume 4)   CIP

∞ This paper meets the requirements of ANSI/NISO Z39.48-1992 (R1997)
Permanence of Paper for Publications and Documents in Libraries and Archives

Contents

The
African American
Encyclopedia

Second Edition

Federal Writers' Project: A federal government program intended to provide employment for American writers, journalists, editors, and research workers in the 1930's. Among those who received work through the project were a number of the time's most prominent African American writers.

From 1935 to 1943, the U.S. government funded an agency known as the Works Progress Administration (WPA), also known as the Work Projects Administration. Part of the New Deal struggle against the GREAT DEPRES-SION, the WPA undertook extensive building and improvement projects to provide work for the unemployed. Among its programs were the Federal Arts Project, the FEDERAL THEATRE PROJECT, the Federal Writers' Project, and the National Youth Administration.

The WPA Federal Writers' Project provided jobs for writers, journalists, editors, and researchers. Operating in all states, the project at one time employed sixty-six hundred people. Under the direction of Henry G. Alsberg, the project produced ethnic studies, folklore collections, local histories, and nature studies—more than a thousand books and pamphlets. The project's most important achievement was the American Guide series, which included guidebooks to every state and territory (except Hawaii); cities such as Washington, D.C., Philadelphia, and New York City; major highways (the Oregon Trail, Ocean Highway, and U.S. 1); and numerous towns, villages, and counties.

WPA regulations called for most of the project's personnel to come from the relief rolls. Some of the most important African American writers involved with the Federal Writers' Project included Claude McKAY, Richard WRIGHT, Ralph ELLISON, and Frank YERBY. In 1941, by the Congressional Emergency Relief Appropriation Act, the project was transferred to state sponsorship.

—*Marjorie Smelstor*

Publication of an affiliate program of the Federal Writers' Project celebrating the seventy-fifth anniversary of emancipation. *(Library of Congress)*

Ferguson, Clarence Clyde, Jr. (b. November 4, 1924, Wilmington, North Carolina): U.S. ambassador to Uganda from 1970 to 1972. Ferguson was also general counsel to the U.S. Commission on Civil Rights during the KENNEDY ADMINISTRATION. In the 1970's he was deputy assistant secretary of state for African affairs and U.S. representative to the Eco-

Clarence Clyde Ferguson, Jr., in 1974. *(AP/Wide World Photos)*

nomic and Social Council of the United Nations. Ferguson also taught law and wrote numerous books and articles on constitutional and international law.
See also: Diplomats.

Fetchit, Stepin (Lincoln Theodore Monroe Andrew Skeeter Perry; May 30, 1902, Key West, Florida—November 19, 1985, Woodland Hills, California): Actor. Stepin Fetchit was Hollywood's first African American star. After his initial great success in the early 1930's, the controversial comedian spent much of his time attempting to refute charges that he portrayed a stereotypical image detrimental to blacks.

Early Years
Born to a mother from the BAHAMAS and a father from JAMAICA, Fetchit grew up in MONTGOMERY, ALABAMA. He joined a plantation-show troupe, the Royal American Shows, sometime around 1914. He performed in MINSTREL and medicine shows using various names, including Rastus, the Buck Dancer; Jolly Pards; and Skeeter Perry. During a difficult period, he got in trouble with the law and served time in jail. After his release, he played the VAUDEVILLE circuit with a partner, Ed Lee. The two were billed as "Skeeter and Rastus: Two Crows from Dixie."

The comedian later claimed that he first heard the name Stepin Fetchit in TEXAS and that it was the name of a racehorse. He wrote a dance song based on the name, and he and his partner used the song in their act. In Tulsa, Oklahoma, a theater manager changed the act's name to "Step and Fetchit." Because of Lee's unreliability, the comedian soon fired his partner, became a solo act, and adopted Stepin Fetchit as his name.

Film Career
In the mid-1920's, Fetchit headed for Hollywood. Although he appeared in his first FILM, *In Old Kentucky*, in 1927, it was the first all-black musical, *Hearts in Dixie* (1929), that won him widespread critical and popular acclaim. Set on a plantation after the CIVIL WAR, *Hearts in Dixie* depicts an idyllic, blissful black life. Clarence Muse starred in the film, but during the filming Fetchit's comic talents so impressed the producers that his supporting role was expanded. Fetchit's characterization of the playful and flirtatious Gummy was highlighted by his strong screen persona and precise comic timing. His success led to a lucrative contract with Twentieth Century-Fox.

In the 1930's, Fetchit became one of the screen's most popular comedians. From 1929 to 1935, he appeared in twenty-six films, receiving feature billing in nine movies in 1934 alone.

Although his characters often had little significance to the plots of the films, scenes were written especially to showcase his talents. Primarily he portrayed a servant who moved in a lethargic manner and seemed ill-suited to perform even the most simple task. The five-foot, ten-inch actor shaved his head and wore ill-fitting, baggy pants. He appeared dim-witted and tended to butcher the English language. The popularity of his characterization influenced the acting styles of such comedians as Willie "Sleep 'n' Eat" Best and Mantan Moreland.

Although he appeared with such stars as Shirley Temple, Janet Gaynor, and Dick Powell, Fetchit was probably best known for his four films with satirist Will Rogers: *Judge Priest* (1934), *David Harum* (1934), *Steamboat 'Round the Bend* (1935), and *County Chairman* (1935). Of these films, *Judge Priest* proved to be the most popular. Directed by John Ford, the movie features Rogers as the title character and Fetchit and Hattie McDaniel as his servants. Although Rogers's character treats Fetchit's with abuse and condescension, most contemporary audiences enjoyed the relationship between the two men.

By the late 1930's, Fetchit's image was being increasingly criticized by African Americans. While some still hailed his comic genius, others accused him of perpetuating the racist tradition of the "coon" from the minstrel-show tradition. Civil rights groups felt that this degrading portrait was particularly inappropriate at a time when they were trying to refute perceptions of blacks as being inferior and when there were few other African American images in the popular media to counter Fetchit's characterization. According to Fetchit, the major studios yielded to these pressures; whatever the reason, he found film work only occasionally after the 1930's.

Personal Life

In 1929 Fetchit married seventeen-year-old Dorothy Stevenson in Los Angeles. A year after their marriage, his wife gave birth to a son. In 1935 Dorothy died, and Fetchit soon married a woman named Bernice, who bore him another son, Donald, in 1938. The couple was divorced in 1942.

It is difficult to separate fact from legend concerning much of Fetchit's personal life, since he seemed to thrive on exaggerated stories about his lifestyle. He boasted of an extravagant house, more than a dozen servants, expensive suits, and a fleet of luxury cars, each with its own elaborately dressed chauffeur. His most famous car was a pink Cadillac with his name written on both sides in neon lights. A sports enthusiast, he purchased blocks of tickets to boxing matches. Newspaper accounts cited his lavish parties, spending sprees, car accidents, and involvement in fights and brawls.

Fetchit formed a production company with the intention of filming the lives of such sports

Stepin Fetchit in *Hearts in Dixie* (1929). *(AP/Wide World Photos)*

greats as boxer Jack JOHNSON and baseball player Satchel PAIGE; however, his fortunes soured. The actor claimed to have earned at least $2 million by the early 1940's, yet he had to file for bankruptcy in 1944, citing $5 million in debts and only $146 in assets.

Later Years

Fetchit moved to CHICAGO and played small nightclubs as a stand-up COMIC between sporadic work in films. His most notable film role of this period occurred when John Ford cast him in *The Sun Shines Bright* (1953), a remake of *Judge Priest*. Continued criticism from the black community dissuaded television executives from showing his films often. When the films were shown, his scenes were sometimes removed.

In the early 1960's, Fetchit joined Muhammad ALI's entourage; he claimed to have taught Jack Johnson's "anchor punch" to Ali. In 1968 Fetchit became the plaintiff in a $3 million lawsuit against the CBS television network and the sponsors of the documentary "Black History: Lost, Stolen, or Strayed," hosted by Bill COSBY. Fetchit claimed that the film's depiction of him as the "symbol of the white man's Negro" cost him job opportunities. The suit languished in the judicial system for six years until a federal judge dismissed the case in 1974, citing that Fetchit's work could be criticized, since he was a public figure and the remarks were not personally directed at him.

In the late 1960's, Fetchit's health began to deteriorate. As a charity patient, he was hospitalized for a prostate operation in Chicago. In 1969 tragedy struck when his thirty-one-year-old son, Donald, went on a shooting rampage on the Pennsylvania Turnpike. The psychologically disturbed young man killed three people, including his wife, and wounded fifteen others before shooting himself.

In the 1970's, Fetchit appeared in two ill-fated films: *Amazing Grace* (1974), with Moms MABLEY, and *Won Ton Ton, the Dog Who Saved Hollywood* (1976). He also garnered recognition for his talents from some members of the black community, recognition for which he had long yearned. In 1974 he was inducted into the Black Filmmakers Hall of Fame, and in 1976 he received a Special Image Award from the Hollywood chapter of the NATIONAL ASSOCIATION FOR THE ADVANCEMENT OF COLORED PEOPLE (NAACP).

Once a devout Roman Catholic, Fetchit converted to ISLAM late in his life. In 1977, a year after suffering a stroke, he entered the Motion Picture Country House and Hospital in Woodland Hills, California, where he spent the final years of his life. At age eighty-three, he died of heart failure and pneumonia.

—Addell Austin Anderson

Suggested Readings:

Bogle, Donald. *Toms, Coons, Mulattoes, Mammies, and Bucks: An Interpretive History of Blacks in American Film.* 3d ed. New York: Continuum, 1994.

Euell, Kim. "Signifyin(g) Ritual: Subverting Stereotypes, Salvaging Icons." *African American Review* 31 (Winter, 1997): 667-675.

Foxx, Redd, and Norma Miller. *The Redd Foxx Encyclopedia of Black Humor.* Pasadena, Calif.: Ward Ritchie Press, 1977.

Landay, Eileen. *Black Film Stars.* New York: Drake, 1973.

McBride, Joseph. "Stepin Fetchit Talks Back," *Film Quarterly* 25 (Summer, 1971): 20-26.

"Whatever Happened to Lincoln (Stepin Fetchit) Perry." *Ebony* (November, 1971): 202.

Fields, Barbara Jeanne (b. Charleston, South Carolina): Historian. Fields earned her B.A. at Harvard University and her M.Phil. and Ph.D. at Yale. As her specialty she took on the study of nineteenth-century American Southern and social history. Her publications include extensive writings on SLAVERY and the CIVIL WAR, including *Slavery and Freedom, on the Middle Ground* (1985). Fields also appeared on Public Broadcasting Service presentations of *The Civil War* (1990) and *The Massachusetts 54th* (1991). Teaching appointments included positions at a number of prestigious schools, including Northwestern University (1974-1978), the University of Michigan (1978-1986), and Columbia University, beginning in 1986.

See also: Fifty-fourth Massachusetts Colored Infantry; Historiography.

Fields, Cleo (b. November 22, 1962, Louisiana): LOUISIANA politician. With his election to Congress in 1992, Cleo Fields became one of the most prominent young African American politicians in Louisiana.

Fields received his B.A. and law degrees from Southern University, a HISTORICALLY BLACK COLLEGE in Baton Rouge. In 1986 he was elected to the Louisiana State Senate, becoming the state's youngest senator. Fields was elected to the U.S. House of Representatives in 1992. After Louisiana governor Edwin W. Edwards announced his decision not to seek reelection, Fields declared his intention to run as a Democratic candidate for the office of governor. No candidate received a majority of the votes in the first election held in 1995, so a runoff election was held in November. In the runoff election, Fields was defeated by Mike Foster, a conservative white Republican.

See also: Congress members; Politics and government.

Fields, Mary (c. 1832, Tennessee—1914, Montana): Pioneer. Fields moved west to MONTANA to work at a school for Native American girls run by a mission. Her rough behavior eventually led to her removal after ten years of service. She became a stagecoach driver and cowhand, and she ran a stagecoach stop in Cascade, Montana. She was the second woman to drive a U.S. mail route, from Cascade to the mission where she had worked. Fields was said to have been able to knock a man down with a single punch, even into her seventies. *See also:* Frontier Society.

Fifteenth Amendment: Adopted on March 30, 1870, the third of the three so-called CIVIL WAR amendments to the CONSTITUTION added after the war.

After the Civil War ended in 1865, Congressional Republicans pushed this amendment so that African Americans would be able to vote. No doubt many RADICAL REPUBLICANS were sincere in supporting African American voting rights on moral grounds. Knowing that many Southern and border states would restrict the African American vote if they had a chance, the Republicans sought to secure African Americans' voting rights by constitutional amendment. Part of their desire to have African Americans able to vote undoubtedly stemmed from the fact these new voters would be overwhelmingly Republican.

Republican expectations were soon disappointed, as the U.S. SUPREME COURT and other white Americans circumvented or simply ignored the constitutional provision. By deciding that primary elections were essentially private nongovernmental group activities, the Court authorized all-white primaries. Democratic nominees, after winning the Democratic Party nomination in "white-only" primaries, could easily win the general election in the strongly Democratic South. By using poll taxes, literacy tests, and outright violent intimidation in many cases, Southern whites increasingly denied African Americans the right to vote.

Starting in 1944, when the Supreme Court outlawed white-only primaries, the situation slowly began to improve. It was not until legislation was passed in the 1960's, however—primarily the VOTING RIGHTS ACT OF 1965,

African Americans in New York City marching to celebrate the ratification of the Fifteenth Amendment in April, 1870. *(Library of Congress)*

with its activist provision of federal election registrars in southern states—that African Americans finally could vote without fear.

—*Richard L. Wilson*

See also: Voters.

Fifty-fourth Massachusetts Colored Infantry: An all-black infantry regiment founded in 1863. This unit was among the first, and the most famous, of the volunteer regiments established within the Union army during the CIVIL WAR. The creation of the Fifty-fourth Massachusetts was, in part, an experiment to determine whether African American troops were as capable in handling themselves in battle as were white soldiers. In battles at Milliken's Bend and at Port Hudson in the West during May and June of 1863, black troops proved themselves fully capable of standing up to the enemy in battle. In the early spring of

1863, Adjutant General Lorenzo Thomas traveled to the Mississippi Valley under orders to organize black regiments that would be assigned to fight (rather than to serve on garrison duty).

The Fifty-fourth Massachusetts Colored Infantry was established through the efforts of the state's governor, John Andrew, a staunch abolitionist. Volunteers were recruited for the regiment from throughout the North and from as far away as Milwaukee; included among the recruits were two sons of Frederick DOUGLASS. Recruitment was so successful that a second regiment, the Fifty-fifth Massachusetts Colored Infantry, was also established. Captain Robert Gould Shaw, a member of a prominent New England abolitionist family, was appointed as head of the Fifty-fourth Massachusetts and was promoted to the rank of colonel. As with other all-black regiments, the commander and other officers were white.

Shaw was determined that his regiment would be prepared for battle rather than placed on display. The men under his command were given extensive training, and Shaw lobbied vigorously for the chance to prove the unit's worth. Finally, in July of 1863, the Fifty-fourth Massachusetts was given orders to join Union troops who were struggling to regain control of Charleston, South Carolina. The entrance to the city's harbor was guarded by Fort Wagner, a strong Confederate earthwork manned by more than one thousand troops. Control of this fort was critical to capturing the city. After aerial bombardment of the fort proved insufficient, Union leaders determined that the fort could only be taken by direct assault. General Quincey Gillmore, commander of the fifteen thousand Union infantrymen assigned to capture the harbor, placed the Fifty-fourth Massachusetts at the forefront of the planned assault, which was scheduled to begin at dawn on July 18.

The frontal attack itself did not secure Union control of the fort. The Confederate troops were securely dug in behind strong breastworks that presented no obvious weakness to be exploited. Nevertheless, the Fifty-fourth Massachusetts did reach the fort's parapet and managed to hold it, despite massive casualties, for nearly an hour before Confederate guns and desperate hand-to-hand fighting drove them back. More than one-quarter of the men in the regiment, including Colonel Shaw, were killed in the fighting. Although they lost the battle, these African American soldiers had demonstrated that, with proper training, they were as capable as any white soldier in fighting for the Union cause.

The significance of the battle at Fort Wagner spread far beyond the Southern theater of the

Romanticized depiction of the taking of Fort Wagner painted in 1890. *(Library of Congress)*

war. Publicity surrounding the battle convinced people on both sides that African American soldiers could, and would, fight. Consequently, much of the antipathy and concern regarding the training and deployment of black soldiers expressed by whites in the North was reduced. The 1989 film *Glory* is a dramatization of the regiment's participation in the Civil War. *See also:* First Rhode Island Regiment; Military; Ninth Cavalry and Tenth Cavalry; Twenty-fifth Infantry; Twenty-fourth Infantry.

Film: From the earliest days of film production in the United States, African Americans played a part in the industry in ways that reflected their status and position in American society. At first they were nearly invisible in film depictions of mainstream American culture. Then they became barely visible as servants; later they became very visible, indeed, but as stereotypical caricatures.

The Silent Film Era

Inventor Thomas Edison, in some of his initial experiments with motion pictures, photographed some African Americans in what he called "interesting side effects" in 1893. In 1903 director Edwin S. Porter made a twelve-minute film called UNCLE TOM'S CABIN—but in his condensed version of the famous story, a white actor in BLACKFACE played the title role. All the black characters in D. W. Griffith's well-known THE BIRTH OF A NATION (1915), too, were played by whites in blackface.

Real African Americans did appear on film during the early silent era, but they were typically presented as insignificant or frivolous, as in Edison's *Ten Pickaninnies* (1904), in which a group of children identified as "snowballs," "coons," "black lambs," and "cute ebonies" frolicked on the screen. Remakes of *Uncle Tom's Cabin* in 1909 and 1913 continued to use white actors, but in 1914, a fourth version starred Sam Lucas, a black stage actor, who

was the first African American to perform a leading role in a film.

Griffith's use of blackfaced actors to depict African Americans in an unfavorable light led the NATIONAL ASSOCIATION FOR THE ADVANCEMENT OF COLORED PEOPLE (NAACP) to picket *The Birth of a Nation*'s New York premiere. Many other protests were staged by civil rights and religious organizations.

Meanwhile, black actors began to appear on screen. Comedian Bert WILLIAMS, for example, appeared in *Darktown Jubilee* in 1914, but the films were written, produced, and directed by white Americans. By the end of the silent era, the stereotypes that were to dominate the depiction of blacks in American films for the next four decades were already established. As film historian Donald Bogle notes, African Americans were confined almost exclusively to portraying "Toms," "coons," "mulattoes," "mammies," and "bucks." As far as the film industry was concerned, these shallow, often slanderous categories adequately covered the range of black experience. Even the most accomplished African American actors were trapped by them.

James B. Lowe, the star of the 1927 *Uncle Tom's Cabin*, was the first black actor to be promoted by Universal Pictures, but he was still playing the archetypal "Tom." Allen Clayton Hoskins became a child celebrity for his work in Hal Roach's *Our Gang* comedies during the 1920's, but he was essentially a type of "coon" character—the childlike, sexless buffoon whose antics were supposed to divert and delight the audience. (Hoskins was originally signed because his hair was so long he could play either a boy or a girl.) When they were not playing prominent stereotypical roles, African American actors were confined to bit parts; accomplished performers such as Rex Ingram, Noble Johnson, and Carolyn Snowden had small roles in such films as *The Ten Commandments* (1923), *The Navigator* (1924), *The Big Parade* (1925), and *King of Kings* (1927).

Hearts in Dixie is the story of a former slave's (Clarence Muse) efforts to educate his grandson. *(Museum of Modern Art, Film Stills Archive)*

The Advent of Sound

A film that revolutionized the motion picture industry, *The Jazz Singer* (1927), was also the final manifestation of the blackface tradition. Al Jolson, the film's white star, appeared on screen in burnt-cork makeup. Jolson was "a classic example of the MINSTREL tradition at its sentimentalized, corrupt best," according to Bogle, and his tremendous popularity launched the musical comedy as a major genre.

The myth of the African American as a musical wonder led the film industry to exploit its possibilities in *Hearts in Dixie* (1929), which featured an all-black cast singing and dancing in the cotton fields of the South, and the much more affecting *Hallelujah!* (1929), directed by King Vidor, which presented a moderately truthful picture of "black grief and passion." *Hearts in Dixie* featured Clarence Muse, Mildred Washington, and Stepin FETCHIT. Fetchit became the biggest early black film performer.

He appeared in twenty-six films between 1929 and 1935, almost always as a servant. For many filmgoers, his apparent jocularity and buoyancy functioned as a kind of comic relief from the anxiety of the GREAT DEPRESSION.

When African American actors were given roles with more dignity, they generally portrayed supportive domestics; for example, Bill "Bojangles" ROBINSON, the great dancer, appeared as a faithful guardian for Shirley Temple in several films. Clarence Muse was one of the most "humanized" black actors; director Frank Capra admired his work. Muse played an important role in *Show Boat* (1936) and cowrote (with Langston HUGHES) the screenplay for *Way Down South* (1939). Muse also wrote the screenplay for *Broken Strings* (1940).

Muse's attempts to gain some degree of control over the filmmaking process were part of a variety of strategies to get beyond the limits imposed by stereotypical characterization. African American filmmakers had been producing independent films since the LINCOLN MOTION PICTURE COMPANY was incorporated in 1916 by actor Noble Johnson and his brother George. The most wide-reaching of these independent efforts was the work of Oscar MICHEAUX, a director who made more than thirty low-budget independent films. From his first feature, *The Homesteader* (1919), through *Betrayal* (1948), Micheaux's films included such actors as Lorenzo Tucker (the "black Valentino") and Bea Freeman (the "sepia Mae West"). Micheaux also gave Paul ROBESON his first role, in *Body and Soul* (1924). Micheaux not only made the most of his extremely limited resources during production but also was ingenious in promoting his films.

On a larger scale, individual actors utilized their skills and wit to combat the confines of their roles. By the sheer magnitude of his physical presence and intelligence, Robeson, who had graduated Phi Beta Kappa from Rutgers University, where he was an All-American football player, dominated the screen in *The*

The Green Pastures recounts Old Testament stories through the eyes of a black Sunday school class. *(Museum of Modern Art, Film Stills Archive)*

feeling and strength of personality that subverted the secondary nature of their positions. Beginning with *Imitation of Life* (1934), Louise BEAVERS exhibited a stoicism and warmth that transcended her "supporting" roles. To fulfill the expectations of the stereotype, Beavers maintained a high-calorie diet, pretended to enjoy cooking, and learned to speak in dialect—subterfuges that enabled her to work steadily from 1932 (when she made ten films) into the 1960's.

Emperor Jones (1933), was unforgettable singing "Ole Man River" in *Show Boat* (1929), and had some fine moments in films he made abroad.

Similarly, Rex Ingram, starring in *The Green Pastures* (1936), a rare major-studio all-black spectacle, surmounted the sentimental story with his dignified acting. Ingram was also effective in many other films, including *Trader Horn* (1931), *King Kong* (1933), *The Adventures of Huckleberry Finn* (1939), *Cabin in the Sky* (1943), *The Thief of Bagdad* (1943), and *A Thousand and One Nights* (1948)—in which, as a genie released from a bottle, he exclaimed, "Free! I'm free at last!"

During the Depression years, African American women were typically cast as maids (unless they were sufficiently light-skinned—as Fredi Washington was—to play tragically ambiguous MULATTO characters). Despite the limited nature of such roles, some black actresses demonstrated a depth of

Hattie McDANIEL, who has been described as "a massive, high-strung mammy figure," also worked extensively; she appeared in eleven films in 1936 alone, and she won an Academy Award as best supporting actress for her role in *Gone with the Wind* (1939). Her Oscar was the first won by a black performer.

When Hattie McDaniel (left) accepted an Oscar from Fay Bainter on February 29, 1940, she became the first African American actor to win an Academy Award. *(AP/Wide World Photos)*

The 1940's Through the 1970's

The portrayal of African Americans as entertainers continued during WORLD WAR II. Both *Cabin in the Sky* and *Stormy Weather*, released in 1943, offered musical diversions. Lena HORNE, Ethel WATERS, and Eddie "Rochester" ANDERSON starred in a triangle romance in the first film. Horne, Fats WALLER, Cab CALLOWAY, Duke ELLINGTON, and Bill "Bojangles" ROBINSON starred in the second, which was loosely based on Robinson's life. After the war, actors such as Canada LEE, who starred in *Home of the Brave* (1949) as a sensitive soldier, were able to develop characterizations that did not depend on the familiar stereotypes.

Real change for African American actors began with the emergence of Sidney POITIER in *No Way Out* (1950), a film that began a series of productions examining racial problems in American society. In *No Way Out*, Poitier played a talented young doctor who is morally superior to the film's bigoted whites. In 1955 Poitier combined anger with poetic sensitivity in *Blackboard Jungle* (1956), in which he played the black counterpart of the James Dean-Marlon Brando rebel and loner.

Poitier's powerful screen presence soon gave him a uniquely high profile for a black actor in Hollywood. He typically played dignified, sensitive, intelligent heroes who served as implicit arguments for equality and integration during the CIVIL RIGHTS movement. He earned an Academy Award nomination for his role in *The Defiant Ones* (1958) and starred in *Porgy and Bess* (1959) and *A Raisin in the Sun* (1961) before winning a best actor Oscar for his performance in *Lilies of the Field* (1963). His success in such films as *A Patch of Blue* (1965), *Guess Who's Coming to Dinner* (1967), *To Sir, with Love* (1967), and *In the Heat of the Night* (1968) enabled him to begin working as a director. He both acted in and directed *Buck and the Preacher* (1972) and a series of social comedies with Bill COSBY beginning with *Uptown Saturday Night* (1974). Poitier's commercial appeal and critical success combined with the social currents of the times to permanently alter the place of blacks in American film.

Melvin VAN PEEBLES's *Sweet Sweetback's Baadasssss Song* (1971) showed a black man who refused to accept any degree of injustice and who was supported by the black community in his resistance. James Earl JONES, who had a small part in *Dr. Strangelove* (1963), portrayed Jack JOHNSON, another outspoken black rebel, in *The Great White Hope* (1970).

The early 1970's saw a wave of films that were nicknamed BLAXPLOITATION films. Gordon PARKS, Sr.'s film *Shaft*, starring Richard Roundtree and with music by Isaac Hayes, was a surprise hit and launched the genre in 1971. While these films showed blacks in strong lead roles, they also served to perpetuate stereotypes of African American behavior. *Shaft*, *Shaft's Big Score* (1972, also directed by Parks, Sr.), and *Superfly* (1972, directed by Gordon Parks, Jr., with music by Curtis MAYFIELD) were highly popular portrayals of the triumphs of strong black heroes. However, the shallowness and violence of the blaxploitation films led to protests; an organization called the COALITION AGAINST BLAXPLOITATION was even formed. By the mid- to late 1970's, the genre had fallen from popularity. The late 1980's and 1990's, however, saw a revival of interest in blaxploitation in the form of spoofs, such as *I'm Gonna Git You Sucka* (1988).

The 1980's and 1990's

The violence and anger of blaxploitation films were echoed but softened with a comic edge by Eddie MURPHY, who became popular in films such as *48 HRS* (1982), *Trading Places* (1983), and *Beverly Hills Cop* (1984) and its sequels. Murphy's performances drew on the satiric slant developed by Richard PRYOR, who costarred in a number of comedy-adventure films such as *Silver Streak* (1976) and *Stir Crazy* (1981).

(continued on page 919)

Notable Films by and About African Americans

Affair of the Skin, An (Zenith International, 1964). Controversial film about an unhappily married white man who has an affair with a model while his wife is away. He makes a black photographer a confidante with whom he discusses sex with his wife.

Amistad (Dreamworks, 1997). Fact-based epic retells the story of the taking of a Spanish SLAVE SHIP by Africans, who were subsequently tried for murder in the United States. Senegalese actor Djimon Hounsou plays Cinque, the leader of the slave revolt. Morgan Freeman plays an abolitionist leader who assists the slaves' legal defense.

Beloved (Touchstone, 1998). Based on the book by Toni MORRISON, an ex-slave (Oprah WINFREY) tries to forget about her past but is tormented by the emotional cost of her and her children's freedom. Cast also includes Danny Glover, Thandie Newton, and Kimberley Elise.

Best Man, The (Universal, 1999). Directed by Malcolm D. Lee. A reunion among college friends (Morris Chestnut, Taye Diggs, and Nia Long) who are attending the wedding of a member of their inner circle. A secret threatens to destroy the wedding and the relationship among best friends.

Beverly Hills Cop (Paramount, 1984). Eddie MURPHY plays a fast-talking Detroit police officer conducting an unauthorized investigation of a complex case in Beverly Hills. The contrast between the street-smart cop and the wealthy, snobbish milieu in which he finds himself provides this film with its best moments. The film inspired two sequels.

Arkent Archive

Bingo Long Traveling All-Stars and Motor Kings, The (Universal, 1976). Billy Dee Williams, James Earl JONES, and Richard PRYOR star in this comedy about a barnstorming baseball team trying to win a place in NEGRO LEAGUE BASEBALL during the GREAT DEPRESSION years.

Bird (Warner Bros., 1988). Exploration of the turbulent life of JAZZ saxophonist Charlie "Bird" PARKER, whose extraordinary musical talent helped launch the BEBOP style. This film explores the dark side of Bird's personality and the addictions to heroin and alcohol that hampered his career as a performer and ultimately caused the physical deterioration that led to his death of a heart attack at the age of thirty-four. Forest Whitaker plays Parker.

Birth of a Race (Frohman, 1918). In response to the negative depiction of African Americans in D. W. Griffith's THE BIRTH OF A NATION (1915), Emmet J. Scott's film offers a positive portrayal of blacks during the Civil War. This film was an artistic and financial failure but proved an inspiration to many black Americans.

Blackboard Jungle (Metro-Goldwyn-Mayer, 1955). Examination of juvenile delinquency in a racially integrated inner-city school, in which a dedicated white teacher (Glenn Ford) struggles to overcome the anarchy threatening his classroom. Sidney POITIER plays the student who torments him but eventually changes his ways. The film's unflinching look at problems confronting inner-city schools and its sensitive treatment of race made it a classic.

Black Girl (Cinerama, 1972). Directed by Ossie DAVIS. Explores the relationship between an African American woman, who feels that she is a failure, and her children.

Black Like Me (Continental, 1964). Based on a 1961 book of the same title by white journalist John Howard Griffin, who traveled through the Deep South after undergoing a process to darken his skin so he could pose as an African American. Although the notion that actor James Whitmore could "pass" as a black man seemed ludicrous, the film had a certain power in revealing the racial bigotry of other whites with whom he came into contact.

Museum of Modern Art, Film Stills Archive

Blacula (American International, 1972). After a modern African prince (William Marshall) is bitten by the legendary vampire Count Dracula (Charles McCauley), he goes on a bloody rampage in Los Angeles in director William Crain's BLAXPLOITATION horror classic.

Boyz 'N the Hood (Columbia, 1991). Written and directed by John Singleton, who became both the first African American director and the youngest director ever nominated for an Oscar, this film explores the struggle of a father (Larry Fishburne) to raise his son (Cuba Gooding, Jr.) decently in the midst of POVERTY and GANG violence.

Bright Road (Metro-Goldwyn-Mayer, 1953). Dorothy DANDRIDGE stars in this touching drama about the relationship between a young black boy and his schoolteacher.

Bright Victory (Universal, 1951). Post-World War II story of a blinded white veteran (Arthur Kennedy) coming to terms with his disability, who reflects on the narrowness and bigotry of his upbringing while forming a friendship with a man (Joe Morgan) who he does not realize is black.

Brother from Another Planet, The (Cinecom International, 1984). Combining elements of science fiction, religion, and social commentary, this innovative film follows the struggle of an extraterrestrial alien (Joe Morton) who lands on Earth while fleeing from a pair of intergalactic slave traders. Members of his race happen to resemble black human beings, and he makes his way to HARLEM, where he is befriended by local residents and learns that enslavement can also take the form of drugs and poverty. The fact that the slaver agents who pursue him happen to resemble white human beings provides a basis for both hilarious confusion and biting satire.

Brother John (Columbia, 1971). Sidney Poitier plays a Messiah-like figure who reappears in the small southern town in which he grew up. His appearance angers the white aristocracy and his strange powers bewilder both his friends and his enemies.

Buck and the Preacher (Columbia, 1972). Sidney Poitier directed himself in this adventure about two former slaves fleeing bounty hunters. As Buck, Poitier is persuaded by the preacher (Harry Belafonte) to join him in his scams. Ruby Dee is also featured.

Cabin in the Sky (Metro-Goldwyn-Mayer, 1943). All-black musical about a woman's high-living husband (Eddie "Rochester" ANDERSON) who falls for the beautiful Georgia Brown (Lena Horne). This film's portrayal of the husband reinforces negative stereotypes of African American men.

Carmen Jones (Twentieth Century-Fox, 1954). For her performance in this black musical, Dorothy Dandridge became the first African American performer ever nominated for a best actress Academy Award. This film tells the story of the beautiful Carmen Jones, who seduces a young soldier then rejects him for a prizefighter.

Claudine (Twentieth Century-Fox, 1974). Memorable look at black family life, starring Diahann CARROLL as a hard-working cleaning woman and single mother fighting to raise her children in the face of social and economic hardships.

Color Purple, The (Warner Bros., 1985). Adapted from Alice WALKER's 1982 novel, this dramatic film is about two sisters and their emotional separation and enduring love. The sisters are played by Whoopi GOLDBERG, who received an Academy Award nomination for best actress, and Oprah Winfrey, who was nominated for a best supporting actress Oscar.

(continued)

Cooley High (American International, 1974). Director Michael A. Schultz's first feature film, this comedy is set in an inner-city CHICAGO high school, whose seniors are preparing for graduation in 1964. Large cast includes Glynn Turman, Lawrence Hilton-Jacobs, Garrett Morris, Cynthia Davis, and Corin Rogers.

Cool World, The (Wiseman, 1963). One of the first feature films shot in Harlem, this drama concerns a fifteen-year-old African American whose only goal is to own a gun—which he believes will win him leadership of his gang and respect from others. Clarence Williams III stars.

Cornbread, Earl, and Me (American International, 1975). The shooting of a high school basketball star by the police and the efforts of his admirers to seek justice are the subjects of this drama adapted from Ronald L. FAIR's novel *Hog Butcher* (1966). Cast includes Moses Gunn, Bernie Casey, Rosalind Cash, Keith Wilkes, Larry Fishburne, and Madge Sinclair.

Museum of Modern Art, Film Stills Archive

Cotton Club, The (Orion Pictures, 1984). Tale set in the Jazz Age focusing on two sets of brothers, one white and one black. Real-life brothers Maurice and Gregory HINES play Sandman and Clay Williams, dancers whose relationship suffers under the strain of Sandman's ambitions. Much of this film is set in the legendary Cotton Club, the white-owned-and-attended club that featured many of the greatest black entertainers of the period. Lonette McKee, Larry Fishburne, Charles "Honi" COLES, and Woody Strode are also featured.

Cotton Comes to Harlem (United Artists, 1970). Directed by Ossie Davis, this action comedy set in Harlem is based on the 1965 novel of the same title by Chester HIMES. Godfrey Cambridge and Raymond St. Jacques play police detectives; comedian Redd Foxx appears in a supporting role, and some of the location shooting was done in the famed APOLLO THEATER.

Crooklyn (Universal, 1994). Directed by Spike Lee. Examines the lives of an African American family living in Brooklyn during the 1970's. The father (Delroy Lindo) aspires to become a jazz musician, while his wife (Alfre Woodard) struggles to support the family of five children.

Darktown Jubilee (1914). One of the earliest feature films to star a black actor, comedian Bert WILLIAMS, this film was controversial in its time because of its positive portrayals of African Americans.

Daughters of the Dust (Kino International, 1992). Written and directed by Julie DASH, this film is set in 1902 on the SEA ISLANDS, off the coast of South Carolina, and explores the lives of the GULLAH, descendants of slaves who have long lived in isolation from the mainland and who have retained their own customs and traditions.

Dead Presidents (Hollywood Pictures, 1995). Directed by Albert Hughes and Allen Hughes. Depicts the tragic journey of a young man (Larenz Tate) to adulthood during the VIETNAM WAR era. After returning from Vietnam, he cannot find a steady job to support his girlfriend and their daughter. He is convinced by his old friends to join them in robbing an armored car containing old paper money that is being returned to the Treasury Department to be destroyed.

Defiant Ones, The (United Artists, 1958). Drama of race relations approaching the issue from the point of view of two convicts, one black (Sidney Poitier) and one white (Tony Curtis), who escape while chained together. Forced by their bonds to work together, they forge a relationship that eventually cuts through racial barriers and prejudices.

Do the Right Thing (Universal, 1989). Produced, written, and directed by Spike Lee, this explosive depiction of racial violence is set during a heat wave in a black Brooklyn neighborhood. Stars Lee, Danny Aiello, Ossie Davis, and Ruby Dee. Lee received an Oscar nomination for his screenplay.

Down in the Delta (Miramax, 1998). Directed by Maya ANGELOU, this film explores black family values. A woman (Alfre Woodard) returns with her two children to her southern roots in an attempt to end her vicious cycle of alcoholism and drug abuse. Al Freeman, Jr., Mary Alice, Esther Rolle, and Wesley Snipes are also in the cast.

Driving Miss Daisy (Warner Bros., 1989). One of the most successful and honored films of its year, this drama, based on a Pulitzer Prize-winning play, explores the growing friendship between an elderly Jewish widow (Jessica Tandy) living in ATLANTA, GEORGIA, and her African American chauffeur (Morgan Freeman).

Duke Is Tops, The (Million Dollar Productions, 1938). Lena Horne made her feature film debut in this film, which helped launch the swing music era of the 1940's.

Edge of the City (Metro-Goldwyn-Mayer, 1957). This film is notable for the natural manner in which it presents the friendship between two men, declining to focus on the fact that one is white (John Cassavetes) and one is black (Sidney Poitier), instead concentrating on their qualities as individuals.

Museum of Modern Art, Film Stills Archive

Emperor Jones, The (United Artists, 1933). Paul ROBESON stars in this adaptation of Eugene O'Neill's play. An African American escapes a chain gang to become the ruler of a Caribbean island, whose people eventually rebel against him.

Eve's Bayou (Trimark Pictures, 1997). Directed by Kasi Lemmons, this film is the story of mothers, daughters, and grandmothers and how they relate to the men in their lives. Stars Lynn Whitfield, Samuel L. JACKSON, and Diahann Carroll.

For Love of Ivy (Cinerama, 1968). In this romantic comedy Sidney Poitier plays a charming gambler who falls in love with a maid (Abbey LINCOLN). Talked into dating her by the teenager brother and sister in the household where she works, Poitier soon finds himself considering abandoning his footloose lifestyle for more domestic comforts.

48 HRS. (Paramount, 1982). This highly successful action comedy marked Eddie Murphy's film debut. Murphy plays a wisecracking convict whom a San Francisco police officer (Nick Nolte) has released from prison for forty-eight hours to help him track down a killer.

Fresh (Miramax, 1994). "Fresh" is a quiet African American youngster who works as a runner for a New York City drug dealer. Although he tries to keep his private life separate from the drug underworld, he cannot keep the violence of the street from ruining the lives of his friends and family.

Get on the Bus (Columbia, 1997). Directed by Spike Lee. The story of fifteen African American men from the South Central area of Los Angeles who are traveling to the MILLION MAN MARCH in Washington, D.C. Andre Braugher, Ossie Davis, and Charles Dutton star.

Glass Shield, The (Miramax, 1995). Written and directed by Charles Burnett, this film explores the pairing of an African American man (Michael Boatman) and Jewish woman (Lori Petty) as rookie police officers assigned to a previously all-white, all-male sheriff's department in California. This film examines prejudice from both black and white perspectives.

Glory (Tri-Star Pictures, 1989). Dramatization of the true story of the FIFTY-FOURTH MASSACHUSETTS COLORED INFANTRY, which fought for the Union in the CIVIL WAR. Denzel WASHINGTON plays an angry runaway slave who enlists; Morgan FREEMAN plays an older enlistee who becomes the regiment's first black sergeant. Washington received an Academy Award as best supporting actor for his performance.

Go, Man, Go (United Artists, 1954). The HARLEM GLOBETROTTERS take center court in this film highlighting their remarkable combination of BASKETBALL skill and showmanship. The story traces the

(continued)

team's struggle to win a place in professional basket-ball at a time when African American athletes could not always compete against white teams.

Gone Are the Days (Trans-Lux, 1963). A preacher (Ossie Davis) stands up to a staunchly segregationist plantation owner, from whom he gets enough money to establish a church. Based on Davis's own play *Purlie Victorious*.

Gone with the Wind (Selznick, 1939). Sympathetic portrayal of the South during the Civil War, based on Margaret Mitchell's best-selling novel. Hattie McDANIEL became the first African American to win an Academy Award, for best supporting ac-

Arkent Archive

tress, for her powerful performance as a maid in Scarlett O'Hara's home. Other African American members of the cast include Butterfly McQUEEN.

Go Tell It on the Mountain (1984). Based on the 1953 novel by James BALDWIN, this television drama is about a young African American man's difficult life with his controlling and harsh stepfather, a stubborn preacher. Cast includes Paul Winfield, Ruby Dee, Rosalind Cash, and Alfre Woodard.

Greased Lightning (Warner Bros., 1977). Directed by Michael Schultz. Richard Pryor stars in this comedic depiction of a race car driver's efforts to surmount the sport's color barrier. Cleavon Little, Pam GRIER, and Beau Bridges costar.

Greatest, The (Columbia, 1977). Muhammad ALI plays himself in this film biography. Tracing Ali's life from his early years as a brash, ambitious young fighter, his rise to success as Cassius Clay, his interest in the teaching of MALCOLM X (James Earl Jones), and the public controversy that resulted from his refusal to enter the Army. This film contains real footage from several of Ali's fights.

Great White Hope, The (Twentieth Century-Fox, 1970). Examination of the life of Jack JOHNSON, the first African American boxer to become world

heavyweight champion. James Earl Jones reprised his stage role as Johnson.

Green Pastures, The (Warner Bros., 1936). Spirited retelling of Old Testament tales as seen through the eyes of a black Sunday school class. Although this film plays on stereotypes of African Americans, it possesses considerable charm and energy.

Guess Who's Coming to Dinner? (Columbia, 1968). Ground breaking in its day for its open treatment of INTERRACIAL MARRIAGE, this film centers on a young white woman (Katherine Houghton) engaged to marry a black doctor (Sidney Poitier). The story focuses on the couple's efforts to win the blessing of the woman's father (Spencer Tracy) for the marriage, an event that tests the older man's liberal convictions, even though his prospective son-in-law's credentials resemble those of a Nobel Prize-winning saint.

Hallelujah! (Metro-Goldwyn-Mayer, 1929). Early sound musical with an all-black cast. An innocent young cotton picker is seduced away from the girl he loves by a dancer named Chick, a situation that leads to tragedy. This film's cinematic merits are often overshadowed by its stereotypical portrayals of African Americans.

Museum of Modern Art, Film Stills Archive

Harlem Nights (Paramount Pictures, 1989). Written and directed by Eddie Murphy, this film is set in Harlem during the 1930's. Murphy and Richard Pryor play father-and-son owners of a casino. The supporting cast includes Redd Foxx, Della Reese, Arsenio Hall, and Jasmine Guy.

Hearts in Dixie (Fox, 1929). Generally upbeat and simplistic look at the lives of southern African Americans, centering on a former slave trying to educate his motherless grandson by sending him to a northern school. Originally categorized as a "novelty" picture, this film features a variety of song-and-dance numbers.

He Got Game (Touchstone, 1988). Spike Lee directed this powerful story about a felon (Denzel Washington) who is offered a chance at a reduced sentence by the governor if he can convince his estranged son to play basketball for the governor's alma mater.

Hero Ain't Nothin' but a Sandwich, A (1977). Drama based on the 1973 novel of the same title by Alice CHILDRESS. Cicely Tyson and Paul Winfield play the parents in a family living in an urban ghetto. The center of the story is a young boy who must deal with a father who has abandoned him, a stepfather, and loneliness.

Higher Learning (Columbia, 1995). Writer-director John Singleton's third effort places the subject of racial and sexual tensions in American society against the backdrop of a mostly white college campus. Omar Epps, Ice Cube, Laurence Fishburne, and Tyra Banks are featured members of this film's black ensemble cast.

Museum of Modern Art, Film Stills Archive

Hollywood Shuffle (Samuel Goldwyn, 1987). Produced, written, and directed by Robert Townsend, this comedy, in which he also stars, follows the fortunes of a struggling young black actor. The lack of quality roles for black actors and the stereotyping of African Americans in films and on television are among the topics that Townsend satirizes in his look at the entertainment industry. Keenen Ivory Wayans, who cowrote the script, had a small role.

House Party (New Line Cinema, 1991). Written and directed by Reginald Hudlin, this film is an African American variation on the popular teenage comedy genre. With all its action taking place within a twenty-four-hour period in the lives of a band of teenagers, this film traces the plans of two rappers who hope that their performance at the party of this film's title will impress two girls. This film was praised for its incorporation of the problems facing black teenagers into its story.

How Stella Got Her Groove Back (Fox, 1998). A single mother (Angela Bassett), joined by a successful businesswoman (Taye Diggs), vacations in Jamaica, where she falls in love with a much younger man.

Their age difference makes for some tough times between them and their families.

Hurricane, The (Universal, 1999). Dramatic film based on the story of boxer Ruben "Hurricane" CARTER, who was falsely accused of murder, convicted, and sent to prison. Denzel Washington plays Carter in a role that was expected to receive Academy Award consideration in early 2000.

I Like It Like That (Columbia, 1994). Writer-director Darnell Martin's debut feature, this comedy/drama drew publicity as the first major studio film directed by an African American woman. The story of a young African American and Latino couple (Lauren Velez and Jon Seda), living in the Bronx and struggling to keep their family together despite economic and sexual pressures. Racial tensions also threaten the couple's survival.

I'm Gonna Git You Sucka (United Artists, 1988). Written and directed by Keenen Ivory Wayans, this send-up of blaxploitation films stars Wayans as a young man searching for a suitably macho role model. He encounters a series of comic characters satirizing such action heroes as Shaft and Super Fly. This film's supporting cast includes Isaac Hayes, Jim Brown, and Clarence Williams III.

Imitation of Life (Universal, 1934). A white woman (Claudette Colbert) goes into business with her black maid (Louise Beavers). Although their business becomes a success, each woman has a young daughter who will grow up to bring her unhappiness. The white woman's daughter falls in love with her mother's fiancé; the black woman's daughter rejects her dark-skinned mother when she discovers that her own light skin will allow her to "PASS" for white. Groundbreaking in its relatively sympathetic treatment of the young black girl's plight, this film was nominated for an Academy Award as best picture.

In the Heat of the Night (Mirisch Company, 1967). A black Philadelphia police pathologist named Tibbs (Sidney Poitier) is mistakenly arrested for murder while visiting relatives in a Deep South town. After being cleared and released, he is assigned by his own superior to remain in the town and assist the bigoted local police chief (Rod Steiger) with the investigation, a situation that both men resent. This film re-
(continued)

ceived five Academy Awards, including best picture and best screenplay. Poitier reprised the Tibbs character in several subsequent series. During the 1990's the original story was adapted for television as a dramatic series in which Howard Rollins played Tibbs.

Island in the Sun (Twentieth Century-Fox, 1957). Set on an imaginary island in the British WEST INDIES, this film deals with the issue of interracial romance. Dorothy Dandridge plays a beautiful young woman who attracts the attention of a white government official, while Harry Belafonte is cast as an island labor leader who begins an ill-fated romance with a white woman.

Jackie Robinson Story, The (Eagle Lion, 1950). Baseball great Jackie ROBINSON plays himself in this biography, which also features Ruby Dee as his wife. Minor Watson plays Branch Rickey, the Brooklyn Dodgers president who hired Robinson in defiance of the color barrier that previously had kept black athletes out of professional baseball.

Jason's Lyric (Polygram, 1994). Explores the impact that a father's tragic death has on the lives of two very different sons—Joshua (Bokeem Woodbine), a gang member and prison convict, and Jason (Allen Payne), a gentle-natured store clerk. Jason's girlfriend Lyric (Jada Pinkett Smith), a young waitress who writes poetry, is a pivotal character in the choice Jason makes to pursue "the good life."

Joe Louis Story, The (United Artists, 1953). Biography of heavyweight boxer Joe LOUIS. Incorporating actual footage of several of Louis's famous bouts, this film balances its portrayal of its subject's athletic prowess with a realistic look at the toll fame took on his personal life.

Jo Jo Dancer, Your Life Is Calling (Columbia, 1986). Richard Pryor directed himself in this semi-autobiographical story about a comedian battling drug abuse. He reflects on his tragic past, beginning with growing up in his grandmother's brothel.

Juice (Paramount, 1992). Directed by Ernest Dickerson. A gritty, chaotic, downbeat, and realistic portrait of life in the streets of Harlem. The lives of four black teenage friends take a tragic turn when a store robbery goes out of control and they find themselves on the run. Starring Omar Epps and Tupac Shakur.

Jungle Fever (Universal, 1991). Written and directed by Spike Lee, this controversial portrait of an interracial romance stars Wesley Snipes as a black married architect and Annabella Sciorra as a white secretary with whom he has an affair, sparking anger from both black and white communities.

Lady Sings the Blues (Paramount, 1972). Diana Ross received an Oscar nomination for her moving performance as singer Billie HOLIDAY in this retelling of the singer's career and tragic life. This film traces Holiday's life, from her childhood through her growing success as a singer to the drug addiction that haunted her. Billy Dee Williams, Richard Pryor, and Scatman Crothers costar.

Lean on Me (Warner Bros., 1989). Morgan Freeman stars in this film based on the true story of New Jersey high school principal Joe Clark, who gained national celebrity by using unconventional disciplinary techniques to turn around a crime-plagued school.

Learning Tree, The (Warner Bros./Seven Arts, 1969). Directed by Gordon PARKS, Sr. Set in Kansas during the 1920's, this film tells the story of a young African American boy's coming of age. It was the first feature film financed by a major Hollywood studio and directed by an African American.

Liberation of L. B. Jones, The (Columbia, 1970). A wealthy African American man (Roscoe Lee Browne) divorces his attractive young wife (Lola Falana) because of her infidelities with white men.

Life (Universal, 1999). Sardonic comedy about a street hustler and naïve bank teller who are framed for murder by a corrupt southern sheriff and sentenced to serve in a Mississippi chain gang. Starring Martin Lawrence and Eddie Murphy.

Lilies of the Field (United Artists, 1964). Sidney Poitier became the first African American to win an Oscar as best actor, for his performance as a traveling handyman in this film. When he arrives at an isolated mission farm in the Southwest run by five German nuns, the Mother Superior insists that he is God's answer to her prayers and begins the gradual process of persuading him to stay long enough to perform all the repairs their mission post needs.

Long Walk Home, The (Miramax Films, 1990). Set in Alabama during the 1955 MONTGOMERY BUS BOYCOTT, this film focuses on the relationship between a white housewife (Sissy Spacek) and her black housekeeper (Whoopi Goldberg). When the housekeeper joins the boycott and begins walking to work, the housewife offers to drive her and is gradually drawn into the Civil Rights movement.

Look Out Sister (Astor, 1948). A largely African American cast performs in this musical satire on Western films. A young man dreams that he is saving the woman whom he loves from an evil rancher, who threatens to foreclose on the ranch where she lives.

Losing Isaiah (Paramount, 1995). Story of a recovering crack addict (Halle Berry) who had abandoned her infant son Isaiah years earlier and later decided to seek parental custody. This film explores the complex issues of TRANSRACIAL ADOPTION.

Lost Boundaries (RD-DR, 1949). In one of the earliest Hollywood films to deal seriously with race, a fair-skinned mulatto couple (Mel Ferrer and Beatrice Pearson) cannot find employment in their small community because of racial prejudice, so they move to New England and try living as "whites." Eventually their past catches up with them.

love jones (New Line, 1997). Romantic tale of blossoming love between two young professional adults. Starring Nia Long and Larenz Tate.

Mahogany (Paramount, 1975). Directed by Berry GORDY, Jr. Diana Ross stars in this melodrama about the life of a FASHION model and clothing designer. This film also stars Billy Dee Williams as the politician Ross loves. This film is notable chiefly for its reteaming of Ross and Williams after their successful pairing in *Lady Sings the Blues* (1972).

Malcolm X (Warner Bros., 1992). Directed by Spike Lee, this epic film biography follows the life of MALCOLM X, played by Denzel Washington, from hustler and convict to charismatic leader to martyred prophet. Other actors include Angela Bassett, Delroy Lindo, Lonette McKee, James McDaniel, and Al Freeman, Jr.

Museum of Modern Art, Film Stills Archive

Man, The (Paramount, 1972). James Earl Jones stars in this intriguing drama about the difficulties facing the first black president of the United States. As the president pro tem of the Senate, the title character suddenly finds himself elevated to the presidency after a series of accidents and illnesses kills or disables everyone ahead of him in the line of succession.

Man Called Adam, A (Embassy, 1966). Sammy DAVIS, Jr., stars in this drama centering on the life of a fictional jazz musician. Haunted by a tragic past, Davis's character faces discrimination and a series of broken romances in his struggle for success. Cicely Tyson, Lola Falana, Jeanette Du Bois, and Ossie Davis are in the supporting cast, and jazz musician Louis ARMSTRONG gives a strong performance as Tyson's grandfather.

Menace II Society (New Line Cinema, 1993): Directed by Allen and Albert Hughes. Examines two young black men living in Los Angeles's WATTS district during the 1990's, when guns, drugs, and senseless violence are the tragic reality in the lives of young black men.

Milk and Honey (Castle Hill, 1989). Relates the experiences of a Jamaican woman who leaves her young son David with her mother while seeking a better life as a live-in nanny for a Toronto couple. Discovering that an immigrant's life has far more hardship than milk and honey, she fights to get the government documents—"landed papers"—that will allow her son to live with her in CANADA.

(continued)

Mississippi Masala (Black River, 1992): In an unusual twist on interracial romance themes, Denzel Washington plays an African American who falls in love with an Asian woman (Sarita Choudhury) whose family settles in a small Mississippi town after being expelled from Uganda during the 1970's.

Mo' Better Blues (Universal, 1991). Writer-director Spike Lee's fourth feature film explores the world of jazz and musicians. Denzel Washington plays a trumpet player whose devotion to his music leaves him little time for the two women in his life. Also featuring Spike Lee, Joie Lee, Wesley Snipes, and Cynda Williams. This film was criticized for its portrayal of two Jewish nightclub owners in a manner which was deemed anti-Semitic.

Native Son (Cinecom, 1986). Adapted from Richard Wright's novel of the same title about a young African American chauffeur, played by Victor Love, who becomes the center of a highly publicized trial after accidentally murdering the daughter of his white employer. Oprah Winfrey, Matt Dillon, and Elizabeth McGovern also star.

New Jack City (Warner Bros., 1991). Directed by Mario Van Peebles, this fictional account of the spread of the drug trade in the United States begins during the early 1980's, when drug dealers discover crack, a potent and cheap form of cocaine. The head of a New York drug consortium (Wesley Snipes), sets up a fortified factory inside a Harlem housing project and terrorizes the residents into accepting his presence. The drug ring is destroyed by a black narcotics detective. Ice-T, Judd Nelson, Allen Payne, and Chris Rock are featured.

Norman . . . Is That You? (Metro-Goldwyn-Mayer, 1976): Redd Foxx and Pearl BAILEY star as the confused parents of a homosexual son with a white lover.

Nothing but a Man (DuArt, 1964): A young man (Ivan Dixon) in the Deep South enters into a troubled marriage with the better-educated daughter (Abbey Lincoln) of a minister. After struggling against racial discrimination in his employment, he leaves his wife. Yaphet Kotto and Gloria Foster also star.

No Way Out (Twentieth Century-Fox, 1950). A young African American doctor (Sidney Poitier) is threatened with violence when he fails to save the life of a white man injured in a gunfight. The dead man's brother incites his gang to violence, and racial hatred on both sides leads to a full-scale riot.

Officer and a Gentleman, An (Paramount, 1982). Louis Gossett, Jr., received an Oscar as best supporting actor for his compelling performance as a tough Navy drill sergeant who represents the best hope that an arrogant recruit (Richard Gere) has for turning his life around.

One Potato, Two Potato (Bawalco, 1964): Story of a marriage between a white woman (Barbara Barrie), who has been deserted by her first husband, and an African American man (Bernie Hamilton) whom she meets at the plant where she works.

Patch of Blue, A (Metro-Goldwyn-Mayer, 1965). Moving and unusual story of a blind white girl (Elizabeth Hartman) who falls in love with a man (Sidney Poitier) without realizing that he is black. Trapped in a bleak, unhappy life with her bigoted mother and grandfather, the woman finds the first love she has ever known with the intelligent, sympathetic Poitier.

Museum of Modern Art, Film Stills Archive

Pinky (Twentieth Century-Fox, 1949). Set in the South, this film examines the life of a young African American woman (Jeanne Crain) called "Pinky" because of her light skin. Returning from a northern nursing school to the home of her grandmother (Ethel Waters), Pinky faces the harsh realities of her situation when she inherits property from a white woman and her white, northern boyfriend proposes marriage. This film was critically acclaimed for its bold handling of a sensitive and difficult subject.

Poetic Justice (Columbia, 1993). Director John Singleton's second feature film deals with an offbeat love affair between a self-styled poet named Justice (Janet JACKSON) and a troubled mailman named Lucky (Tupac SHAKUR). Although the two are initially hostile toward each other, they become romantically involved as Lucky attempts to reach past Justice's loneliness.

Porgy and Bess (1959). This adaptation of George and Ira Gershwin's Broadway musical is set in a poverty-stricken tenement called Catfish Row, where Porgy (Sidney Poitier) falls in love with Bess (Dorothy Dandridge) and kills her former lover (Brock Peters). Sammy Davis, Jr., Diahann Carroll, and Ivan Dixon also are featured.

Posse (PolyGram, 1993). Directed by Mario Van Peebles. A band of African American soldiers deserts the battlefields of Cuba during the SPANISH-AMERICAN WAR with captured gold and journey to the American West. The film draws parallels between the American West and modern urban violence, with references to the 1992 LOS ANGELES RIOTS.

Preacher's Wife, The (Touchstone, 1996). An angel (Denzel Washington) returns to earth to help save a church, its minister (Courtney B. Vance), and his disheartened wife (Whitney Houston).

Purple Rain (Warner Bros., 1984). A showcase for the  talents of rock star PRINCE, this film is a semi-autobiographical look at a young musician's life and career. Morris Day and Jerome Benton play Prince's musical rivals, Apollonia Kotero plays the woman he loves, and Clarence Williams III plays his brutal father.

AP/Wide World Photos

Rage in Harlem, A (Miramax, 1991). Set in Harlem in 1956, this film tells the story of a con woman (Robin Givens), who has fled Mississippi with stolen gold. Also featuring Forest Whitaker, Gregory Hines, and Danny Glover. Adapted from a novel by Chester Himes.

Ragtime (Paramount, 1981). Adaptation of E. L. Doctorow's best-selling 1975 novel, interweaving fact and fiction in a re-creation of American life in the early twentieth century. The most prominent among the novel's many interlocking stories that was used in the film is that of Coalhouse Walker, Jr., (Howard Rollins), a fictional RAGTIME pianist who is driven to become a revolutionary after a series of racial incidents leads to the death of the woman (Debbie Allen) he loves.

Raisin in the Sun, A (Columbia, 1961). Portrait of an urban African American family. After Lena Younger (Claudia McNeil) receives ten thousand dollars in insurance money, a family quarrel erupts as her daughter (Diana Sands), her son (Sidney Poitier), and his wife (Ruby Dee) fight over how to spend the money.

Reivers, The (Cinema Films, 1969). Engaging portrait of life in the South that highlights a pervasive atmosphere of racial injustice. Adapted from *The Reivers* (1962) by William Faulkner, this film is set in Mississippi and Tennessee in the early twentieth century.

River Niger, The (1976). Deals with the problems facing a Los Angeles poet and house painter (James Earl Jones), his wife (Cicely Tyson), who suffers from CANCER, and the rest of their African American community.

Rosewood (Warner Bros., 1997). Fictionalized account based on the true story of an all-BLACK TOWN which became a victim of a white lynch mob. Starring Ving Rhames, Don Cheadle, Esther Rolle, and Elise Neal.

Sankofa (Burkina Faso/Germany/Ghana, 1993). Creative depiction of the journey of a woman back to slavery. This film's title is taken from a West African name for a mythological bird that looks into the past in order to prepare for the future. This film earned critical acclaim for its unflinching examination of the complexities of the African slave trade.

School Daze (Columbia, 1988). Produced, written, and directed by Spike Lee. The rivalry between light- and dark-skinned African Americans is the controversial topic of Lee's second feature film. A musical set in a

Museum of Modern Art, Film Stills Archive

(continued)

fictional black college, this film follows the conflicts between the light-skinned "Wannabees" and the darker-skinned "Jigaboos." Larry Fishburne, Giancarlo Esposito, Tisha Campbell, Kadeem Hardison, Jasmine Guy, and Ossie Davis are members of the all-black cast.

Set It Off (New Line, 1996). Story of four women who, for various reasons, join together to rob banks in Los Angeles. Starring Jada Pinkett Smith, Vivica A. Fox, QUEEN LATIFAH, Kimberly Elise, and Blair Underwood.

Shadows (Lion, 1961). Directed by John Cassavetes. After a light-skinned African American woman falls in love with a white man, she neglects to tell him that she is black—not out of shame, but because she feels that the fact is not important. When the man discovers the truth, however, she learns that matters of skin color are never unimportant in America.

Shaft (Metro-Goldwyn-Mayer, 1971). Directed by Gordon Parks, Sr., this is the first film in a popular series featuring Richard Roundtree as a cool, streetsmart private eye named John Shaft. The plot revolves around the kidnapping of the daughter of a Harlem mobster and Shaft's efforts to find her.

She's Gotta Have It (Island Pictures, 1986). Written, edited, produced, and directed by Spike Lee, this is the story of a young woman, Darling (Tracy Camila Johns), juggling three lovers (Lee, Tommy Redmond Hicks, and John Canada Terrel). *She's Gotta Have It* was Lee's breakthrough picture and the start of greater acceptance of black filmmakers.

Museum of Modern Art, Film Stills Archive

Show Boat (Universal, 1936). Adaptation of the 1927 musical. The story revolves around the show boat's star performer (Helen Morgan), an African American "passing" for white.

Six Degrees of Separation (Metro-Goldwyn-Mayer, 1993). Will Smith plays Paul, a young homosexual who passes himself off as the unacknowledged son of actor Sidney Poitier in order to ingratiate himself with a rich white couple. Explores how perceptions of race and class affect the way individuals treat each other and perceive themselves.

Skin Game, The (Warner Bros., 1971). Entertaining comedy set in the Old South. A pair of white and black con men (James Garner and Lou Gossett, Jr.) runs a scam that involves Garner selling Gossett into slavery, Gossett escaping, and the pair splitting the proceeds. The interplay between the two actors is central to this film's appeal.

Slaves (1969). Ossie Davis stars in this remake of *Uncle Tom's Cabin* as a masochistic slave who takes over the Big House on the plantation on which he works with a mysterious female slave played by Dionne Warwick.

Soldier's Story, A (Columbia, 1984). Adaptation of Charles Fuller's play *A Soldier's Story* (1981), set during WORLD WAR II. An unpopular African American officer is murdered on a segregated army base and another black officer (Howard Rollins) is assigned the difficult task of investigating the crime.

Song of the South (RKO Radio-Disney, 1947). Based on Joel Chandler Harris's Uncle Remus stories, this partly animated musical features James Baskett as Uncle Remus, the amiable black storyteller, and Hattie McDaniel as Tempy, the maid. Often criticized for its romanticized portrayal of the Old South.

Soul Food (Twentieth Century-Fox, 1997). The bonds of an African American family are tested after their matriarch dies. Starring Vanessa L. Williams, Nia Long, Vivica A. Fox, Michael Beach, and Mekhi Phifer.

Sounder (Twentieth Century-Fox, 1972). This portrayal of black family life among SHARECROPPERS during the Depression received Oscar nominations for best picture, best actor, best actress, and best screenplay. The story profiles a proud, hardworking

Museum of Modern Art, Film Stills Archive

couple who struggle to maintain their dignity and provide for their children in the face of overwhelming hardships. Kevin Hooks, Cicely Tyson, and Paul Winfield star.

Stir Crazy (Columbia, 1980). Directed by Sidney Poitier. Richard Pryor and Gene Wilder reteamed to make this prison comedy. Falsely accused of bank robbery, they receive life sentences and must use their wits to adapt to prison life. This film's chief appeal lies in the comedic talents of its stars.

St. Louis Blues (Paramount, 1958). Biography of bluesman W. C. HANDY, starring Nat "King" COLE as Handy and featuring a stellar cast that includes Eartha KITT, Ella FITZGERALD, Mahalia JACKSON, Ruby Dee, and Pearl Bailey, who perform many musical numbers.

Stormy Weather (Twentieth Century-Fox, 1943). Showcase for the talents of Lena Horne and dancer Bill "Bojangles" ROBINSON, this film also includes in its cast Cab CALLOWAY and his band, Dooley Wilson, Ada Brown, the Nicholas Brothers, Coleman HAWKINS, and Fats WALLER, performing "Ain't Misbehavin'." The story is told in flashbacks as the retired Corky (Robinson) reminisces about his career and his on-

again/off-again romance with Selina (Horne). Loosely based on Robinson's life.

Straight out of Brooklyn (Samuel Goldwyn, 1991). Written and directed by Matty Rich, this bleak story of a young black man's attempt to free himself from a life of poverty by committing a crime marked Rich's feature film debut. Longing to free himself from a dismal future and a family life marked by his father's anger and domestic violence, the teenager plans a crime that he hopes will make him rich.

Superfly (Warner Bros., 1972). Directed by Gordon Parks, Jr. One of the first of what would be labeled "blaxploitation" pictures, this film tells the story of a drug pusher (Ron O'Neal) who plans to leave his chosen profession once he gets rich from one last deal.

Sweet Sweetback's Baadasssss Song (Yeah, 1971). Melvin Van Peebles directed himself as an African American man who kills two racist police officers and manages to escape the law.

Take a Giant Step (United Artists, 1958). Singer Johnny Nash plays a troubled black teenager from an affluent family who searches for a place for himself in both the black and the white communities. This film lacks dramatic impact, but it is earnest and well intentioned in its treatment of the young man's problems.

Tales from the Hood (Savoy, 1995). Directed by Rusty Cundieff. This anthology of horror tales lightly spoofs the stories made popular by television series such as *The Twilight Zone* and *Tales from the Crypt.* Cundieff puts his own African American spin on the horror genre, combining gangsta rap and other elements of black popular culture to liven up conventional horror plots.

Tap (Tri-Star Pictures, 1989). Gregory Hines stars as a former convict who is torn between returning to a life of crime and pursuing a career as a tap dancer. A standout among the supporting players is Sammy Davis, Jr., making his final film appearance. This film also features appearances by such famed tap dancers as Harold Nicholas, Howard "Sandman" Sims, Bunny Briggs, and Jimmy Slyde.

To Kill a Mockingbird (Universal, 1962). Adapted from Harper Lee's novel, this sensitive and powerful film tells the story of a southern town torn apart when a black sharecropper (Brock Peters) is accused of raping a white woman during the 1930's. It explores the complexities of life in a small community in which warmth and hospitality exist side by side with racial hatred and violence. Gregory Peck won an Academy Award for his performance as the lawyer who defends the accused black man.

To Sir with Love (Columbia, 1967). Set in a London slum, this film centers on the efforts of a black

(continued)

teacher (Sidney Poitier) to reach a class of troubled, economically disadvantaged, white students. Slowly earning their respect through a combination of humor, discipline, and understanding, the teacher manages to educate his students while instilling in them a sense of

Museum of Modern Art, Film Stills Archive

purpose and self-respect. In many ways, this film was an analogue of the 1955 film *Blackboard Jungle*.

To Sleep with Anger (Samuel Goldwyn, 1990). Written and directed by Charles Burnett. This original, offbeat film is set in Los Angeles, where a family's life is disrupted by the arrival of a friend (Danny Glover) from the South. Embraced by some members of the family and mistrusted by others, the visitor is an enigmatic figure, by turns sinister and seemingly magical.

Up Tight (Marlukin, 1968). In a story set in Cleveland shortly after the assassination of Martin Luther King Jr., Raymond St. Jacques leads a group of African American revolutionaries well armed with guns and slogans. Ruby Dee and Julian Mayfield costar.

Uptown Saturday Night (Warner Bros., 1974). Directed by Sidney Poitier. This popular comedy stars Poitier and Bill Cosby as friends out on the town for the night without their wives. When thieves steal Poitier's wallet, which contains a valuable lottery ticket, the men enlist the aid of private eye Richard Pryor. The strong supporting cast includes Harry Belafonte, Roscoe Lee Browne, Paula Kelly, and Flip Wilson.

Waiting to Exhale (Twentieth Century-Fox, 1995). Tale of four women and their relationships with the men in their lives and with each other. Starring Angela Bassett, Whitney Houston, Lela Rochon, and Loretta Divine.

Walking Dead, The (Savoy, 1995). This action film focuses on five marines—all but one of whom are African American—sent on a suicide mission to rescue survivors of a prisoner-of-war camp during the VIETNAM WAR. The cast includes Joe Morton, Allen

Payne, Eddie Griffin, and Vonte Sweet, each of whose stories is personalized through flashbacks.

Watermelon Man (Columbia, 1970). Directed by Melvin Van Peebles. A white insurance salesman's comfortable suburban life is shattered when he wakes up one morning to find that he has become black. This film's humor lies both in actor Godfrey Cambridge's reaction to his character's situation and in the ways in which his family, friends, and co-workers respond to his change.

What's Love Got to Do with It (Touchstone, 1993). Based on rock legend Tina TURNER's 1986 autobiography *I, Tina*. After meeting musician Ike Turner (Larry Fishburne), young Tina (Angela Bassett) launches not only a professional career but also a romantic liaison. Chronicling the demise of that relationship as a result of Ike's drug addiction, infidelity, and persistent abuse of his wife, this film shows Tina finding the strength to end the marriage and rebuild her career as a solo performer during the early 1980's.

Which Way Is Up? (Universal, 1977). Directed by Michael Schultz, this comedy follows the fortunes of a farm worker who becomes a labor leader and is then co-opted by management as part of a quota hiring program. Starring Richard Pryor, Lonette McKee,

Museum of Modern Art, Film Stills Archive

and Margaret Avery. Pryor plays three roles: the farm worker, his father, and a corrupt minister.

Why Do Fools Fall in Love (Warner Bros., 1998). Story of teen singing sensation Frankie LYMON, played by Larenz Tate, and his three wives. Halle Berry, Vivica A. Fox, and Lela Rochon costar.

Wiz, The (Universal, 1978). Adaptation of the Broadway musical based on L. Frank Baum's children's classic, *The Wizard of Oz*. In this all-black story set in New York City, Dorothy (played by an obviously adult Diana Ross) learns that she can find what she is looking for within herself. The cast includes Michael JACKSON, Nipsey Russell, Lena Horne, and Richard Pryor.

Wood, The (Paramount, 1999). On their friend's wedding day, three old friends recollect growing up together in Inglewood, Calif., during the 1980's. Cast includes Taye Diggs, Omar Epps, and Richard T. Jones.

World, the Flesh, and the Devil, The (Metro-Goldwyn-Mayer, 1959). A black coal miner (Harry Belafonte) and a white woman (Inger Stevens) and man (José Ferrer) are the only survivors of a nuclear holocaust. They must deal with issues of survival and racism while trying to rebuild their lives.

Until the mid-1980's, when filmmakers such as Spike LEE, Robert Townsend, John Singleton, and Carl Franklin began to direct films from material they developed about the African American experience, major black actors worked largely in films produced and directed by whites. Danny GLOVER and Whoopi GOLDBERG won recognition for their roles in director Steven Spielberg's *The Color Purple* (1985), based on the novel by Alice WALKER. The film created a dramatic rendering of life in the black community. In the 1980's African Americans in Hollywood at last began to be cast in roles that were not conspicuously race-conscious, such as Glover's villain in *Witness* (1985), Goldberg's character in *Ghost* (1990), and Lou GOSSETT, Jr.'s characters in *An Officer and a Gentleman* (1982) and *Iron Eagle* (1986).

Through all these changes, the dynamics of racial politics often continued to place black actors in variants of old stereotypes in such films as *Street Smart* (1987; in which Morgan FREEMAN played a pimp) or *Driving Miss Daisy* (1989; in which Freeman played a servant). Among Glover's roles, racial identity figured in the western *Silverado* (1985) and the heartland saga *Places in the Heart* (1984). One of the most respected actors of the 1990's proved to be Denzel WASHINGTON, who won an Academy Award for his work in *Glory* (1989) and high praise for his

acting in *Mississippi Masala* (1991), Spike Lee's *Mo' Better Blues* (1990) and *Malcolm X* (1992), and *The Hurricane* (1999).

Nonetheless, black actors continued to be frequently relegated to roles as pals or hoodlums. African American-themed films in the early to mid-1990's were mostly in a comedic farce or action vein. Examples include *House Party* (1990), *Menace II Society* (1993), and *Friday* (1995).

The release of *Waiting to Exhale* in 1995 signaled a change. The film examined the romantic relationships of, and the friendships between, four very different women. Almost every African American man or woman could relate to a character in the film. The late 1990's saw nonviolent dramatic films that further ex-

(continued on page 921)

Denzel Washington (left) and Morgan Freeman (second from left) in *Glory* (1989), a film about African American soldiers in the Civil War. *(AP/Wide World Photos)*

Documentary Films

Black Rodeo (Cinerama, 1971). Set during a black rodeo staged in New York in 1971, the film incorporates footage of rodeo events, interviews with the participants, and comments on the history of black COWBOYS in the Old West.

Bus, The (1964). Follows Martin Luther KING, Jr.'s 1963 MARCH ON WASHINGTON, a defining moment in the Civil Rights movement.

Color Adjustment (1992). Directed by Marlon T. RIGGS and narrated by Ruby Dee, this documentary deals with the evolution of African American depictions on television, from AMOS 'N' ANDY through *Julia*, *Roots*, and THE COSBY SHOW.

Eight-Trey Gangster: The Making of a Crip (1993). Exploration of the experiences and social environment influencing the life of a Los Angeles GANG member.

Eyes on the Prize: America's Civil Rights Years; Part 1 (1987); Part 2 (1989). Television film examining the social and emotional impact of the Civil Rights movement from 1954 to 1964 and the movement's aftermath in the years from 1966 to 1980.

Library of Congress

First World Festival of Negro Arts, The (UNESCO, 1968). Focusing on an arts festival held in Dakar, Senegal, this film explores the contributions made by black people from around the world in art, literature, dance, and music.

Fundi: The Story of Ella Baker (1981). Profile of civil rights leader Ella BAKER, who was a director of the SOUTHERN CHRISTIAN LEADERSHIP CONFERENCE and a founder of the STUDENT NONVIOLENT COORDINATING COMMITTEE.

Hoop Dreams (1994). Critically praised exploration of the constantly changing prospects of two high school basketball stars through the years in which

they aspired to play in the National Basketball Association. The failure of director Steve James's documentary—which took more than three years to film—to receive an Academy Award nomination stirred a controversy over the awards' selection process.

Jack Johnson (1971). Review of the life of heavyweight boxing champion Jack JOHNSON. Actor Brock Peters provided the voice of Johnson and Miles DAVIS the film's musical score.

Arkent Archive

Listen Up! The Lives of Quincy Jones (Warner Bros., 1990). Quincy JONES's long and remarkable career is the subject of this documentary, which weaves together interviews with Jones, his friends, and his colleagues, and film clips representative of his musical work. Interview subjects include Ray CHARLES, Miles Davis, Ella FITZGERALD, Barbra Streisand, Steven Spielberg, Jesse JACKSON, and Frank Sinatra.

Panther (Polygram Films, 1995). Written, produced, and directed by the father-son team of Melvin and Mario Van Peebles, this film focuses on the most idealistic years of the BLACK PANTHER PARTY, before violence and dissension led to its demise. It retells the story with energy and potent rhetoric of black empowerment and self-respect.

Paul Robeson: Tribute to an Artist (1979). Examination of the life of actor/singer Paul Robeson, whose strong left-leaning political beliefs got him into trouble. Nominated for an Academy Award as a short documentary.

National Archives

Promised Land, The (1995). Ambitious study of the movement of African Americans from the rural MISSISSIPPI Delta to the urban North between 1940 and

1970. Provides oral testimony and vignettes of the lives of black SHARECROPPERS, describes the WORLD WAR II conditions that prompted their exodus, and provides insights into their new lives in CHICAGO. The film also traces the triumphs of the Civil Rights movement and the demoralizing cycle of POVERTY and violence that later trapped many blacks in inner cities.

Quiet One, The (1948). Set in New York City, this film provides a look at the life of an African American youth trying to stay out of mischief after being placed in a home for troubled boys.

Save the Children (Paramount, 1973). Film record of the Black Exposition in Chicago sponsored by Jesse Jackson's Operation PUSH (People United to Save Humanity). The film's roster of musical acts includes Marvin GAYE, Isaac Hayes, the Jackson 5, Roberta FLACK, Quincy Jones, Curtis MAYFIELD, GLADYS KNIGHT AND THE PIPS, and Sammy DAVIS, Jr.

Some of My Best Friends Are White (Roeback-British Broadcasting Corporation, 1967). Made-for-television documentary exploring race relations in the United States through interviews with middle-class blacks. Filmmaker Gordon PARKS, Sr., is among those interviewed in this examination of the often-ignored African American middle class.

We've Come a Long, Long Way (Negro Marches On, 1945). Piecing together newsreel footage and photographs, this film traces the achievements of African Americans in a variety of fields, illustrating their contributions to American life.

---

plored relationships among African American people. This aspect of African American life has often been ignored by the film industry. Even crossover stars such as Denzel Washington have not been offered romantic leads in films produced by white Hollywood. Washington once commented that, despite a rumor that he did not want to do love scenes, "The truth is, a good love story has not come my way in all these years. But I'm dedicated to doing one soon."

In 1997 *love jones* explored the sexual tension and growing relationship between characters played by Nia Long and Larenz Tate. *Soul Food* (1997), a surprise hit, centered on an African American family's triumphs and tragedies. However, when director George Tillman, Jr., told studio executives of his idea for a possible follow-up to *Soul Food*, they rejected it, telling him he was "pushing black love too far." Although the film was a box-office disappointment, an African American love story was the focus of the 1998 release *How Stella Got Her Groove Back*, which centered on the burgeoning relationship between a successful career woman (Angela Bassett) and a much younger man (Taye Diggs).

Two 1999 films explored the theme of African American relationships. *The Wood* depicted the relationship of three high school friends through flashbacks and present-day

Director Spike Lee emerged as the leading African American filmmaker in the late 1980's. *(Universal City Studios, Inc.)*

scenes as one of the friends prepared for his wedding day. *The Best Man* studied the relationships among a group of college friends reunited at the wedding of one of the group's inner circle. The film was directed by up-and-coming director Malcolm D. Lee, a cousin of Spike Lee.

By the 1990's the film industry was beginning to accept films whose roles paid no regard to color. One example was Cuba Gooding, Jr.'s performance in *Jerry Maguire* (1996), which won him an Academy Award for best supporting actor. Will SMITH had several leading roles that could have been played by actors of any color, including his leading roles in the blockbusters *Independence Day* (1996) and *Men in Black* (1997). In 1999 Smith achieved a breakthrough of a kind in *Wild, Wild West* by playing Jim West—a character made famous by a white actor in the 1960's television series on which the film was based.

Regardless of the continuing limits on the number of roles available for African Americans, by the end of the 1990's, possibilities for blacks in Hollywood were greater than ever before. This was true partly because of the creative imagination demonstrated by a new generation of directors but also because, as Sidney Poitier said of his and following generations:

> Guys like me and Canada Lee and Rex Ingram and all of the black actors of my generation may not have made the best foundation. But we made the best foundation that we could, and they will build on that.

—*Leon Lewis*
—*Updated by Andrea E. Miller*

See also: Black Film and Video Network; Black Filmmakers Foundation; Film directors; Performing arts; Women filmmakers.

Suggested Readings:

Anderson, Lisa M. *Mammies No More: The Changing Image of Black Women on Stage and Screen*. Lanham, Md.: Rowman & Littlefield, 1997.

Bogle, Donald. *Blacks in American Films and Television: An Encyclopedia*. New York: Simon & Schuster, 1988.

_____. *Brown Sugar: Eighty Years of America's Black Female Superstars*. New York: Harmony, 1980.

_____. *Toms, Coons, Mulattoes, Mammies, and Bucks: An Interpretive History of Blacks in American Films*. 3d ed. New York: Continuum, 1994.

Cripps, Thomas. *Slow Fade to Black*. New York: Oxford University Press, 1977.

Diawara, Manthia, ed. *Black American Cinema*. New York: Routledge, 1993.

Harris, Erich L. *African-American Screenwriters Now: Conversations with Hollywood's Black Pack*. Los Angeles: Silman-James Press, 1996.

Jones, G. William. *Black Cinema Treasures: Lost and Found*. Denton: University of North Texas Press, 1991.

Martinez, Gerald, Diana Martinez, and Andres Chavez. *What It Is, What It Was! The Black Film Explosion of the '70s in Words and Pictures*. New York: Hyperion, 1998.

Rhines, Jesse A. *Black Film, White Money*. New Brunswick: Rutgers University Press, 1996.

Richards, Larry. *African American Films Through 1959: A Comprehensive, Illustrated Filmography*. Jefferson, N.C.: McFarland, 1998.

Smith, Valerie, ed. *Representing Blackness: Issues in Film and Video*. New Brunswick, N.J.: Rutgers University Press, 1997.

Watkins, Samuel C. *Representing: Hip Hop Culture and the Production of Black Cinema*. Chicago: University of Chicago Press, 1998.

Film directors: In 1992 black director Spike LEE led a Harvard University seminar on African American cinema. Among the works included in the seminar were films by Melvin VAN PEEBLES (*Sweet Sweetback's Baadasssss Song*, 1971), Gordon PARKS, Sr. (*Shaft*, 1971),

Michael Schultz (*Cooley High*, 1975), Paul Schrader (*Blue Collar*, 1978), Reginald Hudlin (*House Party*, 1990), Charles Burnett (*To Sleep with Anger*, 1990), John Singleton (*Boyz 'N the Hood*, 1991), and Lee himself (*She's Gotta Have It*, 1986).

The films presented ranged from the work of Hollywood's first major recognized black director, Parks, to the work of a young Academy Award nominee, Singleton. They suggest a continuity of issues and of styles on the part of blacks behind the camera in a white-dominated industry. Yet the differences between the first wide-distribution, black-directed cinema of the 1970's and the black films of the late 1980's and early 1990's point to the complexities of African American involvement in the FILM industry.

Early Black Directors

In the early silent-movie days of Hollywood, African Americans had to struggle to gain realistic representations in films made by white directors and producers. However, while Hollywood continued to produce films with racist messages and stereotypical black characters, small, independent black studios sprang up around the country to produce "race movies" that played to black audiences.

The early directors of such films included Emmett J. Scott and George and Noble Johnson. The range of subjects and technological limitations these directors faced is exemplified by the work of Oscar MICHEAUX, who made his career with a series of low-budget black features between 1919 and his death in 1951. Responding to Hollywood models, but without their resources, Micheaux contrasted establishment depictions of domestics and comics with stories of the black bourgeoisie featuring black (or MULATTO) stars. However, his thirty-odd films included a range of themes: Paul ROBESON debuted in *Body and Soul* (1925) as both bourgeois hero and doubtful preacher, while *Within Our Gates* (1920) de-

Director Gordon Parks (sitting), Sr., working on the set of *The Learning Tree* in late 1968. *(AP/Wide World Photos)*

picted a lynching. Films such as *The Homesteader* (1918), *Birthright* (1924), *Ten Minutes to Live* (1932), and *God's Step Children* (1937) appealed to black audiences, although the market for race films was dwindling by the time of Micheaux's 1948 film *Betrayal*. Micheaux's films are rarely seen by modern audiences. Cultural critic bell hooks has suggested the need to reexamine his unique perspectives and "politics of pleasure and danger."

Mainstream Opportunities

The Civil Rights movement and the resulting growth in opportunities for blacks eventually had an impact on Hollywood production and direction as well as acting and marketing. Photographer and author Gordon Parks, Sr., became the first mainstream black director with *The Learning Tree* (1969), based on his own autobiographical book. More commercial success followed for Parks with the action films

Shaft (1971) and *Shaft's Big Score* (1972), although Parks proved unable to escape the films' black macho themes. He was able to exert greater control over his more independent artistic projects such as *Leadbelly* (1976). Parks also directed documentaries and productions for the Pubic Broadcasting Service. His son, Gordon Parks, Jr., directed several films, including *Superfly* (1972).

Melvin Van Peebles and his actor-director son, Mario Van Peebles, also contributed to two generations of black film. Melvin Van Peebles began his career in Europe as a writer and director (*The Story of a Three-Day Pass*, 1968). His best-known work, *Sweet Sweetback's Baadasssss Song*, was an independent 1971 production that changed the direction of black cinema with its emphasis on urban life, sex, and violence. He later directed his attention to theater and television. Mario Van Peebles has directed several films, including the high-grossing action film *New Jack City* (1991), *Posse* (1993), *Panther* (1995), and *Love Kills* (1998).

Inspired by Van Peebles and Parks, black directors explored a range of genres in the 1970's. However, they were often restricted by the expectations of audiences and the film community itself; both expected black directors to produce violent BLAXPLOITATION films.

After the hit *Car Wash* (1976), Michael Schultz's projects included the unsuccessful *Sergeant Pepper's Lonely Hearts Club Band* (1978) and then a reemergence with *Livin' Large'* (1991). His work in the late 1990's primarily centered on directing television movies and television series. Charles Burnett, a graduate of the University of California at Los Angeles (UCLA) film school, gained critical acclaim with films such as *Killer of Sheep* (1977) and *My Brother's Wedding* (1984) before reaching a wider popular audience with his psychological drama of urban family and folk life, *To Sleep with Anger* (1990). Burnett went on to direct *The Glass Shield* (1994), *When It Rains* (1995), and *The Wedding*, a 1998 television miniseries.

Black Women Directors

While black men were achieving some success as directors, black women gained little access to directorial control. The first commercial Hollywood feature directed by a black woman, *A Dry White Season*, was not made until 1989, and the film's director, Euzhan Palcy, was a Martinican who already had established herself by making French films. Black women have achieved more success and recognition as documentary and independent filmmakers. Julie DASH, a member of Burnett's UCLA generation, made films exploring African American women's experiences and aesthetics; her works range from *Four Women* (1978) to *Daughters of the Dust* (1992), a feature on GULLAH family life on the SEA ISLANDS at the end of the nineteenth century. Her short film *Illusions* (1982), which deals with a black Hollywood executive "PASSING" for white, was named the best black film of the decade by the BLACK FILMMAKERS FOUNDATION. In the late 1990's, Dash's work included films for television.

Other black female directors include Kathleen Collins (director of several films, including *Losing Ground*, 1982), Ruby Oliver (*Love Your Mama*, 1990), Michelle Parkerson (*But Then, She's Betty Carter*, 1980), Ayoka Chenzira (*Hairpiece: A Film for Nappy-Headed People*, 1982, and *Alma's Rainbow*, 1994), Saundra Sharp (*Back Inside Herself*, 1984, and *Picking Tribes*, 1988), and Camille Billops (*Older Women and Love*, 1987, *Finding Christa*, 1991, and *Take Your Bags*, 1998). In 1997 a promising directorial debut was made by Kasi Lemmons with a film she also wrote, *Eve's Bayou*. The continuing problems that black female directors face in obtaining funding, distribution, and recognition underscore their continuing dual limitation by race and gender within the film establishment.

1980's and 1990's

Spike Lee, a graduate of the New York University film school, emerged as the best-known

John Singleton, the first African American to earn an Academy Award nomination for directing, in 1991. *(AP/Wide World Photos)*

African American director of the 1980's and 1990's. His student film *Joe's Bed-Stuy Barbershop: We Cut Heads* (1982) and his first popular success, *She's Gotta Have It* (1986), became low-budget classics, providing innovative visions of culture and community that were both wry and critical. In *School Daze* (1988) Lee attacked the codes of color and class in black colleges before taking on more controversial images of race, class, and violence in *Do the Right Thing* (1989) and interracial relationships in *Jungle Fever* (1991). He also explored the life of a JAZZ musician in the more lyrical *Mo' Better Blues* (1990) and paid tribute to one of his heroes in *Malcolm X* (1992). Lee went on to direct numerous films in the 1990's, including *Clockers* (1995), *Get on the Bus* (1996), *He Got Game* (1998), and *Summer of Sam* (1999). In public life, Lee was outspoken and sometimes confrontational about the claims and rights of a new black cinema.

In the 1990's, both a larger number and a wider variety of black directors took center stage. John Singleton's exploration of opportunities and despair in a LOS ANGELES ghetto in *Boyz 'N the Hood* (1991) gained him an Academy Award nomination for his first film. Singleton went on to direct *Poetic Justice* (1993), *Higher Learning* (1995), and the critically acclaimed *Rosewood* in 1997. Both Lee and Singleton also moved their work into other genres such as music videos and advertising.

Matty Rich became known as a low-budget outsider for his angry depiction of New York street life, *Straight out of Brooklyn* (1991). Rich's second film, *The Inkwell*, a coming-of-age drama set in the 1970's, was released in 1994. The box-office impact of Reginald and Warrington Hudlin's *House Party* (1990), the return from television of Bill Duke with the 1991 film *A Rage in Harlem*, the tender vision that emerged from Robert Townsend's satiric *Hollywood Shuffle* (1987) and his more emotional *The Five Heartbeats* (1991), the debates over Isaac Julien's *Looking for Langston* (1989), and the enthusiastic critical reception of Dash's *Daughters of the Dust* suggest the wide range of themes and expressions that black cinema began to explore. Nevertheless, male black directors often drew criticism for their emphasis on urban action movies and for the fact that their films frequently lacked strong female roles.

The late 1990's saw the emergence of several young black directors who tended to focus on African American relationships and families rather than on the urban action and comedy plots of the early 1990's. Among them were George Tillman, Jr., who wrote and directed the commercially successful *Soul Food* (1997), Rick Famuyiwa, the cowriter and director of *The Wood* (1999), which examined the relationship between a group of African American high-school friends, and Malcolm D. Lee (a cousin of Spike Lee), writer and director of *The Best Man* (1999). The film explored the relationships among several col-

(continued on page 927)

Notable Film Directors

Carroll, Vinnette (b. Mar. 11, 1922, New York, N.Y.): Broadway's first African American female director, Carroll is best known for her long association with New York City's Urban Arts Corps. Their most notable productions, both written by Carroll, are *Don't Bother Me, I Can't Cope* (1972) and *Your Arms Too Short to Box with God* (1975). Both use distinctive black theatrical forms and traditions influenced by the rituals and musical styles of the African American church.

Duke, William "Bill" (b. February, 1943, Poughkeepsie, N.Y.): In addition to television and theater performances, Duke appeared in numerous films. He honed his directing skills on such television series as *Knots Landing* and *Miami Vice*. He also directed *The Killing Floor* (1984) and other dramas for television. His feature film directorial debut was the 1991 film *A Rage in Harlem*. His other feature credits include *The Cemetery Club* (1992), *Deep Cover* (1992), *Sister Act 2: Back in the Habit* (1993), and *Hoodlum* (1997). His honors include an American Film Institute Award in 1980.

Franklin, Carl (b. Apr. 11, 1949, Richmond, Calif.): Franklin has directed a number of programs for television. He has directed such feature films as *Devil in a Blue Dress* (1995) and *One True Thing* (1998). Franklin has also appeared in a variety of television programs.

Gray, F. Gary (b. 1970): Gray began his directing career as a director of videos for the music industry. His directorial skills were in demand by some of the biggest celebrities in HIP-HOP and RAP music. He has also directed several successful films, including *Friday* (1995), *Set it Off* (1996), and *The Negotiator* (1998).

Hudlin, Reginald (b. 1962, East St. Louis, Ill.): Hudlin's short film created for his thesis at Harvard University garnered an Academy Award and was developed into a feature film, *House Party* (1990), which he produced with his older brother, Warrington. Hudlin and his brother created a company they named Hudlin Brothers, Inc. which is also known for creating music videos of many popular hip-hop artists. Other films Hudlin has directed include *Boomerang* (1992) and *The Great White Hype* (1996).

Hudlin, Warrington (b. East St. Louis, Ill.): Hudlin studied film at Yale University and began his career making documentaries. In 1978 he cofounded the New York-based Black Filmmaker Forum, a national arts service organization that attempted to develop black independent cinema. Hudlin works with his brother, Reginald, creating feature films and music videos. Together they produced the 1990 feature *House Party.*

Lee, Spike. *See main text entry.*

Rich, Matty (Matthew Satisfield Richardson; b. Nov. 26, 1971): A writer, producer, and actor, Rich became the youngest member of an elite group of young black filmmakers with his first film project, *Straight Out of Brooklyn* (1991), which was released to critical acclaim. Some events in the film mirror incidents in Rich's own life. His next project was *The Inkwell* (1994).

Poitier, Sidney. *See main text entry.*

Schultz, Michael A. (b. Nov. 10, 1938, Milwaukee, Wisc.): Schultz began the transition from THEATER to film direction in 1971 with a television adaptation of Lorraine Hansberry's *To Be Young, Gifted, and Black.* He directed his first feature film, *Cooley High,* in 1974. The other films he directed include *Car Wash* (1975), *Greased Lightning* (1977), *Which Way Is Up?* (1977), *Sgt. Pepper's Lonely Hearts Club Band* (1978), and *Krush Groove* (1985). In 1991 Schultz released *Livin' Large.* That same year, he was inducted into the Black Filmmakers Hall of Fame. His honors include an Obie Award for best direction and a nomination for a Tony Award as best director. He also directed *For Us, the Living* (1983) for television.

Singleton, John (b. 1968?, Los Angeles, Calif.): After graduating from the University of Southern California's School of Cinema/Television in 1990, Singleton signed a three-year deal to make films for Columbia Pictures. Within months, he was given a six-million-dollar budget to begin working as director on *Boyz 'N the Hood,* which was released in 1991. His second film, *Poetic Justice,* was released in 1993. Other films Singleton has directed include *Higher Learning* (1995), *Rosewood* (1997), and *Shaft*

(2000). Singleton also wrote the first three films he directed.

Townsend, Robert (b. Feb. 6, 1957, Chicago, Ill.): In 1987 Townsend directed comedian Eddie MURPHY's concert film, *Raw*. That year, he cowrote, directed, and starred in the hit comedy *Hollywood Shuffle*, along with friend Keenen Ivory Wayans. The film's success established Townsend as one of the most talented, insightful directors of the time. Over the next few years, Townsend opened his own studio, Tinsel Townsend, and wrote, directed, and produced *The Five Heartbeats* (1990), *The Meteor Man* (1993), and *B.A.P.S.* (1997).

Van Peebles, Melvin. *See main text entry.*

Van Peebles, Mario (b. Jan. 15, 1957, Mexico City, Mexico): The son of Melvin VAN PEEBLES, Mario Van Peebles began his directing career in 1989 in such television series as *21 Jump Street*, *Wiseguy*, *Booker*, and *Gabriel's Fire*. In 1991 he directed his first feature-length film, *New Jack City*. The film grossed $23 million and had the distinction of being fifth on the list of all-time box-office hits by black directors. Other films directed by Van Peebles include *Posse* (1993), and *Panther* (1995). Van Peebles has also had supporting roles in numerous films and television shows.

Museum of Modern Art, Film Stills Archive

Whitaker, Forest (b. July 15, 1961, Longview, Tex.): An actor, director, and producer, Whitaker has been involved in numerous television and feature film productions. In 1993 he directed his first movie, *Strapped*, for cable television. Other films directed by Whitaker include *Waiting to Exhale* (1995) and *Hope Floats* (1998).

Women filmmakers. *See main text entry.*

lege friends who were reunited at the wedding of one of their college classmates.

—*Gary W. McDonogh*
—*Updated by Andrea E. Miller*

See also: Black Film and Video Network; Performing arts; Women filmmakers.

Suggested Readings:

Acker, Ally. *Reel Women*. New York: Continuum, 1991.

Bambara, Toni Cade. "Reading the Signs, Empowering the Eye: *Daughters of the Dust* and the Black Independent Cinema Movement." In *Deep Sightings and Rescue Missions: Fictions, Essays, and Conversations*, edited by Toni Morrison. New York: Pantheon Books, 1996.

Bobo, Jacqueline. *Black Women Film and Video Artists*. New York: Routledge, 1998.

Bogle, Donald. *Blacks in American Films and Television: An Encyclopedia*. New York: Garland, 1988.

Cripps, Thomas. *Making Movies Black: The Hollywood Message Movie from World War II to the Civil Rights Era*. New York: Oxford University Press, 1993.

_____. *Slow Fade to Black*. New York: Oxford University Press, 1977.

Dash, Julie, Toni Cade Bambara, and bell hooks. *"Daughters of the Dust": The Making of an African American Woman's Film*. New York: New Press, 1992.

Moon, Spencer. *Reel Black Talk: A Sourcebook of Fifty American Filmmakers*. Westport, Conn.: Greenwood Press, 1997.

Smith, Valerie, Camille Billops, and Ada Griffin, eds. Black Film Issue. *Black American Literature Forum* 25, no. 2 (Summer, 1991).

Finley, Clarence C. (b. August 24, 1922, Chicago, Illinois): Business executive. When he was made executive vice president of Burlington House Products Group in 1974, Clarence Finley became one of the most important black business executives in the United States. Finley's position was the second highest in his product group hierarchy in a company with 1970 sales of about two billion dollars.

Finley started work with Charm-Tred Company in 1942 as a file clerk. He had advanced to the position of paymaster at the carpet company by 1943, when he was drafted. He returned to the company after completing his military service and by 1951 had been promoted to controller. He earned a B.S. in accounting in 1951 from Northwestern University and later attended John Marshall Law School.

Burlington House bought Charm-Tred in 1959, and Finley became a division vice president in 1961. He advanced to Charm-Tred division president in 1970 before being named as the product group executive vice president. Later Finley became senior operating executive of Burlington Carpet Divisions and was in charge of Charm-Tred.

See also: Business and commerce.

Fire Baptized Holiness Church of the Americas: Church founded in 1908 by Bishop and Sister W. E. Fuller. It was formerly known as the Colored Fire Baptized Holiness Church (founded in 1898). In the 1990's there were approximately fifty congregations in the United States, and the church held a national convention every four years. Church doctrine is the same as that of the International Pentecostal Holiness Church. The church founded the semiannual publication *True Witness*.

See also: Pentecostalism; Religious publishing.

First Rhode Island Regiment: From 1778 to 1781, the only predominantly African American regiment in the Continental Army. Originally a white regiment, in 1778 the First was reorganized as a black regiment with white officers. Many of its men were slaves who were purchased by the state and were promised their freedom at the end of the war. The regiment lost its unique character in 1781 when the First and Second Rhode Island regiments were combined.

See also: American Revolution; Military; Patriots.

Fishburne, Laurence, III (b. July 30, 1961, Augusta, Georgia): Actor. Born in Georgia to parents who later were divorced, Laurence John "Larry" Fishburne grew up under his mother's care in Brooklyn, New York. He began his acting career on the New York stage at the age of ten. His early appearances included work on the daytime television soap opera *One Life to Live* when he was eleven years old. He made his FILM debut at age twelve as the character "Me" in *Cornbread, Earl and Me* (1975).

In 1976 Fishburne performed in a production with the Negro Ensemble Company. His big break came when director Francis Ford Coppola cast him to play a crazed soldier in *Apocalypse Now* (1979), a role Fishburne secured by lying about his age. After spending eighteen months in the Philippines filming *Apocalypse Now*, Fishburne returned home eager to tackle more Hollywood roles. He later appeared in three other Coppola films: *Rumble Fish* (1983), *The Cotton Club* (1984), and *Gardens of Stone* (1987). Fishburne was eventually cast in the role of Swain in Steven Spielberg's 1985 film adaptation of Alice WALKER's novel *The Color Purple* (1983).

In Spike LEE's *School Daze* (1988), Fishburne played the Afrocentrist character Dap Dunlop. Appearing opposite Gene Hackman in *Class Action* (1990), Fishburne made the most of his small supporting role as a young attorney. On television, he gained visibility as the

Laurence Fishburne as Othello in the 1995 film adaptation of William Shakespeare's play; Kenneth Branagh played Iago. (*Museum of Modern Art, Film Stills Archive*)

character Cowboy Curtis on the popular Saturday morning children's series *Pee-wee's Playhouse*.

Although Fishburne began his career in a series of supporting roles, often playing the heavy, he established himself as a more sympathetic film lead as the principled father in *Boyz 'N the Hood* (1991). Fishburne had met film director John Singleton while working on *Pee-wee's Playhouse*, and Singleton wrote the role of Furious Styles, a model father who steers his son away from Los Angeles gang life, with Fishburne in mind. He gained further attention with his performance in the Tina Turner film biography, *What's Love Got to Do with It* (1993). His portrait of 1960's pop star Ike Turner, which captured the musician's charismatic confidence while chronicling his descent into violence and drug abuse, was central to the success of the film. The film reunited Fishburne with Angela Bassett, who had played his estranged wife in *Boyz 'N the Hood*.

Fishburne also continued to hone his skills in the THEATER. He starred as a loose-cannon former convict in the 1990 world premiere of August WILSON's *Two Trains Running* at Yale Repertory Theater and re-created the role on Broadway, winning a Tony Award for the role in 1992.

In 1993 Fishburne took on the role of a brash African American speed chess player who befriends and instructs a young white chess prodigy in the film *Searching for Bobby Fischer* (1993). Fishburne then appeared in *Higher Learning* (1995), John Singleton's caustic film about the racial and sexual prejudices that affect life on a college campus. As the bow-tie-wearing professor Maurice Phipps, Fishburne appears supercilious but wise. He had a starring role in the sleek film-noir thriller *Bad Company* (1995), directed by Damian Harris. Fishburne played Nelson Crowe, a cynical former Central Intelligence Agency operative who is hired by an industrial espionage company. Later that same year Fishburne received critical acclaim for his performance in the title role in a film version of William Shakespeare's *Othello*, playing opposite Kenneth Branagh as Iago. Fishburne also had a lead role in the HBO made-for-television film *Tuskegee Airmen* (1995), a fictionalized account of the wartime accomplishments of the all-black fighter squadron. Other films in the late 1990's included *Hoodlum* (1997) and *The Matrix* (1999).

Fisher, Elijah John (August 2, 1858, La Grange, Georgia—1913): Clergyman. Fisher worked in a Baptist parsonage as a boy slave and in the mines of Alabama. In his early twenties, Fisher became the pastor of a number of small country churches, and in 1889 he was called to be pastor of Mount Olive Baptist Church in ATLANTA, GEORGIA. At the age of thirty, Fisher enrolled in Atlanta Baptist Seminary. He pastored churches in Nashville, Tennessee, and then went to Olivet Baptist Church in CHICAGO, ILLINOIS, in 1902. He was an active member of the REPUBLICAN PARTY and gained national attention for publicly criticizing Booker T. WASHINGTON for failing to speak out against LYNCHING. Fisher's life is chronicled in *The Master's Slave: Elijah John Fisher* (1922), written by his son, historian Miles Mark Fisher.

See also: Baptists.

Fisher, Rudolph (May 9, 1897, Washington, D.C.—December 26, 1934, New York, New York): Author and physician. A Phi Beta Kappa student, Fisher published his first story, "The City of Refuge," in the *Atlantic Monthly* (February, 1925) while in medical school. Later in 1925 "High Yaller" was awarded the Spingarn Prize. Identified with the HARLEM RENAISSANCE, Fisher wrote realistically and satirically of urban black life, emphasizing the spiritual loss experienced by African Americans who abandon their ancestral ways.

See also: Literature.

Fishermen and whalers: African Americans have made important contributions to the commercial fishing and whaling industries. In turn, those industries have played important roles in African American history. In New England whaling fisheries, black Americans made up a significant proportion of the crews. Blacks formed a large proportion of the crews on fishing fleets based in the South as well. They contributed much of the labor and brought a number of innovations to the fishing industry. For example, the toggle harpoon was developed by Lewis TEMPLE, whose parents were slaves. Some blacks labored in related industries, building ships, making rope, and working for merchants and chandlers who sold provisions to fishing and whaling ships.

African Americans were able to use the fisheries to their advantage in a number of ways. SLAVE RUNAWAYS used the anonymity of seafaring life to hide from their former owners, and the extensive travels of the fleets allowed many blacks to escape to other countries. In their travels to and from ports in the South, free black seamen assisted in the escape of many slaves and nourished the desire for freedom in the minds of others. The fisheries presented employment opportunities for black Americans in an era when most other industries denied them such opportunities. At the same time, the teamwork required in the fisheries fostered a certain level of equality among black and white crew members that was difficult to find elsewhere. A few African Americans worked their way into supervisory positions in the fisheries, and a number of these individuals became captains and owners of fishing or whaling ships. Some of these men used their position and influence to enhance conditions for other black Americans.

Slavery and the Fisheries
The island of Nantucket in Massachusetts was the center of North American commercial whaling for the first several decades of its existence. Led by its Quaker population, Nantucket harbored deep antislavery sentiments and supported the ABOLITIONIST MOVEMENT. Escaped slaves were willingly hidden by many members of the community, and the whaling and other seagoing ventures of the port gave a ready exit (temporary or permanent) from the country if discovery was imminent. Because whaling ships desperately needed manpower, few questions were asked of would-be whalers. Black men were assumed to be free, and thus employable, on the basis of minimal evidence.

Whalers advanced the antislavery cause in many ways. Nantucket's slave population—Indian and black—was freed in the aftermath of a 1769 legal decision involving an escaped slave named Prince Boston. A Quaker whaling captain, Elisha Folger, had employed Boston on his ship despite is status as a known runaway. Although Boston's owner sued for his return and for his earnings from the whaling cruise, the court decided in favor of Folger and Boston. Some time later, Boston's grandson, Absolom, used the courts again in an effort to give black children the right to attend Nantucket's schools. Another escaped slave who had worked as a Nantucket whaler was Crispus ATTUCKS, one of the first to fall in the Boston Massacre and thus the AMERICAN REVOLUTION. Noted orator Frederick DOUGLASS had escaped from SLAVERY and was employed in the whaling industry when he first spoke publicly, advocating the abolition of slavery; his audience included many whalers and other seamen.

This panel in Charles S. Raleigh's 1879 painting *Panorama of a Whaling Voyage in the Ship Niger* shows an African American sailor clinging to the boat being wrecked by a sperm whale. *(New Bedford Whaling Museum)*

Evidence of the impact that free black fishermen and whalers had on slave conditions in the South is clearly seen in the Negro Seamen Laws that many southern states enacted before the CIVIL WAR. Fearing that free black seamen would encourage or actively assist slaves to escape and stimulate rebellion among them, legislators in these states passed statutes that required the incarceration of black whalers until their ships left port. Undoubtedly, these laws were based on past behavior of many free blacks who, sometimes with the help of their white shipmates and captains, had assisted slaves in escaping. Some historians believe that this seagoing route freed as many slaves (if not more) as the better-known UNDERGROUND RAILROAD to Canada. Certainly any association that slaves had with free blacks would have encouraged them to stop thinking of slavery as inevitable.

Blacks and Whites at Sea
White fishermen and whalers were probably not more enlightened in racial attitudes than other people of their time. Whaling and fishing jobs were available to African Americans because insufficient numbers of white men were interested in these positions. The jobs were difficult and dangerous, with long periods of time spent at sea and away from family.

Compared with other jobs that black men could secure in the eighteenth, nineteenth, and early twentieth centuries, however, fishing and whaling jobs paid well. In addition, the teamwork and cooperation required to bring in a fishing net or capture a whale placed the crew members' performances on public display. Ship captains and first mates could not deny a job consistently well done by a black seaman, nor could his shipmates. In some cases, skill and diligence gave black seamen the opportunity to advance to positions of authority. Some became first mates; others became captains, commanding their own whaling or fishing ships. Comparable positions were much more difficult for black men to obtain in other occupations of the time.

Despite this favorable picture of seafaring life with respect to other occupations, African Americans were not treated as equals by white Americans in the fisheries. Many whaling and fishing ships were segregated, with blacks being given poorer living quarters. Various economic strategies on the part of fleet owners and other merchants prevented the black (and white) crew members from reaping the full benefit of their pay. In addition, the proportion of black captains and mates was exceptionally low compared with their representation within the ships' crews. The advantage of employment in the fisheries was only a comparative one. Jobs were available because no one else wanted them, and although in theory advancement was possible for blacks, it was actually achieved by very few.

Paul Cuffe

One of the great African American success stories from the whaling and fishing ranks is that of Paul CUFFE (spelled Cuffee in some

sources). Born the son of a former slave and a Wampanoag Indian woman in 1759, Cuffe began his career on a whaling ship and eventually accumulated his own fleet of whaling and merchant vessels. He was among the first and most successful African American (and American Indian) entrepreneurs.

Cuffe was also conscious of the problems faced by his fellow black Americans. After working diligently to alleviate the inequalities he observed, Cuffe concluded that African Americans could never obtain full equality in the United States. He became instrumental in the COLONIZATION MOVEMENT, an effort to send free blacks to colonize parts of Africa, particularly the area that became known as Sierra Leone. Cuffe transported colonists in his ships and at his own expense. Although the colonization effort did not measurably improve conditions for blacks in America, it did exemplify the concern many successful black whalers and fishermen had for their fellow African Americans.

Consequences

Whaling and fishing gave African Americans opportunities that few other occupations afforded them early in the history of the United States. Many black men took advantage of the chance to work as crewmen on the ships and contributed important technical innovations; some moved into positions of responsibility, and a handful became exceptionally successful in their own right. As blacks associated with these industries became involved in the efforts to abolish slavery, they provided powerful evidence of the capacity of African Americans to contribute as independent citizens.

In 1922 the fishing sloop *Wanderer* had a predominantly black crew. *(New Bedford Whaling Museum)*

—*Carl W. Hoagstrom*
See also: Business and commerce.

Suggested Readings:

Bolster, W. Jeffrey. *Black Jacks: African American Seamen in the Age of Sail*. Cambridge, Mass.: Harvard University Press, 1997.

Farr, James B. *Black Odyssey: The Seafaring Traditions of Afro-Americans*. New York: Peter Lang, 1991.

Garrity-Blake, Barbara J. *The Fish Factory: Work and Meaning for Black and White Fishermen of the American Menhaden Industry*. Knoxville: University of Tennessee Press, 1994.

Malloy, Mary. *African Americans in the Maritime Trades: A Guide to Resources in New England*. Kendall Whaling Museum Monograph Series No. 6. Sharon, Mass.: Kendall Whaling Museum, 1990.

Putney, Martha S. *Black Sailors: Afro-American Merchant Seamen and Whalemen Prior to the Civil War*. New York: Greenwood Press, 1987.

Fisk Jubilee Singers: Group founded as a choir in 1871 to raise funds for FISK UNIVERSITY. George L. White, treasurer of and music teacher at the university, created the Jubilee Singers shortly after the founding of Fisk University in Nashville, TENNESSEE. The Jubilee Singers came into being in response to a financial crisis at Fisk. White believed that the hearts and wallets of northern donors could be mined for funds through Negro spirituals and work songs sung by young, effervescent black students. Like HOWARD UNIVERSITY, HAMPTON INSTITUTE, ATLANTA UNIVERSITY, and other black institutions founded during RECONSTRUCTION, Fisk faced such severe financial problems that it became impossible to meet minimal faculty and administrative financial obligations, much less to undertake library and physical plant development.

The Jubilee Singers immediately established their credentials. With funds borrowed from teachers and other concerned citizens of Nashville, they made their first northern tour, eventually appearing at the National Council of Congregational Churches Meeting in Oberlin, Ohio, in 1875. There they held an audience captive with spirituals and work songs. The fame of the group spread rapidly as it graced many halls in the Northeast through the sponsorship of the country's most distinguished Protestant pastor, Henry Ward Beecher of Brooklyn. Within a short period, the singers had raised approximately $150,000, a portion of which was designated for the construction of Jubilee Hall at Fisk.

The Jubilee Singers toured England, Germany, France, and other European countries, introducing Negro spirituals to their first worldwide audience at the end of the nineteenth century. They performed in Washington, D.C., for President Ulysses S. Grant. Their success inspired groups at other predominantly black schools and became a model of the philosophy of self-help which was critical to black survival following emancipation. They helped make spirituals an international concert genre. Other groups that followed their example include the Hampton Singers of HAMPTON INSTITUTE in Virginia and choirs from HOWARD UNIVERSITY and TUSKEGEE INSTITUTE.

See also: Gospel music and spirituals.

Fisk University (Nashville, Tennessee): Institute of higher education. Founded in 1866 by missionaries, Fisk School—incorporated as Fisk University a year later—was named in honor of Clinton Fisk of the Tennessee FREEDMEN'S BUREAU. It was part of the parallel school system, segregated between white and black students, that characterized the education of African Americans in the United States for many decades after emancipation. Fisk's first students ranged in age from seven to seventy, as African Americans of all backgrounds and kinds of experience tried to secure an education and advance their newly acquired freedom and dignity.

Southern philanthropists selected Fisk as a model institution for black HIGHER EDUCATION. This private school became, in 1930, the first black institution accredited by the Southern Association of Colleges and Schools. It remained a strong liberal arts institution while other HISTORICALLY BLACK COLLEGES, such as TUSKEGEE INSTITUTE, followed the industrial model. Fisk's reputation is based on high standards of scholarship and a commitment to the preparation of leaders. Its core curriculum emphasizes critical, expressive, and scientific inquiry. A very selective admission process keeps enrollment low; about nine hundred students attended in the 1990-1991 academic year. In 1975 a chapter of the Mortar Board National Honor Society was installed, the first at a predominantly black institution.

Located on a 40-acre campus, Fisk was placed on the National Registry of Historic Landmarks in 1978. Its historical significance and architecture attract many visitors. Jubilee Hall may be one of the most famous residence halls in the world—the first erected in the South for the education of African Americans. It was constructed with the proceeds of the 1871 FISK JUBILEE SINGERS' tour, which raised funds to keep the school open and in the process introduced much of the world to black spirituals. The Jubilee Singers' gospel music remains part of Fisk's musical tradition and cultural heritage. The student press published the first student newspaper at a black college, the *Fisk Herald*, as well as the earliest writings of W. E. B. DU BOIS, Fisk's most famous alumnus (class of 1888).

Other important African Americans have been associated with this institution. Arna BONTEMPS, Sterling A. BROWN, Robert HAYDEN, and James Weldon JOHNSON served as faculty; Booker T. WASHINGTON served on its board of trustees, married a Fisk graduate, and sent his children to Fisk; its first black president (selected in 1947), Charles S. JOHNSON, helped conceive the field of sociology;

and Thurgood MARSHALL was an early participant in C. S. Johnson's Race Relations Institute. Among African American physicians, dentists, and lawyers practicing in 1990, about one in six was a Fisk graduate.

The library's special collections are recognized internationally and include the manuscripts of W. E. B. Du Bois, Langston HUGHES, Charles S. JOHNSON, and Aaron DOUGLAS, as well as papers of Marcus and Amy Jacques GARVEY. Also noteworthy are its impressive black oral history archive and its large collection of volumes, newspapers, and dissertations on Africans and their descendants in America and the Caribbean.

Fitzgerald, Ella (April 25, 1917, Newport News, Virginia—June 15, 1996, Beverly Hills, California): JAZZ singer. Vocalist Ella Fitzgerald was one of the most important jazz artists of the twentieth century. Respected by jazz musicians as a skilled improviser, she also had an ability to communicate with popular audiences.

Early Success
Ella Fitzgerald's father died when she was very young, and she moved with her mother to the outskirts of New York City and lived with her aunt, Virginia Williams. As the GREAT DEPRESSION began, the family's financial situation became desperate. As a youth, Ella earned money by running errands for gangsters, and she occasionally helped prostitutes by keeping track of police patrols. In her memoirs, she described her early life as "interesting." In spite of the poverty with which she struggled every day, Ella was deeply inspired by the cultural environment of HARLEM, New York, and by the great performers who regularly appeared there.

Although she participated in music programs at her school, Ella was first attracted to dancing. At age fifteen, on a dare from some friends, she entered a talent contest at the famous APOLLO THEATER in Harlem. She had intended to dance in the contest, but when she actually found herself in front of an audience, she decided to sing instead. Ella performed some material by Connee Boswell, a popular vocalist whom she admired. The audience demanded three encores, and Ella won the $25 first prize; in addition, she gained some valuable exposure. She soon began to sing with local groups.

In 1935 another important opportunity arose when several musicians managed to present Fitzgerald to Chick WEBB, a famous drummer and bandleader who was playing at the SAVOY BALLROOM. Although Webb's group was not known for using female vocalists, he changed his mind when he heard Ella, and she began her professional career as a member of his orchestra. Webb became Ella's mentor—as well as her legal guardian for a brief period, since eighteen-year-old Ella's mother had recently died. She went on tour with the orchestra, and in 1937 recorded "A-Tisket, A-Tasket," a mildly flirtatious, humorous novelty piece that sold over a million copies in 1938. Even after achieving stardom, Ella still turned to Webb for musical guidance and remained the featured vocalist for his group.

A New Style
Webb died in 1939. Although Ella continued to lead the band for a time, the group broke up in 1941. She began recording for Decca Records and performed with other artists such as the INK SPOTS and Louis Jordan. She remained popular and had more hit records, but Fitzgerald became interested in a more musically challenging and modern style of jazz that was emerging at the time.

This style, created in after-hours improvisation sessions by musicians frustrated by the limitations of popular taste, emphasized instrumental virtuosity and complex musical structures. Many musicians were intimidated

Legendary jazz singer Ella Fitzgerald in 1963. *(AP/ Wide World Photos)*

by this style, which became know as BEBOP, and most vocalists would not even attempt it. Ella, however, was attracted by its spontaneity and energy, and she was able to assimilate the new style by using her voice in a purely instrumental manner. She adapted and modernized the jazz tradition of SCAT SINGING that had first been recorded by Louis ARMSTRONG in the 1920's. (Armstrong and Fitzgerald recorded together in the 1950's.) By singing wordless syllables instead of lyrics, a singer can be much more free to create spontaneous rhythms and rapid melodies.

Ella's natural musicality, creativity, and technique (which included a two-and-one-half-octave range) made it possible for her to interact with musicians on their own terms. She began singing with trumpeter Dizzy GILLESPIE, one of the leading advocates and creators of bebop. Fitzgerald began incorporating the more modern style into her own performances and was encouraged in this direction by producer Norman Granz, sponsor of the Jazz at the Philharmonic concerts. Granz, who eventually became Ella's personal manager, arranged for her international tours and live concerts with Gillespie and others. Ella remained under contract with Decca Records for several more years. From 1948 to 1952, Ella performed with the jazz combo of her husband, bassist Ray Brown.

In the 1950's, Fitzgerald began recording for Verve, Granz's record company. She completed a series of "American songbook" recordings that featured the works of Cole Porter, Duke ELLINGTON, the Gershwin brothers, and others. These recordings (which did not emphasize her instrumental-style improvisation) became very popular with the general public and were accepted by modern jazz fans as well. Many listeners regard them as her finest work. In the 1970's, Granz arranged for her to record in a more improvisational style for his Pablo label. On these albums, she achieved a beautifully effective balance between her instrumental and lyrical styles.

First Lady of Song

Ella eventually recorded more than seventy full-length albums and thousands of songs, spanning half a century of American musical history. She performed with nearly all the great jazz musicians of her time and was popularly referred to as the First Lady of Song. In addition to her thirteen Grammy awards, she won the Kennedy Center for the Performing Arts' Medal of Honor Award, the National Academy of Recording Arts and Sciences' lifetime achievement award, and many other awards. She was awarded more than a dozen honorary doctorates and served as a role model for countless musicians.

Her voice, which retained its youthful, innocent sound throughout her long career, has been described as "pure" by many listeners. A long-running television commercial of the 1970's depicted her breaking a glass by singing an extended high note. Because of health problems, Ella Fitzgerald stopped performing in 1989. She died in 1996.

—John Myers

See also: Music.

Suggested Readings:

Colin, Sid. *Ella: The Life and Times of Ella Fitzgerald*. London: Elm Tree Books, 1986.

Gourse, Leslie, ed. *The Ella Fitzgerald Companion: Seven Decades of Commentary*. New York: Schirmer, 1998

Nicholson, Stuart. *Ella Fitzgerald : A Biography of the First Lady of Jazz*. New York: Scribner, 1994

Fidelman, Geoffrey Mark. *First Lady of Song; Ella Fitzgerald for the Record*. Secaucus, N.J.: Carol Publishing Group, 1994.

Flack, Roberta (b. February 10, 1939, Asheville, North Carolina): Singer. Flack grew up in Arlington, VIRGINIA, where she was introduced to music as a young girl. Although the excellence of her voice was recognized by her teachers and peers, she preferred to study for a teaching career rather than aim toward musical performance. She earned a master's degree in music education from HOWARD UNIVERSITY (1958). In the early 1960's, she taught music, math, and English at a segregated high school in Farmville, NORTH CAROLINA.

Flack moved to the Washington, D.C., area. She continued teaching and began to pursue singing as an avocation. As her performing experience increased, she developed a following of fans. Her debut album, *First Take*, was released in 1969. Her repertoire reflected her versatility and included ballads, soul, and rock. As she continued to record for Atlantic Records, her recognition increased, capped by her appearance on Bill COSBY's *Third Bill Cosby's Special*, a nationally televised show in 1970 that brought her immediate national attention. In 1971 her rendition of "The First

Roberta Flack with Grammy Award she won for "Killing Me Softly with His Song" in 1974. *(AP/Wide World Photos)*

Time Ever I Saw Your Face," from *First Take*, was heard on the sound track of the Clint Eastwood film *Play Misty for Me*. The song reached the number-one position on the popular music charts. During that year, she also won a Grammy Award for record of the year. She had more number-one hits with "Killing Me Softly with His Song" (1973) and "Feel Like Makin' Love" (1974).

Flack released other successful albums and eventually moved into record production. In addition to her singing, she studied acting and dancing. She also completed work for a doctorate in linguistics at the University of Massachusetts at Amherst.

Flake, Floyd Harold (b. January 30, 1945, Los Angeles, California): U.S. representative from New York. Flake graduated from Wilberforce University in 1967, completed theological studies at Payne Theological Seminary in Ohio in 1970, and pursued graduate studies at Northwestern University from 1974 to 1976. Flake's subsequent academic career included service as assistant dean of students at Lincoln University in Pennsylvania and as university chaplain and director of the Afro-American Center at Boston University. In 1976 Flake became pastor of the Allen AFRICAN METHODIST EPISCOPAL CHURCH in Jamaica, New York. During his ten years at Allen AME Church, Flake was active in various community projects involving housing rehabilitation, creation of a senior citizens' center, and establishment of home health care services.

Flake's first congressional campaign began when he ran in the Democratic primary race to fill the remaining congressional term of the late Joseph Addabbo in the spring of 1986. Flake lost the primary to Alton Waldon, Jr., who won the special election in June. Waldon was seated in the Ninety-ninth Congress shortly before its final session. In their rematch in the September Democratic primary election, Flake defeated Waldon. Flake then won election to the congressional seat in November of 1986. Flake served as a member of the House Committee on Banking, Finance, and Urban Affairs; the House Committee on Small Business; and the House Select Committee on Hunger. He was elected to a number of additional terms as a U.S. representative from New York. Flake left Congress in 1997, becoming a full-time minister.

See also: Congress members; Politics and government.

Flipper, Henry Ossian (March 21, 1856, Thomasville, Georgia—May 3, 1940, Atlanta, Georgia): First African American to graduate from the West Point MILITARY academy. Flipper was born a slave but was purchased by his

Henry Ossian Flipper, the first African American to graduate from West Point. *(National Archives)*

father, who also had been a slave. Flipper graduated from West Point in 1877. James W. Smith, another African American, had been admitted before Flipper but left the academy in 1874 without receiving a degree. Flipper was dismissed from the military in 1881 on charges of conduct unbecoming an officer. The charges were related to failure to deliver checks to the chief commissary. After his dismissal, Flipper worked as a public surveyor and an engineer for various mining companies.
See also: Engineers.

Flora, William (1755, Portsmouth, Virginia—1820, Portsmouth, Virginia): Revolutionary war hero. Flora was a member of a band of colonial troops at the Battle of Great Bridge in December, 1775. The outnumbered American troops were forced to withdraw. Flora was the last to leave, firing several shots at advancing British troops before following the retreat of

his comrades. American troops eventually won the battle. Flora also served on a gunboat during the WAR OF 1812.
See also: American Revolution; Military; Patriots.

Florida: The fourth most populous state in the United States in 1997, Florida had a population estimated at 14.7 million people. The CENSUS OF THE UNITED STATES estimated the state's African American population that year to be about 2.3 million, or roughly 15 percent of the total population.

Juan Garrido, a free black Spanish conquistador, became the first known person of African descent to enter Florida, when he arrived with Ponce de Leon's expedition in 1513. Almost two hundred years later, the first free BLACK TOWN within the present-day United States, Gracia Real de Santa Teresa de Mose, was started two miles north of St. Augustine. The first black slaves were brought to Florida from southern Spain in 1526. The slaves rebelled and settled with local Indians, becoming part of the area's population of MAROONS, or runaway slaves.

Until 1763 Florida was under the rule of Spain. Under Spanish rule, people of African descent had opportunities for freedom and for participation in society, economics, and government. FREE BLACKS could compete with whites for jobs, for example, and Spanish personalism linked slave masters to slaves as godparents.

Florida was under British rule from 1763 to 1783. During that period, vast PLANTATIONS were established, and slaves were imported from West Africa. By the time of the AMERICAN REVOLUTION, blacks outnumbered whites in the area by three to one. From 1784 to 1819, Florida was once again under Spanish control. During this period colonial Florida became a haven for runaway slaves from the American South.

In 1819 the United States purchased Florida from Spain. It was organized as a territory in 1822. After it became part of the United States, race relations there took on the pattern set in other Southern states, in which the harsh English slavery tradition was the standard. Florida was admitted to the union as a slave state in 1845.

After the CIVIL WAR ended in 1865, African Americans played a significant role during RECONSTRUCTION, helping to elect Republicans to office. One African American served three terms in Congress; another served as secretary of state. As late as 1870, seventeen African Americans served in the state house of representatives. In 1900 African Americans constituted 44 percent of the state's population; however, they had been virtually disfran-

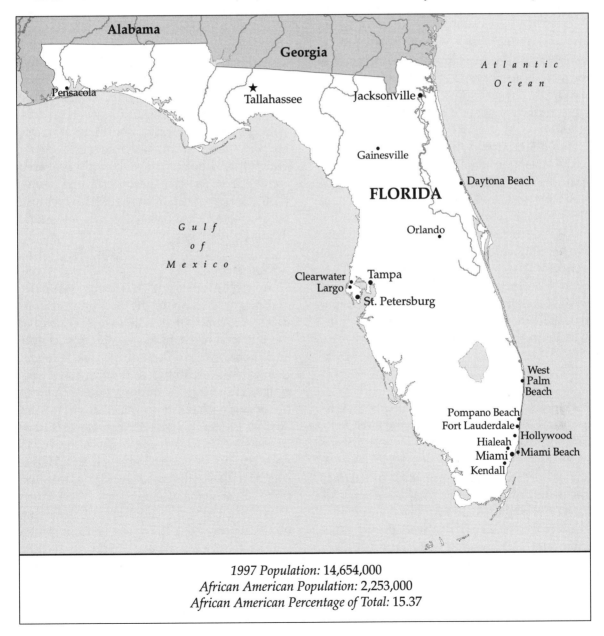

1997 Population: 14,654,000
African American Population: 2,253,000
African American Percentage of Total: 15.37

chised by the end of the nineteenth century through poll taxes and all-white primaries. Despite these restrictions, two blacks served on the city council in Palatka until 1920.

African American participation in Florida politics increased following the CIVIL RIGHTS movement of the 1960's. Voter registration increased from 191,663 in 1962 to 499,534 in 1982, and African Americans had become actors in the political process once again. In 1968 the first African American since Reconstruction was elected to the Florida legislature. In the 1990's fifteen African Americans served in the state house of representatives and five in the senate. In 1992 three African Americans were representing Florida in the U.S. Congress.

In 1975 an African American was appointed to the state's supreme court, while in 1978 an African American was appointed secretary of state. In 1990 an African American became chief justice of the state's supreme court. Florida's African Americans have periodically formed political coalitions with another ethnic minority, Hispanics. In addition, Florida's African Americans have formed ties with more recent black immigrants from the Caribbean, especially those from HAITI, to become significant actors in the politics of the state.

—*William V. Moore*

Folklore: Many folktales associated with African American culture evolved from West African stories and tales. Folktales were one of the most important of the West African literary and cultural forms of expression. With acting, gesturing, and singing, West Africans elevated storytelling to an art. As a favored evening entertainment, the traditional tales compared with those in early European culture in that the stories tried to explain natural phenomena in human terms. Stories were told about the world's creation, about where humans came from, about ancestors, about gods

and the spirit world, and more. Other stories included tales about legendary heroes and heroic deeds, magic, and witches. Many of the stories included lessons.

Folktales
The tales demonstrate how much Africans valued their families, their children, their society, and the natural world. Many such stories were allegorical and could be understood on at least two levels: as children's stories and as allegories that pertained to the adult world.

In the West African tales, animal stories were beloved; trickster roles abounded—rabbits, spiders, and the Nigerian tortoise, for example. They had character traits such as wisdom, patience, cunning, and inner strength. Usually, they also were mischievous, roguish, guileful, and boastful and thereby provided comic relief. Generally in some form of trouble with stronger animals, the heroes always outwitted their foes and usually got a reward at the end of the tale.

African Origins
Although European cultural forms eventually overpowered many of the African traditions that slaves brought with them to America, the folktale was resistant to change. In structure and motif, African American tales followed their African prototypes. Indeed, most specialists in folklore, anthropology, and African history agree that the American slave tales are African in origin. Some African scholars have traced specific American tales back directly to such regions as Ghana, Senegal, and Mauritius and to such ethnic groups as the Ibo (Igbo), Ewe, Ashanti, and Hausa.

Among the American slave folktales, one obvious proof that they sprang from Africa is the retention of African animal characters, including elephants and monkeys. For example, "Nelephant avec Baleine," a tale recorded in Louisiana, told how a trickster rabbit fooled an elephant and a whale; the story

In Walt Disney's 1947 film *Song of the South*, James Baskett played Uncle Remus, reciting folk tales illustrated by animated sequences. *(Museum of Modern Art, Film Stills Archive)*

is identical to one recorded in 1828 in Senegal.

The famous slave tale of the tarbaby comes from the Ewe tribe's story "Why the Hare Runs Away." Forest animals set a trap for the hare after he tricked them and took their water. They made an image of the hare and covered it with bird lime. When the real hare approached the image, the hare greeted the dummy as his brother, but the image was silent. The hare threatened to strike his rude, unfriendly brother if he did not speak; when the dummy hare remained silent, the hare struck the image, and his right hand remained stuck in the bird lime. One after the other, the hare struck with his remaining limbs, which became stuck as well. Substitute "tar" for "bird lime," and one has the African American slave tale about the tarbaby. Most of the other Uncle Remus stories collected by Joel Chandler Harris can also be traced to African prototypes.

Hidden Meanings

A major purpose of the American tales, and perhaps of the African originals, was to teach young people how to survive and cope with a hostile world. Some tales, for example, allowed the symbolic expression of covert aggression toward a slave master; others explained the plantation system and how best to avoid punishment within it. Some stories enabled slaves to make fun of themselves, even to the point of laughing at their very existence. Additionally, the tales, particularly those featuring animals, allowed slaves to escape reality for a time and live in a fantasy world where wishes came true and where the symbol of the slave beat the symbolic form of the master.

"Brer Rabbit," the hero of many such stories made famous in Harris's collections, with cunning, persistence, and bravery always defeated the representatives of the white world. Such stories did entertain, but they did more: They taught some survival lessons and heightened African Americans' self-esteem. They included therapeutic psychological devices for repressing violent anger and projecting it in a way conducive to both survival and mental health—and provided recreation as well. During the slave era, owners accepted the African American animal stories as harmless; many even allowed slave storytellers to tell their tales for the entertainment of white children. That the tales actually projected the experiences and hopes of the slaves apparently went unnoticed.

Many African American folktales did not involve animals but nonetheless dealt with survival and self-esteem. Their characters were more realistic, and many took the master to task—such as the "Jack" or "John" series, in which the protagonist is the wish-fulfillment hero of the slaves. John, in acting more ignorant and humble than he really was, often made a fool of his master. John lied, ran away, discoursed on freedom, was perhaps caught and beaten, but inside, he continued to hate his master and harbored a desire for revenge. In one John episode, the slave asked God to come for his master right away, because he was evil and needed to go to hell. In yet another story, the slave protagonist asked God to kill all the white "folks" and leave all the "niggers." Sometimes John had experiences with the Devil himself.

Some folktales containing enormous exaggeration were called "lies" by the folk themselves and included stories that humorously explained creation, the origins of humankind, the ways of women, and so on. Additionally, the voluminous body of "preacher" tales represents another form of African American folklore. These include stories not only by but also about preachers. That black ministers should be singled out was no surprise, given the historical importance of the church to African Americans.

Some of the African American tales involved conjuring, witchcraft, and other forms of magic. One story related that a very old slave was a "conjure man" and that his wife was a witch; when they had a son, they taught him to conjure, too. One night, the father and son visited their overseer's house; at the front door, they turned into puffs of air and slipped in through the keyhole. Then they took the overseer and his son outside, without the two waking up. The old man then touched both whites with his magic staff; the overseer turned into a bull, and the old man jumped on. The white man's son became a bull yearling, and the slave child jumped on. The slaves then rode to a wheat field that belonged to someone who had once hurt the old man. He touched a wheat stalk with his staff, and the whole field was immediately blighted. As the story concluded, the next day the overseer and his son were so tired that they knew witches must have been riding them, but they could never find out who the witches were.

African American folklore is also found in devil stories (such as "The Word the Devil Made Up"), ghost stories (such as "The Hairy Toe" and "Hold Him, Tab"), religious testimonials (such as "God Struck Me Dead"), sermons (such as "Behold the Rib" and "Sister Lucy"), spirituals (such as "Do, Lord, Remember Me" and "No More Auction Block"), rhymes (such as "When I Go to Marry" and "I'm a Round-Town Gent"), ballads and work songs (such as "John Henry"), the BLUES, and other forms.

Scholarship

In nineteenth- and early twentieth-century studies of African American folklore, authors for the most part denied the African cultural heritage of black Americans, instead setting the folktales in the context of white Eurocentric values and traditions. Many scholars apparently assumed that the violent political, economic, and social subordination of a people automatically also meant their cultural subordination. In the late twentieth century, however, many scholars began to revise the Eurocentric viewpoint. Historians and social scientists began to find Africanisms that had survived centuries of bondage and another century of second-class citizenship. Soon it was discovered that—as with the animal stories—many forms of the folktales had come from Africa almost unchanged. The folktales not only show that slave stories had antecedents in Africa but also prove that SLAVERY could not destroy the creativity or spirit of African Americans.

—*James Smallwood*
See also: African cultural transformations; African heritage; African languages and American English; Literature.

Suggested Readings:
Abernethy, Francis E., ed. *Juneteenth Texas: Essays in African American Folklore*. Denton: University of North Texas Press, 1996.
Abrahams, Roger D., ed. *African Ameican Folktales: Stories from Black Traditions in the New*

World. New York: Pantheon Books, 1999.

Billingslea-Brown, Alma J. *Crossing Borders Through Folklore: African American Women's Fiction and Art*. Columbia: University of Missouri Press, 1999.

Blassingame, John W. *The Slave Community: Plantation Life in the Antebellum South*. New York: Oxford University Press, 1972.

Crowley, Daniel J. "Negro Folklore: An Africanist's View." *Texas Quarterly* 5 (Fall, 1962): 65-71.

Ogunleye, Tolagbe. "African American Folklore: Its Role in Reconstructing African American History." *Journal of Black Studies* 27 (March 1997): 435-455.

Pinckney, Roger. *Blue Roots: African-American Folk Magic of the Gullah People*. St. Paul, Minn.: Llewellyn, 1998.

Pyatt, Sherman E., and Alan Johns. *A Dictionary and Catalog of African American Folklife of the South*. Westport, Conn.: Greenwood Press, 1999.

Sundquist, Eric J. *The Hammers of Creation: Folk Culture in Modern African-American Fiction*. Athens: University of Georgia Press, 1992.

Foodways: Food is much more than a means of sustaining life. A culture's habits and customs centering on food are also a means of maintaining community and cultural integrity.

Food customs can serve as an important link with the past, a way of ensuring cultural as well as physical survival. They can also be a route to the rediscovery of ethnic roots and to the achievement of autonomy and success. Such successes as Sylvia's, a famous soul-food restaurant in the HARLEM area of New York City, and the Glory line of canned ethnic foods, show the extent to which African American foodways have taken their place as a valued part of American cuisine. On the other hand, nutritional deficiencies associated with the African American diet have caused numerous health problems through the years. Some traditions leading to these deficiencies are related to the conditions under which the ancestors of modern African Americans received their food supply. Historically, deficiencies were also simply connected to the POVERTY faced by generations of rural African Americans after the end of SLAVERY.

The majority of African Americans are the descendants of West Africans. West Africans were sold by slave traders to Europeans when the New World was beginning to be settled and colonized, particularly after the middle of the seventeenth century. However, many of the more recent black immigrants to the United States come from other regions, such as the Caribbean, South America, and parts of Africa that were not involved in the slave trade. Thus the diet and food preferences of African Americans vary greatly and derive from a variety of sources.

Foodways Under Slavery
The fact that the first African Americans came to the New World as slaves had a major effect on the food products that they were given. On one hand, the colonial plantation owners saw the slaves as chattel of considerable economic value, and they therefore wished to ensure their health and vitality. On the other hand, the fact that the slaves were viewed as a commodity meant that no more should be spent on their maintenance than was necessary in order to sustain life. In part from ignorance of the principles of good nutrition, but also because of a desire to minimize expenditures, plantation owners fed slaves a diet consisting largely of fatty pork, cornmeal, hominy, sweet potatoes, sometimes molasses, and some greens.

Food for the slaves in the field had to be easily carried, a fact that explains the prevalence of corn pone, biscuits, and hoecakes in the diet. Some slaves were allowed to keep gardens and to hunt and fish, a situation that

Slaves planting rice on a North Carolina plantation. *(Library of Congress)*

can slaves to the shores of America. Boiling and frying in palm oil were frequent methods of cooking, and it was common to dip small portions of food in a sauce. Stews that had a mucilaginous stickiness were preferred dishes. After arrival in the New World, many Africans shared their native cooking traditions with other African groups. Some also learned from Native Americans to prepare indigenous New World foods.

The Culinary Tradition

African Americans embarking on careers in cooking, both under slavery and after independence, created a vibrant cuisine that maximizes the use of low-cost food sources. Under slavery, many black cooks were valued for their ability to prepare fine meals that enhanced the tradition of hospitality that characterized white society in the antebellum American South. In many respects, the southern kitchen was the focal point of cultural exchange during this period. During the CIVIL WAR, many cooks for both the Union and Confederate armies were African Americans. The Cajun and Creole cuisines that developed during this period included a number of dishes typical of the black population, including jambalaya and gumbo, which featured the okra and rice that were common African American foodstuffs.

Following the emancipation of the slaves after the end of the Civil War in 1865, many African American army cooks found employment as chefs in restaurants, where they discovered increasing appreciation for their skill in the preparation of food. Other newly freed African American cooks opened small diners and restaurants throughout the country, specializing in the dishes that were typical fare of African Americans. This style of dining became known as "SOUL FOOD" and became popular in the latter half of the twentieth century. Because of the importance of religion and fam-

enabled them to vary their diet with the addition of small game and salted or dried fish. Occasionally chickens and other small livestock were consumed. Milk was seldom available to the slaves; this was actually fortunate, because of the lactose intolerance that is a pervasive dietary characteristic of black people, as it is with most nonwhites. The result of a diet that was high in salt and fat, lacking in vitamins D, C, A, the B-complex vitamins, and complete proteins, was a frequent incidence of such diet-related diseases as pellagra, kwashiorkor, and TUBERCULOSIS, and a high rate of INFANT MORTALITY. The eating of clay or dirt, a practice called pica, was one response to the lack of minerals in the diet.

Some of the foodstuffs familiar to West Africans were desired and cultivated by the newly settled African slaves in the New World. Such Old World foods as yams, okra, watermelon, squash, and native greens were grown and eaten by the slaves in their new surroundings. Other foods originating in the New World had already been introduced to Africa by the time the slave ships arrived on the coast. Thus chilis, manioc, peanuts, and tomatoes had become staple crops in Africa before the arrival of many of the African Ameri-

ily to African American culture, the Sunday dinner, often featuring fried or roast chicken, became a tradition among African American families.

Renewed African Roots

Many African Americans have made an effort to rediscover their roots through foods and foodways typical of their ancestral lands in Africa. The yam, manioc root, tropical oils and nuts, black-eyed peas, and Old World spices are all used. They help create a cuisine that combines well with traditional African American foods from the South. Together the traditions combine to form a new and unique cuisine that combines visual appeal, taste, and a more balanced diet than was possible under slavery.

With a growing economic and population base, and with greatly improved nutritional knowledge, many African Americans have maintained their African food heritage while avoiding some of the dietary pitfalls—such as excessive salt and fat—of the diet of their forebears. The popularity of African and soul food cookbooks attests a growing awareness of the diversity and taste of this reinvented cuisine.

A New Old Tradition

Among the most cherished of ethnic food customs are those associated with the celebration of holidays, particularly those most meaningful to members of a given group. It was relatively late in the African American experience that such an ethnic holiday began to be celebrated. This holiday is KWANZAA, a week-long celebration that takes place from December 26 to January 1. It has been celebrated only since 1966.

The holiday is based on the mystic number seven and is derived from a Swahili word from East Africa, *kwanza*, meaning the first fruits of harvest. It acknowledges a debt to the agricultural laborers who provide the food supply in all cultures. As a family holiday, it centers on a celebration of family and community. Kwanzaa features foods that have become loved by the African American community over time as well as dishes that originated in the African homeland.

The African American Legacy

Inevitably, in the course of centuries of contact, African American foodways have affected the diet and culture of the white population of the United States, particularly in the South. Many classic southern dishes, such as Hoppin' John, southern fried chicken, and sweet potato pie, originated from recipes devised by African American cooks who were incorporating the foodstuffs typical of the black population. One of the best-known of these foodstuffs in modern America is the peanut, which was once thought to be a food source best suited for livestock. It was research carried out by the African American food scientist George Washington CARVER at the TUSKEGEE INSTITUTE in Alabama that elevated

Foods used to celebrate Kwanzaa are displayed at an exhibition in St. Louis, Missouri, in December, 1997. *(AP/Wide World Photos)*

Mississippi's first African American catfish farmer, Ed Scott, and his daughter fry fish at the Southern Foodways Symposium held at the University of Mississippi in October, 1999. *(AP/Wide World Photos)*

this legume to the rank of valuable dietary resource, both in the United States and internationally. The quintessentially American peanut butter sandwich and a host of other derivatives of the peanut owe a huge debt to Carver's work. Carver also benefited the agricultural development of the southern United States through his experiments with other food crops, such as the sweet potato and soybean.

—*Gloria Fulton*

Suggested Readings:

Copage, Eric V. *Kwanzaa: An African-American Celebration of Culture and Cooking.* New York: William Morrow, 1991.

Harris, Jessica B. *A Kwanzaa Keepsake: Celebrating the Holiday with New Traditions and Feasts.* New York: Simon & Schuster, 1995.

Kiple, Kenneth F., and Virginia Himmelsteib King. *Another Dimension to the Black Diaspora: Diet, Disease, and Racism.* London: Cambridge University Press, 1981.

Mack-Williams, Kibibi. *Food and Our History.* New York: Rourke, 1995.

McIntosh, Elain N. *American Food Habits in Historical Perspective.* Westport, Conn.: Praeger, 1995.

National Council of Negro Women and Cassandra Hughes Webster. *Mother Africa's Table: A Collection of West African and African American Recipes and Cultural Traditions.* New York: Doubleday, 1998.

Piersen, William Dillon. *Black Legacy: America's Hidden Heritage.* Amherst: University of Massachusetts Press, 1993.

Woods, Sylvia, and Christopher Styler. *Sylvia's Soul Food: Recipes from Harlem's World Famous Restaurant.* New York: Hearst Books, 1992.

Football: Black Americans have been involved in the sport of football since its inception during the last quarter of the nineteenth century. As in other SPORTS, however, segregation and RACIAL DISCRIMINATION limited black participation in football at predominantly white colleges, and at the professional level, for nearly a century. During that period, football became increasingly popular at all-black high schools, colleges, and universities. When racial barriers in U.S. society at last began to fall after WORLD WAR II, major university football programs began recruiting African American athletes in ever-larger numbers; when those black players completed their college eligibility, professional teams drafted many of them. By the 1970's, black players had become an important force in all the major college conferences and in the National Football League (NFL). Football in the United States has since provided an opportunity for a fortunate few black men to gain an EDUCATION and to escape from POVERTY.

Pre-1945 Era College Football
Modern football evolved from a game played on November 13, 1875, between teams from Harvard and Yale Universities. College stu-

(continued on page 948)

Football Records and Achievements by African Americans

RUSHING LEADERS

American Football League/American Football
  Conference

Year	Player, Team	Yards
1962	Cookie Gilchrist, Buffalo Bills	1,096
1963	Clem Daniels, Oakland Raiders	1,099
1964	Cookie Gilchrist, Buffalo Bills	981
1965	Paul Lowe, San Diego Chargers	1,121
1966	Jim Nance, Boston Redskins	1,458
1967	Jim Nance, Boston Redskins	1,216
1968	Paul Robinson, Cincinnati Bengals	1,023
1970	Floyd Little, Denver Broncos	901
1971	Floyd Little, Denver Broncos	1,133
1972	O. J. Simpson, Buffalo Bills	1,251
1973	O. J. Simpson, Buffalo Bills	2,003
1974	Otis Armstrong, Denver Broncos	1,407
1975	O. J. Simpson, Buffalo Bills	1,817
1976	O. J. Simpson, Buffalo Bills	1,503
1978	Earl Campbell, Houston Oilers	1,450
1979	Earl Campbell, Houston Oilers	1,697
1980	Earl Campbell, Houston Oilers	1,934
1981	Earl Campbell, Houston Oilers	1,376
1982	Freeman Macneil, New York Jets	786
1983	Curt Warner, Seattle Seahawks	1,449
1984	Earnest Jackson, San Diego Chargers	1,179
1985	Marcus Allen, Los Angeles Raiders	1,759
1986	Curt Warner, Seattle Seahawks	1,481
1987	Eric Dickerson, Indianapolis Colts	1,011
1988	Eric Dickerson, Indianapolis Colts	1,659
1989	Christian Okoye, Kansas City Chiefs	1,480
1990	Thurman Thomas, Buffalo Bills	1,297
1991	Thurman Thomas, Buffalo Bills	1,407
1992	Barry Foster, Pittsburgh Steelers	1,690
1993	Thurman Thomas, Buffalo Bills	1,315
1994	Chris Warren, Seattle Seahawks	1,545
1995	Leonard Martin, New England Patriots	1,487
1995	Curtis Martin, New England Patriots	1,487
1996	Terrell Davis, Denver Broncos	1,538
1997	Terrell Davis, Denver Broncos	1,750
1998	Terrell Davis, Denver Broncos	2,008
1999	Edgerrin James, Indianapolis Colts	1,553

National Football League/National Football
  Conference

Year	Player, Team	Yards
1957	Jim Brown, Cleveland Browns	942
1958	Jim Brown, Cleveland Browns	1,527
1959	Jim Brown, Cleveland Browns	1,329
1960	Jim Brown, Cleveland Browns	1,257
1961	Jim Brown, Cleveland Browns	1,408
1962	Jim Brown, Cleveland Browns	1,863
1964	Jim Brown, Cleveland Browns	1,446
1965	Jim Brown, Cleveland Browns	1,544
1966	Gale Sayers, Chicago Bears	1,231
1967	Leroy Kelly, Cleveland Browns	1,205
1968	Leroy Kelly, Cleveland Browns	1,239
1969	Gale Sayers, Chicago Bears	1,032
1970	Larry Brown, Washington Redskins	1,125
1971	John Brockington, Green Bay Packers	1,105
1972	Larry Brown, Washington Redskins	1,216
1973	John Brockington, Green Bay Packers	1,144
1974	Lawrence McCutcheon, Los Angeles Rams	1,109
1976	Walter Payton, Chicago Bears	1,390
1977	Walter Payton, Chicago Bears	1,852
1978	Walter Payton, Chicago Bears	1,395
1979	Walter Payton, Chicago Bears	1,610
1980	Walter Payton, Chicago Bears	1,460
1981	George Rogers, New Orleans Saints	1,674
1982	Tony Dorsett, Dallas Cowboys	745
1983	Eric Dickerson, Los Angeles Raiders	1,808
1984	Eric Dickerson, Los Angeles Raiders	2,105
1985	Gerald Riggs, Atlanta Falcons	1,719
1986	Eric Dickerson, Los Angeles Raiders	1,821
1987	Charles White, Los Angeles Raiders	1,374
1988	Herschel Walker, Dallas Cowboys	1,514
1989	Barry Sanders, Detroit Lions	1,470
1990	Barry Sanders, Detroit Lions	1,304
1991	Emmitt Smith, Dallas Cowboys	1,563
1992	Emmitt Smith, Dallas Cowboys	1,713
1993	Emmitt Smith, Dallas Cowboys	1,486
1994	Barry Sanders, Detroit Lions	1,883
1995	Emmitt Smith, Dallas Cowboys	1,773
1995	Emmitt Smith, Dallas Cowboys	1,773
1996	Barry Sanders, Detroit Lions	1,553
1997	Barry Sanders, Detroit Lions	2,053
1998	Jamal Anderson, Atlanta Falcons	1,846

SCORING LEADERS

American Football League/American Football
  Conference

Year	Player, Team	Points
1960	Gene Mingo, Denver Broncos	123
1962	Gene Mingo, Denver Broncos	137
1975	O. J. Simpson, Buffalo Bills	138
1982	Marcus Allen, Los Angeles Raiders	84

(continued)

National Football League/National Football Conference

Year	Player, Team	Points
1958	Jim Brown, Cleveland Browns	108
1964	Lenny Moore, Baltimore Colts	120
1965	Gale Sayers, Chicago Bears	132
1968	Leroy Kelly, Cleveland Browns	120
1975	Chuck Foreman, Minnesota Vikings	132
1976	Mark Moseley, Washington Redskins	97
1979	Mark Moseley, Washington Redskins	114
1982	Wendell Tyler, Los Angeles Raiders	78
1983	Mark Moseley, Washington Redskins	161
1987	Jerry Rice, San Francisco 49ers	138
1994	Emmitt Smith, Dallas Cowboys	132
1995	Emmitt Smith, Dallas Cowboys	150
1995	Emmitt Smith, Dallas Cowboys	150

RECEIVING LEADERS

American Football League/American Football Conference

Year	Player, Team	Catches
1960	Lionel Taylor, Denver Broncos	92
1961	Lionel Taylor, Denver Broncos	100
1962	Lionel Taylor, Denver Broncos	77
1963	Lionel Taylor, Denver Broncos	78
1965	Lionel Taylor, Denver Broncos	85
1970	Marlin Briscoe, Buffalo Bills	57
1974	Lydell Mitchell, Baltimore Colts	72
1975	Lydell Mitchell, Baltimore Colts	
	Reggie Rucker, Baltimore Colts	60
1976	MacArthur Lane, Kansas City Chiefs	66
1977	Lydell Mitchell, Baltimore Colts	71
1979	Joe Washington, Baltimore Colts	82
1980	Kellen Winslow, San Diego Chargers	89
1981	Kellen Winslow, San Diego Chargers	88
1982	Kellen Winslow, San Diego Chargers	54
1984	Ozzie Newsome, Cleveland Browns	89
1985	Lionel James, San Diego Chargers	86
1987	Al Toon, New York Jets	68
1988	Al Toon, New York Jets	93
1989	Andre Reed, Buffalo Bills	88
1990	Haywood Jeffires, Houston Oilers	
	Drew Hill, Houston Oilers	74
1991	Haywood Jeffires, Houston Oilers	100
1992	Haywood Jeffires, Houston Oilers	90
1993	Reggie Langhorne, Indianapolis Colts	85

Year	Player, Team	Catches
1994	Ben Coates, New England Patriots	96
1995	Carl Pickens, Cincinnati Bengals	99
1995	Carl Pickens, Cincinnati Bengals	99
1996	Carl Pickens, Cincinnati Bengals	100
1997	Tim Brown, Oakland Raiders	104
1998	O. J. McDuffie, Miami Dolphins	90
1999	Jimmy Smith, Jacksonville Jaguars	116

National Football League/National Football Conference

Year	Player, Team	Catches
1962	Bobby Mitchell, Washington Redskins	72
1966	Charley Taylor, Washington Redskins	72
1967	Charley Taylor, Washington Redskins	70
1968	Clifton McNeil, San Francisco 49ers	71
1970	Dick Gordon, Chicago Bears	71
1972	Harold Jackson, Philadelphia Eagles	62
1973	Harold Carmichael, Philadelphia Eagles	67
1974	Charles Young, Philadelphia Eagles	63
1975	Chuck Foreman, Minnesota Vikings	73
1976	Drew Pearson, Dallas Cowboys	58
1977	Ahmad Rashad, Minnesota Vikings	51
1978	Rickey Young, Minnesota Vikings	88
1979	Ahmad Rashad, Minnesota Vikings	80
1980	Earl Cooper, San Francisco 49ers	83
1983	Roy Green, St. Louis Cardinals	
	Charlie Brown, Washington Redskins, and Earnest Gray, New York Jets	78
1984	Art Monk, Washington Redskins	106
1985	Roger Craig, San Francisco 49ers	92
1986	Jerry Rice, San Francisco 49ers	86
1987	J. T. Smith, St. Louis Cardinals	91
1988	Henry Ellard, Los Angeles Raiders	86
1989	Sterling Sharpe, Green Bay Packers	90
1990	Jerry Rice, San Francisco 49ers	100
1991	Michael Irvin, Dallas Cowboys	93
1992	Sterling Sharpe, Green Bay Packers	108
1993	Sterling Sharpe, Green Bay Packers	112
1994	Cris Carter, Minnesota Vikings	122
1995	Herman Moore, Detroit Lions	123
1995	Herman Moore, Detroit Lions	123
1996	Jerry Rice, San Francisco 49ers	108
1997	Herman Moore, Detroit Lions	104
1998	Frank Sanders, Arizona Cardinals	89
1999	Muhsin Muhammad, Carolina Panthers	96

dents around the nation, including those at HISTORICALLY BLACK COLLEGES and universities, quickly adopted the game. By the 1880's, many colleges and universities had hired coaches and arranged games between their varsity squads and teams from other schools. On December 27, 1892, a team from Biddle Memorial Institute in NORTH CAROLINA traveled to Salisbury, North Carolina, to play Livingston College in the first game between black colleges (Biddle won by a score of 5-0).

During the 1890's, several black men played for predominantly white college teams, but during the succeeding half-century, only a handful of African Americans participated in football at the major-college level. Before radio and television made football a lucrative fund-raiser for universities, very few schools offered scholarships for star players. The cost involved in preparing for and attending predominantly white institutions of higher learning virtually guaranteed that major-college teams would be all-white, with very few exceptions.

Discrimination and prejudice further limited black access to major-college sports. As the twentieth century progressed, many northern colleges and universities began to schedule football games against their southern counterparts. In many cases, the administrators of southern schools refused to allow their teams to play against teams that had black players. In most such cases, coaches on northern teams benched their black players when competing against southern schools.

Early Professional Football

Legal discrimination also greatly limited black participation in professional football before 1946. In the years before the founding of the NFL in 1921, several black men played for various professional football teams. Between 1921 and 1933, a total of thirteen African American athletes played on NFL teams, the first being Fredrick Pollard.

After the 1933 season, owners of NFL franchises made a "gentlemen's agreement" to stop using black players. The owners maintained that they were concerned for the safety of African American players who might be attacked on the playing field by white players or fans. For the next twelve years, there were no black players on NFL teams, but a number of professional all-black teams played football, and many black men played for minor-league teams in the professional Pacific Coast League.

Postwar College and Professional Football

After World War II, black athletes began, slowly at first but finally in large numbers, to penetrate the ranks of both major-college football programs and professional teams. This reversal of prewar trends resulted in part from the unrelenting efforts of CIVIL RIGHTS groups and in part from the changing postwar economic situation. While groups such as the NATIONAL ASSOCIATION FOR THE ADVANCEMENT OF COLORED PEOPLE (NAACP) continued to challenge segregation and discrimination in the nation's courts, college football became the country's second-highest revenue-producing sport, behind professional BASEBALL. Major-college teams began recruiting outstanding African American players in order to field winning (and thus revenue-producing) teams.

Owners of NFL franchises, eager to get their share of the burgeoning entertainment dollars of the postwar economic boom, began drafting black stars from the major-college teams. The Los Angeles Rams management broke the agreement that had kept black players out of the NFL since 1933 by drafting Kenny Washington and future film actor Woody Strode of the University of California at Los Angeles (UCLA) in 1946. Other professional teams quickly noted that the presence of black players on the Rams attracted large numbers of newly affluent black fans to their games. NFL franchises across the nation followed the Rams' lead in drafting black players. The success of black stars on professional teams helped convince franchise owners to begin recruiting on black college campuses. Between 1946 and 1960, eighteen players from small black colleges joined NFL teams.

Despite the broadening opportunities for talented African American football players in the postwar period, blacks still suffered from

949

Running back Jim Brown (no. 32) led the National Football League in almost every rushing category during a nine-year career that ended in 1965 and was still regarded as the greatest player in history at the end of the twentieth century. *(AP/Wide World Photos)*

discrimination at both the college and professional levels. Major universities in the South steadfastly refused to accept black students, much less black athletes, and often refused to allow their football teams to compete against teams that had black players. As late as 1955, Governor Marvin Griffin of GEORGIA refused to allow Georgia Tech to play the University of Pittsburgh in the Sugar Bowl because Pittsburgh had a single black player.

The 1960's and 1970's

The 1960's saw tumultuous racial conflict in the United States that often erupted into violence and death. As many white Americans resisted black demands for equality in society at large, white administrators and coaches continued to recruit only a handful of black student-athletes and to relegate black football players to a few positions on the team. Black athletes continued to be graduated at rates significantly lower than their white counterparts. At most major universities in the South, football teams continued to be all white, despite the fact that many outstanding black football

players were born and raised in southern states. On NFL teams, black players continued to receive lower pay than their white teammates, and African Americans still played only certain positions. Not until 1989, when the Los Angeles Raiders hired Art Shell, did the modern NFL have its first black head coach.

The status of African Americans in college and professional football improved dramatically in the 1970's. Federal laws eliminated vestiges of legal discrimination against black people, forcing state universities throughout the South to admit black students. Federal programs provided massive funds for disadvantaged students to attend college. Equal-opportunity laws resulted in growing numbers of black people moving into administrative and coaching positions in universities. Ever-increasing competition to produce winning football teams at both the college and professional levels led to a torrent of black players entering college programs throughout the nation and being drafted into the NFL. By the 1980's, football had become a major avenue for black athletes to escape from the poverty cycle and to achieve wealth and acclaim. Nevertheless, as several sociologists have pointed out, the integration of football in America has proved to be a mixed blessing to the black community.

During the 1990's the numbers of African Americans playing football increased and were especially evident at the professional level. By the end of the decade 67 percent of the players in the National Football League were black, and the number of black players in major college programs was clearly rising. The representation of black players in the so-

(continued on page 960)

Notable Football Players and Coaches

Allen, Marcus (b. Mar. 26, 1960, San Diego, Calif.). Allen played college ball at the University of Southern California and blocked for Charles White when White won the Heisman Trophy in 1979. In 1981 Allen became the first running back in National Collegiate Athletic Association (NCAA) history to break the 2,000-yard mark, gaining 2,342 yards, and own his own Heisman Trophy. He joined the NFL's

Los Angeles Raiders

Raiders in 1982 as the tenth player chosen in the National Football League (NFL) draft. After leading the league in touchdowns his first year, with 14, he was named rookie of the year. At the end of his second season he set a Super Bowl record of 191 rushing yards against the Washington Redskins and was named most valuable player (MVP) of the game. In 1985 he became the first Raider to lead the NFL in rushing, caught 67 passes, and was named league MVP. After an apparent falling out between with Raider team owner Al Davis, Allen signed with the rival Kansas City Chiefs. When he retired from playing in 1997, he had 12,243 career rushing yards and 123 touchdowns. He then went into broadcasting at CBS.

Anderson, Jamal (b. Sept. 30, 1972). After earning all-Western Athletic Conference honors as a senior running back at the University of Utah, Anderson was made the number 201 overall pick in the 1994 NFL draft by the Atlanta Falcons. In 1996 he had a breakthrough season after being made a starter, rushing for 1,055 yards and catching 49 passes. After posting another 1,000-yard season in 1997, he rose to the level of elite players in 1998, leading the National Football Conference in rushing with 1,846 yards and taking the Falcons to their first Super Bowl. Two games into the 1999 season, however, he suffered a season-ending injury.

Brown, Jim. *See main text entry.*

Brown, Robert (b. Dec. 8, 1941, Cleveland, Ohio). After playing tackle at the University of Nebraska,

Brown became the NFL's number-one draft pick in 1964. While playing for the Philadelphia Eagles, he was selected to play in six Pro Bowl games between 1965 and 1972.

Campbell, Earl (b. Mar. 29, 1955, Tyler, Tex.). An All-American fullback and running back at the University of Texas, Campbell won the Heisman Trophy in 1977. He was the number-one draft pick in 1978, signing with the Houston Oilers. In 1980 he rushed for 1,934 yards, his career best. He led the NFL in rushing yards for four straight seasons, from 1978 to 1981. He gained a total of 9,407 yards and scored 74 touchdowns over his career. He was elected to the Pro Football Hall of Fame in 1991.

Cowlings, Al (b. June 17, 1947, San Francisco, Calif.). Cowlings gained national attention in June of 1994, when he accompanied his friend, accused murderer O. J. SIMPSON, on a slow drive on Los Angeles freeways while police followed. Cowlings talked Simpson out of committing suicide and urged him to surrender to the police. Cowlings and Simpson were boyhood friends who had played football together in high school and at the University of Southern California (USC). At Simpson's request, the Buffalo Bills made Cowlings their first-round draft pick in 1970. Cowlings played defensive end for several professional football teams before retiring in 1979.

Cunningham, Randall (b. Mar. 27, 1963, Santa Barbara, Calif.). The brother of former Patriot fullback Sam Cunningham, Randall Cunningham played quarterback for the University of Nevada at Las Vegas and was drafted by the NFL's Philadelphia Eagles in 1985. During his third season he became starting quarterback and was the first NFL quarterback since 1972 to lead his team in rushing—a feat he accomplished four seasons in a row. With a career rushing average of 6.5 yards per carry and a career passing rating of 81.4, Cunningham had a great ability to improvise on the run. However, by

Philadelphia Eagles

(continued)

the end of 1995 season his skills seemed to have diminished, so he retired and went into broadcasting. A year later, however, he signed with the Minnesota Vikings as backup quarterback. When an early-season injury knocked quarterback Rob Johnson out of the lineup early in the 1998 season, Cunningham got the starting job and had his best season by far. With the help of three exceptional receivers, including Randy Moss, he passed for 3,704 yards and 34 touchdowns to post an exceptional 106.0 passing rating, while leading the Vikings to a 15-1 regular season mark. Six games into the following season, however, he was performing so inconsistently that he willingly surrendered his starting job to his own backup, Jeff George.

Davis, Ernie (Dec. 14, 1939, New Salem, Pa.—May 18, 1963, Cleveland, Ohio). Davis was the first African American to win college football's Heisman Trophy. He attended Syracuse University, where he was an All-American in both football and lacrosse. He was the first pick in the NFL's 1961 draft and would have played professional football for the Cleveland Browns, but he developed leukemia before his first season. Although he never played a professional game, Davis was inducted into the Pro Football Hall of Fame in 1987.

Davis, Terrell (b. Oct. 28, 1972). A running back drafted out of the University of Georgia in 1995, Davis made an immediate contribution to the Denver Broncos by rushing for 1,117 yards and catching 49 passes in his rookie season. His offensive production increased during each of his next three seasons. He led the American Football Conference in rushing yards in both 1996 and 1997, then became the fourth player in NFL history to rush for more than 2,000 yards in 1998, when he was voted league MVP. In both the 1997 and 1998 seasons he helped quarterback John Elway lead the Broncos to Super Bowl championships, and he was named the MVP in the 1998 Super Bowl. An early-season injury sidelined him during the 1999 season, but by the end of the year he appeared ready to return for the 2000 season at full strength.

Dickerson, Eric (Eric Demetric Johnson; b. Sept. 2, 1960, Sealy, Tex.). While playing at Southern Methodist University, Dickerson set Southwestern Conference records in career rushing yards (4,450) and touchdowns (48). After the Los Angeles Rams

picked him number two overall in the 1983 NFL draft, he was an instant success, leading the league in rushing, setting a record for most carries in a season, and being named *Sporting News* player of the year. In 1984 he rushed for 2,105 yards, breaking O. J. Simpson's eleven-year-old record. In 1985 he led the Rams to the conference finals with more than 1,200 yards, although he missed training camp and the first two games of the regular season because of a contract dispute. While at the top of his game in 1986, he became dissatisfied with his team and contract, so the Rams traded him to the Indianapolis Colts. There he led the league in rushing in 1987 and 1988 but earned the reputation of a troublemaker. In 1992 the Colts traded him to the Raiders. After several more trades, Dickerson retired from playing for medical reasons. He was later elected to the Pro Football Hall of Fame.

Dorsett, Tony (b. Apr. 7, 1954, Aliquippa, Pa.). Averaging 141.1 yards rushing per game in four years at the University of Pittsburgh, Dorsett was the first collegiate running back with four 1,000-yard seasons and the first to rush for more than 6,000 career yards. He led the Panthers to the national championship in 1976 and was that year's Heisman Trophy winner. The Dallas Cowboys chose him in the first round of the 1977 NFL draft. After being named rookie of the year, he was later selected to four Pro Bowl teams and played in two Super Bowls, including the 1978 win over the Denver Broncos. In 1985 he became the sixth NFL player to gain 10,000 career rushing yards. He finished his career in 1988, retiring after playing one season for the Denver Broncos. He was inducted into the Pro Football Hall of Fame in 1994.

Eller, Carl (b. Jan. 25, 1942, Winston-Salem, N.C.). After an All-American college career, Eller went on to become one of professional football's most respected players as a defensive end for the Minnesota Vikings, for whom he played from 1964 to 1978. He was named to All-Pro teams four times and appeared in six Pro Bowls, while helping to lead the Vikings to four Super Bowls. He finished his sixteen-year career with the Seattle Seahawks in 1979, then went on to a career in drug and alcohol counseling, developing some of the principles of sports psychology.

Farmer, Forest Jackson. *See main text entry.*

Faulk, Marshall (b. Feb. 26, 1973). After tying or breaking 19 NCAA records during a three-year career at San Diego State, Faulk was made the number two overall pick in the 1994 NFL draft by the Indianapolis Colts. During his first pro season he rushed for 1,282 yards and was voted NFL offensive rookie of the year. That season he also set four records in the Pro Bowl, in which he was named MVP. Although he consistently ranked among the league leaders in combined rushing and receiving yards over the next several seasons, the Colts traded him to the St. Louis Rams at the start of the 1999 season after drafting Edgerrin James. At St. Louis Faulk quickly blossomed into one of the league's dominant offensive players: He rushed for 1,381 yards and caught 87 passes for another 1,048 to win league offensive player of the year honors, and he helped rookie quarterback and league MVP Kurt Warner lead the Rams to their first Super Bowl title in early 2000.

Gaither, Alonzo "Jake" (Apr. 11, 1903—Feb. 18, 1994). Gaither led the Florida A&M Rattlers to numerous Negro Collegiate Football championships while he was head coach, from 1945 to 1969. In 1970 he became the first African American elected to the Orange Bowl Committee. He was inducted into the National Football Foundation Hall of Fame in 1975.

George, Eddie (b. Sept. 24, 1973). After winning the 1995 Heisman Trophy as a running back at Ohio State University, George was made the number fourteen pick overall in the NFL draft by the Houston Oilers, who had selected quarterback Steve McNair the previous year. During his rookie season he rushed for 1,368 yards and was voted 1996 American Football Conference rookie of the year. He rushed for similar yardage in each of the next three seasons, during which the Oilers moved to Tennessee and became the Titans. In his fourth season, he and McNair led the Titans to the 2000 Super Bowl.

Green, Darrell (b. Feb. 15, 1960, Houston, Tex.). Green was selected in the first round of the 1983 NFL draft by the Washington Redskins after playing cornerback at historically black Texas A&I University. In his rookie season, he set the Super Bowl punt return record and was named to the all-rookie team. He also won the title of the NFL's "fastest man" the first of three times in a series of 60-yard dash competitions. Green used his speed off the football field as well. He was part of a 4×100-meter relay team that set a world record at the 1983 World Championships, and he won a gold medal in the same relay event at the 1984 Olympics. Injuries interrupted his career several times, but he nevertheless set a team record for career interceptions (40) in 1995 and was still going strong in 1999, when he intercepted three passes.

Green, Dennis (b. Feb. 17, 1949, Harrisburg, Pa.). Green began his football playing career at Iowa State University. After graduating in 1971, he became a starting tailback for the British Columbia Lions of the Canadian Football League (CFL). While head coach of Northwestern University (1980-1985), he was named Big Ten coach of the year in 1982. From 1986 to 1988, he was receivers coach for the San Francisco 49ers. In 1989 he became head coach at Stanford University. Three years later he was named head coach of the NFL's Minnesota Vikings. After posting mostly most lackluster records, Green saw his coaching reputation shoot up greatly in 1998, when the team compiled a 15-1 regular season record.

Greene, Mean Joe (b. Sept. 24, 1946, Temple, Tex.). Charles Edward Greene played as a defensive tackle for the Pittsburgh Steelers from 1969 to 1981. A first-round draft choice out of North Texas State University, he was defensive rookie of the year in 1969. He led the Steelers to four Super Bowl victories during the 1970's and played in ten Pro Bowls. He was named to the Pro Football Hall of Fame in 1987 and served as an assistant coach with the Steelers.

Grier, Roosevelt (b. July 14, 1932, Cuthbert, Ga.). One of the finest defensive linemen in NFL history, Grier was a star tackle for the New York Giants (1955-1962) and Los Angeles Rams (1963-1968). In 1968 he served as a bodyguard for Robert F. Kennedy during the presidential primary campaign. When Kennedy was assassinated the night he won the California primary, Grier personally disarmed his assailant. After his football career, Grier became a singer, actor, and community activist.

AP/Wide World Photos

(continued)

Griffin, Archie (b. Aug. 21, 1954, Columbus, Ohio). While playing for Ohio State University, Griffin won the Heisman Trophy in 1974 and 1975, becoming the first—and only, through 1999—player to win it twice. He was selected by the Cincinnati Bengals in the first round of the 1976 NFL draft and played as a running back. He was inducted into the College Football Hall of Fame in 1986.

Harris, Franco (b. Mar. 7, 1950, Fort Dix, N.J.). After helping Penn State University win the 1970 Orange Bowl and 1972 Cotton Bowl, Harris joined the Pittsburgh Steelers as a running back in 1972. He rushed for more than 1,000 yards in seven of his first eight seasons. He also helped the Steelers win Super Bowls in 1975, 1976, 1979, and 1980 and won MVP honors in the 1975 game. Known for remarkable balance and durability, he caught 307 passes for 2,287 yards over his career. He was later elected to the Pro Football Hall of Fame.

Harris, James (b. July 20, 1947, Monroe, La.). Trained as a quarterback by Grambling coach Eddie Robinson, Harris believed that he never reached his potential, in part because of his race. When he became available to play pro football, a few teams asked him if he would shift from quarterback to wide receiver or defensive back. Harris declined and was not chosen in the NFL draft until the Buffalo Bills picked him in the eighth round. He played ten seasons for Buffalo, the Los Angeles Rams, and San Diego Chargers.

Hayes, Bob. *See Track and Field table entry.*

Jackson, Bo (b. Nov. 30, 1962, Bessemer, Ala.). One of only a handful of athletes to play two professional sports at the major league level, Jackson won a Heisman Trophy for his football feats at Auburn University in 1985 and was the number one pick, by the Tampa Bay Buccaneers, in the NFL draft. However, he chose to forgo professional football, in favor of baseball, and signed with the Kansas City Royals. In 1987 he signed a contract with the Los Angeles Raiders football

Arkent Archive

team that permitted him to complete the baseball season before reporting for football. Despite the fact that he never played a complete football season in the NFL, he quickly established himself as one of the league's dominant running backs. During the 1990 season he was selected to play in the Pro Bowl, but he suffered a career-ending hip injury in the American Conference championship game against Buffalo. The following year he was waived by the Royals and underwent hip-joint replacement surgery. Despite the gravity of this procedure and the danger of permanent disablement, Jackson returned to major league baseball in 1993 as a designated hitter for the Chicago White Sox and startled the sports world by hitting a home run in his first at-bat. After playing for the California Angels in 1994 he retired from active sports competition.

James, Edgerrin (b. Aug. 1, 1978). After playing for the University of Miami, James was drafted by the NFL's Indianapolis Colts in 1999. Many observers criticized the Colts for drafting James above Heisman Trophy-winning running back Ricky Williams of Texas; however, James led the league in rushing during his first season and was a unanimous rookie of the year selection.

Joiner, Charlie (b. Oct. 14, 1947, Many, La.). After playing football for Grambling State University, Joiner was drafted as a defensive back by the Houston Oilers in 1969. He was traded to the Cincinnati Bengals in 1972, where he stayed until 1975. He joined the San Diego Chargers in 1976. He participated in 180 consecutive regular-season games and appeared in the 1976, 1979, and 1980 Pro Bowls. When he retired in 1986, he held the league's record for career pass receptions, 750. He was later elected to the Pro Football Hall of Fame.

AP/Wide World Photos

Kelly, Leroy (b. May 20, 1942, Philadelphia, Pa.). As a running back for the Cleveland Browns, Kelly led the NFL in rushing in 1967 (1,205 yards) and 1968 (1,239 yards). In 1965, in his second year out of Morgan State College, he led the league in punt returns, with a 15.6-yard average. In ten years as a professional, he gained 7,274 yards, had 27 100-yard rushing games, and went to the Pro Bowl for six straight years, 1966-1971. He was inducted into the Pro Football Hall of Fame in 1994.

Lane, Dick "Night Train" (b. Apr. 16, 1928, Austin, Tex.). Lane began playing professional football in 1952, after his discharge from the Army. He was on the All-Army team in 1949 and 1950. He set a record for pass interceptions in his rookie season with the Los Angeles Rams in 1952. He played for the Chicago (later St. Louis) Cardinals from 1954 to 1959, and for the Detroit Lions from 1960 to 1965. He was named All-Pro defensive back three times and was inducted into the Pro Football Hall of Fame in 1974.

AP/Wide World Photos

Little, Floyd (b. July 4, 1942, New Haven, Conn.). Little was a running back at Syracuse University, where he broke many of Ernie Davis's rushing records. He started his college career by scoring five touchdowns in a single game against Kansas in 1964. In 1965 he led the nation with 19 touchdowns. In 1967 he was the first draft choice of the Denver Broncos of the American Football League (AFL). He played in two AFL all-star games. After the AFL and NFL merged in 1970, he was selected to three NFL All-Pro teams. He led the league NFL in rushing in 1971, and in touchdowns in 1973. After he retired the following season, the Broncos retired his uniform number, 44. In 1980 Little was inducted into the College Football Hall of Fame.

Lott, Ronnie (b. May 8, 1959, Albuquerque, N. Mex.). After graduating from the University of Southern California in 1981, Lott was drafted by the NFL's San Francisco 49ers, for whom he played on four Super Bowl Championship teams. A defensive back, he became the 49ers' all-time leader in interceptions (51) and in interceptions returned for touchdowns (5). He was named defensive back of the year in 1983 by the NFL Alumni Association. In 1991 he joined the Los Angeles Raiders, then moved to the New York Jets two years later. After retiring

from play, he became prominent sports broadcaster and analyst on Fox Sports. A Pro Bowl selection nine times, he was elected to the Pro Football Hall of Fame in January, 2000.

Marshall, Jim (b. Dec. 30, 1937, Danville, Ky.). After earning All-American honors at Ohio State University, Marshall began his professional career in 1959 in the Canadian Football League. The following year he was drafted by the NFL's Cleveland Browns. In 1962 he was traded to the Minnesota Vikings. He later set an NFL record for the most consecutive games played (282) and was on the 1969 and 1970 Pro Bowl teams. During the 1999 season, the Minnesota Vikings honored Marshall in a public ceremony retiring his jersey number.

McNair, Steve (b. Feb. 14, 1973). During his exceptional senior season at Alcorn State University, McNair won the Walter Payton Award as top Division I-AA player and the Eddie Robinson Trophy as the top black college player. He finished third in the Heisman Trophy voting—an unprecedented achievement for a small-college player. Afterward, the NFL's Houston Oilers (later the Tennessee Titans) made him the number three overall pick in the NFL draft. In his second pro season, he became the team's starting quarterback and began posting strong quarterback rating marks for his passing, while leading the league in quarterback rushing yardage. During the 1999 season he and running back Eddie George led the Titans to a 16-4 record, including a Super Bowl appearance. McNair's last pass in the championship game was caught one yard short of what would have been a winning touchdown as time ran out. McNair himself set a Super Bowl record for quarterback rushing yardage.

Mitchell, Bobby (b. June 6, 1935, Hot Springs, Ark.). A football and track star at the University of Illinois, Mitchell was drafted by the Cleveland Browns in 1958. He played 48 consecutive games at halfback, alongside Jim BROWN. In 1961 he was traded to the Washington Redskins, becoming the team's first black player. He played wide receiver until 1968, when he joined the Redskins' personnel staff. He made the All-Pro Team from 1962 through 1964 and played in the Pro Bowl from 1961 through 1964. In 1983 he was inducted into the Pro Football Hall of Fame.

(continued)

Monk, Art (b. Dec. 5, 1957, White Plains, N.Y.). After playing college ball at Syracuse University, Monk was picked by the Washington Redskins in the first round of the 1980 NFL draft. During his rookie season he led the team with 58 receptions. He also led the team in receptions in 1981 and 1982, but a broken ankle kept him out the Redskins' Super Bowl win over the Miami Dolphins. In 1984 he set an NFL record with 106 catches. He played in the 1984, 1985, and 1986 Pro Bowls. Although knee problems hampered his 1987 season, he caught an important pass in the Redskins' Super Bowl victory over the Denver Broncos. In 1992 Monk became the NFL's career receptions leader when he caught his 820th ball. After a salary dispute with the Redskins, he joined the New York Jets in 1994. After sixteen seasons in the league, he retired in 1995 with 940 career receptions—a figure that ranked second in league history in 1999.

Moon, Warren (b. Nov. 18, 1956, Los Angeles, Calif.). After a stellar college career at the University of Washington, Moon ignored the NFL draft and signed with the CFL's Edmonton Eskimos, whom he led to an unprecedented five straight Grey Cup championships (1978-1982). When his CFL contract expired in 1982, he became the object of a bidding war among NFL teams and signed with the Houston Oilers. He led the Oilers to the playoffs in nine straight seasons; however, a lack of postseason success led the Oilers to trade him to Minnesota Vikings, whom he then led to their first playoff appearance in two seasons.

AP/Wide World Photos

Moon's selection to the 1995 Pro Bowl team was his eighth straight—a league record for quarterbacks. He later played two seasons with the Seattle Seahawks and signed as a backup quarterback with the Kansas City Chiefs in 1999.

Moore, Lenny (b. Nov. 25, 1933, Reading, Pa.). After playing college ball at Pennsylvania State University, Moore joined the NFL's Baltimore Colts in 1956. During twelve seasons, he became one of pro football's best runners and pass receivers. He caught a career total of 363 passes, rushed for 5,174 yards, and

scored 63 touchdowns. He was inducted into the Pro Football Hall of Fame in 1975.

Page, Alan (b. Aug. 7, 1945, Canton, Ohio). The first defensive player ever to win the NFL's MVP honor (1971), Page was a member of one of the finest front fours in football history and led the Minnesota Vikings to four Super Bowls. He was inducted into the Pro Football Hall of Fame in 1988. A graduate of the University of Notre Dame and the University of Minnesota Law School (1978), he became assistant attorney general for the state of Minnesota in 1987.

Parker, James Thomas (b. Apr. 2, 1934, Macon, Ga.). After playing offensive guard and defensive linebacker for Ohio State University, Parker was the first-round draft choice of the Baltimore Colts in 1957. He participated in Pro Bowl games from 1959 through 1966 and played central roles on the Colts' conference championship teams in 1958, 1959, 1964, 1965, and 1967, his last year of play. He was inducted into the Pro Football Hall of Fame in 1973.

Payton, Walter. *See main text entry.*

Perry, Joe (b. Jan. 27, 1927, Stevens, Ark.). One of pro football's all-time great running backs and one of the first African Americans to play pro football, Perry played for the San Francisco 49ers (1948-1960, 1963) and Baltimore Colts (1961-1962). Despite numerous injuries, he was known as a durable player. In 1953 he rushed for 1,018 yards to lead the league and was named to the All-Pro team. In 1954 he rushed for 1,049 yards, becoming the first runner to gain 1,000 yards in consecutive seasons. When he retired in 1963, he was pro football's all-time rushing yardage leader. He was elected to the Pro Football Hall of Fame in 1969.

Pollard, Fritz. *See main text entry.*

Powell, Art (b. Feb. 25, 1937, Dallas, Tex.). One of pro football's all-time finest receivers, Powell caught 469 passes during his career. After starting with the Philadelphia Eagles in 1959, he established an AFL record with 81

AP/Wide World Photos

touchdowns from 1960 to 1967. He retired at the end of the 1968 season, after playing for several teams in the AFL and the NFL.

Rashad, Ahmad (b. Nov. 19, 1949, Portland, Oreg.). Born Bobby Moore, Rashad earned All-American honors playing halfback at the University of Oregon and began his pro career in 1972 as a wide receiver. He played with the St. Louis Cardinals, Buffalo Bills, Seattle Seahawks, and Minnesota Vikings. As a Viking, he compiled 5,489 receiving yards and was named to four consecutive Pro Bowls (1978-1981). In eleven professional seasons, he averaged 13.8 yards per catch, scored 44 touchdowns, and led the NFL in receptions in 1977 and 1979. In 1983 he began working for NBC Sports as an announcer.

Rice, Jerry (b. Oct. 13, 1962, Starkville, Miss.). Rice played college ball at Mississippi Valley State University, where he set 18 Division I-AA records. After the San Francisco 49ers drafted him in 1985, he earned conference rookie of the year honors. The next season he caught 86 passes for 1,570 yards and scored 16 touchdowns. Although the 1987 season had only twelve games, Rice set a single-season record with 22 touch-

downs and was voted conference MVP. Despite injuries in 1988, he caught 64 passes and had a remarkable postseason that included MVP honors in the 49ers' Super Bowl victory. He also scored three touchdowns in the 49ers' repeat Super Bowl victory the next year. In 1994 he set a league record with 139 career touchdowns, and the following season he added career records in both receptions and receiving yards. In 1997 a knee injury kept him out of 13 games and ended his streak of 189 consecutive games played. However, he bounced back with solid seasons in 1998 and 1999. By the end of the 1999 season, his accumulated career receiving records appeared unbreakable. They included 11 Pro Bowl selections, 1,206 pass receptions, 18,442 receiving yards, and 169 touchdowns.

Robeson, Paul. *See main text entry.*

Robinson, Eddie (b. Feb. 12, 1919, Jackson, La.). The head football coach of Grambling State University from 1941 to 1997, Robinson became the all-time winningest coach in college history in 1985 when Grambling beat Prairie View A&M to give him his 324th victory. He retired with a career record of 408 wins, 165 losses, and 15 ties, as well as eight national black college championships. He was succeeded as Grambling's coach by former NFL star Doug Williams.

Rodgers, Johnny (b. July 5, 1951, Omaha, Nebr.). One of college football's best punt returners, Rodgers won the Heisman Trophy in 1972 for his play with the University of Nebraska. He helped Nebraska win national titles in 1970 and 1971, and he starred in the 1973 Orange Bowl defeat of Notre Dame, throwing a 52-yard touchdown pass and catching a 50-yard touchdown pass. In 1973 he won the CFL's rookie of the year award, while playing for the Montreal Alouettes, where he stayed until 1976. He played for the NFL's San Diego Chargers in the 1977 and 1978 seasons, but he was hampered by injuries.

Sanders, Barry (b. July 16, 1968, Wichita, Kans.). When Sanders won the Heisman Trophy in 1988 his statistics at Oklahoma State University were unprecedented in college football. He established 34 NCAA records, including 2,628 rushing yards and 3,250 all-purpose yards. In his first season with the Detroit Lions, he rushed for 1,470 yards, scored 14 touchdowns, and was named rookie of the year. In 1994 he led the league with 1,883 rushing yards and was the first player to be unanimously elected to the All-Pro team since 1987. Through the 1990's he was consistently among the league leaders in rushing yardage. In 1999 Sanders shocked the football world by announcing his retirement before the start of the season, even though Walter PAYTON's career rushing record was within range: Sanders's career total was 15,269 yards, only 1,457 shy of Payton's record total.

Sanders, Deion (b. Aug. 9, 1967, Fort Myers, Fla.). Sanders was drafted out of high school by baseball's

(continued)

Kansas City Royals but instead enrolled at Florida State University, where he starred in football and baseball. In 1988 the New York Yankees drafted him, but he stayed at Florida State and won the Jim Thorpe Award as the best defensive player in college football. In 1989 the Atlanta Falcons picked him in the NFL draft, and he soon began playing for both the Yankees and the Falcons. After the Yankees released him in 1990, he signed with the Atlanta Braves. He initially had a small role with the Braves but had a fine 1991 season with the Falcons. In 1992, however, he starred in the World Series with the Braves and made All-Pro during his truncated football season. In 1994 the Braves traded Sanders to the Cincinnati Reds; when the season was ended by a strike, he signed as a free agent with the San Francisco 49ers, whom he helped lead to a Super Bowl victory. The next season he signed with the Dallas Cowboys, whom he also helped win a Super Bowl title; he was still with the team in 1999. Meanwhile, he played a few more seasons of baseball before deciding to concentrate on football.

Sapp, Warren (b. Dec. 19, 1972). An All-American defensive tackle at the University of Miami, Sapp was made the number twelve pick overall in the 1995 NFL draft by the Tampa Bay Buccaneers. During his first five seasons he became a perennial team leader in tackles, forced fumbles, and sacks and developed into one of the most feared defensive players in the league. In 1998 he signed a six-year contract extension with the Buccaneers that made him the second-highest-paid defensive player in the league. During the 1999 season he posted 12.5 sacks and helped lead his team to its best record ever and the National Football Conference championship game.

Sayers, Gale (b. May 30, 1943, Wichita, Kans.). After earning All-American honors as a halfback at the University of Kansas, Sayers was drafted by the Chicago Bears in 1965. During his rookie season he scored 22 touchdowns—an NFL record—including six in one game, and was named rookie of the year. In 1971 he retired to avoid the danger of further damage to an

National Football Foundation Hall of Fame

injured knee. During his brief but spectacular career, he held nine NFL records; he carried the ball 991 times for 4,956 yards, scoring 56 touchdowns. The Professional Football Writers of America voted him the greatest halfback in the first fifty years of professional football in 1969, and he was elected into the Pro Football Hall of Fame in 1977. The story of Sayers's friendship with teammate Brian Piccolo, who died from cancer at twenty-six, was portrayed in the 1970 television movie *Brian's Song*.

Shell, Art (b. Nov. 26, 1946, Charleston, S.C.). After playing tackle for Maryland State Eastern Shore College, Shell was drafted by the Oakland Raiders in 1968 and played for them through 1982. He made the Pro Bowl teams every year from 1973 to 1979 and in 1981 and was a key player in two Raider Super Bowl victories. After he retired as a player, he became an offensive line coach for the Raiders, who had moved to Los Angeles. In 1989 the Raiders made him the first African American head coach in modern NFL history. That same year he was inducted into the Pro Football Hall of Fame. He led the Raiders to the American Football Conference championship game in 1991 but was fired after the 1994 season. He later worked as an assistant coach for the Kansas City Chiefs and Atlanta Falcons.

Simpson, O. J. *See main text entry.*

Singletary, Mike (b. Oct. 9, 1958, Houston, Tex.). While playing for Baylor University, Singletary was voted Southwest Conference player of the year in 1979 and 1980. He was drafted by the Chicago Bears in 1981. Though considered too small, at six feet tall, to play linebacker, he soon proved his detractors wrong. As the team's defensive captain and signal caller, Singletary served as the Bears' field coach. In 1986 he helped lead the Bears to a victory over the New England Patriots in the Super Bowl. He was later elected to the Pro Football Hall of Fame.

Smith, Bruce (b. June 18, 1963). One of the most dominant defensive ends in modern NFL history, Smith was made the number one pick of the 1985 draft by the Buffalo Bills and was named American Football Conference defensive rookie of the year. Afterward, he became a perennial all-pro and Pro Bowl player and helped lead the Bills to an unprecedented four-straight Super Bowl appearances, through the

1990-1993 seasons, and was still performing well in the 1999 season.

Smith, Emmitt (b. May 15, 1969, Pensacola, Fla.). After playing for the University of Florida, Smith was the number seventeen pick in the 1990 NFL draft. During his rookie season with the Dallas Cowboys, he earned league rookie of the year honors and played in the Pro Bow. In 1991 he became the first Cowboy to lead the league in rushing, with 1,563 yards. After two more years of league-leading rushing, he was named league MVP in 1993. He was also named MVP in the first of three Super Bowls he helped the Cowboys win. In 1995 he set a single-season NFL record with 25 rushing touchdowns and completed his fifth consecutive 1,000-yard rushing season. Despite mounting problems faced by the Cowboys in ensuing years, Smith continued to be productive through the 1999 season.

AP/Wide World Photos

Taylor, Charley (b. Sept. 28, 1942, Grand Prairie, Tex.). A star athlete for Arizona State University, Taylor was the Washington Redskins' first draft choice in 1964, when he was named NFL rookie of the year. He caught 53 passes that season, an NFL record for a running back. He was then switched to wide receiver. After playing in eight Pro Bowls and one Super Bowl, he retired from football in 1977. He was inducted into the Pro Football Hall of Fame in 1984.

Taylor, Lawrence. *See main text entry.*

Thomas, Thurman (b. May 16, 1966, Houston, Tex.). After playing running back at Oklahoma State—which also produced Barry Sanders—Thomas was drafted into the NFL by the Buffalo Bills in 1988. He soon became known as the top all-purpose running back in the league. In 1994 he rushed for more than 1,000 yards for the sixth consecutive season, beating O. J. Simpson's team record. In 1996 he upped that record to eight consecutive seasons and set a team record with 82 career touchdowns. He was named league MVP in 1992 and helped lead the Bills to four-straight Super Bowl appearances, 1991-1994.

Tunnell, Emlen (Mar. 29, 1925, Bryn Mawr, Pa.—July 23, 1975, Pleasantville, N.Y.). A 1967 inductee into the Pro Football Hall of Fame, Tunnell began his career in 1948 by walking unannounced into the New York Giants office and asking for a job. He then became the Giants' first African American player. He played in NFL championship games in 1956, 1958, 1960, and 1961, and in nine Pro Bowl games. He retired in 1961, after eleven seasons with the Giants and three with the Green Bay Packers.

AP/Wide World Photos

Walker, Herschel (b. Mar. 3, 1962, Wrightsville, Ga.). The winner of the 1982 Heisman Trophy while at the University of Georgia, Walker set ten NCAA records, including most carries (994) and most yards gained rushing (5,259) during his three years there. He left college in 1983 to play for the New Jersey Generals of the United States Football League (USFL). He led that league in rushing in 1983 and was third in 1984. In 1985 he set a single-season record for rushing with 2,411 yards gained. Additionally, he has been in the top five nationally in track and field for the 60-yard dash and competed in the 1992 Winter Olympics as pusher for the U.S. bobsled team. He played several seasons in the NFL, for the Dallas Cowboys and Minnesota Vikings, leading the league in rushing in 1988.

Ward, Charlie. *See entry in Basketball Players table.*

Warfield, Paul (b. Nov. 28, 1942, Warren, Ohio). Warfield was a first-round draft choice for the Cleveland Browns after he graduated from Ohio State University in 1964. He played in four NFL championships with Cleveland and was named All-Pro, in 1968 and 1969, before being traded to the Miami Dolphins in 1969. He then helped the Dolphins reach the playoffs five years in a row. While with the Dolphins, he made All-Pro in 1971, 1972, and 1973. He signed with the Memphis Southmen of the short-lived World Football League in 1974 and retired in 1977. He was elected to the Pro Football Hall of Fame in 1983 and named to the AFL-NFL 1960-1984 all-star team.

(continued)

Washington, Kenny (Aug. 31, 1918, Los Angeles, Calif.—June 24, 1971, Los Angeles, Calif.). Washington starred at halfback for UCLA from 1937 to 1939, gaining All-American honors in his last year and breaking the all-time UCLA rushing record with 1,915 yards. He and UCLA teammate and future film actor Woody Strode became the first African Americans to play in the NFL after World War II. Washington played for the Los Angeles Rams from 1946 until 1948, and led the NFL in rushing average in 1947.

AP/Wide World Photos

Watts, J. C., Jr. *See main text entry.*

White, Reggie (b. Dec. 19, 1961, Chattanooga, Tenn.). After playing college ball at the University of Tennessee, White signed with the Memphis Showboats of the USFL in 1984 before being selected in the first round of the NFL supplemental draft by the Philadelphia Eagles. Released by the Showboats in 1985, he began playing as a defensive end for the Eagles in September of that year. He had an outstanding career in Philadelphia, playing in the Pro Bowl in seven consecutive seasons and establishing an NFL all-time sack record. After being granted free agency in 1993, he signed with the Green Bay Packers for the 1993-1994 season and helped lead them to a Super Bowl championship in 1997.

Williams, Doug (b. Aug. 9, 1955, Zachary, La.). Williams played college football at Grambling State University, under the legendary Eddie Robinson, whom he would eventually succeed as Grambling's coach. Named an All-American quarterback his senior year, he finished fourth in the Heisman Trophy balloting. In the 1978 NFL draft he was selected in the first round by the Tampa Bay Buccaneers, then a weak expansion team. Williams was only the second African American quarterback drafted in the first round (following Eldridge Dickey in 1968). Williams led the Buccaneers to their first three playoff appearances. However, after a contract dispute in 1982, he signed with the Oklahoma Outlaws of the fledgling USFL. When the USFL folded in 1985, Williams and many other talented players were out of work. The following year he signed with the Washington Redskins as a backup quarterback and saw action in only one play. By the end of the 1987 season, however, he was Washington's starting quarterback, and he led the team to a resounding Super Bowl victory over the Denver Broncos. The first African American ever to start at quarterback in a Super Bowl, he was named the game's MVP. Chronic injuries hampered Williams's play in the ensuing seasons, so he retired at the end of the 1989 season. After Robinson retired as Grambling's coach in 1997, Williams replaced him.

Young, Buddy (Jan. 5, 1926, Chicago, Ill.—Sept, 4, 1983, Terrell, Tex.). After a successful college career in track and football, the five-foot, four-inch Young played professional football with the New York Yankees from 1947 to 1949, then played in the NFL with the New York Yanks from 1950 to 1951 and the Dallas Texans in 1952 (both franchises failed). The Baltimore Colts had Young from 1953 to 1955. He compiled 9,601 total yards and scored 44 touchdowns in nine seasons, retiring with a record 27.7-yard average on kickoff returns.

Younger, Paul "Tank" (b. 1925?). One of the best players in the black college system, Younger scored 60 touchdowns and was a two-time All-American at Grambling State University. He joined the Los Angeles Rams in 1949 as the first player from a HISTORICALLY BLACK COLLEGE signed by an NFL team. In 1951 he was named All-Pro outside linebacker, the first African American to receive the award.

called skill positions was also dramatically increasing. During the 1999 season, for example, as many as ten different black quarterbacks started games during the campaign, and two of the four teams that reached conference finals in early 2000 were led by black quarterbacks. Ironically, Florida State's Charlie Ward, the first black quarterback to win the Heisman Trophy, which goes to the best player in college football, chose to play professional basketball after winning the trophy in 1992. The late 1990's also saw some increase in the repre-

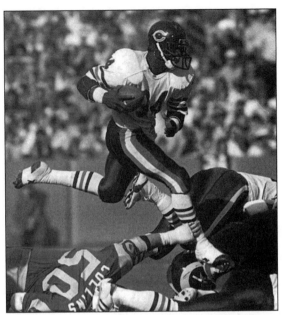

The NFL's all-time leading ground gainer, Walter Payton carrying the ball in 1984. *(AP/Wide World Photos)*

sentation of African Americans in the coaching ranks. However, their number was still so small that when the Green Bay Packers fired head coach Ray Rhodes at the end of the 1999 season, Jesse JACKSON's RAINBOW COALITION publicly protested the move.

—Paul Madden
—Updated by Christopher E. Kent

See also: Segregation and integration.

Suggested Readings:

Alexander, Caroline. *Battle's End: A Seminole Football Team Revisited.* New York: Alfred A. Knopf, 1995.

Ashe, Arthur R., Jr. *A Hard Road to Glory.* 3 vols. New York: Warner Books, 1988.

"Black Football Players Tell Why Integration Doesn't Always Work off the Field." *Jet* (October 7, 1996): 52-55.

Chalk, Ocania. *Black College Sport.* New York: Dodd, Mead, 1976.

Henderson, Edwin B. *The Negro in Sports.* Washington, D.C.: Associated Publishers, 1939.

Holland, Dobie. "Pro Football Celebrates Fifty Seasons of Integration." *Jet* (October 9, 1995): 52-55.

Hurd, Michael. *Black College Football, 1892-1992: One Hundred Years of History, Education, and Pride.* Virginia Beach, Va.: Donning, 1993.

Jones, Wally, and Jim Washington. *Black Champions Challenge American Sports.* New York: David McKay, 1972.

Olsen, Jack. *The Black Athlete: A Shameful Story.* New York: Time-Life Books, 1968.

Forbes, James A., Jr. (b. 1935, Burgaw, North Carolina): Minister. Forbes came to prominence when, on June 1, 1989, he became the first black senior pastor at Riverside Church in NEW YORK CITY, the most prestigious Protestant pulpit in the United States.

Forbes was born the son of the Reverend James Forbes, Sr., former bishop of the Original UNITED HOLY CHURCH. Reared in the PENTECOSTAL tradition, Forbes graduated from HOWARD UNIVERSITY in 1957 and Union Theological Seminary in 1962. After serving as pastor to several churches in the South, Forbes did graduate study at Colgate-Rochester Seminary. He earned a doctorate at that institution in 1975 and earned certification in clinical pastoral education from the Medical College of Virginia. He taught at Union Theological Seminary from 1976 to 1989.

Riverside Church, associated with the United Church of Christ and American Baptist Church, was founded by the Rockefeller family in the 1920's. The prestigious church has been associated with the most liberal wing of American Protestantism. Forbes was preceded at Riverside Church by Harry Emerson Fosdick, a champion of liberalism against fundamentalism, and the Reverend William Sloane Coffin, whom Forbes replaced.

Although Forbes's theological background in the Pentecostal community would seem to place him outside the church's liberal tradition, he made a name for himself as a charismatic and committed preacher. By the 1990's he was often listed in surveys of the greatest contemporary American preachers. Forbes's most important contribution to religious life in the United States was his urging of the Christian church in general to respond to difficult problems such as POVERTY and drug use. He was at the forefront of church leaders urging the religious community and the nation to respond to the crisis caused by ACQUIRED IMMUNODEFICIENCY SYNDROME (AIDS). He searched for ways for his religious community to respond honestly, faithfully, and productively to events in the larger community and the world.

Forbes also emerged as an important essayist and speaker who addressed issues of concern to the church and to the African American community. He became a regular contributor to *The New York Times Book Review*, and he gave the Lyman Beecher Lecture at Yale University in 1986. Colleges and universities such as Lehigh, Richmond, Trinity, Colgate, and DePauw granted Forbes honorary degrees.

Ford, Barney (d. 1902): Businessman. Ford escaped from SLAVERY and is believed to have then run a station of the UNDERGROUND RAILROAD in CHICAGO, ILLINOIS. He traveled to COLORADO in 1860. Ford was politically active in Denver, fighting to keep Colorado from being granted statehood until African American citizens there had been given the right to vote. He built the Inter-Ocean Hotel, which later served a prestigious clientele, in Denver. Some time prior to that, he had amassed a fortune in Nicaragua.

Ford, Harold (b. May 20, 1945, Memphis, Tennessee): First African American elected to Congress from TENNESSEE. Ford was educated at Tennessee State University (B.S., 1967) and HOWARD UNIVERSITY (M.B.A., 1982). He originally prepared for a career as a mortician. He managed a funeral home owned by his father before entering politics. Ford grew up in a politically active family—one brother served in the Tennessee legislature and another on the Memphis city council. Ford's own political career began early, when he was elected to the state legislature in 1970. He quickly established himself as an effective legislator, and within two years, he had become the DEMOCRATIC PARTY whip in the Tennessee House of Representatives. In 1974 he challenged incumbent Republican congressman Dan H. Kuykendall in Tennessee's Eighth District and won a narrow victory.

In Congress, Ford became a prominent member of the CONGRESSIONAL BLACK CAUCUS and made a reputation for himself as an authority on welfare and employment questions, eventually becoming chairman of the House Human Resources Subcommittee. Ford was a major participant in attempts during the 1980's to bring about welfare reform, arguing for changes in the law that would make two-parent families eligible for welfare assistance when the principal breadwinner was out of work.

In 1987 Ford was indicted by a federal grand jury on bank fraud charges involving loans he accepted from Knoxville, Tennessee, bankers; it was alleged that he never intended to repay the loans. After lengthy legal maneuvers, the case was tried in Memphis in 1990 and ended in a hung jury. Federal prosecutors announced their determination to retry the case, but the difficulties of finding a jury unaffected by publicity generated by the case caused delay.

Under House rules, Ford had to give up his subcommittee chairmanship until his legal difficulties were resolved. The adverse publicity had little immediate effect on his local popularity, however. In 1990 he was renominated with 69 percent of the vote and reelected with 58 percent. Ford's problems increased in 1992, when he was named as one of the worst abusers in the House check-bouncing scandal, having written 388 overdrafts on his House bank account. At his second fraud trial, in 1993, Ford was acquitted by a jury consisting of one black and eleven white jurors.

Ford continued serving in Congress until his retirement in 1996. His son was elected to the seat he had held, becoming the first African American to succeed his father to Congress.

See also: Congress members; Politics and government.

Foreman, George (b. January 22, 1948, Marshall, Texas): Professional boxer, minister, and actor. George Foreman began his BOXING career while in a Job Corps training program at the Grant's Pass, Oregon, Conservation Camp. He entered and won the Corps's Diamond Belt tournament. Subsequently he entered the Golden Gloves competition but lost in a split decision. In 1968, as a member of the U.S. boxing team at the Olympic Games held in Mexico City, he won a gold medal in the heavyweight division.

After winning nineteen out of twenty-two amateur matches in two years, Foreman turned professional in 1969. In less than four years, he won thirty-seven straight professional bouts. On January 22, 1973, in Kingston, Jamaica, Foreman faced Joe FRAZIER for the heavyweight championship of the world. He defeated Frazier by a technical knockout in the second round.

Foreman defended his title three times. In his first bout as champion on September 1, 1973, in Tokyo, Japan, Foreman knocked out José Roman in the first round. Six months later, on March 26, 1974, in Caracas, Venezuela, Ken Norton lasted only two rounds. Then, on October 30, 1974, in Kinshasa, Zaire

George Foreman in 1976, a year before he retired from the ring. *(AP/Wide World Photos)*

(later Democratic Republic of the Congo), Muhammad ALI reclaimed the heavyweight title by knocking out Foreman in the eighth round. Over the next few years, Foreman did little fighting. After losing a bout to Jimmy Young in 1977, he retired with a professional record of forty-five wins and two losses. He became a preacher in HOUSTON, TEXAS.

Ten years later, Foreman returned to the ring, primarily fighting lesser-known boxers. He had difficulty getting fights with major contenders because young up-and-coming boxers knew that he still had a powerful punch and did not want to risk shortening their own careers. Finally, at the age of forty-two, Foreman got another chance to reclaim the title. On April 25, 1991, in a highly celebrated heavyweight title fight in Atlantic City, NEW JERSEY, Foreman went twelve rounds with heavyweight champion Evander Holyfield. Although he lost in a decision, Foreman held his own against the much younger Holyfield, proving to his detractors that he was a worthy contender.

In the earlier days of his boxing career he had been cast in the role of villain because of his dark and foreboding countenance. In the 1990's, however, Foreman shed his earlier street-fighter image and captured the imagination of boxing fans and the general public. Foreman became a media star and a highly sought-after personality, serving as a spokesperson for Doritos snack food and a number of other business concerns, including an auto repair company and some restaurant chains. He

Foreman's knockout of Michael Moorer on November 5, 1994, made him the oldest boxer ever to hold the world heavyweight championship. *(AP/Wide World Photos)*

shrewdly parlayed his advancing age and underdog status into an acting career. As a pudgy, affable man in his forties, Foreman wryly poked fun at his own bulging waistline. In 1993 ABC television sought to capitalize on Foreman's new popularity by launching the short-lived situation comedy *George*, starring Foreman as a former boxer turned househusband. Foreman also served as a boxing analyst for HBO sports television.

Foreman also continued to demonstrate devastating punching power. Following his 1991 loss to Holyfield, he worked his way through the ranks of heavyweight contenders, recording one victory after another while awaiting the opportunity to once again vie for a heavyweight title, which he had not held since losing to Muhammad Ali in Zaire in 1974. Foreman finally got his second title shot when he met International Boxing Federation (IBF) champion Michael Moorer in November, 1994, at Caesar's Palace in Las Vegas. In front of a capacity crowd and a worldwide closed-circuit television audience, forty-five-year-old George Foreman knocked out the IBF champion in the tenth round and became the oldest man ever to hold a heavyweight title.

Then, at age forty-six in April of 1995, Foreman became the oldest man to defend the heavyweight title successfully when he won a split decision against a lightly regarded but skilled German fighter named Axel Schultz. The bout, however, was shrouded in controversy. Foreman did not fight again until November, 1996, when he defeated Crawford Grimsley; the fight was tough for Foreman, as was his defeat of Lou Savarese in May, 1997. Foreman wanted to fight Holyfield or Mike TYSON before retiring, but neither fight came to pass. Finally, in November, 1997, he lost a controversial decision to Shannon Briggs and announced his retirement, two months before his forty-ninth birthday. Subsequently, a January, 1999, bout between Foreman and Larry Holmes (Foreman at age fifty and Holmes at forty-nine) was scheduled for the Houston Astrodome, but financial backers pulled out and the fight was canceled.

—*Updated by Joel N. Rosen*

Forman, James (b. October 4, 1928, Chicago, Illinois): CIVIL RIGHTS activist. When James Forman was eleven months old, the harsh economics of the ghetto in CHICAGO forced his parents to send him to live with his maternal grandmother in rural Marshall County, MISSISSIPPI, a mile south of the Tennessee border. Only other African Americans lived near the farmstead, and only black children attended a nearby school. Nevertheless, even before he began school, Forman had his first brush with segregation and RACIAL DISCRIMINATION. After a trip to Chicago to visit his mother, he stopped in MEMPHIS to visit an aunt.

After being given a nickel, five-year-old James went to the nearest drugstore, sat down at a counter, and spun in his seat until a white waitress came; after he ordered a soft drink, the waitress vanished into a back storeroom. When she returned, she brought with her a black man who led James to a back room, explaining that he could not sit at the counter because he was a "nigger." Forman, crying, ran from the store. The incident was the first of many times that Forman would be confronted with and insulted by white racism. This first encounter left him so shocked that he suppressed the memory of it until his graduate school days; he remembered the incident only as he was writing a paper on race relations.

Education and Early Employment
In 1935 Forman returned to Chicago to live with his parents and was soon enrolled in the second grade at the private, all-black St. Anselm's Catholic School. Later, he attended the public Betsy Ross Grammar School and a local high school, from which he graduated in 1947. Almost immediately afterward, he joined the Air Force. After being mustered out of the service, Forman lived for a time on the West Coast, where he attended the University of Southern California. After experiencing police brutality that bordered on torture, however, Forman suffered until his nerves snapped. His mother then took him back to Chicago to begin a slow recovery, after which he enrolled at Roosevelt University. After graduating in 1957, he accepted a teaching job in Chicago, but he soon began graduate work at Brown University in Providence, RHODE ISLAND. After spending almost a year at Brown, Forman in 1958 became a correspondent of the CHICAGO DEFENDER; his first assignment was to go to Little Rock, Arkansas, and report on the desegregation struggle there.

Civil Rights Activism
After Little Rock, Forman went to Fayette County, TENNESSEE, where a racist white citizens' council was working to evict black

James Forman in 1963. *(AP/Wide World Photos)*

sharecroppers who dared ask for their rights; Forman helped organize a relief effort on behalf of the sharecroppers. When blacks in neighboring Haywood County were stripped of their land, Forman enlarged his humanitarian work to include them, too. Disunity among the local African American community, however, made the protests ineffective; eventually, the racists won, and the dispossessed sharecroppers drifted away, family by family.

The LITTLE ROCK CRISIS and the Tennessee troubles further radicalized Forman, and from 1958 onward he became a soldier in the civil rights struggle. By the 1970's Forman had worked with most of the major civil rights organizations in the country, including the CONGRESS OF RACIAL EQUALITY (CORE), which he said was dominated by whites, the SOUTHERN CHRISTIAN LEADERSHIP CONFERENCE (SCLC), which he said was dominated by conservative preachers, and the NATIONAL ASSOCIATION FOR THE ADVANCEMENT OF COLORED PEOPLE (NAACP), which he said was dominated by middle-class African Americans.

SNCC Activism
After the STUDENT NONVIOLENT COORDINATING COMMITTEE (SNCC) coalesced in 1960, Forman rushed to Nashville to join the movement; soon he emerged as one of its most effective leaders. He participated in the FREEDOM RIDES into the heart of the South to test court-ordered integration of public interstate transportation. He also helped to lead the student-engendered sit-in movement, which spread in 1960 and 1961 to include hundreds of protests in at least twenty-seven states. Like other civil rights workers, Forman often had to put his body on the line, and he was frequently arrested. White law officers wishing to break up peaceful SIT-INS often prosecuted Forman for contributing to the delinquency of minors, because many youngsters were involved in the protests. In 1962 and 1963,

Forman continued to organize protests—in Atlanta, Savannah, and Rome, GEORGIA; Greenwood, Mississippi; Danville, VIRGINIA; Cambridge, MARYLAND; Selma, ALABAMA; and elsewhere.

In 1964 Forman was named SNCC's executive secretary, a post he held until 1966. During his tenure, he continued to help organize and to participate in all manner of protests, including voter-registration drives in Mississippi and Alabama. Forman and other activists saw their work rewarded with many victories in the mid-1960's, including the Civil Rights Act of 1964 and the Voter Registration Act of 1965.

By 1966 radicals, angry because the movement had not secured enough gains on bread-and-butter economic issues, emerged in SNCC. Such leaders as H. Rap BROWN and Stokely CARMICHAEL began the now-famous chants of "Black power" and "Burn, baby, burn." The radicals soon gained power in SNCC. After Carmichael replaced John LEWIS as SNCC's chairman, Forman lost his job as executive secretary; however, for a time he continued as a member of SNCC. He also became a member of the BLACK PANTHER PARTY, but he soon resigned over differences with the party's leaders. In 1969 he was appointed director of SNCC's international affairs.

Soon SNCC faded as a national power, in part because of ideological and personality struggles within the organization between radicals who advocated the use of violence to achieve reform and moderates who called for nonviolence. In addition, SNCC became the target of government harassment; the combined external and internal pressures ended SNCC's effectiveness.

Post-SNCC Work
By that time, Forman had moved into a new position with a new organization. In April, 1969, he became acting chairman of the Black Economic Development Conference, a group sponsored by the twenty-three national com-

munity and religious organizations of the Interreligious Foundation for Community Organization (IFCO). As he fulfilled his new duties, he also wrote the BLACK MANIFESTO, in which he highlighted the past injustices perpetrated by white Americans upon African Americans and then demanded reparations.

He found a national forum for his manifesto when, in May of 1969, he burst into New York's interracial, interdenominational Riverside Church, made a speech from near the altar, and demanded $500,000 from white churches and synagogues to atone for past exploitation of blacks, especially for the role of white churches in helping to perpetuate slavery. Forman later demanded that Riverside Church give 60 percent of its income to IFCO, that it give the organization office space and telephone service at the church, and that it give IFCO unrestricted use of the church's radio station. Additionally, Forman demanded that religious groups finance cultural, educational, and industrial programs for African Americans.

Although the white-run Washington Square United Methodist Church of New York City eventually donated $15,000 for African American programs, and although the National Council of Churches and a few other white-directed churches set up agencies to advance money to disadvantaged groups, little came of the Black Manifesto; very little money actually ever changed hands. Further, not all black leaders supported Forman's demands. Joseph JACKSON, who headed the Black National Baptist Convention, strongly criticized the National Council of Churches for even reacting to the manifesto. Nevertheless, Forman's forceful statement did appear to raise white America's level of awareness about the black community's economic plight.

Forman had an additional impact on the protest movement as the author of numerous books. Forman's *The Making of Black Revolutionaries: A Personal Account* (1972) was favor-

ably received by most readers. Writing in *The New York Times*, reviewer Thomas Lask praised the volume as an important work that told what it was like to be black in a society dominated by whites. By the mid-1970's, Forman, like many of the early civil rights leaders, had faded from the public eye; the movement's great age was over. Still, Forman is remembered as one of the premier leaders of the movement.

—*James Smallwood*
See also: Segregation and integration.

Suggested Readings:
Carson, Clayborne. *In Struggle: SNCC and the Black Awakening of the 1960s.* Cambridge, Mass.: Harvard University Press, 1981.
Forman, James. *High Tide of Black Resistance and Other Political and Literary Writings.* Seattle, Wash.: Open Hand, 1994.
_____. *The Making of Black Revolutionaries.* New York: Macmillan, 1972.
Garrow, David J., ed. *We Shall Overcome: The Civil Rights Movement in the United States in the 1950's and 1960's.* 3 vols. New York: Carlson, 1989.
McEvoy, James, and Abraham Miller, eds. *Black Power and Student Rebellion.* Belmont, Calif.: Wadsworth, 1969.
Sitkoff, Harvard. *The Struggle for Black Equality, 1954-1980.* New York: Hill & Wang, 1981.

Forrest, Leon (January 8, 1937, Chicago, Illinois—November 6, 1997, Evanston, Illinois): Writer and educator. Equally successful in creative writing and journalism, Forrest wrote novels that reflect his appreciation of oral tradition.

As a boy growing up on the South Side of CHICAGO, Forrest read Bible passages to his grandmother and received exposure to both Roman Catholicism and Protestantism; these religious traditions would influence his writing later. At school he participated in both creative and journalistic endeavors. Storytellers on both sides of his family background influenced his early development and his deep appreciation for oral tradition and its literary possibilities.

In high school, Forrest won several poetry and essay contests and was a reporter for the school newspaper. He completed college work at the University of Chicago. While serving in the U.S. Army, he wrote feature stories for the *Spearhead*, the newspaper of the Third Armored Division. After his military service, he wrote for a community weekly, the *Bulletin Booster*, and for MUHAMMAD SPEAKS, a Black Muslim publication of which he became managing editor in 1972. His first novel, *There Is a Tree More Ancient than Eden*, was published in 1973, the year he received a professorial appointment at Northwestern University in Evanston, Illinois. Subsequent novels included *The Bloodworth Orphans* (1977), *Two Wings to Veil My Face* (1983), and *The Furious Voice for Freedom* (1995). Forrest received a number of literary awards during his lifetime. He also pursued a career as an educator.

—*Victoria Price*

See also: Black press.

Forten, James (September 2, 1766, Philadelphia, Pennsylvania—March 4, 1842, Philadelphia, Pennsylvania): Businessman and CIVIL RIGHTS leader. Forten was born to free parents. He studied briefly as a child at a school run by Anthony Benezet, a Quaker leader in the ABOLITIONIST MOVEMENT. After his father died, Forten began working at a grocery store to support his mother.

Forten enlisted in the Navy at the age of fifteen, serving as a powder boy. His ship, the *Royal Louis*, was captured by the British during the AMERICAN REVOLUTION. Forten spent seven months in prison after the capture, then lived in England for a year. While there, he met many prominent abolitionists, including Granville Sharpe.

Upon his return to the United States, Forten was apprenticed to sailmaker Robert Bridges. By 1786 he was foreman of the sail loft. He became owner of the business in 1798, when Bridges retired. He invented and patented a device for handling sails and became one of the major sailmakers in Philadelphia. By 1832 he had amassed a fortune of more than $100,000. He used the money earned in his business to promote abolition, women's rights, the temperance movement, the peace movement, and equal rights for African Americans.

Forten used Richard ALLEN's church, the BETHEL AFRICAN METHODIST EPISCOPAL CHURCH, to address black audiences. Stating that the United States was now their home, he urged free blacks to resist the AMERICAN COLONIZATION SOCIETY's attempts to get them to migrate to Africa. Forten joined with Richard Allen and Absalom JONES in protest movements against discrimination and segregation. He wrote a series of letters demolishing the arguments of whites who wanted to limit the number of free blacks who entered Pennsylvania. With Jones, he filed a petition on January 2, 1800, in the House of Representatives, seeking legislative relief from the slave trade, the FUGITIVE SLAVE ACT, and SLAVERY.

The first of the large national conventions held by black leaders to air their grievances began on August 10, 1817, with Forten as its chair. He was prominent at meetings of the Negro Convention, beginning in 1830, and was one of the primary monetary contributors to abolitionist William Lloyd GARRISON's *The Liberator*, which began publishing in 1831. In 1833 Forten helped organize the AMERICAN ANTI-SLAVERY SOCIETY. He was active in that organization, which promoted equal rights for African Americans as well as emancipation, until 1841, when he became ill. In 1839 he founded the American Moral Reform Society to promote temperance.

Fort Huachuca (near Sierra Vista, Arizona): U.S. Army post established in ARIZONA in 1877. Fort Huachuca was one of a string of outposts established during the U.S. Army's campaigns against the Apache. All of the four segregated regiments of African American soldiers authorized by Congress after the CIVIL WAR were garrisoned at Fort Huachuca at some time during their existence. During the 1890's, elements of the Ninth Cavalry and the TWENTY-FOURTH INFANTRY were assigned to the fort. The Tenth Cavalry occupied the post from 1911 to 1931, and the TWENTY-FIFTH INFANTRY was stationed there from 1929 to 1943. The installation served as a training site during WORLD WAR II when members of the Twenty-fifth Infantry were assigned as cadre for the African American soldiers of the NINETY-SECOND DIVISION and NINETY-THIRD DIVISION. Upon completion of their training, these all-black divisions served in the European and Pacific theaters, respectively. Still in active use as the base of the U.S. Communications Command, Fort Huachuca has several of the original fort buildings still standing, and its museum contains exhibits on black MILITARY history in the West.

See also: Buffalo soldiers; Frontier Society; Frontier wars; Ninth Cavalry and Tenth Cavalry.

Fortune, Amos (1710—1801, Jaffrey, New Hampshire): Businessman. Fortune began his work life as an indentured servant in BOSTON, MASSACHUSETTS. After purchasing his freedom in 1770, he moved to Jaffrey, NEW HAMPSHIRE, where he prospered after founding his own tannery and book bindery. Once Fortune had become rich, he began aiding less fortunate African Americans. After his widow, Violet (Baldwin) died, the Fortunes' estate was divided, with part given to the local black church and the remainder given to the integrated local school. Fortune had also founded the Jaffrey Social Library in 1795.

Fortune, T. Thomas (October 3, 1856, Marianna, Florida—June 2, 1928, Philadelphia, Pennsylvania): Journalist and CIVIL RIGHTS organizer. Fortune was born to slave parents. He attended a FREEDMEN'S BUREAU school and later learned the printer's trade in Jacksonville, FLORIDA. In 1876 Fortune entered the preparatory department at HOWARD UNIVERSITY in WASHINGTON, D.C. He had planned to study law at Howard but abandoned his plans for lack of money. While in the nation's capital, however, he received practical experience in what would be his life's work when he worked for the *People's Advocate*, a local black paper.

In 1879 Fortune moved to New York City, where he became a printer. Soon, he also became a part owner of *Rumor*, a weekly tabloid, which later became *The Globe*, with Fortune as editor. After *The Globe* folded, he started the *New York Freeman*, which later became known as the NEW YORK AGE. He edited this newspaper, which he owned jointly with Jerome B. Peterson. *New York Age* became a leading black newspaper primarily because of Fortune's editorials, which denounced RACIAL DISCRIMINATION and demanded full equality for African Americans.

Toward the end of the nineteenth century, when race relations were deteriorating, black leaders sought means of coping with the growing tide of discrimination. Some suggested colonization, while others suggested accommodation. Fortune, however, demanded integration as the only viable solution to racism and segregation. In 1890 he helped organize the National Afro-American League. This organization, in many respects, foreshadowed the civil rights organizations of the twentieth century, since it opposed all forms of discrimination and demanded full civil rights, better schools, and fair wages. By 1893 the league, whose membership was composed almost exclusively of northern blacks, was defunct as a result of limited appeal and a lack of funds. Fortune, however, had become one of the best known and most articulate race spokesmen in the North. He played a major role in the founding of the National Afro-American Council in 1898. That group was a forerunner of the NIAGARA MOVEMENT.

As a respected journalist, Fortune worked as an editorial writer for the *New York Sun*, a leading daily paper during the 1880's. From 1919 until his death, he also wrote editorials for the *Norfolk Journal and Guide*, a major black newspaper. In 1923 he became the editor of *The Negro World*, a publication of Marcus GARVEY'S UNIVERSAL NEGRO IMPROVEMENT ASSOCIATION (UNIA). He also wrote a number of books, including *Black and White: Land, Labor, and Politics in the South* (1885) and *The Negro in Politics* (1885).

See also: Segregation and integration.

Forty acres and a mule: While its exact origins are undocumented, this slogan appears to have come into use in 1865. On January 16 of that year, Union general William T. Sherman issued Special Field Order No. 15 to establish a coastal reservation for freed slaves. Under the order, each family was to receive forty acres of land. Later, Sherman agreed to loan army mules to help these settlers till the soil.

The idea of distributing to emancipated slaves parcels of land on which to begin their free lives was promoted by some federal government leaders, notably Thaddeus Stevens, a leader of the RADICAL REPUBLICANS in Congress, at the end of the CIVIL WAR and early in the RECONSTRUCTION era. (Strictly speaking, the land was not to be given but to be leased or sold at very low cost.)

The legislation that created the FREEDMEN'S BUREAU in 1865 gave the bureau the authority to distribute parcels of land of up to forty acres to freed slaves. The land that was to be redistributed in this way was southern land that had either been abandoned or been confiscated from plantation owners. Ownership of a small amount of land actually was transferred under the Freedmen's Bureau, but resistance from whites (southerners and some northerners) soon led the government to end the policy. Moreover, virtually all the distributed parcels were returned to their original white owners or fell into the hands of speculators. The phrase "forty acres and a mule," though not entirely accurate (not all parcels distributed by the bureau were as large as forty acres, and no mules were involved), became widely used in reference to the bureau's initial land-transfer mandate.

Foster, George Murphy "Pops" (May 19, 1892, McCall, Louisiana—October 30, 1969, San Francisco, California): JAZZ musician. Foster was the younger brother of banjo player and guitarist Willard Foster and is considered by many to be the first famous double bass player in jazz history. By the age of ten, Foster moved with his family to New Orleans, where he took up first the cello and three years later the string bass. He attended New Orleans University, where he studied music, claiming that he received marks simply for playing in night shows around town.

In 1914 Foster left home for the opportunity to play in bands in the burgeoning riverboat trade. He performed with renowned musicians such as trumpeters Joe "King" OLIVER and William "Bunk" JOHNSON. By 1916 he was back in NEW ORLEANS, working as a longshoreman by day and in the clubs in Storyville, the celebrated jazz district, by night until the unofficial home of the jazz world was closed down in 1917 following a political dispute.

Foster's playing style made him the most sought-after bass player of the period. He had the ability to blend into virtually any band's style, whether it was the rough, funky blues of Frankie Dusen's Eagle Band or the more traditional dance style of John Robichaux's outfit. Foster's first recording session took place in 1924 in St. Louis, Missouri, with Charlie Creath's Jazzomaniacs. Because recording capabilities in those days were limited, capturing a string bass was next to impossible.

A significant number of King Oliver Creole Jazz Band recordings with Foster on bass were made in the 1930's for the Gennett label. These recordings, reissued in the 1980's, are fine representations of the depths of Foster's talent. Through the middle of the twentieth century, Foster continued to perform with various bands throughout the world. His age and experience made him the elder statesman of jazz music, a label he wore proudly until his death.

Foster, Henry Wendell, Jr. (b. September 8, 1933, Pine Bluff, Arkansas): Physician. Foster earned a degree in biology from Morehouse College in Atlanta in 1954. He was the only African American in his class at the University of Arkansas Medical School, from which he graduated in 1958. Foster completed his medical internship in DETROIT and then spent two years in the U.S. Air Force as a medical officer. After one year in MASSACHUSETTS, he moved to Nashville, TENNESSEE, to work at the MEHARRY MEDICAL SCHOOL. Foster divided his time between Meharry and John Andrew Memorial Hospital in Tuskegee, Alabama.

Foster became a highly respected member of the medical community and was recognized for his work with poor and disadvantaged people. In 1987 he developed the "I Have a Future" program. This program counseled teenagers living in Nashville housing projects to practice sexual abstinence and to focus on education. President George Bush praised the program in 1991, hailing it as one of the "Thousand Points of Light" in the

Henry Foster, Jr., in 1995. *(AP/Wide World Photos)*

United States. In February of 1995, President Bill Clinton nominated Foster for the position of surgeon general, an office that requires the confirmation of the U.S. Senate.

The surgeon general is the highest-ranking public health official in the United States. Considered by many to be a largely ceremonial position, the office became the focus of national attention during the 1980's because of publicity surrounding Reagan appointee C. Everett Koop. In response to the growing crisis concerning ACQUIRED IMMUNODEFICIENCY SYNDROME (AIDS), Koop had advocated his support for public service announcements encouraging the use of condoms in halting the spread of AIDS. The post again became embroiled in controversy during the tenure of Clinton appointee Joycelyn ELDERS. The outspoken Elders enraged conservatives with her remarks regarding sex education for teens, remarks which led President Clinton to request Elders's resignation in December of 1994.

Clinton hoped that nominating the politically conservative Foster would mollify conservatives dissatisfied with Elders's performance.

The Foster nomination quickly became entangled in the national debate over abortion and in the approaching presidential election of 1996. Although Foster received the support of prestigious groups such as the American Medical Association (AMA), conservative groups were extremely critical of the president's decision to nominate a physician who had performed abortions. Foster originally contended that he had performed fewer than a dozen abortions, but records eventually revealed that he had performed several more. Foster's nomination was placed in further jeopardy when he was accused of involvement with the infamous Tuskegee experiments (or Tuskegee study), in which black men infected with syphilis were not given medical treatment. Foster angrily condemned these charges as false accusations designed solely to block his nomination.

Senators Bob Dole and Phil Gramm, both candidates for the Republican presidential nomination in 1996, sought to gain the support of conservative voters by blocking Foster's confirmation in the Senate. Gramm promised a filibuster to prevent the nomination from coming to a vote. Dole used a parliamentary tactic known as a procedural vote to prevent the Senate from debating the nomination. Dole's strategy worked, and Foster's nomination for the office of surgeon general was defeated.

At a subsequent press conference, President Clinton expressed his disappointment and indicated that Foster would be offered another position in the government. In January of 1996, the Clinton administration announced that Foster would serve as a senior presidential adviser on the issue of TEENAGE PREGNANCY, an appointment similar to that held by Lee Brown as head of the Office of National Drug Control Policy. In this post, Foster served as a liaison to a new nonpartisan coalition called the National Campaign to Reduce Teen Pregnancy. Public figures serving on the the coalition's board included former surgeon general C. Everett Koop, former United Nations ambassador Andrew YOUNG, and actor Whoopi GOLDBERG. He maintained an office in the Department of Health and Human Services to coordinate his work as adviser to the president.

See also: Medicine.

Foucha v. Louisiana: U.S. SUPREME COURT insanity defense case decided in 1992. In 1984 Terry Foucha, an African American, was declared not guilty by reason of insanity for the crimes of aggravated burglary and illegal discharge of a firearm. For eight years he was confined to a mental institution, after which time he declared himself sane and requested release from the hospital. The state of LOUISIANA argued that Foucha had committed acts of violence while institutionalized, and medical evidence supported the belief that he would be a danger to society if released. The state recommended that Foucha continue to be detained in the mental institution until it could be proved that he was no longer a threat to society.

The U.S. Supreme Court overturned the state ruling, claiming that such an action defied the due process clause by confining a sane person for an indefinite period of time, in effect punishing someone who had never been convicted.

—Rose Secrest

Fourteenth Amendment: Amendment to the U.S. Constitution ratified on July 9, 1868. The single most important and far-reaching amendment to the Constitution, except for those of the Bill of Rights, the Fourteenth Amendment clearly established the goal of equality for all persons in the United States by making all citizens citizens both of the nation and of the states in which they reside. No longer allowed to treat some U.S. citizens as second-class persons, states were required to extend to all their citizens the privileges and immunities they had in all other states. States were denied the ability to take life, liberty, or property without due process of law and were required to guarantee citizens equal protection of the law. In constitutional theory, the Fourteenth Amendment sought to overcome the fundamental U.S. SUPREME COURT ruling in

President Bill Clinton cuts a ribbon to open an exhibit celebrating the Fourteenth Amendment at the new Thurgood Marshall Federal Judiciary Building on February 3, 1999. *(AP/Wide World Photos)*

Barron v. Baltimore (1833) that the Bill of Rights protected citizens only from actions of the federal government and did not protect them from actions of their state government.

After the Civil War ended in 1865, a number of Supreme Court decisions overturned congressional legislation aimed at providing improved legal status for the newly emancipated African American slaves. It was primarily these court actions that led to the proposal of the Fourteenth Amendment in Congress. The so-called RADICAL REPUBLICAN leadership in the U.S. Congress pushed the Fourteenth Amendment not only as a means to reverse Supreme Court decisions but also as a way to protect rights for African Americans as well as all Americans by writing guarantees of equality into the U.S. Constitution. The Republican congressional leadership insisted that the former Confederate states (except already readmitted Tennessee) adopt the Fourteenth Amendment as a condition for readmission to the union—an incentive that ensured its adoption.

Despite the high hopes of the framers of the amendment that it would protect the equality of all U.S. citizens, the courts' interpretation of the language of the Fourteenth Amendment meant that this goal was not achieved. In the post-Civil War era it was largely used to protect property rights, and a series of Supreme Court decisions had largely emasculated the amendment by 1900. Effective implementation of the amendment's goals was delayed for many years.

The impact of the Fourteenth Amendment was felt in the twentieth century with the expansion of the "incorporation" doctrine. The U.S. Constitution's Bill of Rights established individual rights and protections for individuals against the actions of the federal government. The incorporation doctrine guarantees these protections also to individuals against actions of state governments. The Fourteenth Amendment specifically reiterated basic tenets of the Bill of Rights, stating that no state shall "abridge the privileges or immunities" of any U.S. citizen; deprive anyone of life, liberty, or property without "due process of law"; or deny any person "equal protection of the laws."

Beginning in the 1920's and 1930's, and increasingly thereafter, the Supreme Court held that this amendment indeed mandated that states conform to the same standards as the U.S. government regarding individual rights. During the mid-twentieth century Civil Rights movement, the Fourteeth Amendment and the incorporation doctrine were important cornerstones upon which the movement could rely.

—*Richard L. Wilson*

Suggested Readings:

Abraham, Henry J., and Barbara A. Perry. *Freedom and the Court*. 6th ed. New York: Oxford University Press, 1994.

Berger, Raoul. *The Fourteenth Amendment and the Bill of Rights*. Oklahoma City: University of Oklahoma Press, 1989.

Fiscus, Ronald J. *The Constitutional Logic of Affirmative Action*. Durham, N.C.: Duke University Press, 1992.

Greenwalt, Kent. *Discrimination and Reverse Discrimination*. New York: Knopf, 1983.

The Four Tops in 1966: (left to right) Abdul Fakir, Levi Stubbs, Lawrence Payton, and Renaldo Benson. *(AP/Wide World Photos)*

Four Tops: SOUL MUSIC vocal group. The group was formed as the Four Aims in DETROIT, MICHIGAN, in 1953 and originally included Levi Stubbs, Abdul "Duke" Fakir, Lawrence Payton, and Renaldo "Obie" Benson. In 1954 the name of the group was changed to the Four Tops. The members had met at a party in Detroit. Their first engagements primarily were garden parties, graduation balls, and talent contests. They relied heavily on gospel music, since each of them had had his first singing experiences in church choirs. The group eventually got the opportunity to perform on the club circuit and developed its distinctive vocal style.

In 1956 the group signed a recording contract with Chess Records. The Four Tops found little success with Chess or a number of other record labels. It was not until the group was picked up by Berry GORDY, Jr.'s MOTOWN record company that its fortunes turned around. The Motown writing and production team of Eddie Holland, Lamont Dozier, and Brian Holland took creative control of the Four Tops and pointed the group toward a more modern soul music sound. With other groups such as the SUPREMES and the Temptations, the Four Tops came to epitomize the Motown sound, a smooth blending of soul and pop that became immensely popular with blacks and whites alike.

In 1964 the group had its first in a string of hits, with Stubbs singing lead on "Baby I Need Your Loving." With Stubbs's dramatic vocal style, the Four Tops continued releasing top-quality records until 1967, when Holland-Dozier-Holland left Motown to form their own label. Some of the other

Four Tops' classic Motown songs were "It's the Same Old Song," "I Can't Help Myself," "Reach Out I'll Be There," "Standing in the Shadows of Love," and "Bernadette."

The group left Motown in 1972 and signed with ABC/Dunhill. The Four Tops had two hits under the new label ("Keeper of the Castle" and "Ain't No Woman Like the One I've Got"). The glory days at Motown had passed, but group members continued to seek creative outlets. Obie Benson cowrote "What's Going On" (1971) with Marvin GAYE. In 1981 the Four Tops had a minor comeback hit with "When She Was My Girl." Stubbs provided the singing voice of the man-eating plant in the 1986 film version of *Little Shop of Horrors*. The group returned to the Motown label for a short time during the 1980's before signing with Arista in 1988.

The Four Tops was one of the most dynamic male soul groups of the 1960's. Even though musical trends changed, it remained true to its Motown roots into the 1990's; the group's records were also prominently featured on the playlists of "oldies" radio stations.

Foxx, Redd (John Elroy Sanford, December 9, 1922, St. Louis, Missouri—October 11, 1991, Los Angeles, California): Comedian and actor. The street-talking, bow-legged comic Redd Foxx made his brand of bawdy humor famous in black nightclubs and in Las Vegas before making his foray into television in the 1960's. Foxx had wanted to be an entertainer since his childhood, and he ran away from home at the age of thirteen to pursue that goal. He spent years performing on street corners and in black VAUDEVILLE, taking various odd jobs to make ends meet. He occasionally was arrested on petty charges for sleeping in hallways or stealing food. He worked briefly at a chicken joint in HARLEM with MALCOLM X, then known as "Detroit Red" (as opposed to Foxx's

nickname of "Chicago Red"). In his autobiography, Malcolm X referred to Foxx as "the funniest dishwasher on earth."

Foxx recorded fifty-four "party records" in the 1950's, containing bawdy comedy routines. He performed steadily in nightclubs, moving up to Las Vegas shows in the 1960's. He made guest appearances on many television shows in the 1960's and 1970's, including *The Addams Family*, *Mr. Ed*, *Green Acres*, *I Love Lucy*, and *The Flip Wilson Show*. It was his own television series, however, that brought him major success.

Foxx struck gold with his portrayal of grumpy junkyard owner Fred Sanford in *Sanford and Son*, which ran from 1972 to 1977. The show also featured costar Demond Wilson (as Fred's son), Whitman Mayo, and guest performances by Slappy White, Foxx's one-time comedy partner. The show was one of the first to feature a primarily black cast, and it helped to open television to less-stereotyped portrayals of minorities. After *Sanford and Son* left the air, Foxx hosted a comedy-variety show called *Redd Foxx*, which lasted less than five months. After some years of tax problems and scrapes with the law in the late 1970's and early 1980's, Foxx attempted a comeback television career with *The Redd Foxx Show*, a situation comedy about a diner/newsstand owner that was on the air only from January to April of 1986. Foxx had more success with the show *The Royal Family*, which premiered in 1991. He died of a heart attack while on the set. The show continued briefly with a modified plot and cast featuring Della REESE, who had costarred with Foxx.

See also: Comedy and humor; Comics, stand-up.

Franklin, Aretha (b. March 25, 1942, Memphis, Tennessee): Singer. Aretha Franklin stands as one of the most enduring musical performers of the twentieth century. Hailed in the 1960's as the Queen of Soul, Franklin made memorable records and performed popular hits, from her first million-selling record in 1967, "I Never Loved a Man (The Way I Love You)," to her hit album of 1985, *Who's Zoomin' Who*, to *A Rose Is Still a Rose* in 1998, with its title song written by Lauryn HILL.

One of Franklin's lasting achievements is that she came to prominence as the embodiment of two major strains of African American music: Such classic recordings as "Respect" and "Since You've Been Gone" combine, both in their arrangements and in her delivery, her gospel music background with a style based in RHYTHM AND BLUES. The passion, pain, and power possessed in her unique voice are another source of the lasting importance of her career. Franklin's recordings stand as a monument both to her striking talent and to African American music.

Gospel Roots

Franklin's musical career has as its foundation the gospel music that was a part of her life from the beginning. Her father was the renowned Reverend C. L. FRANKLIN of DETROIT's New Bethel Baptist Church. His influence in her life and career are central: She not only was raised by him after her mother left when she was a child but also was exposed to important performers as a result of her father's prominence; through him, she came to know such gospel greats as Mahalia JACKSON and Clara WARD. Significantly, another visitor to the Franklin home was Sam COOKE, who achieved success as a member of the gospel group the Soul Stirrers before moving away from gospel to attain great popularity with rhythm-and-blues-tinged popular music—developments similar to the later growth of Aretha's career.

Aretha would sing for these visitors. One means by which her father would encourage her to develop her piano playing (she became an accomplished pianist as well as a singer)

and singing was by playing records for her by Mahalia Jackson and Clara Ward and asking her to emulate them. Considering her musically rich environment, it is not surprising that her singing talent flourished. She sang in her father's church (she sang her first solo at ten) and performed on bills with gospel greats as a result of her father's conducting services around the country. Consequently, gospel music provided a monumental influence on her career—an influence that lasted even after she left the gospel field.

Early Recording Career

When Franklin was eighteen, she decided to change from singing gospel to singing secular music. Though some of her father's church congregation—and, in fact, Mahalia Jackson—were against this move, Aretha's father supported her in her decision. In fact, he later arranged for her to make a demo record and went with her to New York, where she met with executives from Columbia Records.

Her years with Columbia, from 1960 to 1966, were marked by promise and frustration. Executives at Columbia wanted Franklin to dilute her gospel and rhythm-and-blues influence to sing mainstream pop. Frustrated with not having any major hits with Columbia, Franklin made what was to become the most important move in her career: She signed with Atlantic Records.

Success at Atlantic Records

Unlike Columbia, Atlantic let Franklin use her gospel and rhythm-and-blues background to create her own unique brand of music. Indeed, Atlantic Records executive and producer Jerry Wexler understood Franklin to be combining the emotions and melodies of gospel with secular popular music. For her first recording sessions for Atlantic, Wexler took Franklin to Muscle Shoals, Alabama, to work with accomplished BLUES musicians. The single that came out of the sessions, "I Never Loved a Man (The

Way I Love You)," was released in February of 1967. It sold an amazing quarter of a million copies in two weeks. The response marked the beginning of the phenomenal popularity of her Atlantic recordings, in which Franklin used her African American musical influences to forge a unique style. From 1967 to the early 1970's, many of Franklin's recordings became instant—and lasting—classics and were awarded gold records: "Baby, I Love You," "(You Make Me Feel Like) A Natural Woman," "Think," and her version of Otis REDDING's "Respect" are some of the hits of this era.

Cultural Significance

The sociological significance of the popularity of Franklin's music during the era of BLACK NATIONALISM and the BLACK POWER MOVEMENT is important. Pride, independence, and self-worth were all emphasized by these movements, and these values found their parallel in Franklin's music: "Respect" expresses a woman's—and, by extension, African Americans'—demand to be treated properly; "Think" displays a similar self-assertive warning that harmony can only be achieved if one is treated with respect. Thus, although both of these songs are literally about a particular male-female relationship, they figuratively make a symbolic commentary about the treatment of African Americans. The apparent meanings of these songs, therefore, broaden to have a resonance that makes them significant to other aspects of American culture.

The cultural importance of Franklin's recordings of the late 1960's and early 1970's is evident in some central ways. First, the fact that she sold millions of records that clearly displayed her gospel and rhythm-and-blues heritage highlighted the centrality of this musical heritage to African American culture and its appeal to the wider American culture.

Aretha Franklin performing at President Bill Clinton's pre-inauguration festivities in January, 1993. *(AP/Wide World Photos)*

Thus, the popularity of Franklin's music can be seen as a celebration and appreciation of African American music by both those within and without the African American community. Furthermore, Aretha's songs of the piercing pain of love, of which "Ain't No Way" is a prime example, provide listeners with the comforting, cathartic, and empathic experience that has always been central to the blues tradition. Also, the power and exuberance with which she sings some songs that contain blues themes—"Since You've Been Gone," for example—is a testament to the enduring importance of her gospel beginnings to her singing style.

The significance of gospel music to Franklin even as she was being hailed as the Queen of Soul is nowhere more evident than in her acclaimed *Amazing Grace* album, recorded in

1972. On this album, recorded live at the New Temple Missionary Baptist Church in Los Angeles, Franklin sang with the great gospel singer and composer James CLEVELAND and the Southern California Community Choir. Franklin's stirring deliveries of "How I Got Over" and "The Old Landmark" have since been emulated by other singers, showing her lasting influence. When one examines Franklin's career, therefore, it is clear that her music has been admired for many reasons.

The second phase of Franklin's career was marked by a stylistic confusion reminiscent of her days with Columbia. As disco music came to replace soul music as the popular musical form of many artists and dominated both the charts and radio airplay in the 1970's, Aretha tried different styles, from dance music to ballads, while gaining neither the critical nor popular reception of her earlier recordings. After meeting with mixed success for most of the 1970's, Franklin left Atlantic and signed with Arista Records.

Comeback in the 1980's

The 1980's marked a resurgence in Franklin's career. Though her third album for Arista, 1983's *Jump to It*, made an impressive showing on the charts, it was with her next album, *Who's Zoomin' Who*, that she gained her greatest popularity since her glory years with Atlantic. Hit singles from the album included the title song and "Freeway of Love," both of which spawned videos that received significant airplay on music television channels, indicating Aretha's popularity with audiences too young to have experienced firsthand her success of the 1960's. Her popularity with a new generation of music fans was also demonstrated by the popularity of her duets with Annie Lennox of the British group the Eurythmics, with whom Aretha recorded "Sisters Are Doin' It for Themselves," and with British pop singer George Michael, with whom she recorded "I Knew You Were Waiting for Me."

Both her renewed popularity and her significance as a cultural and musical icon were symbolized by her inclusion in fellow Arista artist Whitney HOUSTON's "How Will I Know" video. When Houston sings "I'm asking you 'cause you know about these things," to a screen projecting Franklin's image, the moment is a tribute from one generation to another, a sign of Franklin's significance to modern singers and audiences, and a symbol of the wisdom and power of Franklin's music: She is one who knows about "these things" such as love, doubt, and pain.

In the 1980's and 1990's Franklin experienced a range of personal triumphs and tragedies. Her marriage to actor Glynn Turman ended amicably during the 1980's. In 1984 her father died after having been in a coma since being shot by a burglar in 1979. Franklin and her father had been very close; his loss, devastating to the entire family, encouraged the singer to find strength in her religious faith and her art.

In 1987 Franklin became the first female singer to be inducted into the Rock and Roll Hall of Fame. A documentary about her life, entitled *Aretha Franklin: Queen of Soul*, was aired on the Public Broadcasting Service in 1988. The documentary includes an interview with legendary Columbia Records executive and talent scout John Hammond. Hammond recalled hearing Franklin's demo record and thinking, "My God, that's the greatest voice I've heard since Billie Holiday."

That same year, Franklin released the album *One Lord, One Faith*—her first gospel album since 1972. Nominated in the category for best soul gospel performance, Franklin received her fifteenth Grammy Award for this album. The year was also marked by tragedy; Franklin's sister Carolyn died of cancer. Within a year, Franklin's brother Cecil, who had been her manager, also died. Franklin dedicated her 1991 album, *What You See Is What You Sweat*, to Carolyn and Cecil.

Continuing Career

Franklin continued to perform and to receive accolades during the 1990's. She was awarded an honorary doctorate from Wayne State University in Detroit, Michigan. In 1992 Rhino Records released a retrospective set of four compact discs entitled *The Queen of Soul*. Franklin was invited to perform at the inaugural celebration held to honor President Bill Clinton in January of 1993. Her decision to wear a fur coat on the occasion had the unfortunate result of angering various animal rights groups. On May 9, 1993, the hour-long television special *Aretha Franklin: Duet* was broadcast. During the special, Franklin sang with such recording stars as Elton John, Bonnie Raitt, Rod Stewart, Smokey Robinson, and Gloria Estefan. At the 1994 Grammy Awards, Franklin was honored with the lifetime achievement award from the National Academy of Recording Arts and Sciences. Franklin was selected as the youngest recipient of the Kennedy Center Honors in December of 1994.

During the 1990's, Franklin focused on making improvements in her personal life. In 1993 she stopped smoking. In 1995 she put together a family album with her sons, completed a cooking video, and released the album *Live at Carnegie Hall*. Her personal finances came under public scrutiny when she was sued by Saks Fifth Avenue for unpaid bills and was ordered by the Internal Revenue Service and the Michigan Department of Treasury to render payment of back taxes. Franklin recovered from these setbacks, however, and was in fine form when she performed at the opening of the Rock and Roll Hall of Fame museum in Cleveland, Ohio, on September 2, 1995.

—*Jane Davis*
—*Updated by Jeffry Jensen*

See also: Gospel music and spirituals.

Suggested Readings:

Bego, Mark. *Aretha Franklin: Queen of Soul.* New York: St. Martin's Press, 1989.

Garland, Phyl. *The Sound of Soul.* Chicago: Henry Regnery, 1969.

Haralambos, Michael. *Right On: From Blues to Soul in Black America.* London: Eddison Press, 1974.

Haskins, James. *Black Music in America.* New York: Thomas Y. Crowell, 1987.

Hochman, Steve, ed. *Popular Musicians.* 4 vols. Pasadena, Calif.: Salem Press, 1999.

Norment, Lynn. "Aretha Roars Back and Gets R-E-S-P-E-C-T." *Ebony* (August, 1998): 90-92.

Shaw, Arnold. *Black Popular Music in America.* New York: Schirmer Books, 1986.

Franklin, C. L. (1915—July 24, 1984, Detroit, Michigan): Minister and CIVIL RIGHTS leader. Franklin founded the New Bethel Baptist Church in DETROIT and was its pastor for thirty-eight years. A dynamic preacher, he made the New Bethel religious community into one of the major African American

The Reverend C. L. Franklin in 1963. *(AP/Wide World Photos)*

Protestant congregations in the United States as well as home to an outstanding choir. He also became a central figure in the Detroit civil rights movement. Franklin is perhaps best known for leading a march of more than 125,000 people on Detroit's Woodward Avenue in June of 1963, along with Martin Luther KING, Jr., shortly before the historic MARCH ON WASHINGTON. The Detroit march was one of the few outstanding successes of the Civil Rights movement in the North.

Franklin's inspirational preaching brought him to national attention through radio broadcasts and more than twenty record albums of his sermons. He attracted mainstream media attention and interest, and some of his recordings were produced and distributed by MOTOWN Records. Franklin is also known as the father of soul singer Aretha FRANKLIN, who got her start in her father's church choir.

In 1979 Franklin was shot in a burglary attempt at his home. He spent the last years of his life in a coma. Although he never attained the fame or had the prestige of King, more than ten thousand people attended his funeral, at which Jesse JACKSON delivered the eulogy. *See also:* Baptists.

Franklin, John Hope (b. January 2, 1915, Rentiesville, Oklahoma): Historian. One of the leading African American historians of the twentieth century, John Hope Franklin enjoyed a long and distinguished career. Franklin's father, Buck Colbert Franklin, was a prominent lawyer in Tulsa, OKLAHOMA, and one of the first African Americans to practice law in that state. In 1921, when Franklin's father established his law practice in Tulsa, which was a segregated city at the time, his office was burned to the ground by a group of race rioters. He later became the first African American in Oklahoma to sit on a U.S. district court bench. John Hope Franklin said in a 1963 interview that his father

scorned segregation as a mark of indignity. He paid no attention to signs marked "Negro" and "White." He went where he pleased, mingling with people like any other man.

Education

Franklin attended Booker T. Washington High School in Tulsa and entered FISK UNIVERSITY in Nashville, Tennessee, in 1931. While at Fisk, he waited tables to earn money and served as president of the student government and of his fraternity. An excellent student, he became fascinated with history, which became his major subject, and graduated with a bachelor's degree, magna cum laude, in 1935.

With the encouragement of one of his professors, Franklin began graduate studies in history at Harvard University, obtaining his master's degree in 1936. He returned to Fisk to teach as a substitute in the department of history and later resumed his graduate studies at Harvard, receiving a Ph.D. in American history in 1941.

Teaching Career

In 1939 accepted a faculty position at St. Augustine's College in Raleigh, NORTH CAROLINA, and began research into the social and economic status of African Americans in North Carolina before the CIVIL WAR. He published essays in several academic journals, eventually collecting them in his book *The Free Negro in North Carolina, 1790-1860* (1943), for which he received wide critical acclaim from his fellow historians. In 1943 Franklin became professor of history at North Carolina College, and in 1947, he left for WASHINGTON, D.C., to accept a professorship at HOWARD UNIVERSITY.

While teaching at Howard, he acted as an adviser to the NATIONAL ASSOCIATION FOR THE ADVANCEMENT OF COLORED PEOPLE (NAACP), helping to draft the legal brief that was submitted to the U.S. SUPREME COURT on segregation in the public schools that resulted in the historic BROWN V. BOARD OF EDUCATION decision of 1954. In 1956 Franklin was appointed professor of history and chair of the department at Brooklyn College in NEW YORK, becoming the first African American to head a college department in that state.

Franklin took a year's leave of absence in 1962 and 1963 to work in England as the William Pitt Professor of History at St. John's College at the University of Cambridge, where he lectured on the U.S. Civil War. Upon returning to the United States, he accepted the position of chair of the department of history at the University of Chicago. Franklin also lectured in Germany, Italy, France, India, Australia, and Nigeria and held visiting professorships at Harvard University, the University of Wisconsin, and Cornell University. He held appointments as the James B. Duke Professor Emeritus at Duke University and as a professor of legal history at the Duke University Law School.

Franklin personally experienced the indignities of racism. During WORLD WAR II, he applied for clerical work in the Navy; he was told that, though he was otherwise well qualified, as a black man he could not join the Navy. The rejection hurt him deeply, but he decided instead to devote his energies to becoming an expert on African American history, a field that was virtually unknown in U.S. colleges and universities.

Scholarly Works

In 1947 Franklin published a landmark book, *From Slavery to Freedom: A History of Negro Americans*, which became a standard text in African American history. In 1985 his *George Washington Williams: A Biography* won wide recognition as a brilliant work on the life and works of WILLIAMS, a long-neglected nineteenth-century black historian who wrote one of the earliest histories of African Americans. Franklin devoted nearly forty years of his life to painstakingly reconstructing Williams's life, starting from Williams's birthplace in a small Pennsylvania town and tracing his moves to MEXICO, Europe, Central Africa, Egypt, and finally England, where Williams died. In 1975, after studying Williams's life for thirty years, Franklin discovered his burial place in an unmarked grave in Blackpool, England, and laid a wreath there in his honor. When the book was published in 1985, a reviewer for *Choice* magazine called it "one of the most exciting biographies recently published."

Franklin's 1989 book *Race and History: Selected Essays, 1938-1988* is a collection of twenty-seven essays that represent fifty years of Franklin's prolific scholarship, with most of the essays devoted to the social conditions of blacks in the South during the nineteenth century. Franklin notes in the book's preface that he felt his research into the past was relevant to the great issues affecting African Americans; he explained that he refrained from actively participating in the CIVIL RIGHTS movement because he felt he could best contribute to the struggle for equality by using his skills as a historian to influence public policy.

In an essay entitled "The Dilemma of the American Negro Scholar," originally written in 1963, he urged African American scholars to "rewrite the history of this country and correct the misrepresentations and falsifications in connection with the Negro's role in our history." A reviewer for *The New York Times Book Review* called the collection "both a meditation on history and a record of an extraordinary life," while *The New Republic* said of Franklin:

> We are dealing here with a historian who spares no effort in pursuit of truth, delights in finding it even when he deplores the truth of what he has found, and never thinks of suppressing it on that account. This is a book packed full of hard truths that needed saying.

A prolific writer throughout his career, Franklin also edited several U.S. history textbooks and contributed articles to more than a dozen books on American history, African American history, and higher-education issues. His other major works include *The Militant South, 1800-1861* (1956); *Reconstruction: After the Civil War* (1961), *The Emancipation Proclamation* (1963), and *Racial Equality in America* (1976). In *The Emancipation Proclamation*, Franklin suggested that Abraham Lincoln's manifesto might eventually "give real meaning and purpose to the Declaration of Independence." In *Racial Equality in America*, Franklin discussed his concept of "equality indivisible"—the idea that equality must not be divided so that it is extended to some at the expense of others. The task of all Americans, he argued, is to overcome the effects of the United States' long heritage of inequality.

John Hope Franklin receiving the Truman Good Neighbor Award in Kansas City, Missouri, in May, 1999. *(AP/Wide World Photos)*

Achievements and Honors

Franklin served as president of the Southern Historical Association in 1970, the Organization of American Historians in 1975, and the American Historical Association in 1979. He also served on the board of directors of the NAACP Legal Defense and Education Fund. In recognition of his many achievements, Franklin received a Social Science Research Council Fellowship in 1945, a Guggenheim Fellowship in 1950, and a President's Fellowship at Brown University in 1952. He was also granted honorary degrees from Morgan State College (1960), Virginia State College (1961), and LINCOLN UNIVERSITY (1961).

Franklin's view of race relations in America, he once said, is a "peculiar" one. He argued that African Americans can progress only to the extent that white Americans advance in understanding that all human beings are equal. Blacks have been hindered in achieving equality, he maintained, because whites have not been advanced enough to let them. A crucial factor in bringing about social change is the recognition of the rightful place of blacks in American history. In time, Franklin wrote, this recognition will provide the United States

> with a lesson in the wastefulness and wickedness of human exploitation that have characterized too much of this nation's past. This is a lesson that must be learned if we are to survive and if we are to win the respect and admiration of the other peoples of the world.

—*Raymond Frey*

See also: Historiography; Intellectuals and scholars; Professors.

Suggested Readings:

Anderson, Talmadge, ed. *Black Studies: Theory, Method, and Cultural Perspective.* Pullman: Washington State University Press, 1990.

Franklin, John Hope. *The Color Line: Legacy for the Twenty-first Century.* Columbia: University of Missouri Press, 1993.

_____. *Free Negro in North Carolina, 1790-1860.* Chapel Hill: University of North Carolina Press, 1995.

_____. *From Slavery to Freedom: A History of African Americans.* 7th ed. New York: Alfred A. Knopf, 1994.

_____. *Race and History: Selected Essays, 1938-1988.* Baton Rouge: Louisiana State University Press, 1989.

_____. *Runaway Slaves: Rebels on the Plantation.* New York: Oxford University Press, 1999.

_____, et al. *African Americans and the Living Constitution.* Washington, D.C.: Smithsonian Institution Press, 1995.

Fredrickson, George M. "Pioneer." *The New York Review of Books* (September 23, 1993): 30-33.

Hine, Darlene C., ed. *The State of Afro-American History: Past, Present, and Future.* Baton Rouge: Louisiana State University Press, 1986.

"John Hope Franklin Has Remained Dedicated to the Truth About Race in America for More than Forty Years." *Jet* (April 13, 1998): 34-35.

Franks, Gary A. (b. February 9, 1953, Waterbury, Connecticut): Politician and U.S. representative from CONNECTICUT. Franks grew up in Connecticut and attended Yale University, where he graduated with a bachelor of arts degree in sociology in 1975. Upon graduation, Franks became a real estate entrepreneur and was president of GAF Realty in Waterbury. As a leading businessman in Waterbury, Franks was a member of the city chamber of commerce and took keen interest in local affairs. He was elected to the board of aldermen for the city of Waterbury in 1985 and served until 1990.

Representative Gary A. Franks, the only Republican member of the Congressional Black Caucus in 1993, when this picture was taken. *(AP/Wide World Photos)*

Franks ran as the REPUBLICAN PARTY candidate for Connecticut's Fifth Congressional District seat in 1990. He was elected on November 6, 1990, and became the first African American to represent Connecticut in the U.S. Congress. He took his seat in Congress in January of 1991 and was appointed to serve on the House Committee on the Armed Services, the House Committee on Small Business, and the House Select Committee on Aging. Franks became a member of the CONGRESSIONAL BLACK CAUCUS, as one of its few Republican members. He became a member of the National Republican Congressional Committee and the Republican Policy Committee. *See also:* Congress members; Politics and government.

Fraternal societies: Fraternal orders, from the Prince Hall Freemasons through lodge and mutual benefit societies to Boulé and the Links, have played a significant role in the African American community. These organizations have been involved in teaching moral values; providing fellowship, benevolence, and mutual aid; advancing civil and human rights; providing mentoring and networking opportunities; and offering funding opportunities for HIGHER EDUCATION.

Black Freemasonry

Prince HALL is considered the founder of black freemasonry. In the 1770's Hall apparently attempted to join a white Masonic Lodge but was denied admittance. However, in 1775, Hall and fourteen other men of color were inducted into a military lodge that was attached to a British regiment under the authority of the Grand Lodge of Ireland. Shortly thereafter, he established the first African lodge in BOSTON. Although Masonry teaches the equality of men, historically the white Masonic Lodges in the United States did not admit African Amer-

icans. (Prince Hall Lodges do admit whites.) Thousands of Prince Hall Lodges developed as a result, and at one time they inducted 30 percent of the African American men in many southern cities and towns. The Prince Hall Masonic fraternity claimed 300,000 members worldwide in 1999.

Until the 1990's, the Grand Lodges of individual states did not recognize the legitimacy of Prince Hall Masonry, and some Grand Lodges, primarily in the southern states, still did not in 1999. In a number of instances Grand Lodges sought legally to enjoin Prince Hall Lodges from using Masonic names, titles, regalia, and emblems.

Many African American fraternal organizations have their roots in Prince Hall Masonry, including the Prince Hall Grand Chapter of the Eastern Star, Heroines of Jericho and Order of Golden Circle (both are societies for women related to black masons), and Knights

Members of a Freemason lodge in Greenville, Mississippi, in the late 1890's. *(Library of Congress)*

of Pythias of North America, Europe, Asia, and Africa. Masonic organizations often employ secrecy and ritual in teaching virtues, morals, and religious values.

Fraternal Benefit Societies

Most fraternal organizations in the United States have had mutual aid as one of their principal functions. Initially, benefit societies provided death benefits to the survivors of deceased members. Early in the twentieth century this welfare function expanded to the point that these organizations largely monopolized the health-insurance market. Many benefit societies excluded African Americans from membership, so they formed their own, including the Improved Benevolent and Protective Order of Elks of the World; Daughters of the Independent, Benevolent, Protective Order of Elks of the World (an auxiliary of IBPOEW for black women); the Knights of Peter Claver, a fraternal order for Roman Catholics; Grand United Order of Odd Fellows in America International; Order of Tabor, Knights and Daughters; the Colored Brotherhood and Sisterhood of Honor; and the Mosaic Templars of America. As life and medical insurance became more affordable and available as an employment benefit, this advantage of lodge membership lost its appeal.

Fraternities and Sororities

The National Pan-Hellenic Council listed nine historically African American COLLEGE FRATERNITIES AND SORORITIES on college campuses in 1999. Alpha Phi Alpha was the first such organization and was founded at Cornell University in 1906. Most of the others were started at HOWARD UNIVERSITY; they include the Omega Psi Phi and Phi Beta Sigma fraternities, and Alpha Kappa Alpha, Delta Sigma Theta, and Zeta Phi Beta sororities. Kappa Alpha Psi and Iota Phi Theta fraternities were first established at Indiana and Morgan State Universities respectively. The first chapter of

Sigma Gamma Rho sorority was at Butler University.

African Americans were prevented from joining fraternities and sororities on many historically white campuses. The historically African American organizations above not only furnished support and fellowship for black students facing discrimination on largely white campuses but also, in some cases, provided the only on-campus housing open to them. In contrast to traditionally white fraternities and sororities, the historically African American sororities and fraternities have made human and CIVIL RIGHTS, social justice, and public service foci of their mission statements and outreach activities.

Organizations for the Social Elite

Another of the attractions of fraternal organizations in the United States has been their ability to bestow social prestige. The opportunity to wear lavish regalia, take on high-sounding titles such as Supreme Potentate or Grand Eminent Commander, and participate in public events was more appealing to earlier generations—especially to men. Although the fraternal secret societies have generally lost their attraction as prestige-granting agencies, there are several organizations that have significant cachet in the African American community.

The Links is the largest and the most influential of elite black women's groups, according to Lawrence Otis GRAHAM's study of the black upper class. The Links was founded in 1946. Its members are expected to engage in substantial volunteer work. The Links is a major sponsor of organizations such as the UNITED NEGRO COLLEGE FUND and the NATIONAL ASSOCIATION FOR THE ADVANCEMENT OF COLORED PEOPLE (NAACP) Legal Defense Fund as well as myriad charities and scholarship programs in the United States and abroad. The Links is also famous for the formal social functions it organizes. The Girl Friends, Inc., is another elite group of black women dedicated to philanthropic as well as cultural and social activities.

One of the most influential black men's fraternal organizations was founded in 1963. One Hundred Black Men is dedicated to improving community life and providing educational and economic opportunities for all African Americans. This organization sponsors antiviolence programs for youth, scholarships, mentoring, and networking opportunities in addition to economic development programs.

Boulé, or Sigma Pi Phi, is the most prestigious of all the elite black men's groups, which also include the Comus Social Club and the Reveille Club in addition to One Hundred Black Men. Boulé dates from 1904 but probably has some earlier roots in the Prince Hall Masons. This organization places emphasis on intellect and tends to draw highly educated, professional, accomplished, and influential black men. Members have included W. E. B. Du Bois and Martin Luther King, Jr. Social action is not the focus of this organization. The National Association of Guardsmen is another elite social organization made up largely of professional black men; it was established in 1933.

Although membership in such elite groups as the Links, Boulé, and One Hundred Black Men is highly valued, in general fraternal organizations, which were at one time fixtures in American society, have become less popular with all races. Fewer men in the prime club-joining age range of thirty-five to fifty-five have an interest in spending their leisure time with other men. Although some of these formerly all-male associations welcome women to their ranks, many continue to report declining membership. Several reasons have been suggested to account for this downward trend. One is the fact that, with a large majority of women in the labor force, men have more responsibilities at home and less time for fraternal and other club activities. Taking an even larger view, sociologist Robert Putnam cites a general decline in social connectedness. He points to suburbanization, with its demands of more commuting time, as one of the forces, but he finds television to be the principal malefactor.

—*Gary A. Cretser*

Suggested Readings:

Beito, David T. "Thy Brother's Keeper: The Mutual Aid Tradition of American Fraternal Orders." *Policy Review* 70 (Fall, 1994): 55-59.

Frost, Dan. "Farewell to the Lodge." *American Demographics* 18 (January, 1996): 40-45.

Giddings, Paula. *In Search of Sisterhood: Delta Sigma Theta and the Challenge of the Black Sorority Movement.* New York: William Morrow, 1988.

Graham, Lawrence Otis. *Our Kind of People: Inside America's Black Upper Class.* New York: HarperCollins, 1999.

Schmidt, Alvin J. *Fraternal Organizations.* Westport, Conn.: Greenwood Press, 1980.

Fraunces, Samuel (c. 1722, British West Indies—October 10, 1795, Philadelphia, Pennsylvania): Patriot. Fraunces migrated to British North America from the West Indies sometime before 1759. He bought a tavern in New York City in 1762. During the American Revolution, his tavern was a favorite gathering place for the Patriots. Later it was at Fraunces Tavern, in 1783, that George Washington turned command over to trusted officers before retiring to Mount Vernon.

Frazier, E. Franklin (September 24, 1894, Baltimore, Maryland—May 17, 1962, Washington, D.C.): Sociologist and educator. Best known for his extensive, groundbreaking studies of the African American family, Edward Franklin Frazier was also an authority on various sociological aspects of African American existence such as education, business, housing, and class structure. The author of landmark studies such as *The Negro Family in the United States* (1939) and *Black Bourgeoisie* (1957), Frazier was elected to the presidency of the American Sociological Society in 1948, the first time that an African American had been elected to head a national professional organization with a predominantly white membership.

Youth and Education

The son of a bank messenger, Frazier was born in BALTIMORE, MARYLAND, where he attended public schools. Upon his graduation from high school, he enrolled at HOWARD UNIVERSITY, from which he graduated cum laude in 1916. Impressively proficient in a broad range of disciplines, Frazier taught mathematics, French, English, and history at Booker T. Washington's TUSKEGEE INSTITUTE in Alabama and St. Paul's Normal and Industrial School in Virginia.

In 1919 Frazier enrolled at Massachusett's Clark University, where he began his first formal study of sociology, still a fledgling discipline at that time. He found himself drawn to sociology; he considered it the social science that came closest to providing explanations of the class and race conflicts that increasingly dominated his thoughts. He wrote a thesis entitled "New Currents of Thought Among the Colored People of America" and earned a master's degree within a year. At Clark, Frazier's career as a sociologist began; he was especially influenced by the teaching of Frank Hankins, who convinced him that the analysis of social phenomena could be carried out on a high intellectual level.

In 1920 Frazier earned a fellowship at the New York School of Social Work, where he conducted a study of New York City's longshoremen. The following year, 1921, he embarked upon a year's study of folk culture at the University of Copenhagen as a fellow of the American-Scandinavian Foundation.

Academic Career

In 1922 Frazier married Ellen Brown of Winston, North Carolina, and accepted a teaching position at Morehouse College in Atlanta. Within two years, he was combining his teaching duties with the directorship of the Atlanta School of Social Work. During this time, Frazier began publishing essays relating to the topics that would occupy him throughout a long career: the African American family, race relations, and the African American middle class. In 1927 he published an essay in the popular journal *Forum* entitled "The Pathology of Race Prejudice," a scathing dissection of bigotry articulated from the authoritative, scholarly perspective of a new social science. When the essay appeared in print, it created an uproar among Atlanta whites, who organized a manhunt for Frazier. He was almost immediately forced to leave Atlanta, relinquishing his administrative and teaching jobs.

Unintimidated by this hostility to his ideas, Frazier then entered a doctoral program in sociology at the University of Chicago, where he studied with Robert Park, an eminent and established sociologist. Park belonged to a group of leading researchers and teachers known as the Chicago School of sociology; the Chicago School's method was marked by the empirical examination of one feature of a population in order to explain elements of the social whole.

After completing his doctorate in 1931, Frazier published his dissertation in 1932 as *The Negro Family in Chicago*. He moved on to FISK UNIVERSITY in Nashville to work as a special lecturer and a research professor in the school's department of social sciences, where a special program of research into African American life was already underway. While at Fisk, he published widely in such journals as *The Nation, Current History,* THE CRISIS, and *Opportunity.* In 1934 Frazier left Fisk to become professor and head of the sociology department at Howard University in Washington, D.C.

It was at Howard University that Frazier

would spend the rest of his professional life, teaching full-time for the next twenty-five years, publishing widely, winning numerous fellowships and awards, and helping to shape the sociological discipline. In addition to governing the department of sociology, he served as director of the school's program in social work and as a resident fellow of the Library of Congress.

Scholarly Works

In 1939 Frazier published his classic study, *The Negro Family in the United States*. In 1940 the book won the Anisfield Award as the most significant work on race relations of the year. Frazier's book delineated a history of African American families since the time of slavery and analyzed the structures of African American families in relation to historical events and trends, such as the mass migration of African Americans to urban centers during the twentieth century. Frazier's sociological preoccupation focused on the ways in which social environments determine the formations and functions of families in different cultures and in different parts of the world. When he examined American culture, he deployed methodologies that he had used in studying cultures in Denmark, Brazil, and Africa. The effects of URBANIZATION upon the reordering of FAMILY LIFE preoccupied him, and in the case of African Americans, Frazier emphasized the social and psychological disorganization that inevitably accompanied families' displacement from rural communities to furious, burgeoning industrial cities.

Investigating Black Family Life

The Negro Family in the United States is usually considered Frazier's most important work, and it was a significant contribution to sociology in a number of respects. Frazier described extensive variations among the behaviors and social classes of African Americans. While the book closely examined the question of insta-

bility in African American families, Frazier took pains to assert that there were stable as well as disorganized family units within the African American community. Such an emphasis upon differentiation could be seen as a rebuke to the widespread tendency of cultural commentators to regard African Americans as a homogenous group.

Further, through meticulous historical research, Frazier provided and substantiated, for the first time, a compelling sense of the disorienting impact of material and social change upon African American families. He offered concrete sociological explanations for an asserted tendency of African American families to deviate from normative American family structures. The more frequent incidence among African American families of SINGLE-PARENT HOUSEHOLDS and common-law marriages, for example, was understandable to Frazier as a social phenomenon. This interpretation functioned as an important remedy to prevailing explanations of unstable African American families that attributed the instability to genetic causes. Such explanations had often been used to describe African Americans as inherently incapable of full participation in modern civilization.

Portrait of the Black Middle Class

Frazier's work on urbanization and the family fueled his interest in the development of the African American middle class and in status distinctions between African Americans. Frazier had demonstrated an interest in the middle class as early as 1925, when he published "Durham: Capital of the Black Middle Class," an essay that celebrated the values of the conservative and well-established African American business class of Durham, North Carolina.

Frazier demonstrated that the movement of African Americans to cities created a basis for increasingly elaborate economic and status distinctions among them. The practice of segregation provided a clientele for growing numbers of African American doctors, lawyers, and businesspeople. Frazier developed a distinction between a thrifty and upstanding black middle class that had been established for more than a generation and a newer middle class of blacks whose rapid upward mobility he viewed as leading to an emphasis on conspicuous consumption. His major study of the middle class, *Black Bourgeoisie* (1957), claimed that the older black middle-class virtues had been displaced by those of a newer, highly mobile urban class of blacks whose morality and interest in education were superficial.

Black Bourgeoisie was Frazier's most controversial book. He wrote it in Paris, far from the society it described, in an effort to achieve stark objectivity. However, the volume was read as a polemic—as an overly dramatized, hostile profile of the recently emergent middle class. Those who objected most strongly to the book were themselves members of the new middle classes, who read Frazier's descriptions as highly exaggerated and unfairly critical. Frazier responded by suggesting that his study was meant to illuminate in a disinterested way the dehumanizing effects of segregation. Although some African Americans might have a vested interest in segregation, he contended, the interests of all would be better served by thoroughgoing integration.

The sociological community criticized *Black Bourgeoisie* on methodological grounds. A highly effective informal essayist, Frazier had given the book a looser structure than he had used for his studies of the family. The information in *Black Bourgeoisie* had not been gathered in a rigidly systematic manner; instead, Frazier offered a kind of cultural commentary. He interpreted the methodological criticisms appearing in sociology journals as masking an implicit objection to the book's unsentimental assessment of middle-class ideology and values.

—*James Knippling*
See also: Intellectuals and scholars; Professors.

Suggested Readings:
Frazier, E. Franklin. *Black Bourgeoisie*. Glencoe, Ill.: Free Press, 1957.
_____. *The Negro Family in the United States*. Chicago: University of Chicago Press, 1939.
_____. *On Race Relations: Selected Writings*. Chicago: University of Chicago Press, 1968.
Kusmer, Kenneth L. "The Black Urban Experience in American History." In *The State of Afro-American History: Past, Present, and Future*, edited by Darlene Clark Hine. Baton Rouge: Louisiana State University Press, 1986.
Platt, Anthony M. "Between Scorn and Longing: Frazier's *Black Bourgeoisie*." *Social Justice* 20 (Spring/Summer, 1993): 129-139.
_____. *E. Franklin Frazier Reconsidered*. New Brunswick, N.J.: Rutgers University Press, 1991.
_____. "Racism in Academia: Lessons from the Life of E. Franklin Frazier." *Monthly Review* 42 (September, 1990): 29-45.

Frazier, Joe (b. January 17, 1944, Beaufort, South Carolina): Boxer. Joseph "Joe" Frazier began his amateur BOXING career in 1958. After winning a gold medal in the heavyweight division at the 1964 Olympics in Tokyo, Japan, he turned professional.

In 1967, when heavyweight champion Muhammad ALI was stripped of his title by the World Boxing Association for refusing military service on religious grounds, Jimmy Ellis was the top-rated heavyweight. Ellis was not universally accepted as champion, however. Frazier defeated Buster Mathis to win the New York State Athletic Commission world heavyweight title in 1968. He finally met Ellis for a title bout on February 16, 1970, in New York City. Frazier scored a fifth-round knockout to become undisputed titleholder.

Eight months later, on November 18, 1970, in DETROIT, MICHIGAN, Frazier knocked out Bob Foster in the second round. On March 8,

Boxer Joe Frazier in 1969, when he held the world heavyweight title. *(AP/Wide World Photos)*

1971, in New York City, Frazier finally met the unbeaten Muhammad Ali, in the first of three fights between the two men. Frazier won in a decision. In 1972 Joe Frazier was challenged by two boxers, Terry Daniels and Ron Stander. Frazier defeated Daniels in the fourth round on January 15 and knocked out Stander in the fifth round on May 25. In his last fight as champion on January 22, 1973, in Kingston, JAMAICA, Frazier suffered a second-round technical knockout at the hands of George FOREMAN.

Frazier fought Ali two more times. In a National Boxing Federation bout on January 1, 1974, in New York City, Ali defeated Frazier in twelve rounds. Then, in a title bout afterwards known as the "Thrilla in Manila" on October 1, 1975, world champion Ali scored a technical knockout against Frazier in the Philippines' capital city.

Frazier also fought Foreman again, on June 15, 1976, in Uniondale, New York. Foreman beat him badly, and Frazier retired from the ring with a career record of thirty-two wins, four losses, and one draw. He came out of retirement in 1981 to defeat Jumbo Cummings, a mediocre opponent.

Other than boxing, Frazier launched lesser careers as an entertainer, performing as the lead singer in a rock-blues group called the Knockouts; as a businessman, in such ventures as a limousine service in Philadelphia; and as manager of his son, prizefighter Marvis Frazier.

Free African Society: One of the earliest African American religious organizations in the United States. Formed in PHILADELPHIA in 1787 as a response to the ejection of Richard ALLEN and Absalom JONES from the main (whites only) floor of St. George's Methodist Church, the society gave its members an autonomous setting for religious worship and community organizing. The Free African Society issued explicit ABOLITIONIST MOVEMENT resolutions and provided a base for the later formation of the fully autonomous AFRICAN METHODIST EPISCOPAL CHURCH.

Free blacks: Despite the existence of SLAVERY, more than one-tenth of all African Americans in the United States were legally free persons during the six decades that preceded the CIVIL WAR. They attained this status through emancipation, MANUMISSION, or self-purchase, or by being born to a free black mother. Yet for most free blacks, freedom offered only limited protection from the effects of racism.

Origins and Growth

Less than a generation after 1619, the year the first African slaves were landed at Jamestown, VIRGINIA, a distinct free black population had emerged within the British colonies on the North American mainland. Enclaves of independent blacks continued to exist throughout the seventeenth century on the eastern shore of Chesapeake Bay and in colonial cities such as Boston, New York, Philadelphia, and Charleston. Yet no more than a few thousand free blacks lived in America in 1770.

A dramatic expansion of the free black population occurred in the decades following the AMERICAN REVOLUTION. This was the result of four factors. First, thousands of slaves were emancipated by the British as a war measure or gained their freedom in return for fighting on the American side. Second, northern state legislatures and courts, animated by the ideals of liberty and equality espoused by the patriots of the revolution, mandated the gradual emancipation of slaves within their jurisdictions. Third, hundreds of slaveowners in the upper South were similarly inspired by revolutionary rhetoric and personally manumitted their black chattel. Finally, several thousand French-speaking mulattoes from the Caribbean migrated to cities along America's Gulf Coast in the wake of a revolution in HAITI.

The first federal census in 1790 enumerated 59,466 free blacks, with slightly more than half of those in the South. Thereafter, the ratio of free blacks remained fairly constant by region, but their numbers grew dramatically, nearly doubling to 108,395 in 1800 and again to 186,446 in 1810. The expansion of the free black population slowed in subsequent decades, but considerable growth still occurred. By 1860 the free black population totaled 488,070, with a slim majority still living in the South.

Socioeconomic Diversity

Free blacks lived in a variety of locales and circumstances. The vast majority resided in the upper South or in cities—from Boston to New Orleans. In the decades following the American Revolution, thousands had migrated to urban centers to find employment, to join larger communities of blacks, or to gain a degree of anonymity. Nearly half of all free blacks lived in urban areas on the eve of the Civil War. BALTIMORE, MARYLAND; NEW YORK CITY; PHILADELPHIA, PENNSYLVANIA; NEW ORLEANS, LOUISIANA; and WASHINGTON, D.C., had the largest populations. Yet free blacks were also scattered in isolated farming communities throughout the Midwest, such as the well-known settlements in Cass County, MICHIGAN.

Most free blacks belonged to the lower classes. They worked as waiters, porters, domestic servants, laundresses, stevedores, sailors, farm workers, day laborers, or cartmen, or in similar occupations. Several thousand were artisans or independent businesspeople—shopkeepers, barbers, tailors, boardinghouse keepers, and real estate brokers. Only a few, such as Philadelphia sailmaker James FORTEN, were persons of means. The most prosperous groups of free blacks resided in the lower South. Those in LOUISIANA and SOUTH CAROLINA had accumulated far more property than the average northern white.

Many of the wealthiest free blacks, moreover, were themselves slaveowners. Some 3,775 free blacks owned more than 13,000 slaves by 1830. A majority of BLACK SLAVEOWNERS purchased fellow African Americans in order to protect family members: Since most southern states banished manumitted slaves, owning spouses or children was a way to keep families together. Other black slaveowners, however, possessed slaves out of economic self-interest. This was particularly true in Louisiana, where forty-four free blacks in eight parishes owned more than a tenth of the black-held slave population in the region. A few black sugar planters in the state, such as Andrew Durnford of Plaquemines Parish, owned in excess of fifty slaves.

Discriminatory Treatment

A matrix of laws and customs prevented free blacks—whether living in the North or the South—from achieving full legal, political, and social equality with whites. For this reason, historians of the African American experience have termed them "quasi-free" or "slaves without masters." Even in the North, state legislatures approved so-called black laws limiting the rights of free blacks. Only five states—all of them in New England—permitted black men to vote on an equal basis with whites in 1860. Several states prohibited them from serving on juries or testifying in court cases involving whites. Others outlawed INTERRACIAL MARRIAGE or MISCEGENATION (sexual relations between the races). Some states excluded blacks from entering their borders or required them to post a substantial bond guaranteeing their good behavior. OREGON, for example, forbade free blacks to own real estate, make contracts, or file lawsuits.

Free blacks lived in a racially separate world, excluded from regular contact with whites in most areas of American society. Custom and prejudice kept the races apart on railroad cars, streetcars, stagecoaches, and steamboats; denied blacks equal access to theaters, restaurants, and employment; and forced them into segregated, and usually inferior, public institutions—schools, hospitals, prisons, and cemeteries. The U.S. SUPREME COURT affirmed such treatment. The majority opinion in the case *Dred Scott v. Sandford* (1857, commonly called the DRED SCOTT DECISION) denied free blacks claims to American citizenship and stated that blacks "had no rights which a white man was bound to respect."

Free blacks in the urban North were frequent victims of white violence. Enmity between the races occasionally erupted into mob attacks on free blacks and the neighborhoods in which they lived. Six RACE RIOTS took place in PHILADELPHIA between 1829 and 1849; similar outbursts occurred in BOSTON, Cincinnati, Providence, New York, and Washington, D.C. Rampaging whites usually sought out the symbols of free black success—churches, businesses, the homes of the black elite, and the meeting places of black self-improvement organizations.

Although not subjected to the same sort of periodic racial violence as their northern counterparts, southern free blacks were no more secure. White southerners became increasingly fearful during the pre-Civil War decades that free blacks would "whisper liberty in the ears of the oppressed," provoking slave insurrections throughout the region. Thus many southerners, including many slaveowners, strongly supported the efforts of the AMERICAN COLONIZATION SOCIETY to settle free blacks in LIBERIA, West Africa. After the unsuccessful Nat TURNER slave revolt of 1831 in Virginia, in which nearly sixty whites were killed, southern state legislatures uniformly approved laws restricting or outlawing manumission and limiting the freedom of movement of free blacks. In the wake of John BROWN's raid at HARPERS FERRY in 1859, these same bodies debated bills to expel or enslave their free black populations. ARKANSAS legislators enacted a law requiring all free blacks to leave the state by January 1, 1860, or become slaves. Southern black men were also particularly vulnerable to LYNCHING by whites.

Institutional Life

Free blacks were usually excluded from or segregated within the dominant institutions of American society. To resist racism and to serve their social, economic, intellectual, and religious needs, blacks established hundreds of independent institutions between 1780 and 1860. Churches were among the earliest and most important of these institutions. Beginning in 1787, thousands of northern blacks abandoned white houses of worship to form separate BAPTIST, METHODIST, PRESBYTERIAN, and EPISCOPAL congregations. Many of those within the Methodist fold eventually joined to create distinctly black denominations, most notably the AFRICAN METHODIST EPISCOPAL CHURCH (1816) and the AFRICAN METHODIST EPISCOPAL ZION CHURCH (1822). Hundreds of black private schools were also organized, often in the basements of African American churches.

In addition to churches and schools, free blacks formed a host of organizations dedicated to assisting free black communities and improving the race. These included burial and insurance societies, benevolent associations to aid the ill and indigent, asylums for orphans and the aged, forums for literary discussion and debate, library companies, and moral reform organizations. By 1840 at least one temperance society was organized in nearly every black community in the North. Hundreds of black men also joined racially separate FRATERNAL SOCIETIES and lodges, especially those organized by the Freemasons and the Odd Fellows.

Free Blacks as Leaders

These institutions and organizations were training grounds for black leaders. As pastors, teachers, and other articulate blacks struggled to create and direct churches, schools, and community associations, they honed speaking and management skills, gained leadership experience, and established credentials as voices in the antebellum movements to end slavery and expand CIVIL RIGHTS and opportunities of free blacks. Eleven times between 1830 and 1855, free black community leaders gathered in national conventions to develop strategies and discuss tactics to improve the condition of the race.

When the end of slavery finally came in 1865, at the Civil War's end, for the other nine-tenths of African Americans, many free blacks helped them prepare to face the challenges that lay ahead. They became effective spokespersons for the race and its concerns. More important, perhaps, many free blacks labored among the former slaves as teachers, preachers, and local political organizers, helping to prepare those emerging from bondage for their new role as independent American citizens.

—*Roy E. Finkenbine*

See also: Abolitionist movement; Religion; Slave resistance; Slave runaways.

Suggested Readings:

Breen, T. H., and Stephen Innes. *"Myne Own Ground": Race and Freedom on Virginia's Eastern Shore, 1640-1676.* New York: Oxford University Press, 1980.

Curry, Leonard P. *The Free Black in Urban America, 1800-1850: The Shadow of the Dream.* Chicago: University of Chicago Press, 1981.

Franklin, John Hope. *The Free Negro in North Carolina, 1790-1860.* Chapel Hill: University of North Carolina Press, 1995.

Horton, James O. *Free People of Color: Inside the African American Community.* Washington, D.C.: Smithsonian Institution Press, 1993.

Horton, James O., and Lois E. Horton. *Black Bostonians: Family Life and Community Struggle in the Antebellum North.* New York: Holmes & Meier, 1979.

_____, eds. *In Hope of Liberty: Culture, Community, and Protest Among Northern Free Blacks, 1700-1860.* New York: Oxford University Press, 1997.

Landers, Jane, ed. *Against the Odds: Free Blacks in the Slave Societies of the Americas.* Portland, Oreg.: Frank Cass, 1996.

Lawrence-McIntyre, Charshee C. *Criminalizing a Race: Free Blacks During Slavery.* Queens, N.Y.: Kayode, 1992.

Wilson, Carol. *Freedom at Risk: The Kidnapping of Free Blacks in America, 1780-1865.* Lexington: University Press of Kentucky, 1994.

Free Christian Zion Church of Christ: Church founded by E. D. Brown on July 10, 1905, in Redemption, ARKANSAS. Brown, an

AFRICAN METHODIST EPISCOPAL ZION CHURCH conference missionary, disagreed with the church's policy of assessing "taxes" on individual churches to support the central church body. The Free Christian Zion Church of Christ was established with a Wesleyan METHODIST doctrine and with a bishop, who appoints ministers and church officers, as head of the church. Local churches were to have a pastor and board of deacons; evangelists were appointed for communities with no churches. The church established *Zion Trumpet* as its publication.

Freedman's Savings and Trust Company:

BANKING institution established for African Americans in 1865, often referred to simply as the Freedman's Savings Bank. As the CIVIL WAR was ending, some northern leaders realized that, at war's end, the freed slaves would need help in handling whatever money they would soon be earning, however small the amounts might be. In addition, many FREE BLACKS in northern states who had joined the Union army had received not only regular pay but also bonuses. For these reasons direction was needed to guide African Americans of the 1860's to financial security.

John W. Alvord, a devoted abolitionist, called a meeting of twenty-two prominent New Yorkers to discuss a plan for a financial institution that would serve the needs of newly free African Americans. The committee agreed on the urgency of the proposition and acted at once. Alvord was sent to Washington, D.C., to ask Congress for a banking charter that would serve black Americans in many states. The bill reached the floor of the Senate on March 2, 1865, but its charter was amended and limited to the D.C. area. On March 3, the bill passed; the amendment that had been added limiting its charter was mistakenly overlooked, so it went into operation as originally designed.

The Freedman's Savings Bank was the first bank since the Second Bank of the United States to have branches in more than one state. By the 1870's the bank had thirty-eight branches in at least fifteen states and Washington, D.C. The bank's expansion was rapid, but the institution was not profitable. The bank was a simple mutual savings bank, and its capital was limited. It was owned by its depositors and financed through deposits made. The bank's small amount of capital created difficulty in finding investments that would be profitable. The majority of depositors had accounts smaller than fifty dollars, and some totaled only pennies. The cost of managing an account was the same no matter its size; therefore, the expenses of the bank were high and led to a narrowing profit margin.

In addition to its high operating costs, the bank did not have enough competent officers or employees. Alvord had become the president of the bank, but he had no qualifications for the position other than good intentions. To entice would-be depositors, many black leaders in communities were hired to work in the bank. Their hearts were in the right place, but their knowledge of the banking industry—and their bookkeeping skills—were generally lacking.

By 1870 the bank's officers, who were under little supervision, had interests of their own they wanted to pursue. They persuaded Congress to change the bank's charter and allow it to invest in real estate and make unsecured loans to railroads and other industries. With this new agenda, the bank rapidly became a highly speculative enterprise. A depression panic hit in 1873, and many of the bank's depositors quickly came to withdraw their money. Trying to restore confidence to the depositors, the bank replaced John Alvord as the bank's president with Frederick DOUGLASS, a greatly respected abolitionist leader. However, Douglass had been misled when offered the presidency of the bank, and he quickly realized that the situation was hopeless. The Freedman's Savings Bank officially closed on July 2, 1874. Many of the bank's depositors never saw a penny of their money, and within black communities resentment over the bank's collapse remained for decades.

—*Valerie Brooke*

Freedmen's Bureau: Arguably the original federal CIVIL RIGHTS agency, the Freedmen's Bureau became synonymous with federal attention to the plight of former slaves in the South immediately after the CIVIL WAR. It was in existence from early 1865 to mid-1872. As its official title—the Bureau of Refugees, Freedmen, and Abandoned Lands—suggests, the bureau's activities extended beyond giving aid to blacks. Indeed, it initially fed, clothed, sheltered, and gave medical care to more whites than blacks. Yet it became identified only with blacks.

President Andrew Johnson solidified the bureau's image as a primarily pro-black organization when he vetoed the act authorizing the bureau's continuation in 1866. (Congress passed the act over his veto.) Johnson charged that, through the bureau, the federal government was seeking "to operate in favor of the colored and against the white race."

Historical Background

Controversy surrounded the bureau from the outset. Congress debated for nearly two years before creating it as a branch of the War Department on March 3, 1865. The act establishing the Freedmen's Bureau authorized federal relief for millions of Americans displaced by the fighting in the mostly southern war zone. Thousands of whites sympathetic to the Union had fled to federal strongholds, and hundreds of thousands of slaves had joined the flight. The exodus swelled after President Abraham Lincoln issued the EMANCIPATION PROCLAMATION in January, 1863.

Private relief agencies at once offered some relief, but the need among whites, called "refugees," and blacks, called "freedmen," overwhelmed volunteer benevolence. The U.S. Army became the chief relief agency, as field commanders dealt with urgent demands. No clear policy directed the effort, however, and significant legal and logistical questions arose.

Fundamental disagreements about the constitutionality of relief measures and emancipation split Congress. The debate hinged on conceptions of property rights and public purpose. The crucial issues were whether the federal government had the authority Lincoln asserted to free slaves and whether the federal government had any duty in regard to slaves freed by government action.

The Democratic opponents of Republican plans for relief argued against establishing the bureau on three counts. First, they contended that the Emancipation Proclamation and federal confiscation acts were unconstitutional. Thus, they said, the proposed bureau illegally interfered with constitutionally protected property—slaves. Second, they asserted that relief of refugees and freedmen represented government action to promote the welfare of a class of persons, not the entire community; further, they said that any such relief was properly a state, not a federal, responsibility. Third, they argued that the bureau would benefit blacks primarily. In the words of a minority committee report in the House of Representatives, the charge was that the bureau would become "a great almshouse department, whereby the labor and property of the white population of the country is to be taxed to support the pauper labor of the freedmen."

Operation

The act authorizing the Freedmen's Bureau succeeded in passing in the House—by a margin of only two votes—and the act's compromise language frustrated much of its promise. The act tenured the bureau for only until one year after the Civil War's end and provided it with a meager structure.

The act decreed that a commissioner was to head the bureau. Under the commissioner were a maximum of ten assistant commissioners, one for each state then in rebellion (the states of the CONFEDERACY). The president was to appoint the assistants, like the commissioner, with the consent of the Senate. The act authorized the secretary of war to assign the commissioner a maximum of ten clerks; the twenty-one authorized positions constituted the entire bureau.

The act authorized the secretary of war to issue "provisions, clothing, and fuel, as he may deem needful for the immediate and temporary shelter and supply of destitute and suffering refugees and freedmen and their wives and children." It also provided that

> the commissioner, under the direction of the President, shall have authority to set apart, for the use of loyal refugees and freedmen, such tracts of land within the insurrectionary states as shall have been abandoned, or to

which the United States shall have acquired title by confiscation or sale, or otherwise.

The act authorized the bureau to give free blacks parcels of land, or set-asides, of up to forty acres, giving rise to the misleading folklore phrase "FORTY ACRES AND A MULE." The set-asides were given for terms of three years. A person receiving a set-aside was to pay an annual rent not exceeding 6 percent of the parcel's 1860 tax assessment or, absent such an assessment, its 1860 estimated value. During the three-year term, the set-aside holder could elect to purchase the land's title. The bureau's two-year extension act, passed over President Johnson's veto on July 16, 1866, added a judicial role to the bureau, allowing it to adjudicate freedmen's rights in specified cases and to act as an agent for blacks in labor contracts.

Outcome

Headed by Commissioner Oliver Otis Howard, a veteran U.S. Army general, the Freedmen's Bureau established itself within six

Reconstruction school administered by the Freedmen's Bureau. *(Associated Publishers, Inc.)*

months as a primary relief organization, feeding and giving medical attention to tens of thousands. By August, 1865, the bureau was serving an average 148,000 rations a day. Such packages consisted of an estimated week's worth of food for one adult. The meat rationed out usually was bacon and other pork; sometimes beef appeared. Flour or bread; corn meal; hulled, dry corn for boiling as hominy; peas; beans; and coffee or tea were also included in the rations.

In 1865 the bureau served a total of 4.5 million rations. It served another 5 million in 1866, 3.5 million in 1867, and 2.5 million in 1868. During its existence, the bureau issued about 21 million rations—15.5 million to blacks and 5.5 million to whites.

The bureau's medical division, under the direction of chief surgeon Caleb W. Horner, erected forty-two hospitals with forty-five hundred beds between June and November, 1865. Its approximately 100 doctors and 350 nurses treated 48,429 patients in those six months—45,898 blacks and 2,531 whites. The bureau had added four more hospitals by September, 1867. The forty-six hospitals were spread throughout fourteen states and the District of Columbia and cost about two million dollars to operate through 1869.

The bureau provided clothing and shelter as part of its food and medical care. Indeed, the items were considered together. Clothing, for example, was often distributed with rations. Thus, the bureau reported a cost of $3,169,325 for food and clothing issued from 1865 to 1871. Likewise, medical facilities sometimes provided shelter.

Editorial cartoon designed to damage a Pennsylvania congressman's chances for reelection in 1866 by linking his name to the unpopular Freedmen's Bureau. (*Library of Congress*)

In addition to providing basic relief, the Freedmen's Bureau pursued the mandate added in the 1866 extension act: It as to help freedmen become self-supporting citizens. A primary means of carrying out the mandate involved creating what proved to be a basis for public EDUCATION in the South. Between June, 1865, and September, 1871, the bureau spent $5,262,511 on schools. It funded all levels and several types of educational institutions: day and night schools, Sunday schools, industrial schools, and colleges and universities. By 1870 the bureau had prompted the creation of 4,239 schools, with 9,307 teachers and 247,333 students.

Many of the oldest HISTORICALLY BLACK COLLEGES and universities trace their origins to the bureau's activities. FISK UNIVERSITY in Nashville, Tennessee, and ATLANTA UNIVERSITY in Georgia had their beginnings in bureau efforts. In part symbolizing the bureau's contribution, HOWARD UNIVERSITY in Washington, D.C., bears the name of the bureau's commissioner.

In labor, land, and legal matters, the Freedmen's Bureau faced barriers too entrenched to overcome. For example, freedmen gained title to relatively little land, as they lacked capital for purchase and as both former owners and speculators pulled the land rights from under blacks. Local and state courts gave blacks no legal redress, and neither blacks themselves nor the bureau had the legal assistance needed to fight such practices. The weight of the system also burdened labor relations. The contract labor system offered no bulwark against traditional landowner powers. In July, 1872, Congress put the increasingly neglected bureau out of business.

The Freedmen's Bureau was a godsend in providing post-Civil War emergency relief. It accomplished important purposes by providing food, clothing, medical care, and shelter. Further, it laid a basis for significant development in education. Yet it failed to do what the 1866 act had mandated—to make blacks' freedom complete. That failure should not be charged against the bureau itself, which did what it was allowed to do. A feeble commitment in Congress and the nation to full and equal citizenship for African Americans hobbled the bureau even before its creation and soon permitted the bureau itself to languish. In many ways, the arguments surrounding the Freedmen's Bureau offered a preview of the affirmative action debate of the 1980's and 1990's.

—*T. J. Davis*

See also: Reconstruction.

Suggested Readings:

Bentley, George R. *A History of the Freedmen's Bureau.* New York: Octagon Books, 1970.

Carpenter, John A. *Sword and Olive Branch: Oliver Otis Howard.* Pittsburgh: University of Pittsburgh Press, 1964.

Cimbala, Paul A. *Under the Guardianship of the Nation: The Freedmen's Bureau and the Reconstruction of Georgia, 1865-1870.* Athens: University of Georgia Press, 1997.

Crouch, Barry A. *The Freedmen's Bureau and Black Texans.* Austin: University of Texas Press, 1992.

Finley, Randy. *From Slavery to Uncertain Freedom: The Freedmen's Bureau in Arkansas, 1865-1869.* Fayetteville: University of Arkansas Press, 1996.

McFeely, William S. *Yankee Stepfather: General O. O. Howard and the Freedmen.* New Haven, Conn.: Yale University Press, 1968.

Nieman, Donald G. *To Set the Law in Motion: The Freedmen's Bureau and the Legal Rights of Blacks, 1865-1868.* Millwood, N.Y.: KTO Press, 1979.

Oubre, Claude F. *Forty Acres and a Mule: The Freedmen's Bureau and Black Land Ownership.* Baton Rouge: Louisiana State University Press, 1978.

Richter, William L. *Overreached on All Sides: The Freedmen's Bureau Administrators in Texas, 1865-1868.* College Station: Texas A&M University Press, 1991.

Freedom National Bank: Founded in 1965 in HARLEM, New York, Freedom National Bank was the first commercial bank in the United States to be established and operated by African Americans. It provided loans to businesses in predominantly black communities of New York City until 1990, when the federal government closed the bank under controversial circumstances.

The Freedom National Bank was founded by a group of black and Jewish investors led by baseball great Jackie ROBINSON. Its mission to provide low-cost loans to homeowners and small investors in the Harlem community earned the favor of local black leaders and boosted black-owned businesses but produced little growth for the bank in its early years. After a near-collapse in 1975, the bank recovered under the leadership of president Sharnia Buford, growing in assets from $35 million to $125 million by 1987. The bank's financial problems resumed in the late 1980's, however, and in 1990 the federal government closed Freedom National Bank permanently. The closing was widely criticized in the black community because of allegations that the Federal Deposit Insurance Corporation (FDIC) acted unfairly by not allowing the bank sufficient time to reorganize and by refusing to reimburse uninsured deposit monies—which the FDIC had sometimes done in other cases.

Freedom National Bank symbolized the push toward black economic self-sufficiency that characterized the CIVIL RIGHTS movement in the mid- and late 1960's. The bank was also significant as a symbol of local pride in Harlem, a predominantly black community whose assets were largely controlled by white interests. Its financial struggles and the questionable nature of its demise called attention to inner-city POVERTY but also fueled bitterness and mistrust among urban blacks.

—*Michael H. Burchett*

See also: Business and commerce.

Freedom Now Party: Political party formed in 1963 during the MARCH ON WASHINGTON. The Freedom Now Party, or FNP, achieved its greatest visibility in MICHIGAN during the 1964 elections. Its goal was to build a national, all-black political party that could serve as an independent power base committed to racial equality.

The FNP's leftist founders included William Worthy, an experienced CIVIL RIGHTS lawyer, and Conrad Lynn. In advocating independent black party politics, an FNP platform statement declared that enforcement of meaningful civil rights laws had ended with RECONSTRUCTION. Racist elements, the platform said, had become entrenched in both the Democratic and Republican parties.

Establishing national headquarters in HARLEM, New York, the FNP set out to build an electoral strategy. In 1963 it unsuccessfully ran candidates in NEW YORK STATE and CONNECTICUT. Strong in militant rhetoric, the organization generated enthusiasm mostly among white leftists and the most radical sectors of the black community. Internal dissension soon developed over charges that the party was being controlled by white radical organizations. This was further complicated when Clifton DeBerry, an African American running as the 1964 presidential candidate of the predominantly white Socialist Workers' Party, took the liberty of associating himself with the FNP without obtaining its permission.

In 1964 the party concentrated its efforts in Michigan. Among FNP organizers in Detroit, a faction emerged that demanded a return to the original intent of creating an all-black party. As tension with the national FNP leadership in New York intensified, the Detroit branch essentially began to operate as an independent organization. The party chairman for Detroit was Albert CLEAGE, a black nationalist and author of *The Black Messiah* (1968). In the 1964 elections, the FNP ultimately sponsored thirty-nine black independent candidates on the ballot, from the Senate seat to the Wayne County drain commissioner. Cleage ran for governor. After the FNP failed to poll even 1 percent of the vote, dissension intensified within its ranks and eventually led to its disintegration.

Freedom rides: Interstate bus rides taken by integrated groups in an attempt to enforce desegregation laws. On May 4, 1961, the CONGRESS OF RACIAL EQUALITY (CORE) initiated a bus ride of an integrated group, known as the freedom riders, from WASHINGTON, D.C., to NEW ORLEANS, LOUISIANA.

The first freedom ride, called the Journey of Reconciliation, had actually occurred years before. That ride took place in 1947 and was designed to test the South's compliance with a 1946 U.S. SUPREME COURT ban on segregation

A fire bomb set this freedom rider bus ablaze near Anniston, Alabama, in 1961; no passengers were injured. *(AP/Wide World Photos)*

in interstate bus travel. New federal interstate travel laws were developed from the 1960 Supreme Court case *Boynton v. Virginia*. The Boynton case resulted in the prohibition of segregation in terminal accommodations as well as on trains and buses. The best-known freedom rides, those that began in 1961, tested this set of laws.

Although the 1961 freedom ride was planned initially to end in NEW ORLEANS, it ended in MISSISSIPPI because of violence. The freedom riders' buses were first attacked by white mobs on an Alabama highway near Anniston and again in BIRMINGHAM, ALABAMA. The buses were bombed with incendiary devices and their windows were broken. Additional violence took place in MONTGOMERY, ALABAMA. Attorney General Robert F. Kennedy dispatched six hundred federal marshals to Montgomery and ordered the National Guard to be called in.

After the violent attacks in Alabama, some members of the original group wanted to discontinue the journey to New Orleans. Members of the STUDENT NONVIOLENT COORDINATING COMMITTEE (SNCC) led the effort to continue to Mississippi. On May 23, 1961, a group of CIVIL RIGHTS activists arrived in Jackson, Mississippi, as a part of the last leg of the freedom ride. When the freedom riders arrived in Jackson, they were arrested and convicted of violating a breach of the peace statute which had been passed by the Mississippi state legislature in 1960 to prevent civil rights activity.

A Freedom Ride Coordinating Committee (FRCC) was organized by CORE, the SOUTHERN CHRISTIAN LEADERSHIP CONFERENCE (SCLC), and SNCC. Through the FRCC, thousands of riders participated in later freedom rides. More than three hundred riders were arrested and incarcerated in Mississippi alone. The freedom rides led to the Interstate Commerce Commission's 1961 ruling that prohibited segregated facilities in interstate travel. This ruling was obeyed more widely than previous ones, but segregation in waiting rooms and terminals persisted. *See also:* Montgomery bus boycott; Segregation and integration.

Freedom's Journal: Newspaper established in 1827. The first BLACK PRESS newspaper published in the United States, *Freedom's Journal* began publishing in NEW YORK CITY on March 16, 1827, after a group of FREE BLACKS gathered to protest the stereotypical depictions—and even vile attacks—that characterized the treatment of blacks in the white press. They decided that they, too, would use the press as a weapon. Pooling their resources, they chose as the editors Samuel Eli CORNISH and John Brown RUSSWURM.

Founded at a time when African Americans were fragmented and needed a sense of community and group identity, *Freedom's Journal* was a medium of advocacy. Millions of African Americans were enslaved, and free blacks were wrestling with issues such as abolition and with proposals for free blacks to emigrate and colonize Africa.

Cornish and Russwurm stated their objectives in the first issue of *Freedom's Journal*: "Too long has the publick been deceived by misrepresentations, in things which concern us dearly, though in the estimation of some mere trifles," they wrote. They vowed to cover any useful information relating to Africa and to prove that African Americans were neither ignorant nor stupid, as they were portrayed in the white press. Everything relating to African Americans also found ready admission, interwoven with principal news of the day.

The AMERICAN COLONIZATION SOCIETY was created to promote and execute a plan to "colonize" regions of western Africa by African Americans, with their consent. Many African Americans saw such efforts as a plot designed to weaken the cohesiveness among African Americans for the liberation of slaves. In its May 18, 1827, issue, *Freedom's Journal* launched an anti-COLONIZATION MOVEMENT campaign. They were denounced by white colonizationists, but the editors boldly defended their position.

Two years after its founding, *Freedom's Journal* closed following a dispute between Russwurm and Cornish over the direction of the paper. Though the paper was short-lived, it paved the way for twenty-four other African American newspapers that were published before the CIVIL WAR. Frederick DOUGLASS's *North Star* (1848) was the most influential.

—*Pearlie Strother-Adams*

Freeman, Jewel Virginia Mulligan (b. November 17, 1917, Kansas City, Missouri): Social worker. Freeman received her master's degree in social work from the University of Kansas in 1956. She served as director at a home for girls and as a clinical social worker with a veterans' registration office before moving into administrative work with the public housing administration and Missouri employment office. She was later a CIVIL RIGHTS and management specialist with the Federal Aviation Administration.

Freeman, Jordan (?—December 6, 1781, New London, Connecticut): Soldier in the AMERICAN REVOLUTION. Like most black infantry soldiers during the Revolution, Freeman was assigned to support, rather than combat, duties. At the Battle of Groton Heights, however, Freeman was caught up in the action as British troops stormed the fortifications at New London. He is credited with killing the British commander in hand-to-hand combat. Freeman himself was later killed in the battle.

Freeman, Morgan (b. June 1, 1937, Greenwood, Mississippi): Actor. Freeman was introduced to the THEATER at the age of eight, when he performed in the school play, *Little Boy Blue*. His performance won him a first-place medal. Years later, after a four-year stint in the Air Force, Freeman began studying acting at Los Angeles City College. After performing several small roles in LOS ANGELES, he moved to NEW YORK CITY.

In 1967 Freeman appeared in an Off-Broadway production called *The Niggerlovers*. This performance led to his Broadway debut as the head waiter in an all-black version of *Hello, Dolly!* (1967) starring Pearl BAILEY. Following this production, Freeman found work infrequently. Stability came in 1971, when he was cast as "Easy Reader" in the public television series *The Electric Company*. He left the show in 1976.

In 1977 Freeman was cast in an Off-Broadway production originally entitled *The Last Street Play*. The following year, New York producer Joseph Papp moved the production, now entitled *The Mighty Gents*, to Broadway, with Freeman and the original cast. It ran for only nine performances, but Freeman's portrayal of a wino earned him a Tony Award nomination as well as Drama Desk and Clarence Derwent Awards. Freeman later won Obie Awards for performances in *Coriolanus* (1980), *The Gospel at Colonus* (1984), and *Driving Miss Daisy* (1987).

Freeman began to find success in his FILM career when he portrayed the streetwise pimp Fast Black in *Street Smart* (1987). He had supporting roles in *Clean and Sober* (1988), *Johnny Handsome* (1988), and *Robin Hood* (1990), and leading roles in *Lean on Me* (1989), *Driving Miss Daisy* (1989), and *Glory* (1989). His roles in *Driving Miss Daisy* and *Glory* garnered Freeman critical acclaim and his first two Academy Award nominations. In the 1990's Freeman costarred with Tim Robbins in the prison

Morgan Freeman in his Oscar-nominated role as chauffeur Hoke Colburn in the 1989 film *Driving Miss Daisy. (AP/Wide World Photos)*

drama *The Shawshank Redemption* (1994), for which his character provided reflective first-person narration, and appeared in *Amistad* (1997), the Steven Spielberg-directed film about the 1839 AMISTAD SLAVE REVOLT.

Free Soil Party: Political party founded in 1848. The party was an amalgamation of representatives from several different political affiliations who shared the conviction that SLAVERY should be the most important political issue in the election of 1848. They set aside their differences and personal agendas to unite in an effort to stop slavery from spreading into new U.S. territory.

The debate over increasing the extent of slave territory was intensified after the MEXICAN-AMERICAN WAR (1846-1848) expanded U.S. territory in the Southwest and California. Proposed resolutions included the Wilmot Proviso, first introduced by David Wilmot of Pennsylvania in 1846, which would exclude slavery in the new territories. The Free Soil Party supported the Wilmot Proviso. It also proposed extending the MISSOURI COMPROMISE OF 1820 line through the new territory to the Pacific Ocean, with all territory north of the line designated as free and all territory south of the line designated as slave. The party favored popular sovereignty, which would let voters in the new territories decide the slavery issue for themselves. The term "free soilers" was already being applied to those who opposed the expansion of slavery.

Supporters of the Wilmot Proviso and of Martin Van Buren for president split from the Whigs and the Democrats and joined with the Liberty Party (founded 1839), under the leadership of Salmon P. Chase. Fifteen thousand supporters came together at the Free Soil convention in Buffalo, New York, in August, 1848. They nominated Van Buren for president and Charles Francis Adams, the son of John Quincy Adams, for vice president. Their platform called for the exclusion of slavery from the new territories and the abolition of slavery in the District of Columbia.

The Free Soilers elected nine congressmen and won 10 percent of the popular vote, including 14 percent of the northern vote, in the presidential race. They did not carry any state. The Whig candidate, Zachary Taylor, was elected. Nevertheless, the Free Soil Party did succeed in bringing the slavery issue to the forefront of the 1848 campaign.

The party ran John P. Hale for president in 1852. He received only 5 percent of the popular vote. The dozen or so Free Soil congressmen, however, held the balance of power in the House of Representatives, and the party was well represented in some state legislatures. The newly formed REPUBLICAN PARTY absorbed the Free Soil Party in 1854.

See also: Abolitionist movement.

Free Southern Theatre: African American THEATER group organized in 1963 in Jackson, Mississippi. Its founders, Gilbert Moses, John O'Neal, and Doris Derby, wanted to develop theater that would address the cultural and political aspirations of African Americans in the southern United States. Its first production, *In White America*, premiered in 1964. The theater relocated to New Orleans in 1965 and disbanded in 1971. Its ideas influenced African American theaters such as the Theater of Afro-Arts in Miami, Florida, Dashiki in New Orleans, Louisiana, and Black Image in Atlanta, Georgia.

Frontier marshals and sheriffs: African Americans made important contributions to the history of the Old West as explorers, fur traders, cowboys, settlers, and soldiers. Some of the most heroic deeds were those performed by the black U.S. deputy marshals who served in Indian Territory (later OKLAHOMA).

In the early 1800's, thousands of Cherokee, Chickasaw, Choctaw, Creek, and Seminole Indians, known as the Five Civilized Tribes, were relocated from their land in the Southeast to Indian Territory. Many African Americans also walked the Trail of Tears, as the long trek was called, as slaves or relatives of the Native Americans.

After the CIVIL WAR, these African American residents of Indian Territory received their freedom. Although they could settle elsewhere, most preferred to remain with the Indians. At this time, thousands of African Americans who had fled the South were beginning to settle in Indian Territory as well.

In attempts to elude capture and conviction, some of the most vicious criminals in the West also entered Indian Territory. Jesse James, the Daltons, the Doolins, and the Cook gang all spent time there, as did black outlaw Cherokee Bill (Crawford Goldsby). Other outlaws included Rufus Buck and Dick Glass, both of whom were of mixed African and American Indian descent. One problem was that although American Indians could legally arrest other Indians, they could not legally arrest white citizens, and white lawmen were not well received in Indian Territory.

In 1875 Isaac Charles Parker, who was soon known as the hanging judge, was appointed to the federal district court at Fort Smith, Arkansas, which had jurisdiction over Indian Territory. Judge Parker appointed two hundred deputy marshals to police the vast territory. Because African Americans were welcome in Indian Territory and some spoke various tribal languages in addition to English, many of the deputy marshals Parker appointed were black.

Black marshals were authorized to carry weapons and to arrest white suspects in the course of their duties. These black lawmen had to outsmart some of the most notorious outlaws on the frontier. Because they had to police enormous areas where it was too expensive to send them out after one criminal, the deputy marshals carried stacks of warrants and went out with a prison wagon for up to a month at a time. They would stop some distance from the hideout of a criminal and prepare to seize the criminal without a struggle, if possible. Once a criminal was caught, he was chained to the wagon. Often several outlaws were chained together.

Bass Reeves, Zeke Miller, and Grant Johnson were three of the U.S. deputy marshals who policed Indian Territory. Their experiences serve to illustrate the typical career of African Americans who were hired to enforce the law on the frontier.

Bass Reeves

Reeves was not an Indian freedman, but rather was from ARKANSAS. After knocking out his master, Colonel George Reeves, Bass Reeves escaped into Indian Territory. He fought with the Union Indians during the Civil War.

Reeves was six feet, two inches tall, and was proud of his bushy mustache. Known as an excellent marksman, Reeves had a reputation of never firing the first shot. According to one account of his law enforcement career, at various times Reeves's hat was shot off his head, his reins were shot from his hands, his buttons were shot off, and his belt was shot off, but he was never seriously injured on the job. He killed fourteen men in the line of duty over the years.

After arresting and chaining up his prisoners, Reeves often lectured them on the consequences of doing right or wrong. He would show up at church services and ask criminals to turn themselves in at the marshal's office in the morning. Because he never learned to read or write, Reeves memorized the handfuls of warrants he carried. According to local legend, only one fugitive ever eluded Reeves.

Occasionally Reeves disguised himself as a tramp or a farmer in order to get close enough to a criminal to make an arrest. One day a war-

The career of Bass Reeves was typical of those of many African Americans who enforced the law on the frontier. *(Western History Collections, University of Oklahoma Library)*

rant came in to the marshal's office for the arrest of Reeves's own son, who had killed his wife in an argument. In his deep resonant voice, Reeves told the marshal to give him the writ; within two weeks, he had arrested and brought in his own son, who had fled instead of turning himself in. (The son served a few years of his prison sentence before being pardoned.) Reeves died in 1910 at the age of seventy-one.

In March, 1992, Bass Reeves became the first African American to be inducted into the Great Westerners Hall of the National Cowboy Hall of Fame.

Grant Johnson

Grant Johnson was a man of mixed African and American Indian parentage. He stood five feet, eight inches tall, and weighed only 160 pounds, which was small for an Indian Territory deputy marshal. He was a handsome man with high cheeks, brown eyes, and a gentle, almost shy manner when he was not in pursuit of bandits. He began working out of Fort Smith in 1887, and Judge Parker regarded him as one of the best deputy marshals. Johnson earned a reputation as an excellent tracker after following two horse thieves over a distance of eighty miles before apprehending them both single-handedly. Johnson was said to have served in his job as deputy marshal for fourteen years before he ever killed a suspect.

Johnson often worked with Bass Reeves. Once they arrested a man accused of murder and brought the man in chains to Eufaula, which was in the area Grant Johnson policed. There, they left the prisoner under guard with another deputy and went to get some breakfast. Johnson and Reeves returned to find that relatives of the prisoner had helped him es-

cape. The escaped prisoner gave himself up to Grant Johnson two years later.

Every year, the Emancipation Day festivities at Eufaula attracted all the area's residents to celebrate at two picnics held on opposite ends of the town. One year, in an effort to maintain peace at both events, Johnson made his presence known by tying up one of his horses at one of the picnics before riding his other horse to the other picnic.

In another incident, a Creek Indian named Amos McIntosh had killed Lee Atkins, another Creek who was also a U.S. deputy marshal. Atkins was not killed on the job, so a jurisdictional dispute was waged over whether the Creek tribal government or the U.S. government should arrest McIntosh. When the dispute was settled in favor of the U.S. government, Grant Johnson was given the writ to serve on McIntosh. Johnson waited a few weeks until McIntosh was lulled into thinking

This group of lawmen photographed at Muskogee in Indian Territory around 1900 includes four African Americans. *(Western History Collections, University of Oklahoma Library)*

that he was not under surveillance. When McIntosh entered town to purchase a coffin for his wife, who died the day before, Johnson calmly walked up and arrested him in the store. Johnson then accompanied McIntosh to his home, where he stayed with him until after the funeral the next day. The following day, Grant Johnson took the murderer to Fort Smith.

One Christmas morning, an Indian was very drunk and began shooting innocent townspeople on Main Street. Grant Johnson, who was nearby, quickly took a horse from the hitching post and galloped after the fleeing man. The horse Johnson was riding began bucking as shots flew by, but Johnson managed to break the man's arm with his first shot. Johnson then arrested him. The townsfolk were so grateful to Johnson for his heroism and for keeping the peace during racial unrest in the days that followed that they took up a collection for him as a token of their appreciation.

Zeke Miller

Zeke Miller was an African American from OHIO who resettled in Indian Territory. Once he arrested three men who had robbed a bank. One of the men was very young. Miller corresponded with the young man while he was in jail and sent him reading material so that he could prepare himself for a better life by the time he was released. Miller and his posse were highly praised by the Missouri, Kansas, and Texas Railway Company after they captured an entire gang of thieves within four hours of a train robbery.

Reeves, Johnson, and Miller were among several black deputy marshals who enforced the law in Indian Territory. Their reputations as fearless trackers determined to enforce the law fairly and bring criminals to justice regardless of race paved the way for many other African Americans who chose to pursue careers in law enforcement.

—*Virginia Melrose Safford*

See also: Frontier Society; Law enforcement; Native American and African American relations.

Suggested Readings:

Burton, Arthur. *Black, Red, and Deadly: Black and Indian Gunfighters of the Indian Territory, 1870-1907.* Austin, Tex.: Eakin Press, 1991.

Katz, William L. *Black Indians: A Hidden Heritage.* New York: Atheneum, 1986.

_____. *Black People Who Made the Old West.* Reprint. Trenton, N.J.: Africa World Press, 1992.

_____. *The Black West.* 3d ed. Seattle, Wash.: Open Hand, 1987.

Porter, Kenneth W. *The Negro on the American Frontier.* New York: Arno Press, 1971.

Ravage, John W. *Black Pioneers: Images of the Black Experience on the North American Frontier.* Salt Lake City: University of Utah Press, 1997.

Frontier society: From the earliest days of American history, African Americans worked, lived, and fought on the frontier. "The frontier" can best be defined simply as the region lying just beyond the last outpost of civilization. Whether enslaved or free, blacks on the frontier generally experienced the same forms of discrimination and prejudice as those faced by blacks in the South. African Americans were denied access to hotels, saloons, churches, and schools by white residents in the West. Before the CIVIL WAR, whites seemed determined to keep both SLAVERY and blacks out of the North and the West. After the Civil War, it became official government policy in states from KANSAS to CALIFORNIA to segregate blacks by law and bar them from political participation. The frontier region shifted rapidly westward until 1893, when the U.S. Census Bureau officially declared that the frontier was closed.

The Fur Trade and African Americans

One of the first thriving enterprises on the frontier involved the trapping of animals prized for their furs. Many fur-trading companies on the early frontier, such as the British-owned Hudson's Bay Company, hired African Americans to work as cooks, servants, interpreters, and trappers. Most of these African Americans had been born slaves and had either escaped or bought their freedom. FREE BLACKS, who constituted some 5 to 10 percent of the African American population in the slave states, faced great hostility and open discrimination in the South. Moving to the farthest reaches of civilization seemed a reasonable alternative to some, and they signed on with fur companies. These black employees generally received less pay than whites and often accepted the most dangerous assignments. A myth developed among the fur trappers and traders that African Americans had a special ability that helped them negotiate and talk with American Indians.

Despite the prejudice displayed by white fur-trading companies, some blacks became successful businesspeople in their own right and opened their own stores and trading posts. In the 1790's, a Haitian-born free black named Jean Baptiste Pointe DU SABLE opened a business in northern Indiana and moved to the region of southern Lake Michigan near the modern city of CHICAGO. Du Sable sold supplies and guns to Indians in the area and opened a hotel. For a brief moment, and for quite possibly the only moment, a multiracial community developed on the frontier. Indians, a few dozen runaway slaves, and some mixed-race (French-Indian) trappers lived together peacefully. They faced less prejudice than future generations of black frontiersmen mainly because few whites lived in the area. When white farmers started moving into the area by 1800, Du Sable and many of his friends moved farther west to IOWA, MINNESOTA, and MISSOURI.

John Jacob Astor's American Fur Company, established in 1808, hired many blacks to work in the Rocky Mountains and the Columbia River region. Edward Rose, a free black from Kentucky, was forced to flee his home state after being accused of a crime. He worked as an interpreter for Astor's firm, but he found the hostility displayed toward him by white employees unbearable. He finally left and lived with the Crow Indians for twenty years, finding their life much more pleasant.

Blacks in Texas

African Americans often found that English-speaking people showed greater prejudice against them than did the French, Spanish, or

Noted for the musicians their family produced, the Shores were among many African Americans who settled in Nebraska in the late nineteenth century. *(Nebraska State Historical Society, Solomon D. Butcher Collection)*

Native Americans. In the Spanish territory of TEXAS, the government conducted a census of citizens. Of the 1,600 residents counted, 450 were listed as black. No one knows exactly how these blacks arrived in Texas, but it seems they lived with equal rights and freedoms as other citizens. They were not considered slaves, because slavery had been outlawed. Segregation came to Texas only with the coming of white Americans in the 1820's. In addition to the free blacks living as citizens of the Mexican province in 1834, more than twenty thousand slaves lived in Texas as the property of U.S. citizens. During the Texas Revolution (1835-1836), many blacks, slave and free, fought against the Mexican government and helped win independence. After the war whites responded by taking away the rights of free blacks and legalizing the slave system. Legal discrimination replaced the openness of previous times.

The Mining Frontier

Lead, gold, silver, and copper mines all had African American employees. The great CALIFORNIA GOLD RUSH that began in 1848 brought thousands of fortune seekers to the West. Hundreds of free black sailors deserted their ships in San Francisco and joined the search for the mother lode. White southerners also flocked to the mining towns in Northern California. Many brought slaves with them, even though California did not officially allow slavery. They worked in the mines for long hours hauling heavy baskets of ore long distances to the mill. Free blacks from the North found jobs as cooks and bootblacks, although skilled trades such as carpentry and masonry remained pure white. In 1850 a construction company offered a job as carpenter to a black worker, but whites said they would refuse to work alongside him. As a result, the company withdrew its offer. Because of such prejudice, blacks worked only in menial, low-paying occupations.

A few slaves used special talents to acquire money. Howard Barnes, a slave from MISSOURI, worked in the mines and cooked for his owner. His master allowed him to earn extra money on the side by baking pies, selling them to miners for a dollar each. With the money earned, Barnes was buying his freedom on the installment plan. By the end of the Civil War, however, he had not fulfilled his contract. Even though the THIRTEENTH AMENDMENT, ratified in 1865, freed all slaves, Barnes's owner sued in court seeking the full amount due him according to the contract. A federal court ordered Barnes to continue payments until the promised obligations had been fulfilled, which did not occur until 1870.

Slaves and free blacks faced open prejudice in the gold fields that sometimes erupted into violence. They usually had to live in separate encampments away from the main tent village occupied by whites. Resentful of the competition offered by a slave labor force, white miners attacked a black settlement in 1850, and burned it to the ground. Many slaves actually gained their freedom by being chased from the mining field by hostile whites.

In some places, African Americans built separate communities. One such community, called Negro Bar, had more than one hundred residents, a saloon, and a gambling casino that grew into one of the largest in the area. Most casinos did not allow black miners to gamble at the same tables as white patrons, although they sometimes provided "colored only" tables that were open to African Americans, along with Chinese and Japanese laborers.

Hotels employed blacks as cooks, barbers, and waiters, but did not allow them to rent rooms, and if they wanted to eat they had to sit at tables right next to the kitchen door. Segregation on the frontier provided as firm a barrier against equality as it did in the South. Although only a few blacks participated in the COLORADO gold rush of the late 1850's, they were forced to live in separate parts of the boom towns or face a violent mob.

The Agricultural Frontier

African Americans played a major role in the cattle industry, especially after the Civil War. Approximately 25 percent of the total number of COWBOYS working in Texas were African Americans, and these black cowboys played an important role in driving herds to market. Because most white Texans hated blacks as much as they hated Yankees, African Americans on cattle drives had to sleep and eat at a distance from the rest of the cowhands.

Beginning in 1869, more than twenty thousand freed slaves left Mississippi and Alabama for a place they hoped could provide them with some justice and civil liberty: Kansas. Known as Exodusters, these black settlers faced bitterness and hostility in their new homes, and the Kansas legislature passed a law that levied a $300 fine against land companies that brought settlers into the state who proved unable to take care of themselves. Black settlers established a few separate BLACK TOWNS in Kansas, such as Spearman and NICODEMUS, KANSAS. In the major cities, including Kansas City and Topeka, segregated schools, offices, and neighborhoods quickly developed.

In the OKLAHOMA Territory, blacks also founded separate communities and black towns in order to protect their freedom and escape discrimination. Some hoped that the territory would be established as an independent home for black citizens, but that dream died when Oklahoma received its statehood in 1907. Southern migrants had developed the all-black communities of BOLEY, OKLAHOMA Taft, Oklahoma, and LANGSTON, OKLAHOMA, by 1885. Taft had a segregated state hospital for the insane and a segregated home for the blind and orphans. Langston became the site of a major black college, Langston University, in 1897. These towns remained segregated into the twentieth century.

Born into slavery, Bose Ikard spent much of his adult life riding with such famous cattle barons as Charles Goodnight and Oliver Loving. Ikard was the real-life model for Jose Deets in Larry McMurty's novel *Lonesome Dove* (1985). (*AP/Wide World Photos*)

The Fight Against Segregation

Most western states denied voting and other civil rights to blacks. African Americans could not vote in California unless they paid a poll tax (which whites did not have to pay). At a Convention of Colored Citizens held in Sacramento in 1856, about fifty delegates decided to fight for the right to vote and to serve on juries. A year later, the state legislature passed a bill excluding additional blacks from settling in the state at a time when African Americans represented less than 2 percent of the population. This law convinced some blacks to leave California for new homes in western Canada.

Just as in the South, western states forbade blacks to give testimony against whites, differing only by adding Indians and Chinese to the excluded list. Some states repealed these restrictions after the Civil War; others, including California and NEVADA, did not. The Nevada law prohibited people more than one-half American Indian or one-eighth black from testifying against a white defendant. The California supreme court found its state law constitutional. Thus, if a black resident was robbed or beaten by a white person, the white would go unpunished unless a white witness appeared to offer testimony. Guilt depended on the color of the witness rather than the strength of the evidence.

Discriminatory laws affected blacks in all frontier states and territories and in all aspects of their lives. In 1888 a NEBRASKA barber refused to shave an African American named Arthur Warwick. Warwick sued under the Civil Rights Law of 1876. When the case came before the Nebraska supreme court, the court ruled against Warwick and stated their support of the right of individual businessmen to choose whom they would or would not serve.

The FIFTEENTH AMENDMENT, added to the Constitution in 1868, prohibited states from using race as a barrier to voting. Poll taxes, however, limited voting rights to those citizens who could afford to pay these taxes, thus preventing most blacks from registering. In western states with significant black populations, including Colorado, Kansas, Oklahoma, Iowa, and California, a few African Americans did register to vote. Black officeholders were nonexistent in the West, however, and white political party leaders in some states (especially Kansas, Iowa, and California) fought to keep African American candidates off the ballots.

Access to equal education was another concern for black residents in the West, which had been hailed as the promised land. Freed slaves who had moved west to escape white supremacy in the South found little change in white attitudes. Western states, including California

and Oregon, established separate school districts based on race even before the Civil War. Emancipation and the postwar amendments to the U.S. Constitution did little to improve the situation.

Blacks in the Army

On July 28, 1866, Congress approved creation of a number of black regiments to be sent to frontier outposts. These regiments were to be commanded by white officers because blacks were considered unsuitable for leadership positions. Most white officers saw these assignments as degrading and undesirable. George Armstrong Custer rejected a command of black troops, and General William T. Sherman complained that former slaves could not be competent soldiers because they were too ignorant and cowardly—this in spite of the fact that 37,300 black soldiers had fought valiantly in Civil War combat. Congress tried but failed to eliminate the black units in 1878. Among the black regiments were the NINTH CAVALRY AND TENTH CAVALRY.

Conditions in most frontier forts were terrible. Troops suffered from bad food, inadequate pay, and abuse by officers. In spite of the hardships they faced, black units received high praise from military inspectors. Officers who commanded black troops came away highly impressed with their abilities. Black desertion rates averaged about 2 percent, compared with 12 percent for white regiments. The ALCOHOLISM rate for white troops was approximately ten times that for African Americans.

Nevertheless, Army officials in Washington remained doubtful of black abilities, and the outstanding records of black units went unnoticed and unrewarded. Army prejudice condemned black soldiers to the lowest ranks and dirtiest, most difficult jobs. In one incident, Army officers actually cooperated with a lynch mob in Montana in 1888, turning a black soldier over to a mob without making any effort to investigate the charges against him. His death symbolized the deep prejudice that infected the Army on the frontier.

—*Leslie V. Tischauser*

See also: Exploration of North America; Fort Huachuca; Frontier marshals and sheriffs; Frontier wars; Military.

Suggested Readings:

Downey, Fairfax. *The Buffalo Soldiers in the Indian Wars.* New York: McGraw-Hill, 1969.

Fowler, Arlen L. *The Black Infantry in the West, 1869-1891.* Westport, Conn.: Greenwood, 1971.

Katz, William L. *Black People Who Made the Old West.* Reprint. Trenton, N.J.: Africa World Press, 1992.

_____. *The Black West.* 3d ed. Seattle: Open Hand, 1987.

Lapp, Rudolph M. *Blacks in Gold Rush California.* New Haven, Conn.: Yale University Press, 1977.

Ravage, John W. *Black Pioneers: Images of the Black Experience on the North American Frontier.* Salt Lake City: University of Utah Press, 1997.

Savage, W. Sherman. *Blacks in the West.* Westport, Conn.: Greenwood Press, 1976.

Frontier wars: From the 1620's onward, African Americans participated in the westward sweep—first of the English colonies and later of the new United States. They were found on every frontier as trappers, traders, and scouts. Some were free; many were slaves accompanying their masters and providing much of the labor that went into the building of the United States. The black frontiersmen who became the most famous, however, were probably those who fought in the post-CIVIL WAR Indian wars of the West. They were called BUFFALO SOLDIERS by the Plains Indians because their curly hair reminded the Indians of buffalo hair. The buffalo soldiers and other black frontiersmen helped to open half a continent to American settlement.

Western Black Regiments

Nearly 180,000 African Americans had fought for the Union army during the Civil War, but most were mustered out of the service once the war ended. There remained a need for a MILITARY presence in the West, where settlers constantly encroached on Indian lands. After the Civil War, however, most whites were not interested in the military life. Many white veterans who had fought in the Civil War would not work for thirteen dollars a month when they could make more money in civilian life.

Some leaders in the American government considered using African Americans to fill the depleted ranks, an idea that began a heated debate in Congress. Critics offered racist diatribes, emphasizing that blacks were ignorant and would not work unless forced. Supporters of the idea simply pointed out that African Americans had been good soldiers in all of the country's previous wars. The latter argument won out, and in 1866 Congress decreed that four black regiments would be organized on a permanent basis—the NINTH CAVALRY AND TENTH CAVALRY, the TWENTY-FOURTH INFANTRY, and the TWENTY-FIFTH INFANTRY, each of which would be commanded by white officers.

Interest in Enlisting

After Congress acted, eager African Americans nationwide rushed to claim the units' four thousand slots, each calling for a five-year enlistment. Many former slaves in the North faced everyday segregation and discrimination in the civilian world; many former slaves in the South were being reduced to a state of peonage and semislavery, entrapped by the SHARECROPPING system. Certainly, they believed, the MILITARY could not be worse: Free housing, clothes, and food and wages of thirteen dollars per month sounded good to many poverty-stricken African Americans.

When the government began its recruiting drive, many African Americans were turned away for being too young or too old; the military would accept recruits only from the ages of eighteen to forty-five. Further, some former slaves had been so badly broken physically that recruiters judged them unfit. Additionally, the military entrants were required to be literate, and most African Americans could not read or write; however, military leaders soon changed the literacy requirement and began accepting illiterates who were to be taught to read and write once they were in the service. The Army assigned special chaplains to each black regiment whose duties included conducting classes in reading and writing.

When the African Americans were mustered in, recruiters faced a decision: Which individuals would become infantry, which cavalry? Most recruiters made their decisions based on the appearance of a man. If a volunteer was tall and heavy, most likely he became an infantryman. If a volunteer was small and seemed well coordinated, he joined the cavalry.

Black Units and White Officers
Once the recruiting drive commenced, the Army had a difficult time attracting white officers to head the units. They knew that the African Americans would see front-line service in the West, and many white officers had had enough fighting during the Civil War and wanted safe duty in the more civilized parts of

Members of the Ninth Cavalry posted on the frontier during the late nineteenth century. *(Library of Congress)*

the country. Further, some white officers refused to lead black units. One such officer was the noted George A. Custer, a Civil War hero. Given white prejudices, the Army developed an incentive program: Those whites who volunteered to serve with black units received higher rank and more rapid promotion.

Some excellent commanders came forward, including two cavalry officers personally recommended by General Ulysses S. Grant: Colonel Benjamin Grierson, who commanded the Tenth Cavalry, and Edward Hatch, who commanded the Ninth Cavalry. Both were Civil War heroes, and both had fought under Grant. Colonel Ranald Mackenzie took over the Twenty-fourth Infantry, and Colonel George Andrews assumed command of the Twenty-fifth Infantry. Originally, all white officers working with the black troops had to be Civil War veterans, but later the Army allowed young West Pointers to become junior officers with the black units. John J. Pershing, later to be famous as one of America's greatest generals, was one of the first junior officers to volunteer; forevermore, he would be known by the nickname "Black Jack" because of his service with the buffalo soldiers.

Although the word "colored" was originally part of the official name of the black regiments (as in Ninth Colored Cavalry), Grierson and Hatch saw no reason for erecting a linguistic color bar. They strongly objected to the word, and soon the Army struck the official usage. Thenceforth, cavalry was cavalry and infantry was infantry, not black or white by name.

Training and Missions

Training for the African American units included instruction in the fundamentals of maneuvering, the use of rifles and revolvers, and the care of mules and horses. Some temporary problems developed. Army policy called for the African American units to use black noncommissioned officers, but many privates, especially those from the South, would not obey them. In slave days, they had learned to take orders from white owners or overseers and believed that it was degrading to take orders from other blacks. Heavy indoctrination solved the problem, as privates were taught that the noncommissioned officers did not give orders but merely spoke for white officers who had military authority to give the orders. Another problem was that the African American sergeants had to handle paperwork, and most could not read or write. The problem soon solved itself, however, when blacks began their classes in reading and writing.

Although the African American regiments were, in the main, blessed with effective and energetic white officers, the units nevertheless knew discrimination based on race. The black regiments tended to get cast-off equipment; inferior arms, ammunition, and horses; poor rations; and poor quarters. Risking charges of insubordination, Grierson appealed repeatedly to General Grant, who served as Grierson's protector and who tried to ensure that the African American units received better equipment, horses, and food.

From 1867 until 1890, buffalo soldiers served all over the West and were stationed in many different garrisons; they made up 25 percent of all troops in the West. They soldiered from Texas to Montana and served in most of the major Indian campaigns, including Red Cloud's War, 1865-1868; the Red River War, 1871-1875; the second Sioux War, 1876-1878; and the Apache uprisings, 1878-1890 (they also fought later in the Spanish-American War and in World War I). In all these actions, African Americans and whites fought together; buffalo soldiers often received the harder, more dangerous assignments because they came to be known as among the best soldiers in the Army. Yet they also were given many jobs, such as garrison duty for the infantry and scouting for the cavalry, that whites simply did not want.

Tactical Roles

Infantry and cavalry played different tactical roles. Infantrymen manned far-flung, isolated garrisons and were assigned to hold back Indians and protect settlers, travelers, hunters, telegraph lines, and railroads. In the field, infantrymen could cause Indians considerable trouble. The Plains Indians were accustomed to fighting other cavalrymen; their tactics were usually not successful against infantrymen, who entrenched and then defended from the entrenchments. Cavalrymen conducted prolonged scouting missions to locate enemies and pursue them in running battles; such tactics eventually forced the Plains Indians onto reservations.

In time, buffalo regiments came to be acknowledged as among the best units in the Army. Whereas white soldiers tended to serve one "hitch" and then move on, many African Americans reenlisted because they viewed army life as better than what they would face as civilians in a white man's world. For the same reason, fewer buffalo soldiers deserted, and they eventually became crack troops. Further, beginning in the 1870's, the Army allowed a small number of African Americans to serve as junior officers with the buffalo units. One was Henry O. FLIPPER, the first black graduate of West Point; another was Charles Young, who attained the rank of colonel.

Certainly, the buffalo soldiers earned their niche in American history. More important, at a time when many whites condemned blacks as inferior, the buffalo soldiers were proving that such ideas had always been wrong.

—*James Smallwood*

See also: Fort Huachuca; Frontier Society; Native American and African American relations.

Suggested Readings:

Carroll, John M., ed. *The Black Military Experience in the American West.* New York: Liveright, 1973.

Foner, Jack D. *Blacks and the Military in American History.* New York: Praeger, 1974.

Fowler, Arlen L. *The Black Infantry in the West 1869-1891.* Westport, Conn.: Greenwood Press, 1971.

Katz, William L. *The Black West.* 3d ed. Seattle: Open Hand, 1987.

_____, ed. *Eyewitness: The Negro in American History.* New York: Pitman, 1967.

Lanning, Michael L. *The African American Soldier from Crispus Attucks to Colin Powell.* Seacaucus, N.J.: Birch Lane Press, 1997.

Leckie, William H. *The Buffalo Soldiers.* Norman: University of Oklahoma Press, 1967.

Taylor, Quintard. *In Search of the Racial Frontier: African Americans in the American West, 1528-1990.* New York: W. W. Norton, 1998.

Fugitive Slave Act: Federal law, passed by Congress in 1793, pertaining to SLAVE RUNAWAYS. It was the United States' first legislation to provide the authority and procedures for returning fugitive slaves, criminals, apprentices, and indentured servants to owners, prisons, and workshops. This act allowed a claimant, through oral testimony or written affidavit from the county and state of origin, to seize a person, bring him or her before a judge, establish ownership, and return the fugitive to the proper authorities. The law established a fine of $500 as penalty for any attempts to conceal a fugitive or obstruct putting a runaway into custody.

The act came about after PENNSYLVANIA authorities tried to extradite a free black man captured and put into SLAVERY by Virginians in 1791. Pennsylvania authorities referred to Article IV, section 2, of the U.S. Constitution, which states that any person held to service or labor in one state who escapes to another state shall be delivered up on claim of the party to whom such service or labor shall be due. (This section of the Constitution was later repealed by the THIRTEENTH AMENDMENT.) When Vir-

Contemporary illustration of a runaway slave hiding from his pursuers. *(Library of Congress)*

ginia's governor refused to return the man and cited no federal law that required such action, Congress enacted the Fugitive Slave Act. Free blacks still were not protected, but runaway slaves were now in increased danger.

The act widened the growing rift between North and South, as southerners sought to strengthen enforcement and northerners resisted. With the legislated end of slave importation in 1808 and the increase in the value of slaves, acrimony grew substantially. Slave catching became a lucrative profession, and more free blacks than ever were snatched into slavery.

In the 1830's, organizations in the ABOLITIONIST MOVEMENT resisted and pushed states to pass personal liberty laws that prevented state authorities from taking an active role in capturing or aiding the apprehension of fugi-

tives. The states with these laws increased penalties for kidnapping. Further, northern states disallowed the use of their jails to detain captured African Americans and, to hamper efforts of slave catchers, several states required trials for alleged runaways.

In 1842 the U.S. SUPREME COURT ruled on an 1837 Pennsylvania case in which Edward Prigg had been found guilty of kidnapping after he returned a fugitive slave to a MARYLAND slaveowner. Prigg sued in federal court. The Supreme Court decided that Prigg was correct under the Fugitive Slave Act but that states did not have to cooperate with the law in any way. Northern states responded with new personal liberty laws. MASSACHUSETTS and VERMONT forbade state officials from imprisoning fugitive slaves or from assisting federal authorities in recapturing them. Debates concerning fugitive slaves resurfaced with passage of the FUGITIVE SLAVE LAW of 1850.

Fugitive Slave Law: Legislation enacted in 1850 that strengthened the FUGITIVE SLAVE ACT of 1793. The Fugitive Slave Law was a part of the COMPROMISE OF 1850, enacted to deal with the question of SLAVERY in the territories. The law stirred the ire of northerners involved in the ABOLITIONIST MOVEMENT.

Southerners insisted that before they agreed to let CALIFORNIA enter the Union as a free state, the North must recognize the right of slaveholders to retrieve their runaway property from above the MASON-DIXON LINE. The personal liberty laws and antislavery sentiment of northern states had effectively defused the 1793 Fugitive Slave Act, but the Fugitive Slave Law brought back its power.

The new law put the burden of enforcement on the federal government. Ironically, even while calling for states' rights and limited federal government, southerners wanted a strong central power to maintain their property rights. The law created new positions of "commissioner" throughout the United States. These officials acted as law enforcement judges who issued warrants and provided legal certificates to slave catchers for the removal of fugitives from North to South. Because the government paid these commissioners ten dollars for every slave returned and five dollars for the release of a falsely seized free black person, there was an economic reason for judging in favor of slave catchers. In the decade after the law's passage, of the 333 fugitives who came before commissioners, 322 were returned to the South.

The Fugitive Slave Law required federal marshals to assist slave catchers and provided a fine of $1,000 against any deputy refusing to do so. Fugitives could not testify on their own behalf and were not guaranteed a trial. Marshals could order anyone deputized on the spot and could arrest anyone who refused to help. The government imposed strict penalties on anyone obstructing an officer, hiding a fugitive, or refusing to aid in the recapture of a slave. No statute of limitations applied. The U.S. Treasury bore the costs of capturing and returning a slave.

Northerners opposed the law by forming vigilance committees to aid fugitives and thwart catchers. Northern resistance filled abolitionist societies and led to thousands of African Americans fleeing to Canada or to Great Britain via the UNDERGROUND RAILROAD. By

A broadside printed in 1850 to call attention to the evils of the federal Fugitive Slave law, this picture shows four African Africans—possibly including some freedmen—being ambushed by armed whites. *(Library of Congress)*

1861 there were fifty thousand black people in Canada.

See also: Slave runaways.

Fuller, Meta Vaux Warrick (June 9, 1877, Philadelphia, Pennsylvania— 1968): Sculptor, illustrator, and writer. Fuller studied at the Pennsylvania School of Industrial Art, Pennsylvania Academy of Fine Art, Academie Colarossi in Paris, and École des Beaux Arts in Paris. During her three-year stay in Paris, Fuller was a student of a number of well-known

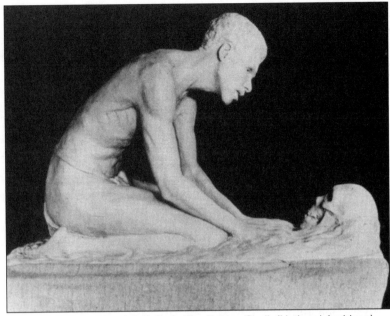

Sculptor Meta Warrick Fuller's *The Talking Skull. (National Archives)*

sculptors, including Auguste Rodin. Rodin's influence is reflected in her early sculptures. In 1910 much of her work was destroyed when her studio burned to the ground. Fuller's work is distinguished by her inspired interpretations of the extremes of humanity.

See also: Sculptors; Visual arts.

Fuller, S. B. (1905, Monroe, Louisiana—October 26, 1988, Blue Island, Illinois): Businessman. Fuller founded the Fuller Products Company, a cosmetics manufacturer, and operated it out of CHICAGO, ILLINOIS. He also served as president, treasurer, and director of Boyer International Labs and as secretary and director of Rose Meta Beauty Products Company. Fuller was active in other business areas as well, including acting as publisher of the PITTSBURGH COURIER.

Funk: Musical genre. Funk evolved from SOUL MUSIC in the late 1960's. In turn, funk provided a basis for 1970's disco music and, eventually, HIP-HOP. Funk may include BLUES, JAZZ, and rock elements.

Artists often said to play varieties of funk include soul pioneer James BROWN, Sly and the Family Stone, George Clinton (with his PARLIAMENT/FUNKADELIC ensemble), and Rick James. Funk is heavily bass-driven. Among the pioneering bassists in funk were Larry Graham (with Sly and the Family Stone) and Bootsy Collins (with Parliament/Funkadelic).

The term "funk" is also used to describe a subgenre of jazz; pianist Horace Silver and drummer Art BLAKEY, for example, rendered jazz versions of funk that included blues and gospel elements. Funk music tends to be heavily rhythmic and, with the exception of some jazz interpretations, is generally not melodically sophisticated. It is feel-good dance music.

Futrell, Mary Hatwood (b. May 24, 1940, Altavista, Virginia): Educator. Futrell's father died when she was five years old. Her mother's emphasis on ED-UCATION spurred her academic achievement. She received a B.A. from Virginia State University and an M.A. from George Washington University, and did further graduate work at Maryland University and the Virginia Polytechnical Institute and State University. She married fellow teacher Donald Futrell in 1977.

As soon as Futrell began her career as a business education teacher at George Washington High

Educator Mary Hatwood Futrell. (© *Roy Lewis Archives*)

School in Alexandria, Virginia, she became involved in professional educators' organizations. She became president of the Education Association of Alexandria in 1973 and served until 1975. She was the first African American to be elected president of the Virginia Education Association (1976). Soon thereafter, she was selected for national duties, serving on the National Education Association (NEA) board of directors (1978) and as secretary-treasurer of the NEA (1980-1983). In 1983 she ran unopposed for president of that almost two-million-member organization and became its longest-serving president, retiring in 1989. During her presidency, she supported higher pay for teachers, urged excellence in teacher preparation on the part of universities, stated that the National Teachers Examination should not be the only criterion for hiring teachers, worked to bring about changes in

funding for education on the federal level, and encouraged parents to become involved in all aspects of their children's education.

Her six-year term encompassed a period of great debate about education. Although the debate itself did not effect some of the changes Futrell encouraged, it did bring about a needed focus on public education. She urged teachers to take an active part in education reform rather than allowing legislators to develop programs. Under her leadership, the movement for equity, or quality education for all students in all schools, was launched.

Futrell was granted honorary doctorates from George Washington University, Virginia State University, and SPELMAN COLLEGE. She was named Outstanding Black Business and Professional Person by EBONY magazine (1984) and one of the country's 100 Top Women by the *Ladies' Home Journal* (1984).

G

Gabriel (Gabriel Prosser; c. 1776, near Richmond, Virginia—October 7, 1800, Richmond, Virginia): SLAVE RESISTANCE leader. Gabriel led one of the major North American slave revolts when he tried to liberate the slaves of VIRGINIA in 1800. His revolt failed, and he was executed.

Background

Most American slaves found subtle ways of revolting against their masters; acts such as breaking tools or stealing produce were common. A few rebelled more emphatically by running away to freedom; a very few planned armed insurrections. This latter type of revolt was hardest to plan and carry into operation, because it obviously depended on the cooperation of large numbers of slaves. Such cooperation was hard to develop, because overseers generally succeeded in keeping groups of slaves isolated, uneducated, and unarmed. Still, a few slaves such as Denmark VESEY and Nat TURNER were able to get armed insurrections organized. Gabriel was another such slave. Although little is known about him, some facts are clear.

Early Life

Gabriel, trained to be a blacksmith, was owned by Thomas Prosser, a young man who had a reputation for treating his slaves very badly. Gabriel grew up on a plantation a few miles from Virginia's new capital, Richmond, and learned to read and write from studying the Bible; he was considered, by whites and African Americans alike, to be very intelligent and a leader. In addition, he was generally well liked and respected within the slave community around Richmond and, even at an early age, was known for his skills in making decisions, delegating authority, and planning. During the height of the diplomatic conflict between the United States and France in 1800 (which threatened to break into actual war), he decided that it was time for the slaves to fight for their liberty, just as the colonists had fought the British for freedom in 1775 and the French peasants had overthrown the Bourbon monarchy only a few years later. Gabriel assumed that once his revolt was underway, other slaves in Virginia would immediately rise against their masters and that France would support the rebellion by supplying arms and food, if not troops.

Preaching Liberation

During the summer months of 1800, Gabriel went among the slaves and preached liberation. His speeches, from all accounts persuasive and powerful, blended rhetoric from the Declaration of Independence, the French Revolution, and the Bible; he stressed that freedom for all people was a God-given right, one that could not be denied by mere men. (This approach backfired occasionally, as many of the slaves around Gabriel had been recently imported from Africa and still had strong connections with their original folk legends and religions.)

Gabriel went on to identify himself with the biblical Samson and, in fact, began to wear his hair long to make the comparison more striking. Martin, Gabriel's brother and a minister, helped Gabriel's cause by using the Scriptures to show parallels between the enslaved Israelites of the Old Testament and the slaves of Virginia; Martin argued that God, who had so forcefully supported the Israelites in times of trouble, would similarly support African Americans in their fight for liberty. He also argued that Gabriel had been chosen by God to lead African Americans to freedom.

Planning the Revolt

After gathering a group of supporters around him, Gabriel started to plan his military strategy. His first goal, he decided, should be the capture of Richmond, then a small town of no more than eight thousand white inhabitants; Gabriel believed that taking Richmond would dishearten whites and knock them off balance. Also, he hoped to seize the arsenal in the town, which could then arm his ill-equipped troops. His second goal would be to inflict as much terror on the whites of Richmond as possible through general slaughter and destruction; his third goal was to have African Americans throughout the state—encouraged by the taking of Richmond—spontaneously rise in revolt against their masters and overseers. Attaining these goals, Gabriel thought, would force the governor of Virginia, James Monroe, to concede to his terms. Optimally, those terms would include the creation of a separate country within the boundaries of Virginia for the newly freed African Americans, though Gabriel was prepared to settle for clearly defined political rights for the liberated slaves. To prepare for the fight, Gabriel spent each Sunday, his day off, in Richmond scouting the layout of the town and learning where its defenses could best be breached. In the meantime, he had his followers make as many crude weapons—primarily clubs and swords made from scythes—as they could.

It is not clear exactly how many slaves Gabriel convinced to join his army; some estimates put the figure at as many as a thousand, others put the figure much lower. At any rate, Gabriel—assisted by his brother Martin, his wife, Nanny, and his primary lieutenant, Jack Bowler—passed the word in the slave community for the army to meet the night of Saturday, August 30, 1800. That afternoon, though, a tremendous thunderstorm ripped through the state, turning the countryside around Richmond where the army was to gather into an impassable morass. Gabriel called off the meeting, rescheduling it for the next night. (Later, many whites—realizing just how dangerous the conspiracy had been and what great peril poorly defended Richmond had faced—called the sudden storm an act of Providence.) Meanwhile, two slaves told their master about the plot; he, in turn, notified the governor, who turned out the militia and declared martial law. All African Americans in the neighborhood of the meeting-place were rounded up, though Gabriel himself was able to escape on a schooner captained by a white sympathizer that took him to Norfolk.

In late September, Gabriel was betrayed by an African American crew member of the schooner who wanted to collect a three-hundred-dollar reward on Gabriel's head. Gabriel was subsequently convicted of revolt. Though he was personally interviewed by Governor Monroe, Gabriel refused to confess to any rebellious activities, much less to inform on others involved in the insurrection. Testimony from informers, though, was enough to convince the whites that Gabriel was the leader of the rebellion and the primary mover behind the planning. On October 7, Gabriel and fifteen of his men were hanged. At least a dozen more African Americans implicated in the rebellion were subsequently executed.

Repercussions

The failed revolt seemed to prove to the majority of Virginia slaveowners the dangers of allowing slaves to become educated or to associate freely with other slaves. Laws restricting African American literacy, for example, became harsher and more rigidly enforced after Gabriel's rebellion. Some owners, though clearly in the minority, argued that the best way to prevent future insurrections would be to ensure better food and shelter for the slaves, along with more humane treatment. Few were courageous enough to call for the outright abolition of slavery.

The name of Gabriel was kept obscure for much of the nineteenth century, for the obvious reason that whites did not want African Americans to admire or to emulate him. Folk stories about Gabriel circulated, however, and in the twentieth century his name became famous as more was written about him.

—*Jim McWilliams*

Suggested Readings:

Bontemps, Arna. *Black Thunder*. New York: Macmillan, 1936.

Egerton, Douglas R. *Gabriel's Rebellion: The Virginia Slave Conspiracies of 1800 and 1802*. Chapel Hill: University of North Carolina Press, 1993.

Furnas, J. C. *The Road to Harpers Ferry*. New York: W. Sloane, 1959.

Genovese, Eugene D. *From Rebellion to Revolution: Afro-American Slave Revolts in the Making of the Modern World*. Baton Rouge: Louisiana State University Press, 1979.

Higginson, Thomas W. *Black Rebellion: A Selection from Travellers and Outlaws*. New York: Arno Press, 1969.

Mullin, Gerald W. *Flight and Rebellion: Slave Resistance in Eighteenth-Century Virginia*. New York: Oxford University Press, 1972.

Sidbury, James. *Ploughshares Into Swords: Race, Rebellion, and Identity in Gabriel's Virginia, 1730-1810*. New York: Cambridge University Press, 1997.

Gaines, Ernest J. (b. January 15, 1933, Oscar, Louisiana): Fiction writer. The publication in 1971 of *The Autobiography of Miss Jane Pittman* established Ernest James Gaines's reputation as a significant African American novelist.

Gaines was born and raised until age fifteen in the bayous of LOUISIANA. His writing focuses on the racial struggle as he witnessed it while growing up. His work emphasizes the

Ernest J. Gaines. *(Jerry Bauer)*

irrationality of that struggle, showing how it threatens to demean, dehumanize, and destroy both the oppressed and their oppressors.

Throughout his novels and short stories, Gaines celebrates the strength and fortitude of his black characters enduring the humiliation leveled at them as they face life in a racist South. He draws directly upon the narrative qualities that characterize storytelling among rural southern blacks, capturing authentically the cadences and structure of their language and the complexity of the social fabric of their lives.

Gaines's first novel, *Catherine Carmier*, was published in 1964, seven years after he graduated from San Francisco State University and after he had studied creative writing at Stanford University for a year. Although the novel does not achieve the artistic level of Gaines's later novels, it foretells the more mature writing that will follow. It deals both with the black-white tensions of Louisiana and with the tensions between blacks and CREOLES that add to the racial complexity of the region. With the publication of this novel, Gaines was appointed writer-in-residence at Ohio's Denison University.

Between 1964 and 1971, Gaines produced and published a collection of short stories, *Bloodline* (1968), and *A Long Day in November* (1971), a children's version of a story first published in *Bloodline*, as well as *Of Love and Dust* (1967), a novel, and his most celebrated novel, *The Autobiography of Miss Jane Pittman*. A television adaptation of that novel was aired by CBS in January, 1974; it won nine Emmy Awards.

The first-person narration of *The Autobiography of Miss Jane Pittman* lends an immediacy to the work, an epic tale related by a hundred-year-old black woman born into SLAVERY. She has lived from before the CIVIL WAR to the CIVIL RIGHTS movement of the 1960's. In this book Gaines achieves his most successful characterization. Using the form of the old woman's reminiscences captured on tape, Gaines stands aside as author, deferring to Miss Jane Pittman's voice.

Other novels followed regularly, including *In My Father's House* (1978), *A Gathering of Old Men* (1983), and *A Lesson Before Dying* (1993). Gaines served as writer-in-residence at Stanford University in 1981 before joining the faculty of the University of Southwestern Louisiana as a professor of English and writer-in-residence in 1983. The recipient of numerous honorary doctorates, Gaines was awarded the prestigious John D. and Catherine T. MacArthur Award in 1993.

—*R. Baird Shuman*

See also: Literature.

Suggested Readings:

Babb, Valerie-Melissa. *Ernest Gaines*. New York: Twayne, 1991.

Gaudet, Marcia, and Carl Wooton. *Porch Talk with Ernest Gaines: Conversations on the Writer's Craft*. Baton Rouge: Louisiana State University Press, 1990.

Hicks, Jack. *In the Singer's Temple: Prose Fictions of Barthelme, Gaines, Brautigan, Piercy, Kesey, and Kosinski*. Chapel Hill: University of North Carolina Press, 1981.

Lowe, John, ed. *Conversations with Ernest Gaines*. Jackson: University of Mississippi Press, 1995.

Gangs: African American gangs have become a serious social and public policy concern. African American street gangs tend to operate in predominantly black urban neighborhoods and target African Americans as their primary victims.

Criminologists and public policy experts agree that many of the difficulties African Americans face in realizing the American Dream of living in a safe and economically vibrant community can be directly attributed to the criminal activities of urban street gangs.

Definition

There is no common definition of the term "gang" that is universally accepted by those who study and investigate street gangs. One definition comes from pioneer researcher Malcolm Klein. Klein defines gangs according to the following three criteria: There is community recognition that the group exists; the group itself recognizes its members as a group, and members commonly adopt a group name as well as symbols and signals; and the group is involved in illegal activities that bring it in conflict with LAW ENFORCEMENT agencies and neighborhood residents.

Historical Background

African American street gangs have existed in some manner since crime statistics began to be reliably recorded near the beginning of the twentieth century. In addition, historians have found evidence of black street gangs operating in several large northeastern cities shortly after the conclusion of the CIVIL WAR. African American gangs originally formed for reasons consistent with those of other ethnic street gangs of that period.

Until the 1950's, most street gangs were what sociologists call conflict gangs. The primary objective of the conflict gang was to engage in territorial wars with similar gangs in their neighborhood. The gang members believed that any groups that attempted to enter their neighborhood or territory were enemies and deserved punishment. These gangs viewed themselves as defenders of their neighborhoods and the limited resources that such neighborhoods offered.

Before the 1950's, African American gangs remained a local neighborhood phenomenon. Although they were routinely arrested for assaulting rival gang members, these street gangs did not generally engage in other serious criminal activity that would provoke a concentrated response from law enforcement officers. Beginning in the mid-1960's, however, African American gangs began to be transformed into criminal gangs, primarily involved in the trafficking and distribution of drugs.

Sociological Factors

Prior to the middle of the twentieth century, black gangs were relatively few in number when compared with those of other ethnic groups; European Americans dominated gang life in the large northern cities. Scholars have identified various explanations for this disparity in gang activity. Ethnic Europeans were the earliest group of minority immigrants to settle into the large urban areas of the northeast and Midwest. Such cities were already populated by Englishspeaking Anglo-Americans who exercised authority in local government. Newer European immigrants, such as the Jews, Germans, Poles, Russians, Slavs, and Italians, did not speak English as their native language. Because they commonly did not share the same physical traits or cultural customs of the dominant Anglo group, these ethnic immigrants were subjected to ridicule and were considered socially inferior. These immigrants encountered widespread discrimination and were forced to settle in ethnic enclaves called ghettos.

Many adolescents living in such ghettos saw little hope of escaping POVERTY and despair and thus turned inward to survive in their own limited social environment. Although forced to live in poverty with immigrants of other cultures, most of these GHETTO youths banded together to form distinct groups. Such groups would protect their members from rivals, who would attempt to

Members of the Los Angeles Crips gang displaying their signs in 1988. *(AP/Wide World Photos)*

deprive them of the limited resources their ghetto offered. These groups evolved into the white conflict gangs that held sway in large American cities until the end of WORLD WAR II.

Although the search for employment had brought many African Americans to northern cities prior to World War II, most African Americans continued to live in the rural southeastern region of the United States. The wartime economic boom prompted millions of rural African Americans to migrate to the great industrial cities of the north in search of higher paying industrial jobs.

Like the European immigrants before them, African Americans faced brutality and discrimination from longtime white residents. African Americans found their experience especially agonizing, because they continued to suffer the indignation of racism and the lingering legacy of SLAVERY. As the nation entered the late 1960's and 1970's, many of the relatively high-paying blue-collar jobs that had attracted black workers began to vanish. The loss of such jobs, combined with other socioeconomic factors, began to weaken the stability of the African American family.

The combination of racism, loss of high-wage industrial jobs, and the fraying of the black family structure led to a phenomenon of social dysfunction called the "underclass." Since the 1960's the economic and social conditions in the urban African American underclass have worsened. A significant amount of underclass behavior that tends to perpetuate social dysfunction, such as the reliance on welfare and criminal activity, has become cyclical and, in some cases, generational.

Sociologist Oscar Lewis called the crushing conditions of inner-city life the "CULTURE OF POVERTY." Another sociologist, William Julius WILSON, defined those living in the culture of poverty as the "truly disadvantaged." The truly disadvantaged exist in an environment in which they occupy the bottom rung of the social economic ladder and are unable to advance. Socially isolated and abandoned to their fate, they are victims of circumstances that prevent them from climbing the ladder to the middle class. Feeling trapped and succumbing to despair, impoverished residents lose confidence in themselves and doubt that society will provide an environment in which they can succeed and prosper.

Wilson further theorized that since the inhabitants of the underclass rarely come in contact with their actual sources of frustration and anger, they direct their hostility at those with whom they have intimate social contact. In the urban environment, those close intimate contacts are rival gangs.

Many young African Americans believe that the only manner in which they can regain the self-worth that the culture of poverty has taken away from them is to involve themselves in the camaraderie of gang life. Furthermore, the affliction of extreme self-doubt, rampant in the underclass, has resulted in the belief that criminal gang behavior is the only avenue to economic survival. This sociological environment has produced the modern rise of large criminal street gangs in inner-city black neighborhoods.

Emergence of Nationally Affiliated Gangs

In the 1990's, two American cities held claim to being the home of nationally recognized black street gangs. CHICAGO is home to the Black Gangster Disciples and Vice Lords, and LOS ANGELES is home to the Bloods and Crips. The Bloods and Crips are the two largest African American street gangs in Los Angeles. Almost all African American street gangs in Los Angeles are aligned with either the Bloods or the Crips.

Gang experts cite numerous origins for the names of the Bloods and Crips. Most believe that the term "Crip" originated when gang members paid homage to a respected gang member who was crippled and walked with a

In July, 1988, leaders of Los Angeles's warring Bloods and Crips gangs met to negotiate a truce. *(AP/Wide World Photos)*

limp. Throughout the 1970's, Crip gang members referred to walking with a distinctive limp and seeking out rival gang members as "crippin'." The term "Blood" is believed to have been adopted from the red color of blood. It also became a popular street term in the 1970's because many black VIETNAM WAR veterans called themselves "bloods." Since the Bloods adopted red as their gang color, the Crips are known for wearing blue.

The Bloods and the Crips originated in the Compton, Watts, and Willowbrook areas of Los Angeles in the late 1960's. The origin of the Bloods is believed to have begun with young African American men from Piru Street in Compton who called themselves the Piru Compton gang. As the membership and territory of the Pirus grew over the years, the gang split into factions called "sets." The "sets" began to be identified as either "Piru" or "Blood." In Los Angeles, the terms "Piru" and "Blood" are the same. The Crips formed in the

same manner as the Bloods, from small neighborhood gangs. Most experts believe that the Crips formed slightly before the Bloods.

The Los Angeles gangs are structured very informally and are simply a composition of independent street gangs that have chosen to ally themselves with either the Blood or Crip factions. Although each small gang probably has some sort of leadership, there is no evidence to suggest that a central Blood or Crip hierarchy exists that controls or directs the independent gangs that call themselves Bloods or Crips.

Large Chicago African American street gangs began to organize in the late 1950's and early 1960's on Chicago's South Side and in neighborhoods to the west. Two African American youths named Eugene "Bull" Hairston and Jeff Fort organized about 250 neighborhood kids from Blackstone Avenue in the Woodlawn neighborhood of Chicago. They called their gang the Blackstone Rangers, in honor of the elite U.S. Army Rangers and Blackstone Avenue. By 1968 the Blackstone Rangers boasted an active membership of four thousand. The Blackstone Rangers evolved into the organized criminal organization the El Ruken. Prior to the organization's demise in the wake of its leaders' convictions on federal firearms violations and conspiracy charges to commit terrorist acts upon the United States, the El Ruken were considered the most notorious and best organized of all African American street gangs in the United States.

During the period that the Blackstone Rangers were active, other small independent Chicago gangs began to organize into the Black Gangster Disciple Nation and the Vice Lord Nation. David Barksdale of the Englewood neighborhood in Chicago organized independent gangs in his area as part of the Black Disciples. In 1974 prison inmate Larry Hoover founded his own breakaway group that evolved into the Gangster Disciples.

The third largest African American street gang in Chicago, the Vice Lords, originated at the Illinois State Training School for Boys at St. Charles. While living at the facility, leader Bobby Gore founded the gang, taking advantage of the fact that many Blackstone Rangers had been imprisoned, leaving the west side of Chicago vulnerable to gang competition.

These young men were charismatic leaders and shrewd organizers. Although they had minimal formal education, they were clever enough to launch financial schemes that embezzled hundreds of thousands of dollars from federal antipoverty programs and private corporate endowments. By establishing quasi-political antipoverty front organizations in addition to other criminal activities, these gang leaders netted huge sums of money to fund their gangs.

The Black Gangster Disciples and the Vice Lords formed an alliance called Nations with which many independent gangs have allied themselves. A number of these gangs are not African American, but ally themselves, at least in theory, with one nation or the other. For example, the Latin Maniac Disciples will ally themselves with the Black Gangster Disciples to war with Latin Kings, who are allied with the Vice Lords. As an example of race and ethnic mixing of gangs that form African American alliances, the gang intelligence unit of the Chicago Police Department reported that the Black Gangster Disciple Nation includes approximately twenty-five mixed race and white gangs in the Chicagoland area.

Each alliance wears distinctive colors and manner of dress. The Black Gangster Disciples' colors are blue and black, and they wear their color apparel in a certain way. The Vice Lords' colors are black and yellow, and they wear their color apparel in another way.

Over the years, many young African Americans have been murdered because they innocently wore the wrong color clothes, wore their clothing incorrectly, or greeted one another incorrectly.

The FEDERAL BUREAU OF INVESTIGATION (FBI) estimates that there are approximately 400,000 gang members in the United States, with nearly 100,000 of these gang members in the Los Angeles and Chicago areas alone. A significant number of them call themselves Bloods, Crips, Black Gangster Disciples, Vice Lords, or a derivative of those names.

Although the media has dramatically portrayed these gangs as nationally organized criminal groups, responsible for sophisticated drug trafficking operations throughout the United States, there is no evidence to support such a conclusion. Headlines and reports citing, for example, the exploits of the Los Angeles-based Crips or the Chicago-based Vice Lords have led to the erroneous conclusion that these gangs actually have headquarters from which they coordinate criminal activities on a regional and national level. That does not appear to be the case. In most cases, only the Chicago gangs seem to have some semblance of control over independent gangs and then only in the Chicagoland area. Nevertheless, the 1996 federal trial of Larry Hoover and his street lieutenants has shed new light on the structure and operation of the Gangster Disciples.

There have been reports that a number of gang members from Los Angeles and Chicago have relocated to areas far from those two cities to establish criminal enterprises and have attached the name of their previous gang for those new operations. Upon further investigation into the motive for such moves, police have found that most relocations were merely a result of a family move, not because of an organized and orchestrated plan by the existing gang to establish a national network of gang chapters.

There is also no evidence that gangs that bear the same name take orders, pay tribute, or are under any operational control to a headquarters or leader, as is the case with organized crime groups. For example, there is no requirement that Crip gang members in MEMPHIS, TENNESSEE, obey an order from a Crip gang member or hierarchy from Los Angeles. In fact, police report that in some rural areas, gangs such as the Black Gangster Disciples are multiracial or white. In almost all cases, the expansive growth of these large gangs is not the result of a systematic intent to establish a national gang network, but simply thousands of independent gangs developing and taking the name of the large gangs and the reputation that comes with it, for their own purposes.

Social Alternatives to Gang Life

Numerous attempts to offer alternatives to gang life by both private and government organizations have been initiated throughout the United States. Alternatives to gang life are provided at both the national and local levels, usually as specialized youth initiatives incorporated under larger antipoverty programs. These programs are typically sponsored or managed by existing social agencies, such as the Boys and Girls Club, the Police Athletic League, the NATIONAL URBAN LEAGUE, the Gang Resistance and Education Program, and similar organizations. These programs attempt to reach children and youth in their early teens before gangs can form a lasting impression.

All these programs have one thing in common. They attempt to demonstrate to the gang or potential gang members that there are realistic alternatives to gang life. Most programs attempt to offer alternatives that meet the general needs that gangs fulfill. Factors such as a need for recognition, self-esteem, and success are identified and addressed. Normally such programs focus on the positive benefits of work, recreation, education, and moral development. These programs pinpoint each need and show youngsters that they can attain all the benefits and status a gang offers, yet they do not have to enslave themselves to the destructive lifestyle that gang membership requires.

Of a more immediate concern, civic organizations and even many large gangs themselves have attempted to deal with the problem of gang violence by initiating positive dialogue among rival gang leaders. During the 1990's, a number of peace summits involving major gangs were held in large cities. In addition, some gangs have allegedly arranged truce agreements in an attempt to lower the level of violence between gangs. The truce between the Los Angeles Crips and Bloods after the 1992 Los Angeles riots is the best-known truce of that type.

Although such peace summits are typically greeted with much fanfare and optimism, there is no evidence to suggest that these events or agreements lead to a reduction of gang criminal activity. In some cases, these summits do effect a temporary reduction of violence between gangs. Most organized crime experts point out that the objective to keep intergang violence to a minimum by gang leaders is simply an indication that gangs are becoming more organized in much the same manner as La Cosa Nostra and the Al Capone gang of the 1920's and 1930's. They held summits and agreed to truces because they realized intergang violence served no business purpose and diminished their ability to make money.

Gangs have spread to almost every corner of America. Although they have not spread in a sophisticated and organized pattern as commonly believed, they have spread nevertheless. Gangs have, in a sense, become fashionable. Criminologists cite examples of music videos and styles of clothing marketed by large retail manufacturers that glorify and encourage gang behavior. It is not uncommon to see white suburban kids dress in the style of inner-city black gang members.

Most public policy scholars believe that gangs are a social phenomenon that has become institutionalized and extremely difficult to eradicate. Experts on gangs and gang life believe that three steps must be taken to destroy street gangs. First, programs must be established to lessen the negative social effects of the culture of poverty among young African Americans. Second, prevention and intervention programs must be established to divert the loyalty of young African Americans away from gangs and toward positive programs that offer a realistic alternative to the destruction and violence common in gang life. Finally, the criminal justice system must be provided resources necessary to apprehend, prosecute, and convict "hard core" gang members, thereby destroying the gang leadership hierarchy and the gang's ability to survive.

—*Joseph G. Andritzky*

See also: Black-on-black violence; Crime and the criminal justice system.

Suggested Readings:

Burris-Kitchen, Deborah. *Female Gang Participation: The Role of African-American Women in the Informal Drug Economy and Gang Activities.* Lewiston, N.Y.: Edwin Mellen Press, 1997.

Hagedorn, John, with Perry Macon. *People and Folks: Gangs, Crime, and the Underclass in a Rustbelt City.* Chicago: Lake View Press, 1988.

Huff, C. Ronald, ed. *Gangs in America.* Newbury Park, Calif.: Sage Publications, 1990.

Jackson, Robert K., and Wesley D. McBride. *Understanding Street Gangs.* Placerville, Calif.: Copperhouse, 1992.

Klein, Malcolm W. *The American Street Gang: Its Nature, Prevalence, and Control.* New York: Oxford University Press, 1995.

_____, Cheryl L. Maxson, and Jody Miller, eds. *The Modern Gang Reader.* Los Angeles: Roxbury, 1995.

Knox, George W. *An Introduction to Gangs.* Rev. ed. Bristol, Ind.: Wyndham Hall Press, 1994.

Phillips, Susan A. *Wallbangin': Graffiti and Gangs in L.A.* Chicago: University of Chicago Press, 1999.

Thrasher, Frederic M. *The Gang.* Reprint. Chicago: University of Chicago Press, 1960.

Garner, Erroll Louis (June 15, 1921, Pittsburgh, Pennsylvania—January 2, 1977, Los Angeles, California): JAZZ pianist. Son of a pianist and classmate of Dodo Marmarosa, Garner reputedly had no formal training. He worked in Pittsburgh ensembles, especially with Leroy Brown's orchestra, from 1938 to 1941. Garner, whose brother Linton also was a pianist, began his New York experience in 1944, when he performed in Fifty-second Street nightclubs such as the Three Deuces and Tondelayo's. He was part of the Slam Stewart Trio, which included Tiny Grimes on guitar and Leroy "Slam" Stewart on bass.

Pianist Erroll Garner in 1962. *(AP/Wide World Photos)*

Garner is known primarily for his work with his own trio, which he formed in the 1940's. Garner won the *Esquire* New Star Award in 1946, the *Down Beat* critics' poll in 1949, and later, between 1956 and 1958, the *Metronome* poll from 1958 to 1960 and the *Playboy* magazine poll for the same period.

Garner developed a unique style of piano playing which involved the use of block chords in a steady rhythmic pattern. During the 1940's, he made a large number of recordings as a leader, including "Erroll's Bounce" (1947) and "Cocktail Time" (1947). Although he recorded for a wide variety of labels, he was for a time exclusively with Columbia records. Some of his later recordings include "Easy to Love/Lullaby of Birdland" (1953), the noted "Misty" (1954), "Concert by the Sea" (1955), and "That's My Kick" (1966). Garner also recorded with Slam Stewart and Charlie PARKER during the 1940's. During the 1950's, Garner became a well-known television personality. In 1948 he was featured at the Paris Jazz Festival. With his trio, he toured Europe during the 1950's. Garner's piano solos were transcribed and published during the 1950's as *Erroll Garner Piano Solos*.

As a composer, Garner is known for "Erroll's Bounce." The film score for *A New Kind of Love* (1963) was composed in part by Garner, whose composition "Misty" became a jazz standard and was used in the 1971 film *Play Misty for Me*.

Garnet, Henry Highland (December 23, 1815, New Market, Maryland—February 13, 1882, Monrovia, Liberia): PRESBYTERIAN minister, orator, and early advocate of BLACK NATIONALISM. Much of Garnet's nationalism was shaped by his pride in his African ancestry, his belief in black independent political action, and the relationship between emerging land monopoly capitalism and the black struggle for political and social equality.

Born a slave in MARYLAND, Garnet was nine years old when his family escaped to freedom in NEW YORK CITY. From 1826 to 1828, Garnet attended the New York AFRICAN FREE SCHOOL. In 1829 while Garnet was working as a cabin boy on a schooner, his family scattered to avoid recapture. In the 1830's, with his family reunited, Garnet studied at the New York Free School and the High School for Colored Youth in New York, the Noyes Academy in Canaan, NEW HAMPSHIRE, and the Oneida Institute in Whitesboro, New York, graduating from the latter in 1839. After graduation, Garnet trained for the Presbyterian ministry under black ABOLITIONIST MOVEMENT leader Theodore S. Wright. Immersing himself in the abolitionist cause, Garnet emerged as a leader in the black community, largely because of his organizational activities and powerful oratory.

By the early 1840's, Garnet, advancing nationalist ideas and organizations, was in the camp of the black nationalists of the day. Inspired by the emancipation and enfranchisement of Caribbean former slaves, Garnet called for a new black militancy and political abolitionism that would lead to emancipation of the slaves, black suffrage, and black control of community institutions. Garnet's prominence increased as he used his pastorate of Liberty Street Presbyterian Church in Troy, New York, for black national and state convention meetings, as well as for harboring escaped fugitives. His advocacy of the Liberty Party and his efforts to organize black New Yorkers to endorse the party, placed him in the vanguard of black abolitionism.

Garnet's independent political action aroused the ire of William Lloyd GARRISON's followers who espoused moral suasion and nonresistance as the ideological and tactical strategies for slave emancipation and social change. Garnet's radicalism was clearly evi-

Although Henry Highland Garnet had earlier been a fervid emigrationist, he did not go to Liberia until President James Garfield sent him there as counsel general in 1881. *(Associated Publishers, Inc.)*

dent in his 1843 "Address to the Slaves" at the National Negro Convention in Buffalo, New York. He argued that slaves could mitigate their oppression by collective resistance.

Garnet founded two newspapers, *The Clarion* and *National Watchman*, in the 1840's, ostensibly to support his ideas. Each died an early death for financial reasons. By the end of the decade, most African Americans had moved closer to Garnet's position of political abolitionism and slave resistance.

By the 1850's, Garnet had identified land monopoly capitalism as the oppressor of the new laboring classes. One economic alternative, for which Garnet hoped, was land redistribution that could develop an economic base in black communities. Another economic and political alternative that Garnet proposed was selective emigration. Garnet supported selected emigration to MEXICO, the WEST INDIES, HAITI, and especially AFRICA. Undoubtedly influenced by LIBERIA's independence in 1847, Garnet remained committed to emigration until the CIVIL WAR. Although his selective emigration plan initially was greeted with dismay in the black community, the passage of the FUGITIVE SLAVE LAW of 1850 swayed many African Americans to his position.

Garnet participated in the international peace and Free Produce movements, believing that war and slavery were products of the same aggressions in society. Upon his return to the United States in the mid-1850's, Garnet founded the African Civilization Society, hoping to "Christianize and civilize" the continent and ultimately end the slave trade. The Civil War curtailed the emigration efforts of the society, which then turned toward social relief for newly freed people. Garnet, as the first black person to sermonize in the U.S. House of Representatives, gave a memorial to abolition in 1865. He continued to work diligently for black causes. President James Garfield appointed him U.S. minister and general counsel to Liberia in 1881. Garnet died shortly after arriving in Liberia.

Garrison, William Lloyd (December 10, 1805, Newburyport, Massachusetts—May 24, 1879, New York, New York): Leader in the ABOLITIONIST MOVEMENT. His newspaper, *The Liberator*, labeled slaveholding a crime.

Committed to social reform throughout his life, Garrison rose to national prominence in the 1830's fighting SLAVERY. His newspaper, *The Liberator*, stirred such abolitionist sentiment that it has been credited with playing a major role in ending slavery in the United States. In 1828, already a veteran reform journalist, Garrison became partners with Benjamin Lundy, a pioneer antislavery propagandist who believed in gradual liberation. In Lundy's newspaper, *The Genius of Universal Emancipation*, Garrison attacked slave dealers so viciously that he was sued for libel.

In 1831 Garrison joined with another American abolitionist, Isaac Knapp, to begin the most influential abolitionist newspaper in the United States, *The Liberator*. The next year, Garrison formed the first society for immediate abolition of slavery, the NEW ENGLAND ANTI-SLAVERY SOCIETY. In 1833 he helped establish the AMERICAN ANTI-SLAVERY SOCIETY, of which he was president for twenty-two years.

Garrison argued that the northern states should separate from the South, and thus he angered northern moderates who sought a compromise solution to the slavery problem. He refused to vote and castigated the U.S. government for permitting slavery. He withheld his attacks only after the secession of the southern states and the outbreak of the CIVIL WAR in 1861. Garrison's dedication to reform was total. He set the tone in the first issue of *The Liberator* when he wrote: "I am in

Abolitionist William Lloyd Garrison. *(Library of Congress)*

earnest—I will not equivocate—I will not excuse—I will not retreat a single inch—and I will be heard!" For more than thirty years he was the dominant voice of abolition in the United States.

—Ellen Powell and John Powell

Garvey, Amy Jacques (1896?, Kingston, Jamaica—July 22, 1973, Kingston, Jamaica): Activist and second wife of Marcus GARVEY. Born Amy Jacques (pronounced "Jakes"), Garvey had a fiery, indomitable spirit that characterized her entire life. She absorbed her spiritedness and knowledge of world affairs from her father, George Samuel Jacques. At an early age, she read international publications with her father who, having lived in Cuba and the United States, would explain the impact of world events upon their lives. Reared in comfortable material circumstances, in a family that owned land and employed field hands, Garvey grew up with the responsibility of handling her father's field workers. This work experience, coupled with her knowledge of international affairs, proved indispensable to her later life's work in the Garvey movement.

Garvey was educated at Wolmer's High School, the leading high school for girls in Kingston, JAMAICA. Following her father's death, she worked for the family lawyer, T. R. McMillan, as a secretary for four years. She was groomed to become the WEST INDIES colony's first female lawyer but grew restless at her job and opted to travel to broaden her horizons. She intended to seek further educational opportunities abroad, but WORLD WAR I prevented her from emigrating to England. Instead, she emigrated to the United States in 1917. At the invitation of a friend, she went to hear Marcus Garvey speak. Their lives were intertwined inextricably from that time.

The Garvey movement, with its black nationalist ethos of pride, self-reliance, and African redemption, fired her imagination. Impressed with her business knowledge, Marcus Garvey enlisted her to restructure his expanding organization, the UNIVERSAL NEGRO IMPROVEMENT ASSOCIATION (UNIA). By 1920 she was instrumental in the management of the BLACK STAR LINE, a shipping company that linked trading throughout the Third World, and had become the secretary of the Negro Factories Corporation, which established manufacturing plants in industrial centers in the United States, the West Indies, Central America, and Africa. She also edited the UNIA newspaper, establishing the relationship of black women to Garvey's BLACK NATIONALISM.

On July 27, 1922, she became Marcus Garvey's second wife. (His first wife was also named Amy.) Faced with impending trial for using the mails for purposes of fraud in that same year, she emerged as his principal advocate and an authority on Garveyism. Upon his subsequent conviction and incarceration at the Atlanta penitentiary, Amy Jacques Garvey became the major political propagandist of both the UNIA and Garvey's plight. In an attempt to provide sustenance to his followers, dispel the impact of his critics, and revitalize the fledgling movement, she edited two volumes of Garvey's work, the *Philosophy and Opinions of Marcus Garvey, Volume I* (1923) and *Volume II* (1925).

After serving less than three years of a five-year sentence, Marcus Garvey was deported in 1927. The couple then moved to Kingston, Jamaica. A continued active political life brought the Garveys into constant confrontation with the authorities. They traveled to Central America, Canada, Europe, and England in an attempt to renew Garveyism. Asthma and political harassment finally drove Marcus Garvey to London, where he died in 1940. WORLD WAR II prevented Amy Garvey from returning to England. Instead, she reared her two sons in Kingston.

Garvey remained a crusader for Garveyism and restoring the image of her husband's ideology and reputation. Her widespread influence included serving as a contributing editor for the black nationalist journal, *The African*, in HARLEM in the 1940's, reorganizing the African Study Circle of the World in Kingston, and lecturing to scholars and college students on the importance of Garveyism. Her unflagging communication to scholars around the world, as well as the 1963 publication of her book, *Garvey and Garveyism*, promoted the resurgence of interest in Marcus Garvey and the Garvey movement.

Garvey, Marcus (August 17, 1887, St. Ann's Bay, Jamaica—June 10, 1940, London, England): Black nationalist leader and official national hero of JAMAICA. Marcus Mosiah Garvey's father, after whom he was named, was a stonemason and an avid book collector. Following his father's death in 1903, Garvey was apprenticed as a printer and quickly earned journeyman and foreman ranks in that trade. His involvement in a typographical union and a printers' strike in 1907 and 1908 caused Garvey to have trouble finding employment in Jamaica. He traveled and worked in Costa Rica, Panama, and elsewhere in Central and South America; he made his way to London, England, in 1912.

In London, Garvey attended college lectures and was strongly influenced by works such as Booker T. WASHINGTON's *Up from Slavery* (1901), the West African journalist Casely Hayford's *Ethiopia Unbound* (1911), and William H. Ferris's *The African Abroad* (1913). These works introduced him to the early pan-African movement. In 1913 Garvey developed an acquaintance with the Egyptian editor Dusé Mohamed Ali (1866–1945), a former actor who had become a journalist and, inspired by the Universal Races Conference held in London in 1911, had founded a monthly magazine called the *African Times and Orient Review*. Working with Dusé Mohamed Ali put Garvey in contact with African nationalists such as Casely Hayford and Attoh Aduma, as well as with Ali's contacts in the United States.

The *African Times and Orient Review* also published Garvey's article "West Indies in the Mirror of Civilization" in October, 1913. Garvey later wrote that his experiences in London determined his decision to become "a race leader":

> I asked, "Where is the black man's government?" "Where is his King and his kingdom?" "Where is his President, his country, and his ambassador, his army, his navy, his men of big affairs?" I could not find them, and then I declared, "I will help to make them."

With great enthusiasm, Garvey returned to his homeland, arriving in Jamaica on July 15, 1914. He formed the nucleus of a new organization in an informal discussion group of equally enthusiastic and race-conscious friends who shared his dream of uplift for people of African descent.

That summer, Garvey met Amy Ashwood at the East Queen Street Baptist Literary and Debating Society. Shortly afterward, with his other friends, they founded the Universal Negro Improvement and Conversation Association and African Communities League, better known as the UNIVERSAL NEGRO IMPROVEMENT ASSOCIATION (UNIA). Early meetings included musical performances, recitations of poems by Lord Byron and Paul Laurence DUNBAR, and addresses by local clergymen and the former mayor of Kingston, Jamaica. Formal debates on political issues were also included in these programs.

Amy Ashwood was very active in UNIA organizing and, despite her parents' objections, she married Garvey on Christmas Day, 1919, in New York City. The couple separated after a few months, however, and were later divorced. In 1922 Garvey married Amy Jacques, another young woman who was a fine public speaker and a leading UNIA figure. This marriage lasted until Garvey's death. Amy Jacques Garvey, who compiled her husband's speeches and articles in two volumes entitled *Philosophy and Opinions of Marcus Garvey* (1923 and 1925), served as Garvey's literary executor and staunch defender until her own death in 1973.

The Garvey Movement

Marcus Garvey's controversial and embattled Universal Negro Improvement Association, dismissed by some as the expression of an extremist ideology, was the most popular black nationalist movement of the first half of the twentieth century. While his detractors felt his claims of an international membership of six million people were not credible, Garvey did enjoy widespread popular sympathy, regardless of the actual number of dues-paying UNIA members.

During the summer of 1914, the ambitious young Garvey wrote to Booker T. Washington and William H. Ferris describing his new organization, and Washington politely responded with an invitation to visit TUSKEGEE INSTITUTE. Ferris was more enthusiastic and encouraging. Arriving in the United States on March 23, 1916, Garvey immediately contacted the militant journalists and scholars who were Dusé Mohamed Ali's American correspondents. In 1917 he established a UNIA chapter in NEW YORK CITY and began publishing the weekly THE NEGRO WORLD, which, by 1920, had an international circulation of more than fifty thousand.

Garvey's UNIA owed its success to the fact that it expressed ideas that were already shared by many African Americans. The UNIA's main platform was what Garvey called "a race consciousness," which meant improved self-esteem and political self-determination for people of African descent on the African continent or in the diaspora of the Caribbean and the United States. "I know of no national boundary where the Negro is concerned," Garvey wrote. "The whole world is my province until Africa is free."

Garvey's ideas, including a call for economic self-sufficiency and outspoken opposition to both American racism and European colonialism, had an affinity with pan-African thought dating to the writings of Martin R. DELANY in the 1860's and Edward Wilmot Blyden in the 1880's. Both men had visited Africa and urged those born in the diaspora to acknowledge kinship with the continent. For many UNIA supporters, Garvey's theme of "African redemption" also offered the possibility of a utopian return to their ancestral homeland. Those who despaired of the prejudice faced by African Americans in the United States periodically suggested emigration, as Henry McNeal TURNER had in the 1870's. There was also a long-standing belief that educated African Americans had a moral duty to assist in the modernization of the continent.

Marcus Garvey at the height of his fame in the early 1920's. *(Library of Congress)*

The Black Star Line

In 1919 the UNIA formed the BLACK STAR LINE, a steamship company intended to establish a black-owned economic base for trade and, eventually, passenger traffic between the diaspora and the African continent. Incorporated in Delaware in June, 1919, the enterprise was, in terms of competing with established shipping companies, unrealistically capitalized at one-half million dollars, with shares offered to the rank-and-file UNIA members at five dollars each. Unseaworthy ships and untrustworthy officials literally sank the endeavor. Purchased for far more than they were worth, the aging ships *Frederick Douglass* and *Antonio Maceo* appeared to be jinxed. The *Antonio Maceo* broke down on her first voyage to Cuba, and the *Frederick Douglass* was sold for scrap when the Black Star Line failed. Another vessel, the riverboat *Shadyside*, purchased for $35,000, sank at anchor in New York. Garvey also admitted losses of up to $45,000 in deals with unscrupulous agents. When the Black Star Line was liquidated in April, 1922, its losses amounted to more than $600,000. In 1923 Garvey was indicted for mail fraud.

Evidence suggests that Garvey's indictment as a result of the Black Star Line's financial problems was partly orchestrated by his many political opponents. In addition to the problems with its other ships, the Black Star Line had attempted to raise funds by advertising the *Phillis Wheatley* (the new name for the SS *Orion*), which had, in fact, not yet been legally acquired. Garvey's political opposition, however, came from all quarters. As early as October, 1919, Justice Department agents were discussing attempts to deport Garvey, while colonial officers in Great Britain and France were engaged in efforts to impede the international circulation of *The Negro World*. The UNIA also was attacked by more conservative CIVIL RIGHTS organizations such as the NATIONAL ASSOCIATION FOR THE ADVANCEMENT OF COLORED PEOPLE (NAACP) and by radical African American groups.

Garvey served as his own attorney during the mail-fraud trial and used the courtroom to expound his ideas and denounce his political enemies. He was convicted despite what some felt was a weak case for the prosecution. He began serving a five-year prison term in 1925 but was pardoned in 1927 and deported from the United States. Traveling to Canada and to Jamaica, Garvey attempted to keep the UNIA organization intact. In 1928 and again in 1931, he traveled to Geneva, Switzerland, hoping to address the League of Nations and petition for land in Africa to establish an independent government. Garvey was elected and served briefly on the Kingston City Council, but he was also imprisoned in Jamaica on a libel charge. In 1935 Garvey resettled in England and continued his attempts to maintain the Universal Negro Improvement Association until his death, following a stroke, on June 10, 1940.

—*Lorenzo Thomas*

See also: Black nationalism; Bruce, John E.; Davis, Henrietta Vinton; Garvey, Amy Jacques; Pan-Africanism.

Suggested Readings:

Clarke, John Henrik, ed. *Marcus Garvey and the Vision of Africa*. New York: Vingtage Books, 1974.

Cronon, Edmund D. *Black Moses: The Story of Marcus Garvey and the Universal Negro Improvement Association*. Madison: University of Wisconisn Press, 1955.

Garvey, Marcus. *Philosophy and Opinions of Marcus Garvey*. 2 vols. Edited by Amy Jacques-Garvey. New York: The Universal Publishing House, 1923-1925. Reprint. New York: Arno Press, 1968-1969.

Harrison, Paul C. "'The Black Star Line': The De-mystification of Marcus Garvey." *African American Review* 31 (Winter, 1997): 713-716.

Hill, Robert A., ed. *The Marcus Garvey and Universal Negro Improvement Association Papers*. 10 vols. Berkeley: University of California Press, 1983-1999.

Hill, Robert A., and Barbara Bair, eds. *Marcus Garvey: Life and Lessons*. Berkeley: University of California Press, 1987.

Lewis, Rupert. *Marcus Garvey, Anti-Colonial Champion*. Trenton, N.J.: Africa World Press, 1988.

Martin, Tony. *Race First: The Ideological and Organizational Struggles of Marcus Garvey and the Universal Negro Improvement Association*. Westport, Conn.: Greenwood Press, 1976.

Satter, Beryl. "Marcus Garvey, Father Divine and the Gender Politics of Race Difference and Race Neutrality." *American Quarterly* 48 (March, 1996): 43-76.

Stein, Judith. *The World of Marcus Garvey: Race and Class in Modern Society*. Baton Rouge: Louisiana State University Press, 1986.

Wintz, Cary D., ed. *African American Political Thought, 1890-1930: Washington, Du Bois, Garvey, and Randolph*. Armonk, N.Y.: M. E. Sharpe, 1996.

Gaston, Arthur George (July 4, 1892, Demopolis, Alabama—January 19, 1999, Birmingham, Alabama): Businessman. Gaston built a

Entrepreneur Arthur G. Gaston in 1963. *(AP/Wide World Photos)*

wide-ranging business empire in which he made millions of dollars for himself. His enterprises engaged in banking, broadcasting, insurance, real estate, and mortuary services, among others.

See also: Business and commerce.

Gates, Henry Louis, Jr. (b. September 16, 1950, Keyser, West Virginia): Scholar and writer.

One of the most influential of African American literary critics, Gates was instrumental in establishing African American writing as an important branch of LITERATURE. Overcoming racism and a serious physical injury sustained at an early age, Gates became one of the most respected and honored scholars in the United States. His many achievements include writing and editing numerous books and articles, reprinting the works of nineteenth-century African American writers, and heading the Department of African American Studies at Harvard University.

Gates was raised in Piedmont, WEST VIRGINIA, where he suffered a hip fracture in 1964 during a football game. He was examined by a white doctor who asked him about his career plans. After learning that the teenager intended to study medicine, the doctor told Gates that he was an "overachiever"; he also told him that his injury was psychosomatic. As a result of this misdiagnosis, Gates grew up with his right leg more than 2 inches shorter than his left leg.

Despite this disability and the racism of others who denied Gates's intellectual ability as the doctor had, Gates achieved outstanding success as a scholar. He graduated with honors from Yale University in 1973 with a degree in history, then won fellowships to Cambridge University in the United Kingdom, where he earned a doctorate in English in 1979. Winning recognition for his articles on African American literature, Gates won grants from the National Endowment for the Humanities in 1980 and the MacArthur Foundation in 1981. Gates served as a lecturer and professor at Yale and Duke Universities and then taught at Cornell University from

Henry Louis Gates, Jr., in 1994. *(Jerry Bauer)*

also edited *Black Literature and Literary Theory* (1984) and was one of the editors of the prestigious *Norton Anthology of Afro-American Literature* (1990). Later in the 1990's Gates was a coeditor, along with Kwame Anthony Appiah, of the 2,000-plus page single volume *Africana: The Encyclopedia of the African and African American Experience* (1999).

One of the most acclaimed books written by Gates is *The Signifying Monkey: Towards a Theory of Afro-American Literary Criticism* (1988), which won the American Book Award. Expanding his influence beyond the academic world, Gates published essays on prominent African Americans in *The New Yorker* and other popular publications; some were later collected in *Thirteen Ways of Looking at a Black Man* (1997). He created the documentary television series *The Image of the Black in the Western Imagination* for PBS in 1982. *Colored People: A Memoir* was published in 1994.

—*Rose Secrest*

See also: Intellectuals and scholars.

1985 to 1988; he was named W. E. B. Du Bois Professor of Literature at Cornell in 1988. In 1986 he received the Zora Neale Hurston Society's award for creative scholarship. Gates became the chair of the highly respected Department of African American Studies at Harvard University in 1991.

Among the many early writings of African Americans edited and reprinted by Gates, one of the most important was *Our Nig: Or, Sketches from the Life of a Free Black* (1983) by Harriet E. Wilson, first published in 1859. Gates established by careful scholarship that this work was the first novel published in the United States by an African American. In a similar manner, Gates preserved the work of numerous early female African American authors in the massive Schomburg Library of Nineteenth Century Black Women Writers, published in thirty volumes in 1988. Gates

Gaye, Marvin (April 2, 1939, Washington, D.C.—April 1, 1984, Los Angeles, California): Motown recording artist. Gaye was the son of a minister and began singing in church as a child. By the 1950's, he was singing in doo-wop groups, and eventually he became a member of the Moonglows, Harvey Fuqua's band.

In 1960 Berry Gordy, Jr., head of Motown Records, hired Gaye to work as a session drummer for Smokey Robinson and the Miracles and as a backup singer for the Marvelettes. Gaye also married Gordy's sister Anna. In 1962 Gaye had what would be the first of more than twenty hit records as a vocalist for Motown, "Stubborn Kind of Fellow." Gaye not only was successful as a solo artist but also achieved success by teaming up to sing duets with major Motown female artists, most notably Tammi Terrell.

By 1971 Gaye had gained artistic control over his career and had begun to write, arrange, and produce his own records. He put out socially conscious songs dealing with major issues of the day, including pollution, POVERTY, and the VIETNAM WAR. "What's Going On" and "Mercy Mercy Me (the Ecology)," both released in 1971, were his major hits of this period. He moved toward frank eroticism with *Let's Get It On* (1973). He continued to develop this erotic strain in his music after leaving Motown for Columbia records in 1982. The result was "Sexual Healing," for which Gaye won a Grammy Award.

In the final years of his life, Gaye was beset with personal and financial problems. His two marriages ended in divorce, and he had tax problems with the Internal Revenue Service. He also developed a cocaine habit and reportedly became suicidal. Gaye was shot to death by his father in a violent quarrel in his father's Los Angeles home. His father was sentenced to five years in prison for voluntary manslaughter.

See also: Rhythm and blues.

Gayle, Addison, Jr. (b. June 2, 1932, Newport News, Virginia): Poet, essayist, and biographer. His biographies include *Oak and Ivy: A Biography of Paul Laurence Dunbar* (1971) and *Richard Wright: Ordeal of a Native Son* (1983). His autobiography, *Wayward Child: A Personal Odyssey*, was published in 1977. Gayle also found success as a teacher, editor, consultant, and reviewer.

See also: Dunbar, Paul Laurence; Literature; Wright, Richard.

Gayle, Helene Doris (b. August 16, 1955, Buffalo, New York): Epidemiologist. As a medical researcher, Gayle has specialized in the study and control of disease epidemics, particularly viral infections among children and adolescents. She received the Outstanding Unit Citation and the Achievement Medal in 1989 from the U.S. Public Health Service. During the early 1990's, her research at the Atlanta-based Centers for Disease Control focused on finding a cure for the virus that causes ACQUIRED IMMUNODEFICIENCY SYNDROME (AIDS). Gayle was a coauthor of "The Epidemiology of AIDS and Human Immunodeficiency Virus Infection in Adolescents," an article published in *The Challenge of HIV Infection in Infants* (1991). She also coauthored an article entitled "Prevalence of Human Immunodeficiency Virus Among College and University Students," which appeared in *The New England Journal of Medicine* in 1990.

See also: Medicine.

Marvin Gaye, holding his first Grammy Award in 1983. *(AP/Wide World Photos)*

Genetic theory of intelligence: Hypothesis that intelligence can be inherited. This theory was advocated most powerfully by William Bradford Shockley, a white physicist. Shockley, who shared the 1956 Nobel Prize in Physics, became controversial in the 1960's because of his views concerning the cause of differences in intelligence test scores between black and white. Shockley, building on the work of Jean Piaget and other child development specialists who attributed many traits to heredity, believed that the higher intelligence quotient (IQ) scores of white children were a result of genetic as opposed to environmental factors.

Shockley also believed that the greater childbearing rate of African Americans and intermarriage between them and whites were threats to the genetic pool of the United States. He became notorious for this theory of "retrogressive evolution," as he called it. Shockley lectured for more than twenty years advocating eugenics, or the science of racial improvement, especially among humans, through the control of hereditary factors. In the mid-1980's, he suggested that legislation be enacted which would pay individuals with IQs below one hundred to submit to voluntary sterilization.

Shockley argued that African Americans were intellectually superior to their African counterparts because they had white genes. Shockley also believed that blood tests could determine the degree of white genetic material that an individual had inherited. He received funding for this eugenics campaign from the Pioneer Foundation, a eugenics organization founded in 1937. Shockley attempted to sue a magazine for libel in 1984, because its science reporter drew parallels between Shockley's views and Nazi studies of Jewish people and retardation.

Both the idea of intelligence as a hereditary trait and the validity of intelligence testing and measurement have been questioned. Although some correlation does exist between racial groups and IQ scores, inheritance of intelligence by individuals has not been proved. Within larger groups, the correlation could be a result of environmental factors prevalent for different groups rather than a result of heredity. Studies of identical twins have showed some evidence of genetic effects on intelligence, but it is clear that environmental factors do play a role. Adding to the debate are arguments concerning the validity of intelligence testing and measurement in general. Many theorists argue that standard intelligence tests are invalid, for a variety of reasons. The norms of the tests may be correct for some groups but not for others, as members of different groups might be expected to have acquired different background knowledge and understanding. Values held by members of different groups can also affect scores. Research has uncovered different types of intelligence, most of which had not been incorporated into standard measures of intelligence during Shockley's time. Such types include creativity, musical aptitude, interpersonal skills, and bodily control. *See also:* Intelligence and achievement testing.

George, Nelson (b. September 1, 1957, Brooklyn, New York): Journalist and cultural critic. The son of Nelson E. and Arizona Bacchus George, young George grew up in Brooklyn. He worked as a part-time staff member on the AMSTERDAM NEWS in NEW YORK CITY from 1977 to 1980 while earning his bachelor's degree from St. John's University. After graduation, he worked for two years on the staff of *Record World* magazine before joining the staff of *Billboard* magazine as its black music editor in 1982. In addition to his work for *Billboard* and later for *The Village Voice*, George became a contributor to ESSENCE, *Musician*, *Rolling Stone*, and *The New York Times*.

Based on musical interests that developed out of his career as a journalist, George began publishing a number of books. His first major

Culture critic Nelson George. *(AP/Wide World Photos)*

publishing success, *Where Did Our Love Go? The Rise and Fall of the Motown Sound*, was published by St. Martin's Press in 1985. The book described the inner workings of MOTOWN Records, which at one time was the largest black-owned business in the United States. George described how company founder Berry GORDY, Jr., succeeded in building the careers of the Miracles, the SUPREMES, the Temptations, and Marvin GAYE during the late 1950's and 1960's before the company began to decline in the mid- to late 1970's. Critics hailed the book not only as a concise history of the firm but also as a lively, well-written story that brought the backstage world of popular music to life.

In *The Death of Rhythm and Blues* (1988), George wrote a cultural history of the development of black music in the twentieth century. He provided fresh information on the artists, arrangers, and record producers who had created RHYTHM AND BLUES, while placing the history of black popular music within the larger context of the struggle for racial pride and equality before the law. George vividly described how rhythm and blues came to dominate the world of popular music, only to become submerged in America's majority white culture. He argued that African American musicians needed to recapture their racial identity if they were to continue their powerful role in black cultural life.

In 1989 George became a regular contributor to *The Village Voice* and broadened the range of his cultural criticism. His 1992 book, *Elevating the Game: Black Men and Basketball*, described how African American players in schoolyards and colleges across the country took over, integrated, and transformed the game of basketball, finally leading to the integration of the National Basketball Association itself. A second book published that same year, entitled *Buppies, B-Boys, Baps and Bohos: Notes on Post-Soul Black Culture*, brought together his *Village Voice* essays on various aspects of black popular music and culture. In 1994 he published *Blackface: Reflections on African Americans and the Movies*, which provided a history and critique of the role of African American actors and directors in the film industry.

Although known primarily for his nonfiction works, George published a novel entitled *Urban Romance: A Novel of New York in the 80's* (1994). The novel's protagonist is a tough music critic reared in working-class Brooklyn who has an affair with a sophisticated suburban-born book editor. Although praised for its picture of the political climate, club scene, and HIP-HOP culture of New York City in the 1980's, the novel did not achieve the commercial success of George's cultural writing and drew criticism for its stilted dialog and unlikely coincidences. In 1996 George published a second novel, *Seduced: the Life and Times of a One-Hit Wonder*, and in 1998 he published *Hip-Hop America*, a nonfiction look at RAP and hip-hop culture.

Georgia: In the late 1990's Georgia was the tenth most populous state in the United States, with a 1997 population of about 7.5 million. The state's approximately 2.1 million African Americans constituted approximately 28 percent of the population of the state, the fourth-highest percentage of the fifty states.

When the Georgia colony was established under the leadership of James Oglethorpe in 1732, it was envisioned as a colony for white yeomen farmers. In 1736 the trustees of the colony formally prohibited African Americans and black SLAVERY there. Despite these restrictions, a few blacks moved to Georgia, and in 1750 the legal restrictions on African Americans and black slavery were removed. In 1776 Georgia's population totaled 40,000, with slightly more whites than blacks. By the time

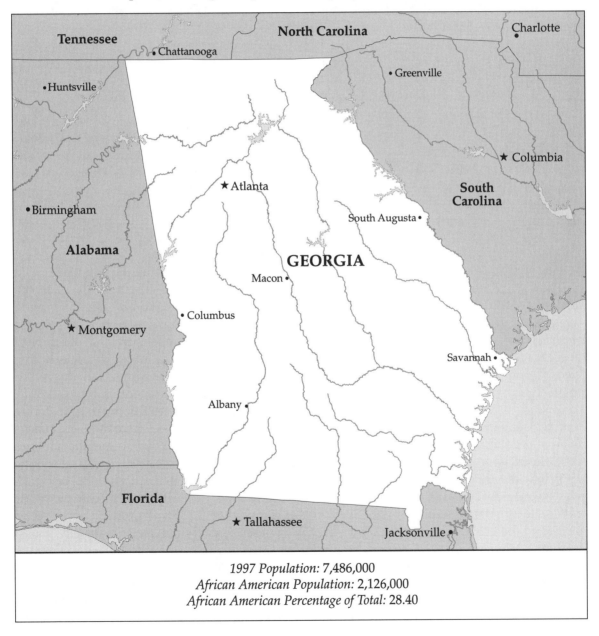

1997 Population: 7,486,000
African American Population: 2,126,000
African American Percentage of Total: 28.40

the CIVIL WAR began in 1861, the percentages were roughly the same, but fewer than 1 percent of the state's blacks were free.

Immediately following the end of the war in 1865, the new government of Georgia repealed slavery. However, as in other southern states, legislation was soon enacted that limited the rights of African Americans. When RECONSTRUCTION was imposed on Georgia in 1867, all male adults, both black and white, were allowed to register to vote. In April, 1867, there were 122,411 whites and 98,507 blacks registered. Blacks constituted 37 percent of the 169 delegates who drew up a new state constitution. In 1868 twenty-nine African Americans were elected to the state house of representative and three were elected to the state senate. Their impact, however, was limited, and by 1870 the Reconstruction government had been defeated. From the 1870's until the turn of the twentieth century, African Americans faced increased opposition in their efforts to vote. By 1908 most had been disfranchised through literacy tests, property requirements, and all-white primaries.

The CIVIL RIGHTS movement of the 1950's and 1960's, led by Georgia native Martin Luther KING, Jr., resulted in major changes in the status of African Americans in the state. The percentage of registered black voters increased from 27 percent in 1965 to 53 percent in 1967, and by the early 1970's African Americans constituted just under 20 percent of the total registered voters. The changing racial climate was recognized by Jimmy Carter, who proclaimed upon being elected governor in 1970 that the time for racial discrimination was over. In 1972 Andrew YOUNG, a former colleague of Martin Luther King, Jr., was elected to the U.S. Congress from Georgia. A year later Maynard JACKSON became the first African American mayor of Atlanta.

In 1984 Robert Benham became Georgia's first African American elected to statewide office when he was elected to the State Court of Appeals. In 1989 Benham became the first African American appointed to the state's supreme court, and in 1995 he became chief justice. By the end of the century, African Americans in Georgia constituted 25 percent of all voters. Of the fifty states, Georgia has the third-highest number of black city and county officeholders. African Americans also constitute 18 percent of the membership of the state senate and 17 percent of the membership of the state house. In 1999 three of Georgia's eleven congressmen were African American. Clearly African Americans have become major actors in the political process of one of the fastest-growing states in the union.

—*William V. Moore*

See also: Disfranchisement.

Gerrymandering: Drawing boundaries of voting or other political districts so that desired voting results are achieved. Politicians have used gerrymandering to dilute the power of African Americans (and other minority groups) by redrawing boundaries to include more white voters in districts that otherwise would have had large concentrations, or even majorities, of blacks. This process virtually can ensure that candidates elected from the redrawn districts will be white or have other properties desired by those drawing the boundaries. It can allow the majority in the overall population to control voting, even in areas where there are concentrations of minority group members. A process with similar results is at-large voting, which mandates that officeholders be elected by a geographically widespread electorate, rather than by local groups. An example would be citywide elections for city council seats, with those receiving the highest number of votes overall being elected. An alternative procedure, one more likely to elect representatives of minority groups, would be to elect one member from each of a number of districts,

The Gerry-mander.

☞ *A new species of Monster, which appeared in Essex South District in January last.*

Early nineteenth-century cartoon satirizing Elbridge Gerry's politically motivated division of Massachusetts into senatorial districts. *(Library of Congress)*

with only the residents of a district voting for their representative.

The term "gerrymandering" comes from the name of Elbridge Gerry, at one time the governor of Massachusetts. He secured passage of a law in 1812 that divided the state into new senatorial districts so as to concentrate supporters of the Federalist Party in only a few. The Federalists were thus ensured overwhelming majorities in those few districts, while Gerry's DEMOCRATIC PARTY was assured of small majorities in a far greater number of districts and thus of a majority in the senate. The redrawn districts had the appearance of a salamander, and the map of them was called a "gerrymander."

As the power of gerrymandering became more obvious, political battles over the districting process began to receive greater attention. In the late twentieth century, REDIS-TRICTING processes received public attention, rather than being matters to be settled by politicians meeting in private. In some cases, districts were redrawn to ensure that minority group members would be elected to certain positions, reversing the traditional intent of gerrymandering.

Gerrymandering is only one of the forms that DISFRANCHISEMENT, or taking away of voting power, has taken. Poll taxes, literacy requirements, grandfather clauses, and even violence against those who attempted to exercise their right to vote were all used in the RECONSTRUCTION period and after. Like the other forms of disfranchisement, gerrymandering gradually was reduced in its effects by the process of protest and legislative reform. A legal campaign by the NATIONAL ASSOCIATION FOR THE ADVANCEMENT OF COLORED PEOPLE (NAACP) led the U.S. SUPREME COURT to outlaw racial gerrymandering in the 1960 case of *Gomillion v. Lightfoot*, and to outlaw at-large elections with discriminatory intent in *White v. Regester* in 1973. In 1982 Congress amended the VOTING RIGHTS ACT OF 1965 to outlaw electoral procedures with discriminatory impact. This was a change from the earlier law, which was stricter in requiring that proof of discriminatory intent be presented before a procedure would be outlawed.

See also: Grandfather clause; Voters.

Ghetto: Urban area settled exclusively or nearly exclusively by members of a single minority group. Seclusion of minorities in ghettos extends back in time at least as far as ancient Rome, with its Jewish ghettos. Ghettos in the United States tend to have high rates of POVERTY and of unemployment. Inhabitants who wish to move out of them often are unable financially to do so.

See also: Housing discrimination; Housing projects.

Gibson, Althea (b. August 25, 1927, Silver, South Carolina): TENNIS player. Gibson was reared in NEW YORK CITY. Because she did not come from an affluent family, her only contact with tennis was through playing paddle tennis on a blocked-off street in Harlem. Through the help of Buddy Walker, a professional heavy-weight boxer and recreation director who saw her play, she got her first racket and received her first professional coaching at the Cosmopolitan Tennis Club in 1942. In 1943, and again in 1945 and 1946, she was the New York State Negro Girls Singles tennis champion. She would later win the women's division for ten consecutive years, beginning in 1948.

A tennis and basketball scholarship enabled her to attend Florida A&M College in Tallahassee. She graduated in 1953. She taught health and physical education at LINCOLN UNIVERSITY, IN JEFFERSON CITY, MISSOURI, FROM 1953 TO 1955.

Gibson's tennis expertise made the United States Lawn Tennis Association lift the color bar and allow her to be the first African American to enter the national tennis championships at Forest Hills, Long Island, in 1950. She played well but won only one match. She was also invited by the U.S. State Department to play tournament tours of Asia, South America, and Europe. In 1951 she became the first African American to play at Wimbledon. In 1957 she became the first African American (and the first black person) to win Wimbledon titles in both women's singles and doubles. New York City welcomed her home with a ticker-tape parade. She won the titles again the following year, and in those same two years (1957 and 1958) she won the U.S. Women's Singles Championship at Forest Hills. She retired from amateur tennis in 1958 to pursue other interests.

To develop her artistic ability, Gibson studied voice, then produced several records and appeared on television. She appeared in the film *The Horse Soldiers* in 1959 and published her autobiography, *I Always Wanted to Be Somebody*, in 1958. Gibson was the first African American to qualify for the Ladies Professional Golf Association (LPGA) circuit, but she never attained the success she had had in tennis.

Gibson earned numerous honors. She was made a member of the New Jersey State Athletic Control Board, was the Associated Press poll woman athlete of the year (1957 and 1958), and was named to the Florida State Hall of Fame, Black Athletes Hall of Fame, South Carolina Athletic Hall of Fame, National Lawn Tennis Hall of Fame, and International Women's Sports Hall of Fame.

Althea Gibson's achievements on the tennis court earned her induction into five different sports halls of fame. *(International Tennis Hall of Fame)*

Gibson, Truman K., Jr. (b. January 22, 1912, Atlanta, Georgia): Government official. During WORLD WAR II, the secretary of war hired a black executive to advise him on matters concerning the use of African Americans in the armed forces. The office of civilian aide to the secretary of war was created on November 1, 1940. William H. HASTIE, the first African American to become a federal appeals judge, was the first to hold this position, under Secretary of War Henry K. Stimson. Gibson was the second to hold this office.

Gibson's tenure in this office began in February, 1943, following Hastie's resignation in January. Gibson's tenure was embroiled in controversy. He allegedly was critical of the performance of black troops, especially the Ninety-second Infantry Division, which he was reported as saying did not perform well under fire. Whites who already were critical of African American soldiers quickly repeated the allegation to indict the courage of black soldiers and to justify the American policy of segregation. Black leaders assailed Gibson, assuming that he had "sold out" his race.

Gibson had not done so, according to his supporters: Critics simply had exaggerated his comments for their own benefit. Gibson had commented on the performance of the Ninety-second Infantry Division, saying that it had been hampered by poor equipment, inadequate training, and limited education. The Army was to blame for the division's performance. This was especially true regarding educational preparedness. Gibson observed that 17 percent of the unit belonged in class five, the lowest literacy class admitted into the Army. In spite of its handicaps, however, Gibson reported that the Ninety-second Infantry Division performed admirably. The members of the unit received more than twelve thousand medals and citations. Gibson's reports were misconstrued, however, and the incident tarnished Gibson's reputation among African Americans. He continued to hold his position as civilian aide to the secretary of war until 1945.

See also: Military; Ninety-second Division.

Gillespie, Dizzy (October 21, 1917, Cheraw, South Carolina—January 6, 1993, Englewood, New Jersey): Composer, bandleader, and trumpeter. The tilted bell of his trumpet and his puffed cheeks when playing made John Birks "Dizzy" Gillespie one of the most visually identifiable of all JAZZ musicians. He was also known for his sense of humor, which he demonstrated in the 1940's by wearing a beret and growing a goatee, thus starting something of a fad and reinforcing his nickname. In the 1960's, he was a nonserious presidential can-

Dizzy Gillespie performing at the Monterey Jazz Festival in 1990 with his famous tilted trumpet. *(AP/Wide World Photos)*

didate. He appeared as a celebrity performer on such television programs as *The Cosby Show* and *Sesame Street*.

Despite the foregoing, Gillespie was fundamentally a serious musician, one of the most significant figures in all of modern jazz. In the early and mid-1940's he, saxophonist Charlie PARKER, pianists Bud Powell and Thelonious MONK, drummer Kenny Clarke, and others established BEBOP, a new approach to jazz which is characterized by harmonic complexity and rhythmical innovation. Technically adept and inventive, unafraid of rapid playing and sustained high notes, Gillespie established the standard for bebop trumpeters such as Fats NAVARRO and Howard McGhee.

Although Gillespie usually led small groups, he also led big bands. His was the first bebop big band, in the 1940's. A later band, in 1956, had the distinction of being the first such group to perform abroad under the auspices of the U.S. Department of State.

In addition to his own musical accomplishments, Gillespie was an important identifier and developer of young talent. For example, pianist John Lewis, vibraphonist Milt Jackson, and Kenny Clarke were members of Gillespie's band in the 1940's. Those three went on to form, with bassist Percy Heath, the Modern Jazz Quartet, one of the most subtle and long-lasting of all jazz groups. Saxophonist James Moody and trumpeter Jon Faddis are just two of the many other substantial musicians whom Gillespie encouraged. Gillespie published *To Be or Not to Bop: Memoirs* in 1979.

See also: Songwriters and composers.

Gilliam, Dorothy Butler (b. 1936, Memphis, Tennessee): Editor and newspaper COLUMNIST. The wife of artist Sam Gilliam, Gilliam graduated cum laude from Lincoln University in 1957 and became associate editor of JET magazine. She served in that position until

1959. After attending journalism school at Columbia University and earning her master's degree in 1961, she joined the staff of *The Washington Post*, serving as a city reporter from 1961 to 1966. She then took a break from newspaper reporting, first to work as a freelance writer and then to host a television interview program in Washington, D.C. In 1972 Gilliam returned to *The Washington Post* as assistant editor of the newspaper's "Style" section, which covers entertainment and cultural activities, and wrote a column at least twice a month.

In 1973, while researching and writing an obituary for actor and singer Paul ROBESON for *The Washington Post* to store and print later upon the star's death, Gilliam began to view Robeson as a kind of unifying force, a symbolic African American whose artistry and dedication to brotherhood could help heal racial wounds. As a result, she wrote *Paul Robeson: All-American* (1976), a biography that reveals how the son of a preacher became a celebrity and explores why Robeson's political stands caused him to be scorned late in life.

As a freelance writer, Gilliam wrote for such national publications as *Redbook*, *McCall's*, and *Columbia Journalism Review*. During the late 1960's, she lectured on the history of the BLACK PRESS at American University and HOWARD UNIVERSITY, and subsequently she taught a summer program for minority journalists at the University of California at Berkeley. Gilliam became a member of the Capital Press Club, the Washington Press Club, the American Federation of Television and Radio Artists, the Women's National Press Club, and Sigma Delta Chi Sorority.

Gilliam's writing honors include a 1961 award from the New York Newspaper Women and awards from the Capital Press Club in 1967 and 1969. The National Association of Black Journalists, the largest minority media organization in the United States, inducted Gilliam into the Journalism Hall of Fame.

Giovanni, Nikki (Yolande Cornelia Giovanni; b. June 7, 1943, Knoxville, Tennessee): Poet. Giovanni graduated from FISK UNIVERSITY with honors in 1967. She helped establish the school's chapter of the STUDENT NONVIOLENT COORDINATING COMMITTEE (SNCC). Her first book was the collection *Black Feeling, Black Talk* (1968). During the late 1960's, she sometimes was grouped with Sonia SANCHEZ, Haki MADHUBUTI (Don L. Lee), and Etheridge Knight, whose work was also published by Dudley Randall's Broadside Press. These "Broadside poets" believed poetry to be a means of political and social revolution. Giovanni wrote in *Gemini: An Extended Autobiographical Statement on My First Twenty-five Years of Being a Black Poet* (1971) that "Objective standards and objective feelings always lead to objectionable situations. I'm a revolutionary poet in a pre-revolutionary world."

Giovanni's means of communicating her revolutionary spirit in poetry include an assertive personal voice, strong direct statement, blunt language, and forceful rhythms, often created by intense use of parallel structure. Her powerful poetry and political message, combined with her public readings, lectures, and teaching—and her many television and radio appearances—made her a well-known literary figure.

The anger evident in her 1960's poems became less strident in Giovanni's later works. She published poetry—some for children—and essays, and works for which she served as editor. Among her poetry volumes of the 1980's and 1990's are *Vacation Time: Poems for Children* (1980), *Shimmy Shimmy Shimmy Like My Sister Kate* (1996), *The Genie in the Jar* (1996), *The Sun Is So Quiet* (1996), and *Blues: For All the Changes* (1999). Her nonfiction work includes *A Dialogue: James Baldwin and Nikki Giovanni* (1972), *A Poetic Equation: Conversations Between Nikki Giovanni and Margaret Walker* (1974), and *Racism 101* (1994).

A PBS special, *Spirit to Spirit: The Poetry of Nikki Giovanni*, was produced in 1986. In 1986 Giovanni became director of the Warm Hearth Writers' Workshop, and in 1991 she edited a collection of writings from the workshop, *Appalachian Elders: A Warm Hearth Sampler* (1991). Giovanni also edited the collection *Grand Mothers; Poems, Reminiscences, and Short Stories About the Keepers of Our Traditions* (1994).

Giovanni served on a number of humanities councils in the 1980's and 1990's and was granted honorary degrees from many universities. Among her awards are the Ohioana Book award (1988) and the Langston HUGHES Award (1996).

See also: Baldwin, James; Literature; Walker, Margaret Abigail.

Glaudé, Stephen A. (b. July 25, 1954, Washington, D.C.): Political appointee. Glaudé graduated from Morgan State University with a bachelor of science degree in 1977. He was founder of the Institute of Life Studies and began serving as its president in 1970, holding this position into the 1990's. In 1977 he was hired as assistant director of the Capitol East Children's Center, a day care facility located in WASHINGTON, D.C. He was named chairman of the board for the center in 1979. Glaudé worked as a vocational evaluator for the D.C. Association for Retarded Citizens from 1979 to 1980. In 1984 he served as chairman and member of the development committee of the Black Child Development Institute. He became a member of the Council for Black Economic Agenda in 1985.

Glaudé's first political appointment came in 1981, when President Ronald Reagan named him to the President's Task Force on Private Sector Initiatives. He was subsequently appointed by President George Bush to serve under Secretary Jack Kemp as assistant for intergovernmental relations and deputy secretary of the Department of Housing and Urban Development.

See also: Housing and Urban Development, Department of; Politics and government.

Glover, Danny (b. July 22, 1947, San Francisco, California): Actor. Danny Glover, who came to prominence during the early 1980's, built a prolific stage and screen career. He often worked on several undertakings simultaneously, and his many FILM and television projects made him one of the busiest actors in Hollywood.

Background
Glover was the eldest of five children. Glover's parents were among those African Americans who journeyed from the South in search of better lives in California. Tall and lanky, Glover grew up believing himself to be unattractive, a belief reinforced by the ridicule he received from other youths who mocked his features.

Glover had no intention of becoming an actor when he enrolled in San Francisco State University in 1965. Content as an economics major, he soon became politically active in black student organizations such as the African Liberation Support Group and the Black Student Union. In 1967 he went to hear black playwright, poet, and activist Amiri BARAKA lecture for the Black Student Union. Baraka announced he was forming a communications program linked to the black community of the Bay Area that would include dance, poetry, music, and drama. In his speech, Baraka stressed the connections between political activism and black THEATER. Baraka was looking for volunteers, and an interested Glover auditioned and won the role of the father in a play called *Papa's Daughter*. The experience assisted Glover in getting over his self-consciousness about his physical appearance.

Glover married jazz vocalist Asake Bomani in 1972; they met while she was a student at San Francisco State University. In 1976 she gave birth to their daughter, Mandisa.

Although he continued to act, Glover earned his degree in economics and began looking for work in that field. He took a job working for San Francisco's city planning department. After working for the department for five years, he found it to be too limiting and unsatisfying. At the age of thirty, Glover quit his position to commit himself to acting. Auditioning for roles during the day, he continued to study acting at night with the Black Actors' Workshop of the American Conservatory Theatre under the direction of South African actor Zakes Mokae.

Breakthrough Stage Roles
In this early part of his career, Glover received several roles on television series, including *Lou Grant* and *B.J. and the Bear*, which kept him and his family financially secure. Desiring to couple his political awareness to his acting career, Glover searched for roles that made a statement regarding social conditions. This attitude forced him to turn down the opportunity for a role on the television series *Hill Street Blues*. Instead, he left California to appear in an Off-Broadway production of *Blood Knot* at the Roundabout Theater. This choice proved to be for the best. *Blood Knot*'s playwright, Athol Fugard, saw part of a rehearsal and was impressed by Glover's performance. Two years later, he contacted the actor in Los Angeles and offered him a role in his new play, *Master Harold . . . and the Boys*. His costar would be Glover's former teacher, Zakes Mokae. Premiering at the Yale Repertory Theatre under the direction of Lloyd Richards, the production was eventually moved to Broadway, ending Glover's years of struggling.

Film Career in the 1980's
After leaving *Master Harold . . . and the Boys*, Glover received numerous film offers, which he attributed to his performance in the play. In 1984 and 1985 Glover appeared in four films: as a ruthless killer in the Harrison Ford police

drama *Witness* (1985), as a sharecropper who attempts to save Sally Field's character's farm in the GREAT DEPRESSION-era drama *Places in the Heart* (1984), as a cowboy in Lawrence Kasdan's *Silverado* (1985), and as the brutal husband of Celie (Whoopi Goldberg's character) in Steven Spielberg's *The Color Purple* (1985), adapted from Alice WALKER's novel.

His performance in *Silverado* was commended for focusing attention on the achievements of blacks in the development of the American West. Ironically, that same year, Glover's portrayal of the cruel, simpleminded Mister in *The Color Purple* led many national black organizations—including the NATIONAL ASSOCIATION FOR THE ADVANCEMENT OF COLORED PEOPLE (NAACP)—to criticize the film for its depiction of black male characters. Some organizations called for a boycott of the film, and the issue exploded into a national debate on Hollywood's treatment of the black image. Glover believes the entire event was fueled by repressed black frustration at Hollywood's stereotypical portrayal of African Americans. Following the controversy, Glover returned to the stage in a Chicago production of Fugard's *A Lesson from Aloes*.

Glover's next major film role was police detective Roger Murtaugh in the Richard Donner action film *Lethal Weapon* (1987). Costarring with Mel Gibson, Glover played a character who was presented as the symbol of stability—a middle-aged, middle-class family man. The role gave Glover another huge commercial success to add to his growing résumé. Glover returned to the role of detective Murtaugh for *Lethal Weapon 2* (1989), *Lethal Weapon 3* (1992), and *Lethal Weapon 4* (1998).

In *The Color Purple* (1985) Danny Glover plays the abusive husband of his child bride (Desreta Jackson). *(Museum of Modern Art, Film Stills Archive)*

Major Television Performances

Glover's more critically acclaimed work has been connected with several major television appearances. In the teleplay *Mandela* (1987), Glover, starring in the title role, once again joined his political beliefs to his acting. Co-starring Alfre Woodard and directed by Philip Saville, *Mandela* was distinguished for its sensitive depiction of future South African president Nelson Mandela's life story. Next, Glover starred in the thirtieth anniversary production of the 1959 play *A Raisin in the Sun*. Directed by former actor Bill DUKE, the cast featured Esther Rolle and Starletta Du-Pois. Glover's third significant television production was a costarring role in the television miniseries *Lonesome Dove* (1989), marking his return to Westerns. His subsequent television project was the prison drama *Dead Man Out* (1989), in which Glover portrayed a court psychiatrist assigned by the state to certify the mental competence of a supposedly insane death-row prisoner. Glover's performance was unanimously declared an excellent piece of work.

Work in the 1990's

In an effort to increase opportunities for African American actors to work on material relevant to their ethnic background, Glover signed with Edward Pressman Productions to star in and serve as executive producer on the film *To Sleep with Anger* (1990). Directed by Charles Burnett, the film—a drama set in South Central Los Angeles—costarred Mary Alice, Carl Lumbly, Vonette McGee, and Paul Butler. Although well-received critically, the film failed financially. In 1990 Glover was inducted into the Black Filmmakers Hall of Fame.

Glover made a number of films immediately following *To Sleep with Anger*—the Vietnam War film *Flight of the Intruder* (1991), a screen adaptation of Chester HIMES's novel *A Rage in Harlem* (1991), which reunited Glover

with director Bill Duke, and the comedy *Pure Luck* (1991, with Martin Short). He also appeared in Lawrence Kasdan's *Grand Canyon* (1992) in the role of Simon, a tow-truck driver who rescues and befriends a white basketball fan stranded in South Central Los Angeles. Other Glover films of the 1990's include *Bopha!* (1993), *Buffalo Soldiers* (1997, for the TNT cable network), and *Switchback* (1997). In 1998 he teamed with Mel Gibson once again for *Lethal Weapon 4* and, in a more serious role, had a major role in the film version of Toni MORRISON's novel *Beloved*.

Private Life

A humanitarian and activist, Glover participated in many charitable causes in the 1980's and 1990's. These activities included serving as honorary cochair of the first Oxfam America Hollywood Hunger Banquet and as a spokesman for the National Association for Sickle Cell Disease. Glover also became involved in both the NATIONAL URBAN LEAGUE and the NATIONAL ASSOCIATION FOR THE ADVANCEMENT OF COLORED PEOPLE (NAACP).

In 1994 Glover went to South Africa twice in his role as a cochair of the Fund for Democratic Elections in South Africa. South Africa's historic post-apartheid elections were held in April, 1994, and Glover was there as an observer. He had previously gone on a fundraising tour in the United States to help raise money for South Africa's African National Congress (ANC) party. Also in 1994, alongside other figures including Harry BELAFONTE, Glover spoke out against U.S. policy regarding HAITI and Haitian refugees.

Glover was named goodwill ambassador of the United Nations Development Programme in 1998-1999. In 1999 he donated $1 million to TRANSAFRICA to launch its two-year "capital campaign" drive. He served as a cochair of the campaign, as did writer Walter MOSLEY.

—Gary Anderson

Suggested Readings:

Belker, Lisa. "Fame and Controversy for Danny Glover." *The New York Times* (January 26, 1986): B21.

Collier, Aldore. "Danny Glover: The Reluctant Movie Star." *Ebony* (March, 1986): 82.

"Danny Glover." *Current Biography* 53 (April, 1992): 29-32.

Hallett, Lisa. "The World According to Danny." *Dial* (February, 1989): 10-12.

Krista, Charlene. "Danny Glover: An Interview." *Films in Review* (April, 1985): 233-235.

Randolph, Laura B. "Oprah and Danny Sizzle in Their First Love Scenes in the Powerful Film 'Beloved.'" *Ebony*, November, 1998, 36-39.

Rosen, Marjorie, and Lois Armstrong. "Danny Glover." *People Weekly* (February 10, 1992): 91-92.

Bernhard Goetz leaving a preliminary court hearing on his shooting case in early 1985. *(AP/Wide World Photos)*

Glover v. St. Louis-San Francisco Railway Company: U.S. SUPREME COURT case regarding RACIAL DISCRIMINATION in employment. On January 14, 1969, the Court reversed lower court rulings that African American employees of the company could not sue for damages. Lower courts had held that the employees had not exhausted administrative remedies within the company. The Supreme Court ruled that the formality, which would have required appeals by employees to the same people who had discriminated against them, were not mandatory in law. Such a formality, the Court said, would only have prolonged the deprivation of the workers' civil rights.

Goetz, Bernhard, case: On December 22, 1984, Bernhard Goetz, a thirty-seven-year-old white man, was riding on a NEW YORK CITY subway train. He was asked for five dollars by four black men who were eighteen and nineteen years old. In response, Goetz shot each of the young men. Barry Allen, Troy Canty, and James Ramseur would eventually walk out of the hospitals to which they were taken. The bullet that hit Darrell Cabey, however, severed his spinal cord and left him paralyzed for life.

Goetz left the scene before he could be arrested, but on December 31 he surrendered to state police in Concord, New Hampshire. He was tried on charges of attempted murder, aggravated assault, reckless endangerment, and illegal possession of a firearm. At the trial, witnesses stated that the young men had been behaving in a rowdy manner and that the train's other passengers had moved to the far end of the car to avoid them. Goetz said that when the men approached and asked for money he believed that they were about to mug him. (Goetz had been attacked and injured in the subway a few years before.) Goetz was ultimately acquitted of all charges except weapons possession, and he served less than nine months in prison. In 1996, however, Cabey was awarded $43 million in a civil suit against Goetz.

The shooting and the court cases that followed drew considerable interest and provoked heated debate. The debate over Goetz's actions tended to focus on whether he was a hero who had stood up to street criminals or a dangerous vigilante who had acted irresponsibly—and murderously—by taking the law into his own hands. The case became known as a significant event in New York City's, and the nation's, history of race relations. Some commentators argued not only that Goetz was a vigilante but also that his actions were the equivalent of a LYNCHING. The amount of public support that emerged for his actions, they said, provided evidence of a racist mob mentality that still existed in the United States.

—*Jonathan Markovitz*

See also: New York City; Race, racism, and race relations.

Goldberg, Whoopi (Caryn E. Johnson; b. November 13, 1949, New York, New York): Actor and comedian. Whoopi Goldberg became a star actor and the most successful black female stand-up comic since Moms MABLEY. Beginning in the 1980's, her career in THEATER, FILM, and television, as well as her humanitarian efforts, were widely chronicled in the media.

Family Life

Goldberg and her brother, Clyde, were reared as Roman Catholics in a single-parent household by their mother, Emma. Goldberg always wanted to be an actor. Growing up in the Chelsea section of Manhattan, she began her acting training at age eight with the Helen Rubenstein Children's Theatre. Educated in parochial schools but a poor student because of an undiagnosed case of dyslexia, she dropped out of high school at the age of seventeen. Within a few years, Goldberg fought an addiction to narcotics, married her drug counselor, and, in 1974, gave birth to a daughter, Alexandrea Martin.

While her child was still a baby, she divorced her husband and traveled with her daughter to CALIFORNIA to seek work as an actor. To supplement her meager earnings in the entertainment field, she depended on welfare and worked variously as a bank teller, a bricklayer, and a cosmetologist at a morgue.

Theater Career

While in New York, Goldberg had worked in the choruses of the Broadway shows *Pippin*, *Hair*, and *Jesus Christ Superstar*. In California, she continued her theater career as a founding member and actor of the San Diego Repertory Theatre. She played various roles not traditionally acted by blacks, most notably the lead character in *Mother Courage and Her Children*. During this period, she decided to change her name to Whoopi Goldberg, since she felt her birth name was "boring."

Goldberg performed with the improvisational company Spontaneous Combustion and as part of a comedy duo before moving to the Bay Area to join Berkeley's Blake Street Hawkeyes. While with the Hawkeyes, she created seventeen characters that she portrayed in a one-woman performance, *The Spook Show*, in 1983. The show toured clubs and theaters, including the Dance Theatre Workshop in Manhattan. There, impressed by Goldberg's virtuosity, director Mike Nichols asked her to allow him to assist in the development of the show for a Broadway engagement. Before accepting his offer, Goldberg returned to Berkeley to perform a show about "Moms" Mabley. Her performance earned for Goldberg a Bay Area Theatre Award.

Broadway Appearance

Under Nichols's supervision, Goldberg created a one-woman show billed as *Whoopi Goldberg* that opened at the Lyceum Theatre on

October 24, 1984. The performance featured six principal characterizations: Fontaine, a drug addict emotionally affected by his European trip to the home where Anne Frank hid from the Nazis; a white teenager who tells how she rid herself of an unwanted pregnancy by using a coat hanger; a nine-year-old black girl who longs to be a blue-eyed blonde; a Jamaican woman who serves as a companion for an elderly, wealthy white man; a young woman with a deformed body who has found romance; and a former black vaudevillian who is now a panhandler.

While Goldberg received mixed notices concerning her material, most critics acclaimed her memorable and adroit characterizations. The show and its star quickly garnered notice, especially in the print media, giving Goldberg the kind of widespread publicity she had been seeking to further her career. In 1985 cable television's Home Box Office (HBO) broadcast the production, and the recording of the show won for Goldberg a Grammy Award.

Beginning Her Film Career

Despite her success, Goldberg did not want to be labeled as a comic; she wanted to be considered an actor. She actively campaigned for and won the role of the lead character in the movie that would launch her film career, *The Color Purple* (1985). Based on the best-selling novel by Alice WALKER, the film tells the story of the emotional and intellectual liberation of a poor southern woman, Celie, who has been mistreated most of her life by men. Besides Goldberg, the film used the talents of director Steven Spielberg, composer Quincy JONES, and actors Danny GLOVER, Margaret Avery, Adolph Caesar, and Oprah WINFREY.

While *The Color Purple* won acclaim from audiences and critics, especially for the performances, the film had detrac-

tors who protested its showing at theaters throughout the country. The protesters charged that the film misrepresented African American life and contained negative depictions of black male characters, who appeared abusive or slow-witted. Goldberg was among those who vigorously defended the film. While the debate did not seem to hurt the film's box-office appeal, the controversy may have affected its chances of winning an Academy Award. Nominated for eleven awards, the film and its cast—including Goldberg, who was nominated in the best actor category—won none.

Despite the controversy surrounding *The Color Purple*, Goldberg became a major star and appeared on the covers of such magazines as *Ms.*, *Rolling Stone*, and *American Film*. *People* named her "one of the most intriguing people of 1985." She appeared in a guest role on television's *Moonlighting* and served as one of the

Whoopi Goldberg, the first female African American actor to win an Academy Award since Hattie McDaniel. *(Whoop, Inc.)*

hosts of the television special *Comic Relief*, a benefit for the homeless. Riding on her popularity, she starred in the film *Jumpin' Jack Flash* (1987). The film proved financially successful despite mixed reviews.

Goldberg became the only black woman to star in Hollywood films in the late 1980's. Critics, however, complained that her movies—*Fatal Beauty* (1987), *Burglar* (1987), *Clara's Heart* (1988), and *The Telephone* (1988)—were of widely uneven quality. By 1989, after Goldberg appeared in the critically panned box-office failure *Homer and Eddie*, reviewers were questioning her judgment in selecting roles appropriate for her talents. An admitted workaholic, Goldberg embraced a variety of artistic endeavors in the 1980's. She recorded a comedy album, *Fontaine... Why Am I Straight?* and beginning in 1988 had a continuing role as Guinan on television's *Star Trek: The Next Generation*.

Career in the 1990's

With the assistance of the film's male lead, Patrick Swayze, Goldberg petitioned the director of *Ghost* (1990) for a supporting role as a spiritual medium. The film earned the largest box-office gross of the year, and Goldberg once again earned the respect of critics and audiences. Her performance garnered her an Academy Award as best supporting actor and gave her the distinction of being the first black woman since Hattie McDANIEL in 1939 to win an Oscar. In 1991 Goldberg acted in two films, *The Long Walk Home*, a drama concerning the 1955 MONTGOMERY BUS BOYCOTT, and *Soapdish*, a comedy about the backstage activities on the set of a television soap opera. In 1992 she starred in the films *Sarafina!* and the very popular *Sister Act*.

By the end of the 1990's, Goldberg's list of achievements and appearances in film and television was somewhat astonishing. She accepted large and small roles alike if the project or part interested her. Her 1990's film work in-

cluded *Made in America* (1993), *Corrina, Corrina* (1994), *Boys on the Side* (1995), *Ghosts of Mississippi* (1996, in which she played civil rights activist Myrlie Evers), *The Associate* (1996), *In and Out* (1997), *How Stella Got Her Groove Back* (1998), and *Girl, Interrupted* (1999).

On television, Goldberg was featured in the short-lived comedy series *Bagdad Cafe* (1990), and in 1992-1993 she hosted her own syndicated talk show, *The Whoopi Goldberg Show*. Other television work, in addition to her recurring appearances on *Star Trek*, included appearances on shows ranging from *Muppets Tonight* to *The Nanny* to *L.A. Doctors*. She appeared on numerous specials, including many comedy performances for the HBO cable network, and was deeply involved in the *Comic Relief* series of HBO specials, which raised money for charity; she hosted the third (1989) through the eighth (1998) *Comic Relief* programs. She became sought-after as a host, hosting the Grammy Awards in 1992 and the Academy Awards in 1994, 1996, and 1999, among other programs. In 1998 she began hosting the game show *Hollywood Squares*.

Goldberg also enjoyed doing voice-over work; she voiced animated characters in *The Lion King* (1994), *A Christmas Carol* (1997), *The Rugrats Movie* (1999), and other films, and in television shows including *Defenders of Dynatron City* (1992) and *A Cool Like That Christmas* (1993). She appeared on the stage in the 1997 Broadway revival of *A Funny Thing Happened on the Way to the Forum*. A memoir, *Book*, was published in 1997.

Personal Life and Awards

Goldberg became an outspoken activist on such issues as drug abuse, the homeless, U.S. policy in Central America, abortion rights, and apartheid in South Africa. Her honors included the 1990 entertainer of the year Image Award, bestowed by the NATIONAL ASSOCIATION FOR THE ADVANCEMENT OF COLORED PEOPLE (NAACP), an honorary doctorate in humanities from Wilson College, and an award for excellence from the Sixth Annual Women in Film Festival in 1990. Throughout the 1990's she received a variety of awards and nominations in addition to her Academy Award for *Ghost*, including Golden Globe, Emmy, and Image Award nominations. In 1998 she won a second NAACP Image Award, for her supporting performance in *How Stella Got Her Groove Back*. Concerning her personal life, after her second divorce (from Dutch cameraman David Claessen), Goldberg vowed that she would never marry again.

—*Addell Austin Anderson*

Suggested Readings:

Edwards, Audrey. "Whoopi!" *Essence*, March, 1985, 84-86.

Erickson, Steve. "Whoopi Goldberg." *Rolling Stone* (May 8, 1986): 38.

Kearney, Jill. "Whoopi: Color Her Anything." *American Film* (December, 1985): 24-26.

Nemy, Enid. "Whoopi's Ready, but Is Broadway?" *The New York Times* (October 21, 1984): B1.

Parish, James R. *Whoopi Goldberg: Her Journey from Poverty to Mega-stardom*. Secaucus, N.J.: Carol, 1997.

Randolph, Laura. "The Whoopi Goldberg Nobody Knows." *Ebony* (March, 1991): 110-112.

"Whoopi Goldberg: Hollywood's Busiest Actress." *Jet* (November 18, 1996): 58-61.

Golden Thirteen of the U.S. Navy: In 1944 the Golden Thirteen became the first African American naval officers in U.S. history. The thirteen included Jesse Walter Arbor, Phillip George Barnes, Samuel Edward Barnes, Dalton Louis Baugh, Sr., George Clinton Cooper, Reginald Ernest Goodwin, James Edward Hair, Charles Byrd Lear, Graham Edward Martin, Dennis Denmark Nelson, John Walter Reagan, Frank Ellis Sublett, and William Sylvester White.

The accomplishments of these men cannot be found on any battleship decoration: None of them could participate in combat during WORLD WAR II because Navy policy prohibited their assignment on any combat ship. As a result, opportunities for the Golden Thirteen were limited to shore duty, small local-defense crafts, and the construction and service fields.

All the men entered the Navy's enlisted ranks in the early 1940's. In 1944 the Navy chose these men and three others to attend an officer training program. All sixteen successfully completed their training, but only twelve were commissioned as ensigns and one as a warrant officer. (The Navy's Bureau of Personnel, for reasons never explained, established a limit of twelve promotees.) As a result, the three who were not commissioned as officers reverted to enlisted status.

Background

Up to 1899, manpower requirements forced the U.S. Navy to accept skilled black seamen, creating a de facto integrated service. In 1899, however, the Navy implemented a "landsman for training" program that provided training for motivated but unskilled recruits. This program expanded the number of available whites for naval service and gradually displaced many blacks. Entry restrictions eventually increased; by August of 1919, the Navy had stopped enlisting black seamen. By 1932 the black naval enlisted force reached its nadir and made up a mere 0.55 percent of the total Navy enlistment force.

The demands of total war in the 1940's, however, forced all branches of the American MILITARY, including the Navy, to increase job opportunities. As the number of black enlisted men increased, President Franklin D. Roosevelt and Adlai Stevenson, assistant to the secretary of the Navy, forced then-secretary Frank Knox to provide a select number of black enlisted personnel the opportunity to become officers. The first group of African

Twelve members of the Golden Thirteen in early 1944: front row, George Clinton Cooper, Graham Edward Martin, Jesse Walter Arbor, John Walter Reagan, Reginald Ernest Goodwin; back row, Phillip George Barnes, Samuel Edward Barnes, Dalton Louise Baugh, James Edward Hare, Frank Ellis Sublett, Charles Byrd Lear. *(National Archives)*

Americans to be commissioned by the Navy became known as the Golden Thirteen.

Training

For two and a half months, the thirteen attended a segregated program at Great Lakes Naval Training Center, Camp Robert Smalls, Illinois. Their classes were held in their own barracks, and the men ate at the general mess before any other groups arrived. This isolation, however, did help the men pull together. In George Cooper's oral accounts, he stated that each man taught the others what he knew. Reggie Goodwin and George Cooper helped with math, Frank Sublett and Dalton Baugh shared their knowledge of boilers, and A. Alves provided information on seamanship. In addition, Reggie Goodwin provided a needed liaison between the black officers-in-training and the Navy's white power structure. By

helping one another, and sustaining proper contacts with supportive white officials, the officer trainees passed their course work. On March 17, 1944, the Golden Thirteen received their commissions without fanfare or a graduation ceremony. This anonymity continued even after the publication of an article in *Life* magazine on April 23, 1944. The article celebrated the integration of the Navy, but Navy policy prohibited the publisher from printing the specific names of the Golden Thirteen. Nevertheless, these men did change the face of America's military.

Common Thread

All of the men were chosen from the enlisted ranks. Ten of the final thirteen had attended college, and two had gone to specialized schools. Samuel E. Barnes was the only member of the Golden Thirteen who had a doctoral degree. Most were athletes and had exhibited leadership qualities that made them stand out as potential officer trainees. The FEDERAL BUREAU OF INVESTIGATION (FBI) checked their backgrounds so thoroughly that bureau officials questioned George Cooper's potential after they found out that he had a skirmish with a white child when he was eight years old. Many of the trainees received short notice to report to the Great Lakes Naval Training Center, and some of them did not know their assignments until they arrived. Ultimately, although all of the Golden Thirteen were qualified as deck officers, none received an assignment to a warship.

Careers

The Navy ended up classifying each man as a "Deck Officer Limited," a classification reserved for officers who could not meet the educational or physical standards required to work on ships. Naturally enough, the men believed that their classification and assignments reflected the Navy's inability and unwillingness to integrate the Golden Thirteen fully into its force structure. The Navy assigned George Cooper, John Reagan, and Frank Sublett to vocational training school at Hampton, Virginia. Four others went to yard and harbor craft duty, while the rest remained at the Great Lakes Training Facility. Only one remained in military service at the end of the war. Dennis Nelson served a full career on active duty; as a lieutenant commander, he attained the highest rank of the group while playing a crucial role in public relations and training. John Reagan, on the other hand, received a recall to active duty. In the fall of 1949, the Navy assigned him to recruitment duty.

The Virginia naval base at Hampton provided some of the Golden Thirteen with their first opportunity to become role models as black officers. As personnel officer, George Cooper confronted perceived racial injustice in a direct manner—he used one-on-one meetings with people to show his own humanity. As the officer-in-charge of an electrical course, John Reagan was convinced that his job description should have also included the title "role model." The officers who had remained at the Great Lakes Training Facility later received a variety of assignments. William White's previous experience as an assistant American attorney led to his assignment to the public relations division at the Great Lakes Training Facility, where he worked specifically with the BLACK PRESS.

In the case of the men assigned to harbor duty, the Navy seemed to prefer pairing them together. Graham Martin and Frank Sublett worked on patrol crafts and yard oilers at Treasure Island in San Francisco Bay. Charles Lear, the only warrant officer, served as a boatswain with Jesse Arbor in Hawaii. Jim Hair and John Reagan served on a yard tugboat in New York City. Dennis Nelson (as personnel officer), Graham Martin (as recreation officer), and Frank Sublett (as executive and supply officer) all worked together in the Marshall Islands at Eniwetok, a staging base for the planned American invasion of Japan.

Although the majority of the Golden Thirteen were shuttled back and forth between assignments on both coasts, there were some officers who went much farther afield. Jim Hair left a harbor tugboat assignment to work on the USS *Mason*, a destroyer escort in the Atlantic. Later, as a deck officer of an amphibious landing vessel in the western Pacific, Hair joined others in providing transportation support for Chinese leader Chiang Kai-shek and his government. Graham Martin served overseas in the Marshall Islands as a straw boss for a stevedore gang, while Charles Lear and Jesse Arbor served in Hawaii and later in Guam as supply and logistics troubleshooters.

Legacy of the Thirteen

On V-J Day, the Navy had 164,942 black enlisted men, constituting 5.37 percent of the total force. Forty percent of these black enlisted men served as steward's mates and messmen. In contrast, approximately sixty black officers (including six women) received their commissions. The numbers were meager, but they represented a crack in the door of segregation. The Golden Thirteen were the first to open this door and pave the way for others.

—*Yolandea M. Wood*

Lee Elder was the first African American to play in the Master's Tournament. *(AP/ Wide World Photos)*

Suggested Readings:

"'Golden Thirteen': First Black Naval Officers Mark Fiftieth Year of Commission." *Jet* (March 28, 1994): 54.

MacGregor, Morris J., Jr. *Integration of the Armed Forces 1940-1965*. Washington, D.C.: Center of Military History, United States Army, 1981.

Nalty, Bernard C. *Strength for the Fight: A History of Black Americans in the Military*. New York: Free Press, 1986.

Stillwell, Paul, ed. *The Golden Thirteen: Recollections of the First Black Naval Officers*. New York: Berkley Books, 1994.

See also: Segregation and integration.

Golf: Although golf has traditionally been regarded as a "white man's game," African Americans have been playing the sport for a long time despite their historically limited access to golf courses, golf lessons, and—for golf professionals—sponsorship money.

In 1896 John Shippen, an African American who was the first professional U.S. golfer, played in the first U.S. Open and led until the thirteenth hole on the final day. Had he won, the history of African American golfers might have been quite different. As it was, many golf courses were segregated until 1956, so African Americans established their own courses, tournaments, and golfing associations. The UNITED GOLFERS' ASSOCIATION (UGA) was formed in 1926 in Stowe, Massachusetts, by Robert H. Hawkins, and "The Champ" golf course in Chicago was opened soon after. Michael Cooper, the first black to qualify for the Arizona State University golf team, was one of the players who honed his skills at The Champ.

It would be many years before racism was eliminated from golf. In order for Bill Wright, a student at Western Washington College, to play in the 1959 National Public Links Golf Championship in Denver, his father had to win a lawsuit charging illegal RACIAL DISCRIMINATION on municipal golf courses. Wright went on to win the tournament. Similar court cases were tried in other places, including BALTIMORE and ATLANTA, during the 1950's. After the battle for integrated public courses was won, racism at private country clubs was the next legal battleground. African Americans have not flocked to private country clubs, however, for reasons that include the

Notable Golfers

Brown, Pete (b. Feb. 2, 1935, Port Gibson, Mo.). Brown began playing professionally in 1954. He won the UNITED GOLFERS' ASSOCIATION (UGA) title in 1961 and 1962, winning the Negro National Open in both years. He joined the PGA tour in 1963 and was the first black golfer to win an official PGA tournament, the Waco Turner Open in 1964. His biggest win was the San Diego Open of 1970, in a sudden-death playoff against Britain's Tony Jacklin.

Elder, Lee (b. July 14, 1934, Dallas, Tex.). Elder began playing professionally in 1959 and joined the PGA tour in 1967. He went on to achieve a number of firsts in golf: the first African American to play in a Masters tournament (1975), the first to break the $100,000 mark in yearly earnings (1976), and the first to make the U.S. Ryder Cup team (1979). As a member of the select group of PGA tour players to win three consecutive events, he also became one of the top fifty all-time money winners.

Elder, Rose Harper. In 1963, while playing in the women's division of the UGA, Elder met her future husband, pro golfer Lee Elder. She continued to play into the 1970's but devoted most of her time to managing her husband's golfing career. She also opened Rose Elder and Associates, a firm involved in public relations, marketing, and promotions.

Peete, Calvin (b. July 18, 1943, Detroit, Mich.). Peete learned to play golf at the age of twenty-three and began playing professionally in 1971, joining the PGA tour in 1975. He consistently ranked among the top ten golfers in four PGA statistical categories: driving accuracy, greens in regulation, scoring, and putting. He was a member of the 1983 and 1985 U.S.

Ryder Cup teams and the 1985 Nissan Cup team. Peete was also the first African American to earn more than one million dollars playing golf and had the most wins on the PGA tour in the four years ending in 1984. He received the Ben Hogan Award in 1983.

Powell, Renee (b. 1946, Canton, Ohio). Powell, whose father had built and maintained a golf course in East Canton, Ohio, began playing professionally in 1967. At one time the only African American on the Women's Professional Golfers' Association (WPGA) tour, she also played in the Ladies' Professional Golfers' Association (LPGA). In 1979 she became a golf instructor at an all-male club in England.

Sifford, Charlie (b. June 2, 1922). Sifford was the first African American officially to break the color barrier of professional golf. In 1957 he won the Long Beach Open, becoming the first African American to win a PGA-sanctioned event. Admitted to the PGA in 1961, he was one of the top sixty money winners on the tour from 1960 to 1969. In 1967 he won the Hartford Open, becoming the first African American to win a regular PGA tour event.

Thorpe, Jim (b. Feb. 1, 1949, Roxboro, N.C.). Thorpe's father worked at a white golf club, enabling family members to master the sport. Thorpe's brother Charles (Chuck) entered the PGA tour first. Thorpe began playing professionally in 1972, and by 1986 he had earned more than a million dollars. In the early 1990's, Thorpe emerged as the number-one African American golfer on the PGA tour.

Woods, Tiger. *See main text entry.*

high cost of membership and the availability of public courses.

After Shippen's golfing success—he played in four more U.S. Opens and finished fifth in

1902—there were few African American professional golfers on the Professional Golfers' Association of America (PGA) tour. The PGA maintained a "white only" clause for membership until 1961. (Two African American women, however—Althea GIBSON and Renee Powell—did play in Ladies' Professional Golfers' Association, LPGA, events.)

Ted Rhodes, who won more than 150 UGA tournaments, played in a few PGA events and in 1949 became the second black professional golfer to play in the U.S. Open. Charlie Sifford was the first black golfer to win on the tour, and he earned more than $200,000 in prize money. Lee Elder became the first black golfer to play in the prestigious Master's tournament, and Calvin Peete became the black player with the most tournament wins and money earned.

Peete's record was expected to be shattered by Tiger WOODS, ranked in early 2000 as the best professional golfer in the world. Unlike his predecessors, Woods had the advantage of participating in outstanding junior programs and intercollegiate competition. In fact, by the 1990's the National Minority Junior Golf Scholarship Association had established programs throughout the United States, and several historically black universities had developed golf programs to develop more African American golfers. The existence of the National Black Golf Hall of Fame and the National Afro-American Golfers Hall of Fame attests to the contributions of African Americans to the game of golf.

—*Thomas L. Erskine*

Suggested Reading:

Robinson, Lenwood, Jr. *Skins and Grins: The Plight of the Black American Golfer.* Chicago: Chicago Spectrum Press, 1997.

Gomillion v. Lightfoot: Landmark 1960 U.S. SUPREME COURT decision ruling racially motivated GERRYMANDERING unconstitutional. The case originated in ALABAMA in 1957, when the state legislature redrew Tuskegee's boundaries to create a white voting majority. African American residents, who had previ-

ously held an electoral majority, challenged the state's action under provisions of the FOURTEENTH and FIFTEENTH AMENDMENTS. After lower courts dismissed their challenge, the Supreme Court considered the case. The Court ruled that Alabama's action violated federally protected rights—particularly the Fourteenth Amendment's equal protection clause. It further ruled that if it could be shown that the state moved the boundaries intentionally to strengthen a white voting bloc, the local redistricting act would be declared void. Finally, the Court sent the case back to the lower courts.

—*Christopher E. Kent*

Goode, Malvin R. (b. February 13, 1908, White Plains, Virginia): Reporter. Goode began reporting on the United Nations for the ABC television network in 1962, becoming the network's first black reporter. He stayed with the network for eleven years. Previously, he had been a reporter with the PITTSBURGH COURIER for fourteen years and had worked in radio news. After he left ABC, he worked as a consultant for the National Black Network. *See also:* Black press.

Gordon, Dexter (February 27, 1923, Los Angeles, California—April 25, 1990, Philadelphia, Pennsylvania): JAZZ tenor saxophonist, soprano saxophonist, composer, and actor. After playing in the early and mid-1940's with musicians such as vibraphonist Lionel HAMPTON and trumpeter Louis ARMSTRONG, Gordon became involved in the new music known as BEBOP, of which he became one of the most significant practitioners. Although his playing on his first recordings as leader in 1943 reveals the strong influence of tenor saxophonist Lester YOUNG, not long thereafter he developed his own individual and unmistakable tone and style, thus influencing other bebop saxophonists, including, in time, such important figures as John COLTRANE and Sonny ROLLINS.

Gordon's most famous early solo, with leader Billy ECKSTINE in 1944, featured interplay between Gordon and tenor saxophonist Gene Ammons on "Blowing the Blues Away." Gordon became one of the first saxophonists to engage regularly in extended solo exchanges with other saxophonists, as he did with Wardell Gray in 1947.

In 1955 Gordon became inactive because of problems with drugs, but when he returned to performing and recording in 1960, he did so with renewed vigor. His albums for Blue Note in the early 1960's are among the most substantial of his career. After his recordings for Blue Note, he moved to Copenhagen, Denmark, where he resided for many years and recorded fairly prolifically. Upon returning to the United States in late 1976, he was received as something of a hero, and his first American performance in years brought him renewed acclaim. Despite his reception, Gordon remained essentially an internationalist.

Toward the end of his life, Gordon also gained notice as an actor. Always an imposing man, tall and handsome, with deliberate speech patterns, he was perfect for the leading role as an aging jazz musician in 'Round Midnight (1986). His performance earned for him an Academy Award nomination for best actor.

Saxophonist Dexter Gordon performing at a jazz festival in the Netherlands in 1987. (AP/Wide World Photos)

Gordon, Edwin Jason (b. October 10, 1952, Cincinnati, Ohio): Publishing executive. Gordon worked for ten years as an associate editor at South-Western Publishing. In 1984 he moved to Harcourt Brace Jovanovich to become senior acquisitions editor. From 1987 to 1989, Gordon was director of San Diego State University Press, leaving to take a position as assistant director of HOWARD UNIVERSITY Press. Gordon remained at Howard University Press through the 1990's, becoming acting director in 1994 and director in 1995.

Gordy, Berry, Jr. (b. November 28, 1929, Detroit, Michigan): Songwriter, record producer, and recording executive. Berry Gordy founded MOTOWN, the most successful African American-owned record company. He and Motown changed the sound of American popular music in the 1960's.

One of eight children, Gordy was reared in DETROIT. His father was a construction contractor who also ran a grocery store and a printing shop; his mother, Bertha, was an insurance agent and was active in the local DEMOCRATIC PARTY. Gordy attended Northeastern High School, dropping out in the eleventh grade to pursue a professional BOXING career

Berry Gordy, Jr., the founder of Motown.

until he was drafted into the U.S. Army. He served from 1951 to 1953, stateside and in Korea, and earned his high school equivalency diploma.

Returning to Detroit, Gordy opened a record store which failed in 1955. He went to work at the Ford Motor Company while writing songs and producing records in his spare time. By 1959 Gordy had scored several hits, including "Lonely Teardrops," sung by Jackie WILSON. He had also, with singer William "Smokey" ROBINSON, Jr., organized his own Motown Records, which eventually included the Motown, Gordy, Tamla, VIP, and Soul labels as well as the Jobete Music publishing firm. Robinson and the Miracles achieved Motown's first gold record with "Shop Around," on the Tamla label in 1960. With a recording orchestra led by Gil Askey and a crew of talented songwriters including the team of Brian Holland, Lamont Dozier, and Eddie Holland, Motown Records produced a sophisticated version of RHYTHM AND BLUES—often with symphonic backgrounds—that became the most popular sound of the 1960's and 1970's. Artists such as Stevie WONDER, Martha and the Vandellas, Marvin GAYE, the Temptations, the Jackson 5, and Diana Ross and the SUPREMES continued to score consistent top-selling records under Gordy's direction.

In 1972 Gordy moved his headquarters to LOS ANGELES, CALIFORNIA, and expanded into television and motion picture production. At that time, Motown was doing more than $50 million in business annually. Motown-produced films such as *Lady Sings the Blues* (1972), nominated for five Academy Awards, and *The Bingo Long Traveling All-Stars and Motor Kings* (1976) found a large and receptive audience. In 1984 Gordy sold a large interest in Motown Industries to MCA, retaining his position as chairman of the board; in 1988 he officially sold Motown to MCA and Boston Ventures for a reported $61 million but kept his production and music publishing companies. Gordy later stated that he felt he had to leave the music business because it was changing so dramatically. Also in 1988, in addition to the many civic and business honors Gordy had received through the years, he was inducted into the Rock and Roll Hall of Fame.

Gordy published a memoir, *To Be Loved: The Music, the Magic, the Memories of Motown*, in 1994. In 1997 he sold half of Jobete, his music publishing firm, to EMI for $132 million; EMI, the world's largest music publishing firm, had five years in which to bid on the other half. (Music publishing firms collect royalties when recordings of the songs they own are sold or played on the radio, and they handle licensing arrangements for song use in films, television, and elsewhere. These firms therefore generate a considerable amount of money. Jobete was earning roughly $15 million annually in the 1990's.

See also: Business and commerce; Recording labels; Songwriters and composers.

Gospel music and spirituals: Gospel music and spirituals are distinctive African American religious art forms that have extensively influenced the MUSIC and culture of the United States. The spirituals are the parent music of gospel music as well as a direct ancestor of JAZZ and BLUES. Originating in SLAVERY, they were collected and popularized by touring African American choirs in the late nineteenth century. Gospel music was a derivative of the spirituals that arose as a para-church movement, beginning in Chicago in the 1930's. At first, gospel music was considered to be unacceptable for performance in church. A quarter of a century after its introduction, gospel music not only had moved into the churches but also was regarded by many to be the quintessential element of African American worship.

Spirituals

African American spiritual music originated in the convergence of African cultural style, the religious fervor of the Second Great Awakening in the United States, and the conditions of slavery in the South. By the nineteenth century, few formal structures of African culture or religion remained intact among slaves of the southern United States. Nevertheless, African cultural traits survived in the lifestyle and expression of slave subculture. Those from whom the slaves had descended lived in a world of sound, a world in which the spoken, chanted, sung, or shouted word was the primary form of communication. Among those Africans brought to the southern United States, that manner of being in the world went underground, emerging in new cultural adaptations.

The work songs of the slave communities, for example, reflected characteristics difficult to explain without reference to African influence. The unique musical character of the spirituals likewise seems to have derived from African origins, even though direct links cannot

be established. If the musical style of the spirituals was derived from African roots, it appears that the revival and camp meeting provided the spirituals with sacred language and imagery. The stories of the Old Testament, the image of God as all-powerful savior, and the instrumentality of music in religious expression were themes common to the experience of the Second Great Awakening, whether the hearer-participant was black or white. In fact, there apparently was a great deal of cultural sharing between European Americans and African Americans in the revival meetings that swept the countryside in the early nineteenth century. The creative genius of the spirituals resided in the use of these two traditions, African style and Euro-Christian story, to interpret the survival conditions of slavery.

Characteristics of the Spirituals

The spirituals were first of all contextual in nature. These slave songs arose out of the general context of slavery, but they were even more particularly contextual than that. One can only guess how the essential melody and lyrics of a song originated. Some suggest that they may have begun in a context of worship in which the chant of the preacher and the response of the congregation were arranged in a repeatable pattern. Once a song took shape, it did not remain static but was always changing as the community altered and re-created it. In this way, the songs moved beyond the worship setting to form a living, communal language expressive of the struggles, the hopes, and the fears of an oppressed people.

Always, the songs communicated the cultural worldview of the singers. The spirituals were almost devoid of feelings of depravity or unworthiness. They were pervaded by a sense of personal worth, transcendence, and ultimate justice. Often, the songs were used for more immediate and functional communication. Many of the spirituals were given veiled

(continued on page 1065)

Notable Gospel Singers and Musicians

Brown, Ruth Weston. *See main text entry.*

Caesar, Shirley. *See main text entry.*

Cleveland, James. *See main text entry.*

Coates, Dorothy Love (b. Birmingham, Ala.). In the 1940's and 1950's, Coates sang with the Harmonettes, Birmingham's most popular gospel act. Her fervent, expressive style exasperated the rest of the group but made her popular with audiences. When the Harmonettes reorganized in 1961, Coates applied the gospel to the conditions of African Americans.

Cooke, Sam. *See main text entry.*

Crouch, Andrae. *See main text entry.*

Dixon, Jessy (b. Mar. 12, 1938, San Antonio, Tex.). A composer, pianist, and gospel music singer, Dixon became director of the Thompson Community Choir in 1964 and made several recordings with the group. That same year, he founded and directed the Omega Singers and the Jessy Dixon Singers. A popular touring act beginning in 1972, his recordings became increasingly popular. His best-known works include "God Can Do Anything but Fail," "There Is No Failure in God," and "The Failure's Not in God, It's in Me."

Dorsey, Thomas Andrew. *See main text entry.*

Gates, J. M. (c. 1885, Atlanta, Ga.—c. 1940, Atlanta, Ga.). A BAPTIST cleric and singer, Gates began preaching in 1910, and in 1914, he became pastor at Mount Calvary Church in Rock Dale Park, ATLANTA, GEORGIA. His preaching and bluesy gospel singing attracted a large audience, and both were released as commercial recordings. The first of his recorded sermons was *Death's Black Train Is Coming* (1926).

Green, Al. *See main text entry.*

Hawkins, Edwin R. (b. Aug. 18, 1943, Oakland, Calif.). Along with his group, the Edwin Hawkins Singers, he achieved international fame in 1969 with the gospel hit "Oh Happy Day." He has recorded numerous albums, both solo and with the Edwin Hawkins Singers as well as with the Edwin Hawkins Music and Arts Seminar Mass Choir, founded in the early 1980's. By the early 1990's, he had earned three Grammy Awards.

Hawkins, Tramaine Davis (b. Oct. 11, 1957, San Francisco, Calif.). Born into a gospel music family, Hawkins recorded her first single at the age of ten. Before launching her solo career in the early 1980's, she sang with the Heavenly Tones and the Edwin Hawkins Singers. She has recorded a number of best-selling albums, among which are *The Joy That Floods My Soul* and *Tramaine Live!*

Holliday, Jennifer (b. Oct. 19, 1960, Riverside, Tex.). Blessed with a powerful, four-octave voice, Holliday replaced Dolores Hall in the musical *Your Arms Too Short to Box with God.* Holliday made her Broadway debut in 1980 to critical acclaim. She was chosen for a starring role in the Broadway musical *Dreamgirls*, which opened in 1981, and won a Tony for her performance. She released the album *Free My Soul* on Geffen Records in 1983.

AP/Wide World Photos

Jackson, Mahalia. *See main text entry.*

Knight, Marie. *See main text entry.*

Martin, Sallie. *See main text entry.*

Tharpe, Sister Rosetta. *See main text entry.*

Tindley, Charles Albert. *See main text entry.*

Ward, Clara. *See main text entry.*

Winans, Benjamin "BeBe," and Cecelia "CeCe" Winans. Part of the gospel-singing Winans family, BeBe and CeCe often sang duets during the lengthy Winans shows. CeCe's powerful voice is considered to be one of the best in the music business, both gospel and secular.

Members of a Charleston, South Carolina, church choir singing at a ceremony in which the state governor signed a bill designating the spiritual South Carolina's official music on July 1, 1999. *(AP/Wide World Photos)*

multiple meanings in a given circumstance. A lyric such as "My God ain't no lyin' man" not only affirmed the trustworthiness of God but also could satirize the slave master, who was, in fact, a "lyin' man" and anything but all-powerful. Lyrics about heaven or the Jordan River typically had double meanings. On one hand, they declared faith in the ultimate deliverance of God. On the other, they could refer specifically to escape to the North across the Ohio River. In such a manner, the spirituals were sung to signal secret meetings or give instructions for escape on the UNDERGROUND RAILROAD.

Moreover, the spirituals were communal in nature. Created and sung in a call-and-response style, they were expressions of community solidarity. Through their songs, the slave communities gave their members support and encouragement in the struggle for survival. The songs built community morale, enlisted in common cause, stated group values, and conspired toward rebellion and es-

cape. At a deeper level, the spirituals passed on a cultural heritage, the verbal stories of which had been lost.

Finally, these slave songs were theologically subversive. On the surface, they sounded passive and submissive to the white slave-owners' religion, but they expressed a view of history and a doctrine of God that undermined the authority of the slave master and of the institution of slavery itself. In the spirituals, God was the sovereign, all-powerful liberator of those in bondage—a God of justice who would vindicate the oppressed.

Revival of the Art Form

After the CIVIL WAR, the spiritual songs all but died out. They had lost much of their function with the abolition of slavery. Many African Americans refused to sing them because they were considered to be the old songs of slavery. The FISK JUBILEE SINGERS are credited with saving the spirituals for posterity. In the
(continued on page 1067)

Notable Gospel Groups

Caravans. Formed in 1952 as a backing group for Robert Anderson, who had left the Roberta Martin Singers, the Caravans soon re-formed under the direction of Albertina Walker. James CLEVELAND contributed musical arrangements, which gave the group a progressive sound. In 1955 Cassieta George was admitted and soon was joined by Dorothy Norwood, Imogene Greene, and Inez Andrews. Andrews was replaced in 1961 by Shirley CAESAR. Over its fifteen-year history, the Caravans boasted at least a dozen name talents, including Delores Washington and Sarah McKissick.

Clark Sisters. A quintet, the Clark Sisters retained the integrity and vigor of traditional gospel while keeping the music fresh and innovative. The group consisted of the five daughters of Mother Mattie Moss Clark: Karen, Jackie, Dorinda, Niecy, and Elbernita (known as "Twinkie"). "You Brought the Sunshine" was a crossover hit in the 1970's and was especially popular in gay discos, partly because of the sisters' ministry to the gay community. The sisters could sing polished five-part harmonies, backed by Twinkie on the organ, break down into scatlike counterpoints to one another or sing "in the spirit" (the pentecostal practice of "speaking in tongues"), then suddenly pull together as a disciplined ensemble.

Dixie Hummingbirds. *See main text entry.*

Jackson Harmoneers. Male group also known as the Five Blind Boys of Mississippi. (The group also recorded under the name Original Five Blind Boys, in friendly competition with another group called the Five Blind Boys of Alabama.) Of the two groups, the Harmoneers are the better known, probably because of the popularity of their lead singer, Archie Brownlee. His falsetto screaming, a first among male gospel groups, endeared him to audiences. Early recordings such as "He's My Rock" (1949), feature singing characteristic of the quartet style of the times: a capella vocal harmonizing dominated by a distinctive lead presence.

Mighty Clouds of Joy. *See main text entry.*

Nightingales. Male group whose membership included Howard Carroll, Julius "June" Cheeks, Carl Coates, Paul Owens, and Jo Jo Wallace. The Nightin-

gales had achieved some recognition before the Reverend Julius Cheeks joined the group in 1946. He left briefly in the late 1940's to perform with the Soul Stirrers but rejoined in the early 1950's. Together they recorded a string of hits, including "Standing in the Judgment," "It Is No Secret," and "See How They Done My Lord." The Nightingales became known for a shouting and preaching style characterized by Cheeks.

Original Gospel Harmonettes. Gospel singing group organized in 1940 in BIRMINGHAM, ALABAMA. It was composed of contralto Willie May Newberry, soprano Vera Kolb, contralto Odessa Edwards, mezzo soprano Mildred Miller Howard, and pianist Evelyn Starks. In 1945 the group was joined by contralto Dorothy Love Coates, a gospel singer and composer whose membership in the group helped get it national attention. The group retired in 1958 but was reorganized in 1961 by Coates. This new group was composed of soprano Cleo Kennedy and contralto Lillian McGriff, in addition to Coates, Newberry, and Howard. This group quickly became popular with such recordings as "Come On in the House" and "I Won't Let Go of My Faith."

Roberta Martin Singers. Group established in 1933 as the Martin-Frye Quartet at the Ebenezer Baptist Church in CHICAGO by Roberta Martin and Theodore R. Frye. With the exception of Martin, who served as the accompanist, this was an all-male group and included Eugene Smith, Robert Anderson, Norsalus McKissick, Willie Webb, and James Lawrence. It was renamed the Roberta Martin Singers in 1935 and by 1940 had expanded to include such female singers as Lucy Smith Colier, Gloria Griffin, Bessie Folk, Deloris Barret, and Myrtle Scott.

Soul Stirrers. Four teenagers formed the original Soul Stirrers in Trinity, TEXAS, in 1926. In 1937 the group made its recording debut, for the Library of Congress. Members of the group at that time included Robert Harris, Ernest Roundless, Silas Crain, Mozelle Franklin, and Jesse Farley. The Soul Stirrers became one of the leading gospel groups in the CHICAGO area. Sam COOKE assumed the lead singer's position for the Soul Stirrers when Harris retired in 1955. In 1989 the Soul Stirrers were inducted into the Rock and Roll Hall of Fame.

Winans. Twins Marvin and Carvin Winans and their brothers Michael and Ronald were initiated into gospel music in church choirs in their hometown of DETROIT. Gospel legend Andrae CROUCH helped them record their first hit, "The Quest Is." The quartet then recorded a number of albums for the gospel label Light Records, including the Grammy-nominated *Introducing the Winans*, *Tomorrow*, and *Long Time Comin'*. The brothers signed with producer Quincy JONES's record label, Qwest, in 1984 and burst into national prominence with *Let My People Go*, the 1985 Grammy Award-winning recording in the Best Gospel Album category.

1870's, they toured to raise money for FISK UNIVERSITY. Confronted at first with discrimination and discouragement, they discovered that crowds warmed to their singing of a selection of spirituals. Soon they were concentrating their concerts on these African American folk songs. Their success prompted the formation of the Hampton Singers from HAMPTON INSTITUTE. These and similar groups introduced the world to spirituals.

Gospel Music

African American spirituals developed in the rural South of the nineteenth century. Gospel music originated in the urban contexts of African Americans a century later. Although Thomas A. DORSEY is generally considered to be its founder and popularizer, gospel music had its genesis in the composed music of Charles TINDLEY, an African American METHODIST preacher who published *New Songs of Paradise* in 1916. Features of the songs in Tindley's collection marked them as distinct from the spirituals and anticipatory of a new genre that would become known as "gospel." These songs were composed by an identifiable composer. They were written down in a relatively fixed form with relatively fixed meaning. Like the spirituals, they were survival songs, but like the blues, they sang of survival in an individualistic urban culture.

Preaching Through Music

Dorsey and others took the music one step further in distinguishing it from the spirituals. His sheet music was written primarily for performers, although it still retained a strong participatory element. In the 1930's and later, choirs, ensembles, and soloists toured large urban centers, gathering people in churches and convention halls to "preach the gospel" through their music. Dorsey named them "gospel songs" because they told "good news." The singers understood their vocation in the same way as the revival preacher. Women such as Willie Mae Ford SMITH and Mahalia JACKSON found vocational freedom through the performance of their music that they would not have had as preachers in the traditional sense. The conventions functioned to socialize and provide ethnic identity for urban African Americans in a context in which communal life was difficult to maintain.

Gospel music also differed from the spirituals theologically. Whereas the stories of the Old Testament dominated the spirituals, the figure of Jesus was central to gospel. Jesus was no longer the warrior king of the spirituals. He was the friend who bore one's burdens, the companion in life's struggles, and the savior who would ultimately receive the faithful in a better life. Willie Mae Ford Smith described her music as a feeling going to the marrow of her bones, giving her the sensation of being able to fly away and forget that she was in the world. Gospel music countered the alienation and despair of the urban context with a personal and spiritual affirmation of human dignity and worth.

The music of Dorsey and his successors, while distinct from the spirituals, maintained points of continuity uniquely African American. God was understood as an immediate, living, all-powerful presence in both. The God of gospel music cares and delivers humankind from the troubles of life. Dorsey's "Precious Lord," written about the death of his wife and child, is illustrative: "Precious Lord, take my hand/ lead me on, let me stand/ I am tired; I am weak; I am worn." Call-and-response patterns, improvisation, body movement, hand clapping, and shouting marked gospel's continuity with and indebtedness to the spirituals.

Gospel's Impact

Like its secular counterparts jazz and blues, gospel music has had a significant impact on modern popular music. Also like jazz and blues, it has continued to develop as a genre in its own right. Since the 1960's, the use of percussive and electronic instrumentation has complemented, if not replaced, the piano. The use of electronic media has expanded gospel's audience and moderated its social and religious particularity.

—B. Edmon Martin

See also: Crouch, Andrae; Rhythm and blues; Soul music.

Suggested Readings:

Abromeit, Kathleen A. *An Index to African-American Spirituals for the Solo Voice.* Westport, Conn.: Greenwood Press, 1999.

Boyer, Horace C. *How Sweet the Sound: The Golden Age of Gospel.* Washington, D.C.: Elliott & Clark, 1995.

Cruz, Jon. *Culture on the Margins: The Black Spiritual and the Rise of American Cultural Interpretation.* Princeton, N.J.: Princeton University Press, 1999.

Du Bois, W. E. B. *The Souls of Black Folk.* Greenwich, Conn.: Fawcett, 1961.

Houston, Cissy, and Jonathan Singer. *How Sweet the Sound: My Life with God and Gospel.* New York: Doubleday, 1998.

Hurston, Zora Neale. *The Sanctified Church.* Berkeley, Calif.: Turtle Island, 1981.

Jones, Arthur C. *Wade in the Water: The Wisdom of the Spirituals.* Maryknoll, N.Y.: Orbis Books, 1993.

Lincoln, C. Eric, and Laurence H. Mamiya. *The Black Church in the African American Experience.* Durham, N.C.: Duke University Press, 1990.

Newman, Richard, and Cornel West. *Go Down Moses: A Celebration of the African-American Spiritual.* New York: Clarkson N. Potter, 1998.

Thurman, Howard. *Deep River and The Negro Spiritual Speaks of Life and Death.* Richmond, Ind.: Friends United Press, 1975.

Gossett, Lou, Jr. (b. May 27, 1936, Brooklyn, New York): Actor. Louis Gossett, Jr., was the only child of Helen (Wray) and Louis Gossett, Sr. Gossett's parents reared him in the ethnically diverse Coney Island section of Brooklyn. As a member of a large extended family, Gossett witnessed several of his relatives—including his own father—fall victim to ALCOHOLISM. Gossett credits his mother as the greatest influence on his life.

An excellent student and athlete in high school, Gossett won letters in track, baseball, and basketball. As captain of the varsity basketball team, he dreamed of playing professional basketball following graduation, but a hernia injury in his junior year forced him to sit out ten games. During that time, his grade-point average dropped severely. Gossett's English teacher, Gustave Blum, recognized Louis's need for another extracurricular activity. A former Broadway director, Blum suggested that Gossett audition for the school production of *You Can't Take It with You.* Although Gossett performed in the play, acting failed to capture his attention, and he returned to basketball.

Theater Career

Impressed by the young man's talents, Blum once again came to Gossett and suggested he audition for the male lead in the Broadway production of Louis Peterson's *Take a Giant Step* (1953). On a lark, Gossett went to the auditions. To his surprise, he was cast over some 450 other actors to play Spencer Scott in the coming-of-age drama. Making three hundred dollars a week, Gossett required a tutor every day after school to help him lose his thick Brooklyn accent. On September 24, 1953, his Broadway debut garnered rave reviews for the novice actor. Major New York THEATER critics heralded his performance as the emergence of a rare natural talent. At the age of seventeen, encouraged by winning the Donaldson Award as best newcomer of 1953, Louis Gossett, Jr., decided he would undertake both basketball and drama in college.

After graduating from Abraham Lincoln High School in 1954, Gossett entered New York University (NYU) on an athletic/drama scholarship. At NYU he studied acting with Frank Silvera and Lloyd Richards. Playing basketball as well, Gossett worked primarily on television until returning to Broadway in the play *The Desk Set* in 1955. Next he performed in two Off-Broadway revivals, *Take a Giant Step* in 1956 and *Lost in The Stars* in 1957.

After receiving his bachelor of arts degree in 1959, Gossett was drafted by the National Basketball Association's New York Knickerbockers, but his former acting teacher, Lloyd Richards, offered him a role in Lorraine HANSBERRY's *A Raisin in the Sun*. Upon accepting the role, he finally relinquished his basketball aspirations to devote himself exclusively to acting. Hansberry's urban drama, now considered an American classic, became a popular as well as a critical success. Gossett's performance as the well-to-do college student George Murchison was singled out for praise by critics. His career seemed to have a promising future.

Throughout the 1960's, Gossett worked mainly on the stage, with the exception of a few television roles and his film debut,

reprising his stage role, in the screen adaptation of *A Raisin in the Sun* (1961). He continued to hone his skills in such Off-Broadway plays as Jean Genet's controversial drama *The Blacks* in 1961, Langston HUGHES's *Tambourines to Glory* in 1963, and Athol Fugard's *The Blood Knot* in 1964. Yet the acclaim garnered from these productions did little to fulfill the expectations his earlier work had created. Since Off-Broadway shows paid little, Gossett began to sing and play the guitar and drums in local New York clubs to supplement his income.

Community Service

In 1966 Gossett saw many of the Lower East Side children in his neighborhood aimlessly playing during school hours. Deciding to do for them what Blum had done for him, he organized the Gossett Academy of Dramatic Arts (GADA). Receiving a $13,500 grant from the Federal Office of Economic Opportunity,

Lou Gossett won an Academy Award for his performance as a tough drill sergeant in *An Officer and a Gentleman* in 1983. *(AP/Wide World Photos)*

Gossett involved the talents of such professionals as playwright Loften MITCHELL and actor Paul Sorvino in introducing the youngsters to the world of theater. GADA offered courses in make-up, acting, playwriting, fencing, voice, and stagecraft. Many skeptics predicted failure for the project, but GADA finished the summer with eighty-five youngsters whose lives had been enriched by exposure to the opportunities of a career in the theater.

Film and Television

Returning to the screen in *The Landlord* (1970), Gossett played a black militant tenant who explodes in anger after he uncovers his wife's (Diana Sands) affair with the white building owner (Beau Bridges). In an otherwise forgettable film, Gossett's performance with Sands is considered a high point. Following this film, Gossett became one of Hollywood's busiest yet most dissatisfied black actors. He appeared in a string of unimpressive films during the peak of Hollywood's BLAXPLOITATION period; all these movies were commercial failures.

A major turning point for Gossett came when he was cast in *Roots*, the 1977 television adaptation of Alex HALEY's best-selling book. Hired to play Fiddler, the friend and mentor to the drama's hero, Kunta Kinte, Gossett created a dignified, highly acclaimed portrayal of a southern plantation house slave. Researching his own family history for authenticity, Gossett drew on personality characteristics from several of his relatives. The performance brought Gossett an Emmy Award, and once again critics wrote articles predicting that he would become a major star.

Although his opportunities increased after *Roots*, and he performed in television projects such as *The Critical List* (1978), *Backstairs at the White House* (1979), and the failed series *The Lazarus Syndrome* (1979), Gossett became frustrated at the stereotypical roles from which he had to choose. With the exception of roles as baseball player Satchel PAIGE in *Don't Look*

Back (1981) and Egyptian president Anwar Sadat in the television miniseries *Sadat* (1983), his job options were limited. Consequently, he began to petition for roles written originally for whites. The part of Sergeant Emil Foley, a tough Marine drill instructor in the film *An Officer and a Gentleman* (1982), was such a role.

Director Taylor Hackford was impressed by Gossett's audition and agreed to cast him in the role. Gossett's film performance earned him an Academy Award as best supporting actor. Winning the award made Gossett only the third black actor to receive an Oscar for acting. Assuming that winning an Oscar, a Golden Globe Award, and a NATIONAL ASSOCIATION FOR THE ADVANCEMENT OF COLORED PEOPLE (NAACP) Image Award for his performance would generate numerous film projects, Gossett was sadly disappointed by the reality. As offers failed to materialize, Gossett fell into depression. Much as his father and uncles had used alcohol to drown their frustrations, Gossett found comfort in alcohol, cocaine, and other narcotics.

After suffering from depression for several years, Gossett finally recognized the severity of his problem. He credits an anonymous group support program for helping him to regain his self-respect. Following completion of his treatment, he again began to work on television and in film, but this time with a new perspective on the important things in life.

Beginning in the late 1980's, Gossett worked on diverse projects, including the science-fiction film *Enemy Mine* (1985), the action-adventure film *Iron Eagle* (1986) and its sequel *Iron Eagle II* (1988), the television adaptation of Ernest J. GAINES's novel *A Gathering of Old Men* (1987), and the teleplay *The Father Clements Story* (1987). As a crime-solving Ivy League anthropology professor in *Gideon Oliver* (1989), Gossett became one of only a handful of black actors to star in a dramatic television series. For his role as a boxer involved in a con game in the film *Diggstown* (1992), Gossett undertook a strenuous training regimen to lose weight and prepare for the film's fight scenes.

In the 1990's Gossett's film work included a third *Iron Eagle* film in 1992 as well as roles in *A Good Man in Africa* (1994), *Managua* (1997, which he also coproduced), and *Legend of the Mummy* (1997). On television he appeared in the miniseries *Return to Lonesome Dove* (1993) and many television films, including *Flashfire* (1994), *Curse of the Starving Class* (1995), and *The Inspectors* (1998). Gossett won a Golden Globe Award for his role in the HBO cable film *The Josephine Baker Story* (1991) and an NAACP Image Award in 1998 for his supporting role in the television series *Touched by an Angel*.

Private Life

Gossett's marriage to his first wife, Hattie, ended in an annulment. His second wife, actor Christina Mangosing, gave birth to their son, Satie. After their marriage ended in divorce, Gossett fought for and won custody of Satie. On Christmas Day in 1987, Gossett married his third wife, actor and singer Cyndi James-Reese. While watching television in 1986, Gossett was moved by the plight of a boy named Sharon who had been featured in a *Good Morning America* feature on the homeless. The boy had been living on the streets of St. Louis with his widowed mother and two brothers. After tracking him down and getting the permission of the boy's biological mother, Gossett brought Sharon to his Malibu home. He and his wife adopted the boy in 1988.

Having conquered many of the problems that once plagued his career, Gossett founded his own production company, LoGo Entertainment, in the hope of increasing the number of opportunities for black actors in feature films and television. In much the same way that he created GADA, Gossett continued to use his resources to create avenues for younger generations of blacks.

—*Gary Anderson*

See also: Image Awards.

Suggested Readings:

Bogle, Donald. *Blacks in American Films and Television: An Encyclopedia*. New York: Garland, 1988.

Collins, Glenn. "Lou Gossett, Jr. Battles the Hollywood Stereotype." *The New York Times* (February 19, 1989): B23.

Klemesrud, Judy. "Earning Sergeant's Stripes for a Movie Role." *The New York Times* (July 25, 1982): B1.

"Louis Gossett, Jr." *Current Biography* 51 (November, 1990): 33-37.

Norment, Lynn. "Lou Gossett, Jr.: The Agony and Ecstasy of Success." *Ebony* (December, 1982): 142.

Stone, Judy. "Lou Gossett: Did We Always Eat Watermelon?" *The New York Times* (August 30, 1970): B13.

Gottingen Street (Halifax, Nova Scotia, Canada): Historic neighborhood in the city of Halifax, located in the Maritime province of Nova Scotia. The street and its surrounding district have been home to a large black community since the conclusion of the AMERICAN REVOLUTION. Unlike many thriving black communities located near urban centers in Canada, most of Halifax's black residents were unable to create a self-supporting black economy and struggled under the burdens of racism and POVERTY during the course of many generations. In the 1990's, local residents began making efforts to preserve the neighborhood's history and its buildings as evidence of the black community's enduring presence in Halifax.

See also: Canada; Historic landmark and neighborhood preservation.

Gourdine, Meredith C. (September 26, 1929, Newark, New Jersey—November 20, 1998, Houston, Texas): Physicist and engineer. Gourdine conducted pioneering research in the conversion of gas to electricity for energy

Meredith C. Gourdine at Caltech in 1958. *(AP/Wide World Photos)*

Gourdine, Simon Peter (b. July 30, 1940, Jersey City, New Jersey): Attorney. After several years as an assistant attorney general for the Southern Judicial District of New York, Gourdine began work with the National Basketball Association (NBA) as assistant to the commissioner, a post he held from 1970 to 1972. He became vice president of administration in 1972 and deputy commissioner in 1974. Gourdine served as commissioner of the NEW YORK CITY Department of Consumer Affairs and as secretary for the Rockefeller Foundation between 1982 and 1986; from 1986 to 1990, he was the director of labor relations for the New York City Transit Authority. In 1990 he returned to work for the NBA as general counsel for the NBA Players Association, and he became a general partner in TCS Television.

use (electrogasdynamics). He developed a device known as the "Incineraid," to remove smoke from buildings, and developed a technique for dispersing fog from airport runways. Gourdine received several patents on gasdynamic products. From 1958 to 1960, he served as senior research scientist at the Jet Propulsion Laboratory (JPL), a research facility operated by the California Institute of Technology and the National Aeronautics and Space Administration (NASA). In 1962 he left JPL to work as chief scientist at Curtiss-Wright Corporation.

After leaving Curtiss-Wright in 1964, Gourdine founded Gourdine Laboratories, his own research and development company, in Livingston, New Jersey. Gourdine has published numerous articles in scientific journals on electrogasdynamics. Although he became blind in 1973 after being diagnosed with diabetes, Gourdine continued his research and launched the Houston-based company Energy Innovations in the late 1970's.
See also: Engineers; Physicists.

Grace, Charles Emmanuel "Sweet Daddy" (Marcelino Manoel de Graca; January 25, 1881, Brava, Cape Verde Islands—January 12, 1960, Los Angeles, California): Religious leader. Grace was a bishop in the United House of Prayer for All People, a pentecostal Holiness sect, from 1926 until his death. His ancestry was Portuguese and African, but he preferred to pass as white when he could. Nevertheless, his followers mostly were African Americans from black ghettos in economically depressed urban areas.

Grace migrated to New Bedford, MASSACHUSETTS, about 1900. He worked as a short-order cook on trains and as a salesman and grocer before developing a religious following. After returning from a trip to the Holy Land in 1921, he established the first missions of the United House of Prayer for All People in Wareham and New Bedford, Massachusetts. Some accounts give 1926 as the date of organization of the first house of prayer, in Charlotte, NORTH CAROLINA. Grace traveled along the East Coast in the late 1920's and found a large group of supporters in NEWARK, NEW JERSEY.

Unlike FATHER DIVINE, a rival religious organizer of the period, Grace did not claim divine status. He adopted the title of Sweet Daddy Grace only after achieving national prominence. At one time, he was the landlord of Father Divine's rented headquarters. Grace did stress, like Father Divine, his own personal abilities to solve problems. He also used his name to imply personal power, as when he claimed that only through Grace could there be salvation. He assured his followers that God was on a vacation and that he would care for humanity in God's absence.

Members of the church were forbidden from smoking, drinking, dancing, or attending public entertainment. Grace offered the services of his claimed healing powers to his followers. Worship services were raucous affairs involving Bible readings, boisterous sermons, and even brass bands and alleged possession of followers by the Holy Spirit on some occasions. Grace himself appeared at many of these meetings. He organized such tangible

Charles Emmanuel "Sweet Daddy" Grace in late 1949, on his return from a tour of France and Italy. (*AP/Wide World Photos*)

services as church cafeterias, retirement homes, insurance, and burial services, but personal testimonials from followers tended to emphasize healing as the main reason for conversion to the faith. Grace is alleged to have cured hundreds of people of various illnesses. Even *Grace Magazine*, the church's publication, was believed to be curative when held directly against the body. Grace also sold commodities such as toothpaste, soap, and cold cream that were supposed to have healing properties.

Grace encouraged donations to his church, to allow its activities to continue as well as to support Grace personally. He developed a flamboyant lifestyle as church membership grew, and followers shared that lifestyle vicariously. Grace at times sported shoulder-length hair and three-inch fingernails painted red, white, and blue. He had an eighty-four-room mansion in LOS ANGELES, and a twenty-two acre estate in Havana, CUBA, as well as numerous other houses. He understood that only through him would his economically disadvantaged followers ever experience such a lavish lifestyle, and he encouraged them to enjoy his life of luxury. Tax problems and other legal entanglements forced him to leave the United States in the mid-1930's, cutting short his rivalry with Father Divine.

Some estimates of church membership have been as high as a peak of three million, spread across sixty cities. The church retained members even after the death of its founder and struggles for power among his successors. Bishop Walter McCullough took over the church in 1962 and became known as Sweet Daddy Grace McCullough, Grace's spiritual son. He converted the church into a Holiness sect, rather than one that worshiped a person. *See also:* Pentecostalism; Religion.

Graffiti and tagging: Originating from the Italian word *graffiare* for "to scratch," graffiti is writing or drawing that appears on public surfaces such as buildings, buses, or bathroom walls. Spray paint or markers are commonly used to write graffiti. Tagging is a form of graffiti in which the writer reproduces the same word or symbol in many places. Most Americans consider graffiti writing to be vandalism, the destruction of public property, but some observers consider graffiti as a form of public art available to anyone regardless of education, training, or social class. Sociologists and psychologists have argued that graffiti is an expression of discontent and rage against an increasingly restrictive and uncaring society.

History

Archaeologists have discovered graffiti in the ruins of the city of Pompeii, which was destroyed in 79 C.E. by volcanic eruption. Romans complained about graffiti in public latrines, and prisoners held in the Tower of London scrawled comments on the walls. Romantic graffiti such as "John Loves Mary" could be found throughout the United States. The nature and popularity of graffiti, however, changed dramatically in the late 1960's with the arrival of the "graffiti artist." In New York City, a Greek teenager wrote "TAKI 123" on a subway wall. The phrase began appearing in subway stations throughout the city. Inspired by TAKI 123, other writers spray painted their logos on walls and subway trains. The more ambitious graffiti artists painted elaborate murals, while the less dedicated merely scrawled their name or their symbol on any available empty space.

The phenomenon was not confined to New York. Large urban centers throughout the United States and Europe experienced an increase in graffiti. As was the case with many fads in the United States, entrepreneurs saw an opportunity to make money from the phenomenon. In the 1980's, several motion pictures featured graffiti writing, most notably the film *Turk 182!* (1985). Stores carried clothing decorated in graffiti style, videotapes about graffiti were produced, and fan magazines on the topic appeared. Dedicated writers spurned the popularity of the graffiti subculture as a product of commercialization.

The popularity of graffiti spawned a burgeoning subculture, which had its roots in the inner-city African American community in the 1970's. Closely tied to RAP music and BREAK DANCING in the 1980's, the subculture was quickly appropriated by Hispanic and Anglo teenagers, usually young men, and spread from the cities into the suburbs. Graffiti writers developed their own language. Any artist was known as a "writer." Small personal symbols were called "tags," and their writers were known as "taggers," whereas large and complex works were called "pieces," short for "masterpieces," and were drawn by "piecers." A group of friends who tagged together was known as a "crew." The act of writing graffiti was a "hit."

Public Response

The explosion of graffiti in the late 1960's and 1970's increased anxiety among the nation's urban dwellers. Already concerned with rising crime, drug use, and juvenile delinquency, New York subway riders saw graffiti as a symbol of social decay and the collapse of authority. In 1984 the New York Metropolitan Transit Authority (MTA) announced that graffiti would no longer be tolerated on its subway cars. Any car marked with graffiti was immediately pulled from service and cleaned. The graffiti removal program was successful but expensive—fifteen hundred workers were hired for the program, and the cleaning costs averaged $10 million a year. Although passengers were pleased with the results, the problem of graffiti was not solved. During 1995, the MTA reported an average of thirty-five hundred graffiti writings per week on its cars, all of which were immediately removed. Moreover, graffiti writers left the subways and turned to the streets, painting and tagging

Graffiti in a low-income housing project in Pacoima, California, defaces a mural celebrating cultural diversity. *(Martin A. Hutner)*

public buildings, commercial businesses, and billboards. Graffiti spread from the nation's largest cities and became a pressing problem in Denver, Colorado, San Antonio, Texas, and scores of smaller cities and towns throughout the country.

As the amount of graffiti soared, so did the cost of removing it. While no exact figures were available, it was estimated that the cost nationwide for cleaning graffiti reached from four billion to seven billion dollars annually by the 1990's. The Los Angeles Metropolitan Transit Authority budgeted $13 million for graffiti removal in 1995. Corporations realized the tremendous profit potential in graffiti cleaning and began research into graffiti-resistant paint and surfacings and the development of new removal processes, such as using lasers to clean graffiti.

Offended by the graffiti, which appeared everywhere, and appalled at the costs of re-

moving it, the public labeled graffiti writers as malicious vandals and began demanding intervention and increasingly stern punishments for graffiti vandalism. Graffiti opponents established the National Graffiti Information Network to distribute information to communities concerned about graffiti. Several cities formed antigraffiti teams. Some cities such as Denver and Los Angeles offered cash rewards to anyone who turned in graffiti writers. Businesses turned to hidden cameras and motion detectors to catch writers, and police departments organized sting operations to catch taggers in the act. One strategy police employed was to whitewash a wall and wait for writers to show up, spray cans or markers in hand. Undercover police officers in California posed as filmmakers working on a graffiti program and caught thirty-one graffiti writers.

Once apprehended, graffiti writers faced serious punishment for their activities. While many were sentenced to community service, especially graffiti removal teams, some writers received long terms of detention, including a California teenager sentenced to eight years in a juvenile facility. California offenders could also have their drivers licenses revoked. New laws were also aimed at the parents and guardians of offenders. In Los Angeles, the parents of two graffiti writers received fines of $38,000 for the damage done by their children.

Additional laws were aimed at preventing access to spray paint and markers, the tools of the graffiti artist. Several cities and states banned the sale of spray paint to minors—in some areas, stores had to keep paint in locked display cases to prevent shoplifting. In 1995 the U.S. Circuit Court of Appeals upheld a CHICAGO ordinance that banned all spray paint and most markers. Concerned that graffiti hurts business, frightens away tourists, and lowers property values, some cities mandated that the owners of property defaced by graffiti were responsible for removing it—the city of St. Petersburg, Florida, required the removal of graffiti within forty-eight hours.

Despairing of a solution to the graffiti problem, some politicians advocated corporal punishment. The 1994 caning of an American teenager in Singapore for spray painting cars and other acts of vandalism shocked many Americans, but others believed that such responses would end the graffiti problem. A bill introduced into the California legislature called for paddling as a punishment for graffiti vandalism, and four major cities in the United States also considered similar ordinances. An alderman in St. Louis, Missouri, claimed that his office received numerous calls in support of such a law, but the city council rejected the proposal on the grounds that it was inhumane. While resistance to corporal punishment remained strong in American communities, the continued problem of graffiti vandalism ensured that such solutions would again be proposed in the future.

An Urban Art Form

Although many Americans considered graffiti vandalism, others viewed it as a modern urban art form that deserved appreciation, respect, and study. The work of many graffiti artists was displayed in art galleries, and several universities allowed graffiti writers to lecture in art classes. Colorful and complex graffiti caught the attention of art critics, who sometimes likened it to the works of modern artists such as Jackson Pollock. In the 1970's, a sociology student convinced several writers to commit their work to canvas and sell it through a corporation called United Graffiti Artists (UGA). Some UGA members went on to become professional artists. Certain graffiti writers became famous for their work, and artists Lee Quinones, Jean-Michel Basquiat, and Lady Pink were celebrated for their talents. The art of Keith Haring was nationally recognized when it appeared on posters and T-shirts. Recognizing the appeal of some graffiti art, major corporations signed some artists to produce material for advertisements.

In an attempt to lure graffiti artists away from illegal activities, some communities developed mural programs. In Los Angeles, the InnerChange program created a summer program centered on the creation of a mural in an alley known as a hangout for drug dealers; similar projects were undertaken in Philadelphia and New York. With permission from building owners, graffiti writers and taggers were invited to design and complete colorful murals which often contained positive social messages aimed at combating violence, drug abuse, child abuse, and the spread of venereal diseases. While the products of these programs were often defaced by unauthorized graffiti within days, participants often reported that the mural projects gave them an outlet for their artistic ambitions and allowed them to make new friends in neighborhoods that were often dangerous.

Popularity of Graffiti

Psychologists and sociologists have long been interested in why individuals are motivated to create graffiti. Investigating the reasons that people draw and write on public surfaces could help resolve the conflict between graffiti as art and graffiti as vandalism and could also suggest possible solutions to the continued destruction of public and private property.

The most common form of graffiti, scrawled on walls of public restrooms, is typically sexual in nature. Psychologists argue that repressed sexuality, sometimes hostile, is readily expressed in the bathroom, which is considered "unclean," as are the sexual thoughts. This explanation does not apply to the more visible forms of graffiti that became popular in the 1970's and 1980's. In those cases the artist attempted to reproduce his tag as many times as possible in numerous locales. The more a tagger's symbol appeared, and the more interesting the location, the higher his standing in the graffiti underworld rose—the most popular artists were knows as "kings." These standards soon led to serious accidents and some fatalities as graffiti artists struggled to write on dangerous overpasses and high billboards.

Social scientists claimed that this form of graffiti artistry could be understood as an expression of identity in an urban environment that ignores the individual. Every time the writer placed his tag on a bench or a wall, it articulated a personal response to an uncaring society. Critics responded that this may have been the case in the early 1970's, a time when urban graffiti was often complex, individualistic, and eye-catching, but the explosion of graffiti writing in the later 1970's and 1980's reduced the artistic and personal aspects of graffiti into conformist behavior best described as vandalism.

Another theory argued that graffiti was a form of resistance to an authoritarian society. American cities had become increasingly segregated, not only racially also but in terms of class and social structure. Public spaces such as parks disappeared with intensive construction and building, and urban areas became a patchwork of private holdings from which most people were excluded. In addition, cities enacted curfews that restricted the movements of young people in the few remaining public spaces. Recognizing that they were not welcome in most of the commercial and public buildings they passed by daily, young city dwellers manifested their anger not through destroying these properties but through altering them and thus making them their own in a limited fashion. According to this theory, graffiti writers were not vandals, but frustrated youths protesting a restricted environment. Proponents of this theory noted that taggers rarely marred private homes, and that in interviews many of them wrote exclusively on city property such as street signs.

Graffiti writing is one way that youths relieved boredom and acted out against authority. Taggers reported that graffiti writing provided them with a sense of daring and excitement which they equated with being an outlaw. Graffiti artists risked beatings and arrests to write their messages, and the element of danger increased their pleasure and desire to continue writing. Several reported that the feeling was similar to an adrenaline rush or drug high; obsessive graffiti artists claimed that they were addicted, and several spent hours each night writing graffiti.

A development in the 1990's suggested that the social dynamics of graffiti artistry were again changing. Previously, graffiti writing had been an individual or small group activity, and was rarely associated with crimes other than illegally marking public property. The rising number of street gangs and gang members in the late 1980's, however, created a new and more menacing form of graffiti designating the boundaries or "turf" of neighborhood gangs. While this form of graffiti had always existed, it had never been predominant.

Graffiti researchers in the 1990's noticed that a greater percentage of the markings were gang related. Study indicated that the graffiti often contained messages regarding drug transactions and other criminal activities. The researchers also noted that those areas with gang tags rarely had any other forms of graffiti, suggesting that gang activity frightened away the more typical graffiti artists.

Graffiti became an increasing source of concern in American life during the 1970's and 1980's. While some defended graffiti as a sign of identity in crowded urban environments, or as a form of art available to everyone, others condemned it as vandalism and as a sign of the increasing failure of American society to control its juvenile population. Even those sympathetic to the plight of urban teenagers despaired over the defacing of architecture, monuments, and public transportation. Although Americans spent billions on intervention and cleaning programs, the problem seemed insoluble. While industry worked to create effective solutions to graffiti, artists devised new ways to make their mark on the nation's public surfaces, turning to drills and glass etching to ensure that their tags would remain visible. Whether the cause of graffiti was a need to express one's individuality, create art, or merely engage in destructive behavior, it remained a source of public debate.

—*Thomas Clarkin*

See also: Gangs.

Suggested Readings:

Abel, Ernest L., and Barbara E. Buckley. *The Handwriting on the Wall: Toward a Sociology and Psychology of Graffiti*. Westport, Conn.: Greenwood Press, 1977.

Barboza, Steven. "A Mural Program to Turn Graffiti Offenders Around." *Smithsonian* 24 (July, 1993): 62-71.

Ferrell, Jeff. *Crimes of Style: Urban Graffiti and the Politics of Criminality*. New York: Garland, 1993.

_____. "Urban Graffiti: Crime, Control, and Resistance." *Youth and Society* 27 (September, 1995): 73-91.

Hager, Steven. *Hip Hop: The Illustrated History of Break Dancing, Rap Music, and Graffiti*. New York: St. Martin's Press, 1984.

Heldman, Kevin. "Mean Streaks: Amped, Angry, and in Your Face, Graffiti Refuses to Die." *Rolling Stone* (February 9, 1995): 43-47.

Henderson, Andre. "Graffiti." *Governing* (August, 1994): 40-44.

O'Brien, Glenn. "Cream of Wheat Paste: Cost and Revs." *Artforum International* 32 (March, 1994): 76-77.

Phillips, Susan A. *Wallbangin': Graffiti and Gangs in L.A.* Chicago: University of Chicago Press, 1999.

Graham, Lawrence Otis (b. December 25, 1962, New York, New York): Attorney, educator, and author. Growing up in Manhattan and in suburban White Plains, New York, Graham was reared in a privileged upper-middle-class family. His father worked in the real estate business and his mother worked as a psychologist. After receiving his undergraduate degree from Princeton University, Graham went on to earn his law degree from Harvard Law School. After joining a Manhattan law firm as an attorney specializing in corporate law, Graham eventually joined the faculty of Fordham University.

Conscious of his economic advantages, Graham also encountered the brutal legacy of racism. Choosing to probe the prevalence of racist attitudes, Graham decided to infiltrate an all-white country club in 1992 by posing as a busboy. He published his observations in an article that appeared in the July, 1992, issue of *New York* magazine. In 1993 he took a leave of absence from his law firm and spent a month living in a run-down apartment in Harlem. Switching between clothing that made him blend in with his surroundings, whether on

GHETTO streets or in midtown museums, Graham encountered the pressures and contradictions of attempting to conform to the expectations of two very different communities. He published his experiences in a book entitled *Member of the Club: Reflections on Life in a Racially Polarized World* (1995). He looked at the workaday world in *Proversity: Getting Past Face Value and Finding the Soul of People, a Manager's Journey* (1997) and at well-to-do black society in *Our Kind of People: Inside America's Black Upper Class* (1999).

Grambling State University: Public, state-supported, coeducational, liberal arts institution founded in 1901 in Grambling, LOUISIANA. One of the best-known HISTORICALLY BLACK COLLEGES, the school was originally established as a private industrial school because African American farmers in rural, northern Louisiana wanted a school where they could educate children in the northern and western parts of the state.

The founder and first president of the institution, Charles P. Adams, was sent by Booker T. WASHINGTON of TUSKEGEE INSTITUTE to start the school. The school developed and flourished during Adams's thirty-five year tenure at Grambling. By 1928, after a few name changes and different locations, the school (then known as Louisiana Negro Normal and Industrial Institute) became a state junior college and offered two-year professional certificates and diplomas. In 1940 a four-year program was initiated, and in 1944 the first bachelor of science degree in elementary education was conferred. The school's name was changed to Grambling College in 1946, after which the curriculum included not only teacher education but also liberal arts, business, and the sciences. After graduate programs in early childhood and elementary education were added to the institution's offerings, the school earned a new position and a new name, Grambling State University, in 1974.

Grambling was able to establish a doctoral program in developmental education and two professional schools—nursing and social work—after receiving significant legislative allocations during the late 1970's. A pivotal event occurred under the leadership of the school's third president, Joseph B. Johnson. In September, 1981, a "consent decree" was signed. It rendered "legal protection for programs and faculties" which the school had been unable to obtain in the past. A part of the University of Louisiana system, Grambling had an enrollment of sixty-two hundred students in 1999; they were pursuing undergraduate, graduate, professional, and continuing education degrees in various disciplines.

In addition to being noted for its academic program, Grambling State University has been acclaimed for its marching band and athletics, particularly its football program. Grambling's legendary football coach, Eddie Robinson, accomplished a feat that no other coach ever had in collegiate football—324 wins—on October 5, 1985. Ten years later, Robinson achieved another collegiate football milestone—he won his four hundredth game.

Although the school's original intent was to foster the educational, cultural, and social growth of young African Americans from north central Louisiana, the university now focuses on meeting the educational demands of a national and international student body. The motto of Grambling State University is "the place where everybody is somebody," which is the institution's guiding philosophy in providing an environment that is conducive to student development.

—*Andrea E. Miller*

See also: Higher education.

Grandfather clause: Part of the "Mississippi Plan" for disfranchising African Americans. The original clause, widely adopted in the

South after Louisiana wrote it into its state constitution in 1898, allowed all male adults to vote, regardless of educational, property, or other qualifications, if their fathers or grandfathers were qualified to vote on January 1, 1867—a time when no freedmen could vote. The U.S. SUPREME COURT outlawed the grandfather clause in GUINN V. UNITED STATES (1915). *See also:* Disfranchisement.

Grandmaster Flash and the Furious Five: Early and influential RAP music group. Members included Joseph "Grandmaster Flash" Saddler, Melvin "Melle Mel" Glover, Danny "Kid Creole" Glover, Eddie "Mr. Ness" Morris, Guy "Rahiem" Williams, and Keith "Cowboy" Wiggins. The group's members grew up together in the Bronx, New York.

Saddler, or Grandmaster Flash, is sometimes credited as the originator of rap; regardless of whether that is literally true, he was certainly one of those (another was Kool Herc) who pioneered and steered the early development of the form. Grandmaster Flash and the Furious Five strongly influenced the direction of rap music.

In 1974 Grandmaster Flash experimented with plugging two turntables into the same amplifier and mixing music segments from the two by switching back and forth between them. Saddler formed Grandmaster Flash and the Furious Five in 1977. The Furious Five provided lyrics by talking over Saddler's sound tracks in catchy, rhymed narratives about their street experiences. The first commercially successful rap record was the Sugarhill Gang's "Rapper's Delight," released on Sugar Hill Records in 1979. Shortly thereafter, Saddler and the group negotiated a recording contract with Sugar Hill Records owner Sylvia Robinson.

In 1981 Grandmaster Flash and the Furious Five had a moderately successful rap hit with the single "Wheels of Steel." Their next record was the 1981 single "The Message," a song about ghetto life, inner-city decay, junkies, hustlers, and other street people. Although it received little airplay, "The Message" went gold and achieved more than one million dollars in sales. It was voted the best single of 1982 by many of the nation's rock music critics and is considered a landmark in the development of rap. The album *White Lines* was released in 1983. The group had split up by the next year but reformed occasionally for live performances.

Grandmaster Flash and the Furious Five was perhaps the top rap act before rap became more mainstream and entered the realms of big business. Several of the group's members went on to record on their own.
See also: Hip-hop.

Granger, Lester Blackwell (September 16, 1896, Newport News, Virginia—January 9, 1976, Alexandria, Louisiana): Government of-

National Urban League director Lester B. Granger. *(Schomburg Center for Research in Black Culture, New York Public Library)*

ficial. Granger was the executive director of the NATIONAL URBAN LEAGUE, which implemented programs designed to advance the political, social, and economic interests of African Americans, from 1941 to 1961. Granger, who graduated from Dartmouth College, was special assistant to the secretary of the Navy during WORLD WAR II and played a key role in the integration of African Americans into the armed forces.

See also: Military.

Granville, Evelyn Boyd (b. May 1, 1924, Washington, D.C.): Mathematician. Granville was the first African American woman to earn a Ph.D. in pure mathematics, from Yale University in 1949. She taught mathematics at various universities, worked for the U.S. Bureau of Standards and Department of the Army, and was a research specialist on the Apollo space project.

Graves, Earl G., Sr. (b. January 9, 1935, Brooklyn, New York): Magazine editor and publisher. Graves graduated from Morgan State College, a historically black institution in BALTIMORE, MARYLAND, in 1958. During the Lyndon B. Johnson administration, Graves joined the staff of Senator Robert F. Kennedy as an administrative assistant and worked from 1965 to 1968 in that capacity.

After Senator Kennedy's assassination, Graves left public service and established a number of independent and successful enterprises. Probably the best known of these is *Black Enterprise* magazine, which first appeared in 1970. The stated purpose of this monthly publication was to offer insight into financial planning and investment and to guide black entrepreneurs in managing their independent businesses and ventures. Although *Black Enterprise* was intended to focus on effective solutions to problems affecting

Earl G. Graves, founder of *Black Enterprise* magazine. (*Earl G. Graves Publishing Company, Inc.*)

the black business community, it also came to enjoy a wide readership outside this community. It became accepted as an authority on the progress of minorities in business, advocating social activism and responsibility to its readership in the black middle class.

Graves's enterprises are widely recognized and admired. In addition to his publishing company and magazine ventures, Graves founded his own marketing and research company and was president of a broadcasting company that operated an FM and an AM radio station in Fort Worth, Texas. In the April 3, 1992, issue of *The Wall Street Journal*, a profile on Graves appeared in a special section on black entrepreneurship. The article discussed Graves's pioneering work in providing assistance to growing black enterprises and noted that Earl G. Graves, Jr., had become senior vice president of his father's publishing company.

Graves also maintained an active presence in the community. Among other positions, he was a member of the economic development board of New York State, a commissioner of the Job Development Authority of New York State, a member of the national board of Interracial Council for Business Opportunity, and a trustee of TUSKEGEE INSTITUTE. He was named as one of the ten most outstanding minority businesspeople in the country by President Richard M. Nixon in 1973.

See also: Business and commerce; Broadcast licensing.

Gray, William H., III (b. August 20, 1941, Baton Rouge, Louisiana): U.S. representative from PENNSYLVANIA. Gray was born in LOUISIANA but spent most of his first eight years in FLORIDA, where his father was a college president. In 1949 the family moved to PHILADELPHIA, where Gray's father was appointed as pastor of Bright Hope Baptist Church, succeeding his own father.

Congressman William H. Gray III (right) presenting an award from the Congressional Black Caucus to Philadelphia 76ers basketball star Julius Erving in 1983. *(© Roy Lewis Archives)*

Gray attended public schools in Philadelphia and graduated from high school in 1959. He was accepted at Franklin and Marshall College, where he studied sociology and was graduated with his bachelor of arts degree in 1963. During his senior year in college, Gray served as an intern for Congressman Robert N. C. Nix, Sr. Despite this early brush with politics, Gray was determined to pursue a career in the ministry and entered Drew Theological School in New Jersey, where he received his master of divinity degree in 1966. Gray earned his master of theology degree from Princeton Theological Seminary in 1970.

While studying at Drew, Gray was appointed assistant pastor of Union Baptist Church in Montclair, NEW JERSEY, in 1964. In 1966 he was installed as senior minister of the church by Martin Luther KING, Jr. While in New Jersey, Gray taught as a lecturer at Jersey City State College, Rutgers University, and Montclair State College, and from 1970 to 1974 he was an assistant professor on the faculty and a director of St. Peter's College.

Gray became active in community affairs in Montclair and was instrumental in founding the nonprofit Union Housing Corporation in order to build affordable housing for low- and moderate-income black residents. In an effort to combat rampant discrimination, Gray brought a suit against a Montclair landlord in 1970, accusing the landlord of refusing to rent to Gray because he was black. The New Jersey Superior Court made a precedent-setting decision to award damages to Gray as a victim of racial discrimination.

After his father died in 1972, Gray was appointed to

succeed him as pastor of Bright Hope Baptist Church. Upon moving to Philadelphia, Gray continued to be active in community causes and developed the Philadelphia Mortgage Plan to assist residents in poor neighborhoods to obtain mortgages in order to purchase their own homes. In 1976 Gray decided to run for public office and challenged his former employer, Congressman Nix, for Pennsylvania's Second Congressional District seat. Although he was narrowly defeated in the 1976 DEMOCRATIC PARTY primary, Gray challenged Nix again in 1978. Gray defeated Nix by earning 58 percent of the vote in the Democratic primary, then went on to beat his Republican opponent in a landslide victory in November.

Gray took his seat in January of 1979 and was appointed to serve on the House Committee on Foreign Affairs, the House Committee on the District of Columbia, and the House Budget Committee. He also served on the Democratic Steering and Policy Committee, which was responsible for nominating congressmen to working committees. In 1981 Gray gave up his seat on the Budget Committee in order to serve on the House Appropriations Committee. During his first term, Gray became vice chairman of the CONGRESSIONAL BLACK CAUCUS. In 1985 Gray was the chief sponsor of the Anti-Apartheid Act, which called for a ban on U.S. bank loans and high-technology exports to South Africa. He was successful in gaining support to override President Ronald Reagan's veto of the act.

In 1983 Gray rejoined the House Budget Committee and became one of its most effective negotiators in engineering behind-the-scenes agreements to convince liberals to accept compromise budget resolutions. He garnered support among influential congressmen in order to win appointment as chairman of the Budget Committee in January of 1985. He was successful in building a coalition of bipartisan support for the budgets passed by Congress in 1985 and in 1987, the latter of

which was complicated by the balanced budget restrictions imposed by the Gramm-Rudman Amendment. In December of 1988, Gray was elected chairman of the House Democratic Caucus, and in June of 1989, he was elected House majority whip. Upon taking this office, Gray became the highest-ranking African American representative in Congress and was considered likely to become the first African American Speaker of the House. On June 20, 1991, however, Gray declared that he would not run for reelection. He had decided instead to accept the position of president of the UNITED NEGRO COLLEGE FUND.

See also: Congress members; Politics and government.

Gray v. Sanders: Voting rights case. In 1962 the U.S. SUPREME COURT ruled, in BAKER V. CARR, that citizens could challenge malapportionment in the courts under the equal protection clause of the FOURTEENTH AMENDMENT. That decision set a precedent for Court-ordered apportionment but left some questions unanswered. The very next year, in *Gray* (1963), the Court ruled that a GEORGIA state election plan that diluted the voting strength of heavily populated counties denied equal voting rights. By an 8-1 vote, the Court established the principle of "one person, one vote." The following year, in WESBERRY V. SANDERS (1964), the Court extended the principle to voting districts for congressional elections.

—*Christopher E. Kent*

Great Depression: The Great Depression began with the stock market crash in late 1929, and it worsened month by month in the early years of the 1930's. After Franklin D. Roosevelt was elected president in 1932, he instituted a variety of programs, collectively called the New Deal, to help provide relief and hope for beleaguered Americans. The Depression lasted through most of the 1930's; some scholars contend that it did not truly end until industrial production in the United States increased because the country entered WORLD WAR II in 1941.

The economic crisis of the 1930's was a time of great hardship for African Americans; they bore a disproportionate burden of the nation's suffering and received less than their fair share of relief payments and opportunities from New Deal recovery programs. The Great Depression worsened the already poor standard of living that many African Americans had endured during the first two decades of the twentieth century. When hard times hit, employers fired black laborers first, and the few companies that hired new workers generally favored whites over blacks. As a result,

The Depression years were particularly hard on African American workers, who were typically the first to lose their jobs and the last to be hired. *(Associated Publishers, Inc.)*

unemployment rates throughout the nation were higher for blacks than for whites.

By 1932 roughly half of all employable African Americans were without work, about double the national average. Skilled black workers who retained their jobs usually experienced sharp wage cuts. As a result of these trends, a high percentage of the African American population received relief payments. Because local officials determined the size of the payments, whites received larger relief payments than blacks in some areas of the South.

The New Deal

In 1930 some 40 percent of African American laborers worked in AGRICULTURE, most of them landless sharecroppers and tenant farmers. The average income of African American farmers was consistently lower than that of their white counterparts. A 1934 study revealed that in some parts of the South black farmers were earning less than $200 per year. The Agricultural Adjustment Administration (AAA), which was intended to provide assistance to farmers by increasing the cost of agricultural products, actually had an adverse effect on black farmers. The AAA paid farmers to take a percentage of their land out of production. This payment system helped the landowner, but not the tenant farmer or sharecropper. Moreover, government payments were made directly to landowners, allowing the unscrupulous among them to cheat their African American tenants. Some landlords went further, evicting their tenants so that they could keep all the payments. Between 1930 and 1940, some 192,000 African Americans

Missouri family that benefitted from the federal government's Farm Security Administration program in 1938. *(Library of Congress)*

stopped tenant farming, compared with 150,000 white tenants who stopped.

African Americans received some relief from other New Deal programs, but they were often the victims of discrimination in the programs' implementation or design. In TEXAS, National Youth Association director Lyndon B. Johnson had to assist poor African Americans secretly, lest he lose his position. Some African Americans dismissed the NRA acronym of the National Recovery Act as standing for "Negroes Ruined Again," because the act's provisions did little to help African Americans realize any wage gains. The NRA established regional wage rates, for example, which meant that workers in the South, where many African Americans lived, received less pay. In addition, NRA wage guidelines did not cover farm work or domestic services such as housekeeping, two professions in which many African Americans labored.

Three New Deal agencies did offer African Americans a share of government assistance. Officials in the Farm Security Administration (FSA), a small agency created to assist landless farmers, worked to include African Americans in their programs. The Public Works Administration (PWA) sponsored several construction projects that benefited African American communities. The PWA also instituted hiring quotas to ensure that African Americans would receive employment on agency projects. The Works Progress Administration (WPA), established in 1935, also provided African Americans with opportunities.

Social Tensions

The economic crisis of the 1930's increased many national social tensions, including those between white and black Americans as both groups struggled to make ends meet. The number of lynchings in the South climbed during the early years of the Depression, from eight in 1932 to nearly thirty the following year. However, in some cases shared difficulties brought African Americans and their white neighbors together. In ARKANSAS, farmers of both races organized the Southern Tenant Farmers' Union (STFU). Approximately one-third of the union's thirty thousand members were African American, and blacks held prominent positions within the union.

African American Response

African Americans did not react passively to the Great Depression. CIVIL RIGHTS organizations struggled on behalf of African American interests. The NATIONAL ASSOCIATION FOR THE ADVANCEMENT OF COLORED PEOPLE (NAACP) investigated the plight of tenant farmers under the AAA and expressed its concerns to government officials and to the public at large. The NAACP also pressed, albeit unsuccessfully, for federal antilynching legislation. However, the problems associated with the Depression led to a crisis within the organization as members disagreed over appropriate responses. African Americans dissatisfied with the NAACP's emphasis on legal issues at the expense of economic development turned to other organizations. The National Negro Congress, which held its first meeting in 1936, called for solidarity with white workers to bring about significant reform.

African Americans within the administration of President Roosevelt also promoted the interests of black citizens. Mary McLeod BETHUNE, for example, a friend of First Lady Eleanor Roosevelt and director of the Office of Minority Affairs with the National Youth Association, became an important black leader during this era. Bethune used her office to operate programs that substantially reduced black illiteracy rates. She also spoke out against LYNCHING and acts of RACIAL DISCRIMINATION. In 1936 Bethune and other black administration officials organized the Federal Council on Negro Affairs. Commonly referred to as the "black cabinet," this group, which had no official standing within the government, brought the needs of African Americans to the attention of New Deal officials.

In Harlem, Major J. Divine—better known as FATHER DIVINE—the founder of a small religious group, sponsored soup kitchens that fed the hungry. His movement spread to other cities. In 1935 the citizens of Harlem expressed their frustration with economic conditions by rioting, the only major racial disturbance of the decade. In Detroit, Wallace D. FARD founded the NATION OF ISLAM, also known as the Black Muslims. Because the group advocated self-reliance within the African American community, Black Muslims were instructed not to accept relief payments from the government.

—Thomas Clarkin

See also: Roosevelt administration, Franklin D.

Suggested Readings:

Bunche, Ralph J. *The Political Status of the Negro in the Age of FDR.* Chicago: University of Chicago Press, 1973.

Sitkoff, Harvard. *A New Deal for Blacks: The Emergence of Civil Rights as a National Issue.* New York: Oxford University Press, 1978.

Sullivan, Patricia. *Days of Hope: Race and Democracy in the New Deal Era.* Chapel Hill: University of North Carolina Press, 1996.

Wolters, Raymond. *Negroes and the Great Depression: The Problem of Economic Recovery.* Westport, Conn.: Greenwood, 1970.

Great Migration: Twentieth-century black migrations to the North represent collectively the most critical mass movement of African American people in history other than the forced migration of SLAVERY. In fact, these migrations were not entirely voluntary, as external dynamics contributed to the African American exodus from the South. Although there was some drift of blacks northward prior to 1900, the most significant numbers came in two waves during the second and fourth decades of the twentieth century. Because of the momentous impact of these migrations on African Americans and on the nation at large, it is important to understand the reasons for the migrations, white and black institutional responses to this exodus, and the known consequences of northern urbanization.

Push and Pull Factors

Black migrants left the South for several reasons. Most studies stress economic troubles and rampant terrorism endured by southern blacks as the main causes. Boll weevils, floods, employer machinations, mechanization, and minimum-wage laws were among many troubles. Racist statutes that sanctioned separate and unequal conditions for blacks and that were buttressed by extralegal white violence added to these troubles. Black migrants told of more-equal opportunity in the North; antiblack violence, at least, was punishable there. Scholar Carole Marks has suggested that black migrants—many of whom were urban, nonagricultural laborers—"left the South not simply to raise their wages but because they were the displaced mudsills of southern industrial development." In addition to resisting the internal violence of POVERTY, southern blacks were concerned about DISFRANCHISEMENT, proscriptions of EDUCATION, and freedom of movement. Finally, white conscriptions and the loss of immigrant labor during WORLD WAR I

opened up northern factory jobs for black workers.

Migration made race a national issue; the sudden presence of blacks and the economic competition they caused forced northern whites to confront their own racism daily. The myth that race was only a southern problem was shattered. According to Nicholas Lemann in *The Promised Land: The Great Black Migration and How It Changed America* (1991),

Panel in painter Jacob Lawrence's 1941 migration series, depicting the Great Migration of African Americans out of the South. *(National Archives)*

"The very notion that an enormous racial problem existed in the North caused the whole consensual vision of American society to crumble." Many African Americans already knew this.

Institutional Responses

White institutions in the North responded in systematic ways. Whites controlled all dominant institutions and acted to protect their privilege. Black industrial workers were assigned the same place on the economic ladder as southern black workers had been—the bottom rung. Although some of the indignities of southern racism were mitigated outside the South, the African American masses were still kept in poverty.

African Americans also desired to seize control of their destinies; black migrants looked to their own institutions for help in their new lives. Those institutions were involved in every facet of movement and resettlement. They represented information networks for the exodus, provided comfort and familiarity, and were sources of information about jobs and of pressure on employers.

Politics, Education, and Housing

In CHICAGO, ILLINOIS, the destination of many black migrants, black institutions also operated as a cog within the machine of Chicago politics, galvanizing and directing the black vote—perhaps too predictably. Without a black power base or effective strategies to insure accountability, black political participation paid minimal dividends to black voters. Even so, the opportunity to vote provided valuable lessons in group politics.

Many black families in the North committed their children to the promise of education, again without significant reward. Although scholars have determined that black children's attendance rates in Chicago public schools matched if not exceeded the rates for white children well into the 1930's, black students were rewarded with embarrassment, harassment, and a white-oriented curriculum.

Finally, housing was almost completely beyond the control of black institutions. Initially, small areas of African American settlement grew into large city sections. The making of the GHETTO was under way. Residential segregation was a major factor in the inability of black migrants to translate their initial advancement into better jobs into fuller participation in the northern economic and political mainstream. In part, that lack of participation stemmed from the relegation of black children to separate schools with inferior resources.

Divisions Within the Black Community

Black institutions were riven by internal division as well. Certainly, the class conflict that strained those institutions represents one context for understanding both the fragile unity and subsequent deterioration of community within the "Black Metropolis." Blacks already in the North had ambivalent feelings toward the newcomers; many were unsure whether the presence of increased numbers of southern blacks, who were often seen as illiterate and poor, would help or hinder black aspirations. In *Black Chicago, 1900-1920: The Making of a Negro Ghetto* (1964), Allan Spear points out that "the old settlers began to formulate a myth that became an article of faith in later years. Discrimination, they argued, was minimal before the Great Migration, and it was the behavior of the newcomers that induced it." Nevertheless, it was Institutional racism that contributed most heavily to intraracial discord. The definitions and deprivations that emanated from dominant institutions were critical sources of intraracial strife, including class divisions.

Carole Marks insists that migration should be examined "from the perspective of underlying structural rather than simply individual factors." If one adds political control and force—which the migrants confronted in machine politics and police power—to racism, economics, and cultural repression in the classroom, a convincing case exists for calling the result "colonialism" in the inner city. African Americans, pushed out of the South by structural factors, confronted the structural factors of colonialism in the North.

Black migrants compared their new wages and work conditions with the conditions of black workers in the South and saw improvement. Unlike white workers, they did not see their fortunes frozen in a time of accelerated capitalist progress. The self-defeating racism of white workers reflected their failure to understand black workers' view of unions. Unions had to prove that they were willing to grant African Americans entry and power. Instead, to most black workers, they seemed primarily concerned about whites.

Consequences

The short-term and long-range consequences of black migration to the North are numerous. Some scholars have focused on black exclusion from power in labor positions. Understanding that such exclusion was a function of both convention and white worker power, these historians suggest that the possibility of upward mobility gave the white worker motivation, provided real advantages when promotions were secured, and helped the modern economic system to develop because it created a black labor supply to fill the bottom jobs.

The long-range consequences of the migrations are still being assessed. The conditions of inner-city urban areas, however, suggest much. Black family income is about 57 percent that earned by white families, the same percentage that was estimated for 1900. Black unemployment is more than double that of whites. The vast majority of students who attend inner-city schools are African American, and most of those children belong to one-parent, low-income families. Crime and drugs are rampant. Middle-class blacks abandoned the inner cities, leaving behind fewer and less-stable institutions and fewer models of mainstream success. The "promised land" has become the "dark ghetto"; a clearer picture of the northern migrations could contribute to an understanding of that decline and serve as a catalyst for change.

—*Fred Lee Hord*

Suggested Readings:

Clark-Lewis, Elizabeth. *Living In, Living Out: African American Domestics and the Great Migration*. New York: Kodansha International, 1996.

Goodwin, E. Marvin. *Black Migration in America from 1915 to 1960: An Uneasy Exodus*. Lewiston, N.Y.: E. Mellen Press, 1990.

Grossman, James R. *Land of Hope: Chicago, Black Southerners, and the Great Migration*. Chicago: University of Chicago Press, 1989.

Harrison, Alferdteen, ed. *Black Exodus: The Great Migration from the American South*. Jackson: University Press of Mississippi, 1991.

Lemann, Nicholas. *The Promised Land: The Great Black Migration and How It Changed America*. New York: Alfred A. Knopf, 1991.

Marks, Carole. *Farewell—We're Good and Gone: The Great Black Migration*. Bloomington: Indiana University Press, 1989.

Sernett, Milton C. *Bound for the Promised Land: African American Religion and the Great Migration*. Durham, N.C.: Duke University Press, 1997.

Trotter, Joe William, Jr., ed. *The Great Migration in Historical Perspective: New Dimensions of Race, Class, and Gender*. Bloomington: Indiana University Press, 1991.

Green, Al (b. April 13, 1946, Forest City, Arkansas): Singer and songwriter. Green became one of the most successful and original figures in SOUL MUSIC during the 1970's. His distinctive vocal prowess aligned him with earlier figures such as Otis REDDING, James BROWN, and Sam COOKE, while his innovative musical style, based on vocal, lyrical, and musical nuance and meaningful repetition without replication, cleared for him a space of his own. *Al Green Is Love* (1975) was one of his most successful albums and remains perhaps the best example of his style.

Green focused on the complexities of romance, as the string of immensely popular singles he released in the 1970's attests. In such songs as "Tired of Being Alone" (1971) and "Let's Stay Together" (1971), Green explored love with insight and originality, thus revivifying one of the most tired concerns of popular music. Green's voice ranges from a high falsetto to a soulful growl worthy of James Brown. Nowhere are his capacities, as well as his eclectic but unified approach, more evident than on *Call Me* (1973), one of the most critically acclaimed and influential soul albums in history. He transforms Hank Williams's "I'm So Lonesome I Could Cry" and Willie Nelson's "Ain't

It Funny How Time Slips Away" from country music classics into soul originals. This is also one of the most consistently excellent albums in a genre in which albums often follow the "hit single plus filler" formula.

Green's musical approach typically centered on medium tempos and meditative instrumentation, leading some to complain of a sameness in his music. Green's music, however, corroborates minimalist composer Brian Eno's assertion that "repetition is a form of change." Green is a master of meaningful nuance, and his work repays repeated listening with renewed insight into a deceptively simple exterior.

In the late 1970's Green became a pastor and directed his distinctive musical approach toward GOSPEL MUSIC. His transitional 1977 work, *The Belle Album*, exemplifies the growing conflict between earthly and spiritual loves, especially on "Belle" and "Feels Like Summer," in which a Christian God is celebrated through, and found within, the physical world. Green's devotion to spiritual concerns became the encompassing concern of his music. For a number of years he limited his appearances primarily to religious services, although he did perform on Broadway in 1982 in Vinnette Carroll's gospel musical *Your Arms Too Short to Box with God*, costarring with Patti LaBelle. In the 1980's Green release a number of gospel albums and won a string of Grammy Awards for his recorded work.

The gospel album *Don't Look Back* was released in 1993, and in 1995 Green released his first nongospel album in almost two decades, *Your Heart's in Good Hands*. In his performances that year he sang both secular love songs and songs of fervent prayer. That same year he won a Grammy Award for "Funny How Time Slips Away," a duet wth Lyle Lovett, and was inducted into the Rock and Roll Hall of Fame.

See also: Gospel music and spirituals; Songwriters and composers.

Singer Al Green holding a Grammy Award he won in 1990. *(AP/Wide World Photos)*

Clifford Scott Green testifying before the U.S. Senate's Judiciary Committee in 1971. *(AP/Wide World Photos)*

Green, Clifford Scott (b. April 2, 1923, Philadelphia, Pennsylvania): Judge. Green became a U.S. district judge in PENNSYLVANIA in 1971. He received his law degree from Temple University in 1951. He also served as a county court judge in Philadelphia (1964-1968) and on the court of common pleas (1968-1971). *See also:* Judges.

Green, Ernest G. (b. September 22, 1941, Little Rock, Arkansas): Investment banker and political appointee. In 1957 Green was one of nine black teenagers to enroll at Central High School in Little Rock, Arkansas. As one of the "Little Rock Nine," Green was one of the four black students who completed coursework and actually received their diplomas from Central High School. Green was awarded the SPINGARN MEDAL in October of 1958, along with the other eight students and Daisy BATES, the head of the Arkansas chapter of the NATIONAL ASSOCIATION FOR THE ADVANCEMENT OF

COLORED PEOPLE (NAACP). He headed north for college and graduated with a bachelor of arts degree in sociology from Michigan State University in 1962. He went on to earn his master's degree in sociology from the university in 1964.

Green moved to New York in 1964 and worked with the joint apprenticeship program, a program which was set up in 1966 to recruit and place young African Americans in apprenticeship programs in the construction trades. The program was cosponsored by the A. Philip RANDOLPH Education Fund and the Workers Defense League. Green became director of the A. Philip Randolph Education Fund in 1968. In 1972 the joint apprenticeship program was renamed the Recruitment Training Program, Inc., and Green served as its executive director. He also was director of the Twentieth Century Fund. In addition to his labor recruiting activities, Green served on the national board of the NAACP.

In 1977 President Jimmy Carter appointed Green to serve as assistant secretary for employment and training at the Department of Labor. Green held this post until 1981. After leaving the Labor Department, Green became a partner in Green and Herman. In 1985 he became founder and owner of E. Green and Associates. He later took a position as an investment banker with Shearson Lehman Hutton, Inc., in Washington, D.C. *See also:* Little Rock crisis.

Green, Henry Morgan (August 26, 1876, Georgia—1939): Physician. Green was president of the NATIONAL MEDICAL ASSOCIATION from 1921 to 1922 and helped found the National Hospital Association in 1923. He also aided in getting a black hospital unit attached to the Knoxville General Hospital. *See also:* Medicine.

Greener, Richard (January 30, 1844, Philadelphia, Pennsylvania—May 2, 1922, Chicago, Illinois): Educator, lawyer, and diplomat. Richard Theodore Greener was the first African American graduate of Harvard University and the first U.S. consul to Vladivostok, Russia.

Greener's early academic training was at OBERLIN COLLEGE in Ohio from 1862 to 1864. After becoming the first African American graduate of Harvard in 1870, he served as principal of the Institute for Colored Youth in PHILADELPHIA for two years and then of the Sumner High School in WASHINGTON, D.C., for a year. Greener earned a law degree from the University of South Carolina in 1876, was admitted to the bar in Washington, D.C., and served as the dean of the law school at HOWARD UNIVERSITY until 1882. As a practicing lawyer, he was a clerk for the first comptroller of the U.S. Treasury.

Although Greener never ran for political office, he participated in numerous national conventions and campaigns for the REPUBLICAN PARTY. In 1896 he was a delegate to the Republican National Convention. Because he spoke in support of many Republican presidential candidates, he was rewarded with various governmental appointments. From 1885 to 1889, he was the chief examiner of the New York City Civil Service Board. In 1898 he was appointed as U.S. consul in Bombay, India, but because of a bubonic plague epidemic there, he left for a similar appointment to Vladivostok, Russia, serving there until 1905. After 1906, Greener worked diligently for the NATIONAL ASSOCIATION FOR THE ADVANCEMENT OF COLORED PEOPLE.

—Alvin K. Benson

See also: Diplomats; Legal professions.

Greenfield, Elizabeth Taylor (c. 1819, Natchez, Mississippi—March 31, 1876, Philadelphia, Pennsylvania): Concert singer. Greenfield is believed to be the earliest African American concert singer. She was born into SLAVERY. Her father was from Africa and her mother was a Seminole Indian. After gaining their freedom, her parents relocated to the West African country of LIBERIA, where many African Americans resettled in the 1840's. Greenfield's mistress, a wealthy landowner, took her to PHILADELPHIA. As a child, Greenfield apparently taught herself to play several instruments, with occasional lessons from local musicians. In 1851 she sang for the Buffalo Music Association and gave other recitals in the area. After getting a manager later that year, she toured throughout the New England area and the Midwest.

In March, 1853, Greenfield reportedly attracted an audience of three thousand (many out of curiosity) when she made her NEW YORK CITY debut at Metropolitan Hall. Shortly after her New York concert, Greenfield departed for England. With the aid of American author Harriet Beecher Stowe, she gave many recitals in England, including a command performance before Queen Victoria in 1854. After her return to the United States, she made several concert tours in Michigan (1855), Wisconsin (1857), and Canada (1863). She sang the arias of Gaetano Donizetti, Vincenzo Bellini, George Frederick Handel, and Giuseppe Verdi. She was known and promoted in the press as the "Black Swan," the African American counterpart to the renowned Swedish soprano Jenny Lind, who was known as the "White Swan." Greenfield was active in the ABOLITIONIST MOVEMENT in her earlier days and sang at several antislavery meetings. She settled in Philadelphia and was a successful voice teacher until her death.

Green v. County School Board of New Kent County: U.S. SUPREME COURT case on RACIAL DISCRIMINATION in schools in 1968. Charles C. Green and other VIRGINIA parents challenged the "freedom of choice" desegregation plan put in place in 1965 by the school board of New Kent County. Beginning in 1965, each African American and white pupil in the county could choose her or his own school under the plan. New Kent County had only two schools, each a combined elementary and high school. Until 1965, one school had been for African American pupils and the other for white children.

Green argued that the school board was continuing to operate a racially discriminatory segregated school system because under freedom of choice no white child had chosen to attend the African American school and 85 percent of the black children still attended the African American school. The U.S. SUPREME COURT ruled the county's freedom of choice plan unconstitutional because it did not lead to a speedy transition to a single nonracially distinct school system.

—*Steve J. Mazurana*

Gregory, Dick (b. October 12, 1932, St. Louis, Missouri): Comedian and CIVIL RIGHTS activist. The son of a domestic worker and a father who was often absent, Richard Claxton "Dick" Gregory grew up in a desperately poor St. Louis, MISSOURI, home. As a teenager, he became noted for his running ability and developed into a high school track star. In 1951 he entered Southern Illinois University on an athletic scholarship; he was named the school's outstanding athlete in 1953. Gregory served a tour of duty with the U.S. Army from 1953 to 1955 and again attended Southern Illinois from 1955 to 1956.

After leaving college, Gregory secured a job with the U.S. Post Office in CHICAGO. He was soon fired, however, because he impersonated his colleagues and because he put all letters addressed to MISSISSIPPI into the overseas mail slot.

A collection of quips from Dick Gregory's stage routines, *From the Back of the Bus* (1962) mixes comic photographs with biting social satire. *(Arkent Archive)*

Comedy Career

Although Gregory's sense of humor failed to mesh with the Post Office, he soon turned an avocation into a vocation; he became a professional entertainer, a stand-up COMIC. Soon after launching his career, he received a big boost when the Esquire Club in Chicago made him the opening act for visiting performers. Later, he appeared at the Apex in Robbins, Illinois, and became that club's master of ceremonies. By 1959 he was back in Chicago, appearing at the Roberts Show Club. In 1960 he went on the nightclub circuit and performed at many noted clubs in such cities as Akron, Milwaukee, San Francisco, and Hollywood. By 1961 he was again in Chicago, appearing at the Playboy Club.

By that time, Gregory had a growing family to support. In 1959 he married Lillian Smith, with whom he had ten children: Michele, Lynne, Paula, Pamela, Stephanie, Gregory, Christian, Ayanna, Miss, and Yohance.

As his nightclub act was becoming more and more popular, Gregory began making guest appearances on national television variety and talk shows. He also began his record-

In April, 1963, Dick Gregory was manhandled and arrested by Greenwood, Mississippi, police while accompanying a group of men attempting to register to vote. (AP/Wide World Photos)

ing career and in time cut many record albums, one of note being *The Light Side, The Dark Side*. At his peak in the mid-1960's, Gregory was earning approximately $350,000 per year. (In his act, he often commented that the United States was the only place in the world where a person had to grow up in a ghetto, had to attend the worst schools, had to ride at the back of the bus, and then was paid $5,000 a night to talk about it.)

Civil Rights Activism
As the Civil Rights movement gathered momentum in the late 1950's and early 1960's, Gregory became an activist and participated in many nonviolent protests and demonstrations. He seemed to make a greater individual impact, however, by incorporating civil rights themes into his nightclub act. As well, he hit the college lecture circuit and gave scores of addresses all across the United States. His speeches, flavored with biting comedy, always had serious overtones, and many college students were influenced by his messages.

Gregory almost lost his life in the WATTS RIOTS in the summer of 1965. He went to a troubled area and found both lower- and middle-class African Americans formed up in several mobs, looting white-owned stores and destroying property. When Gregory tried to disperse one group, he was shot. Although he recovered, at least thirty-four died in the rioting before authorities restored order.

Showing no fear, Gregory risked his life time and again in the Civil Rights movement. For example, in June of 1966, he rushed to join James MEREDITH, who had been shot by Aubrey Norvell, a white man. When shot, Meredith was engaging in a 225-mile "freedom walk" from Memphis, Tennessee, to Jackson, Mississippi. After Norvell shot Meredith, the trek attracted national attention. In addition to being joined by Gregory, Meredith found himself surrounded by such civil rights leaders as Martin Luther KING, Jr., Floyd B. McKISSICK, and Stokely CARMICHAEL. Between 1962 and 1974, he was jailed twenty times for his actions in demonstrations.

When President Lyndon B. Johnson escalated and widened the VIETNAM WAR, Gregory joined the antiwar movement. In 1965 he participated in several teach-ins, seminars in which notables from various fields joined college professors and students to speak out against the war. One of the more famous of the teach-ins that Gregory attended was a two-day affair organized on the campus of the University of California at Berkeley. At least twelve thousand students heard speakers such as Gregory, Norman Mailer, and Isaac Deutscher condemn the war.

On two occasions, Gregory went on prolonged fasts to protest the war. The first, in November of 1967, lasted forty days; the second, in June of 1968, lasted forty-seven days. In 1971, in his third fast, he banned solid food only; for a time he existed on fruit juices to show support for American prisoners of war in Vietnam.

In addition to working on behalf of civil rights and against the Vietnam War, Gregory also became a published author, with many of his books having racial or civil rights themes. His books include *Nigger: An Autobiography* (1964), *What's Happening?* (1965), and *Dick Gregory's Political Primer* (1972). Other works include *The Shadow That Scares Me* (1968), *Write Me In!* (1968), and *No More Lies: The Myth and the Reality of American History* (1971).

Political Forays

Gregory made a foray into politics in 1967 when, as a write-in candidate against Chicago's incumbent mayor Richard J. Daley, he received 22,000 votes. In 1968 Gregory broke with the political establishment by becoming the presidential nominee of the Peace and Freedom Party, a fledgling splinter group of the Peace and Freedom Party that was pro-

civil rights and antiwar. After receiving 148,622 popular votes, Gregory went to Washington, D.C., took an "oath of office," and declared himself U.S. "president-in-exile." When the 1968 Democratic National Convention met in Chicago, he led street demonstrators through police barricades and was arrested.

Although Gregory's Peace and Freedom Party made little impact nationally, he continued speaking out on issues of the day. In 1968 alone, he spoke on 150 college campuses in thirty-six different states. In June of 1969, he attended the World Assembly of Peace in East Germany, where he maintained that racism was a primary cause of most wars.

By 1973 Gregory had abandoned his nightclub career and was devoting his time to his college lecture tour. In 1974 he spoke on three hundred different campuses. Even as he was on tour, he continued to find time to write politically oriented works: *Up from Nigger* (1976, with James R. McGraw) and *Code Name Zorro: The Murder of Martin Luther King, Jr.* (1977, with Mark Lane). In 1974 Gregory also produced *Dick Gregory's Bible Tales, with Commentary*.

Entrepreneur

In 1973 Gregory launched a new business career when he published his *Dick Gregory's Natural Diet for Folks Who Eat: Cookin' with Mother Nature*. Soon, he developed into an articulate spokesman on health and nutrition. A major breakthrough came in 1984, when he began marketing his Slim-Safe Bahamian Diet, the first of a line of products developed by the Chicago-based Dick Gregory Health Enterprises. Success was almost immediate; by 1988, the company had $3 million in sales. All manner of natural food product developments followed and were market successes. The encouraged Gregory decided in 1989 to establish a health resort; he paid $7 million for a beachfront hotel near Walton Beach, Florida, naming the new acquisition Dick Gregory's Diet and Health Resort and Beachmark Inn. For his guests, he established a two-week program geared to safe weight loss. Remaining true to his past as social activist, Gregory earmarked 10 percent of his resort's rooms for the poor who could not afford to pay his fees.

As his health-fitness empire grew, Gregory also branched into the field of ALCOHOLISM and drug addiction and recovery. In 1988 he bought twenty condominiums in New Orleans; later, he also bought a 1,000-acre campground site in Missouri's Ozark Mountains. Both sites were to become rehabilitation centers.

Among Gregory's many awards, he particularly valued EBONY's Heritage and Freedom Award, which he received in 1978 in recognition of his contributions to the Civil Rights movement.

—*James Smallwood*

See also: Comedy and humor.

Suggested Readings:

Branch, Taylor. *Parting the Waters: America in the King Years, 1954-1963*. New York: Simon & Schuster, 1988.

_____. *Pillar of Fire: America in the King Years, 1963-65*. New York: Simon & Schuster, 1998.

Forman, James. *The Making of Black Revolutionaries*. New York: Macmillan, 1972.

Garrow, David J., ed. *We Shall Overcome: The Civil Rights Movement in the United States in the 1950's and 1960's*. 3 vols. New York: Carlson, 1989.

Gregory, Dick. *Nigger: An Autobiography*. New York: Dutton, 1964.

_____, with James R. McGraw. *Up from Nigger*. New York: Stein and Day, 1976.

Manly, Howard. "Gregory Buys Hotel and Fattens His Diet Empire." *Black Enterprise* (March, 1989): 22.

Neary, John. *Julian Bond: Black Rebel*. New York: William Morrow, 1971.

Gregory, Frederick Drew (b. January 7, 1941, Washington, D.C.): Astronaut. Gregory was reared in Washington, where he graduated from Anacostia High School in 1958. He received his B.S. from the U.S. Air Force Academy in 1964 and a master's degree in information systems from George Washington University in 1977.

After his graduation from the Air Force Academy, Gregory entered pilot and helicopter training programs. He received his wings in 1965 and was assigned as a helicopter rescue pilot. Gregory served for a year in Vietnam, flying 550 combat missions, and was assigned briefly as a missile support helicopter pilot upon his return to the United States. He retrained as a fixed-wing pilot in 1968 and attended the U.S. Naval Test Pilot School from September, 1970, to June, 1971. Gregory became a test pilot for helicopters and fighter planes at Wright Patterson Air Force Base in Ohio, then was transferred in 1974 to the National Aeronautics and Space Administration (NASA) Langley Research Center in Hampton, Virginia. He was a test pilot there until selected for the astronaut program in January, 1978.

Gregory's first mission as an astronaut was as pilot of the space shuttle *Challenger*, launched on April 29, 1985. During that weeklong mission, crew members carried out a variety of scientific experiments. Gregory commanded the shuttle *Discovery* on its five-day mission beginning on November 22, 1989, and commanded the shuttle *Atlantis* on its mission launched on November 24, 1991. The latter mission deployed the defense support program satellite and carried out experiments to evaluate the ability of spaceborne observers to gather information about ground troops, equipment, and facilities. Upon completion of his third mission, Gregory had logged more than 450 hours in space. In 1992 he became associate administrator of NASA's Office of Safety and Mission Quality in Washington, D.C.

Gregory also wrote or cowrote several papers in the areas of aircraft handling qualities and cockpit design and logged a total of more than sixty-five hundred hours of flying time in more than fifty types of aircraft. His military honors and awards include the NASA Outstanding Leadership Award, the Defense Superior Service Medal, two Distinguished Flying Crosses, and sixteen Air Medals. He was also the recipient of the National Society of Black Engineers Distinguished National Scientist Award (1979).

See also: Aviators and astronauts.

Grier, Pam (b. May 26, 1949, Winston-Salem, North Carolina): Actor. Grier is best known as the "queen of the BLAXPLOITATION films" of the 1970's. She emerged as a box-office attraction in such action films as *Foxy Brown* (1973), in which she played the title role. Grier was cast in numerous cartoonish roles that required her to disrobe and to commit acts of needless violence. She performed more serious roles in the 1970's and early 1980's, including that of Charlotte in *Fort Apache, the Bronx* (1982). Her performance in the 1997 film *Jackie Brown* was considered a successful comeback.

Griffey, Ken, Jr. (b. Nov. 21, 1969, Donora, Pennsylvania): Professional BASEBALL player. Under his father's guidance, George Kenneth Griffey, Jr., developed into one of the top prospects in the country as a teenager. He was drafted into the major leagues at seventeen years of age. Two years later he became the youngest player in the major leagues and quickly established himself as one of the premier players in the American League.

His father, Ken Griffey, Sr., had just begun his first minor league season when Ken, Jr., was born in 1969. Griffey was called up by the Cincinnati Reds in 1973. He went on to become one of the best players in professional baseball, playing an integral role in the Reds' World Series championships in 1975 and 1976.

The younger Griffey, nicknamed "Junior," grew up at the ballpark, watching and learning from his father's teammates on the Cincinnati Reds, New York Yankees, and Atlanta Braves.

Griffey was unable to compete in athletics during his freshman year at Archbishop Moeller High School in Cincinnati because of poor grades, but he became an outstanding athlete by his junior year. Although he was a star wide receiver on the school's state championship football team, Griffey dropped football during his senior year to concentrate on baseball. After batting .484 over the course of

Pam Grier and Richard Pryor in *Greased Lightning* (1977). *(AP/Wide World Photos)*

Ken Griffey, Jr., hitting a grand slam home run on April 29, 1999, during his last season with the Seattle Mariners. (AP/Wide World Photos)

Batting above .300 with power and making spectacular catches in the field during his rookie season, Griffey, Jr., received more write-in votes for the 1989 all-star game than any other player. The following year he became the first Mariner ever voted to the all-star game, a feat repeated each year until an injury in 1995 ended his streak. He also won Gold Gloves in 1990, 1991, and 1992. During 1993 Griffey established his superstar credentials by batting .309 with 45 home runs and 109 runs batted in, and tying a major-league record with home runs in eight consecutive games. That year, Griffey joined hall of famers Joe DiMaggio, Ted Williams, Ty Cobb, and Mel Ott as the only players to drive in 100 runs in three consecutive seasons before their twenty-fourth birthdays.

The 1994 season was a remarkable one, with Griffey locked in a race with Matt Williams and Frank Thomas, each vying to break Roger Maris's record of 61 home runs in a single season. When the season ended seven weeks early with a player's strike on August 12, Griffey already had 40 home runs. Although he was occasionally criticized for not playing hard, his production continued to climb. In 1995 he helped the Seattle Mariners become a playoff contender by leading them to victory in the American League West division.

Griffey continued putting up big numbers throughout the 1990's. After Mark McGwire moved from the American League to the National League in the middle of the 1997 season, Griffey won American League home run titles in 1997 (56 home runs), 1998 (56), and 1999 (48), and took the 1997 title in runs batted in with 147. He also continued to bat for average and play exceptional defensive ball. McGwire broke Maris's single-season homer record with 70 home runs in 1998 and followed with 65 in 1999. He led Griffey 522-398 in career home runs going into the 2000 season. Nevertheless, Griffey—because of his greater youth—

twenty-four games in his senior year—with 7 home runs and 28 runs batted in (RBIs)—Griffey was selected by the Seattle Mariners as the first pick in the major league amateur draft.

Following an argument with his father in the off-season, Junior attempted suicide in January, 1988. After reconciling with his father, the younger Griffey quickly moved through the minor league ranks and won the starting job in center field for the Mariners in 1989. With Griffey, Sr., again playing for Cincinnati that year, it was the first time a father and son had played in the major leagues at the same time. More improbably, the senior Griffey was picked up in August by the Mariners, who fielded the famous father-son team during 1989-1990.

was widely considered the better long-term prospect to reach Hank Aaron's all-time record of 755 home runs.

At the end of the 1999 season, the Mariners offered Griffey the most lucrative contract in the history of major league sports. Nevertheless, he turned them down and demanded to be traded to a team closer to Florida, where his family was living. As one of the most productive players of modern times, he naturally attracted the interest of many teams. However, so great was his market value that it proved difficult for the Mariners to find a team that could both meet its terms and satisfy Griffey's needs. In early 2000 a deal was worked out that sent Griffey to the Cincinnati Reds in the National League.

Griffin v. Prince Edward County School Board: U.S. SUPREME COURT school desegregation case in 1964. In an effort to avoid carrying out the school desegregation mandated by the 1954 U.S. Supreme Court decision in BROWN V. BOARD OF EDUCATION, Prince Edward County, VIRGINIA, closed its public schools in 1959.

In general, in the aftermath of the 1954 decision, school boards in Virginia attempted to avoid desegregation of the public schools. After Prince Edward County closed all public schools, white children were educated in private academies operated under the Prince Edward Foundation, which received state support. From 1959 until 1963 African American children received no education. In 1963 "free schools" were set up to provide some schooling for those children.

When suit was brought before the Virginia supreme court, that court ruled that the Virginia constitution did not require states or counties to provide money to public schools. When the case was appealed to the U.S. SUPREME COURT, the Court ruled that state and local governments are indeed responsible for

educating all citizens. In the aftermath of this decision, the Prince Edward County public schools were integrated. The decision confirmed that school desegregation would be required in all parts of the United States.

—*Annita Marie Ward*

Griffith-Joyner, Florence (December 21, 1959, Los Angeles, California—September 21, 1998, Mission Viejo, California): Champion TRACK AND FIELD sprinter. Griffith-Joyner began running track at the age of seven. At the age of fourteen she won the Jesse OWENS National Youth Games. After enrolling at California State University, Los Angeles, in 1979 to train with the distinguished coach Bob Kersee, she followed him to the University of California at Los Angeles.

In 1984 she won a silver medal in the 200-meter dash at the Los Angeles Olympic Games. Afterward, she went into semi-retirement and worked as a customer service representative and hair stylist. In 1987 she began training again with Kersee and her husband, Olympic gold medalist Al Joyner, brother of heptathlon champion Jackie JOYNER-KERSEE. She dominated the 1988 Summer Olympics in Seoul, South Korea, by smashing two sprint records, while winning gold medals in the 100- and 200-meter dashes and the 400 meter relay. During the competition she set Olympic records in the 100 meters (10.62 seconds) and 200 meters (21.34, also a world record). She also bettered Wilma RUDOLPH's 1960 record medal total by adding a silver medal in the 1600-meter relay. For these achievements, Griffith-Joyner received the Jesse Owens Award, bestowed on the year's best track and field athlete, and the Sullivan Award, awarded to the nation's most exceptional amateur athlete. She also received the Associated Press's female athlete of the year award. In 1995 she was inducted into the USA Track and Field Hall of Fame.

Florence Griffith-Joyner (right) hands off the baton to teammate Evelyn Ashford in the 4x100 meter relay won by the American women in the 1988 Olympics. *(AP/Wide World Photos)*

Griffith-Joyner was also known for her commitment to community service and her work with children. In 1989 she was awarded the Harvard Foundation Award for her many contributions to the public. Among other activities, Griffith-Joyner was serving as the cochair of the President's Council on Physical Fitness and Sports at the time of her death. As the 2000 Olympics approached, her Olympic and world records in the 100 and 200 meters still stood.

—*Andrea E. Miller*

Popularly known as "FloJo," Griffith-Joyner was also known for her unconventional track uniforms and six-inch-long, decorated fingernails. Finding conventional track uniforms uncomfortable, she raced in colorful bodysuits. In 1989 she retired from track in order to dedicate more time to coaching her husband; pursue opportunities in acting, modeling, and writing; and oversee endorsement deals.

Nine years later, at the age of thirty-eight, she died in her sleep of an apparent heart seizure. Her death revived rumors of steroid use that had first surfaced at the 1988 Olympic trials in Indianapolis, where she lowered the women's 100-meter sprint record to an almost unbelievable 10.49 seconds. However, she had passed eleven drug tests in 1988 and consistently denied using performance-enhancing drugs. An autopsy on her body revealed no traces of illegal or prescription drugs.

Griggs v. Duke Power Company: U.S. SUPREME COURT case regarding employment testing. The Court ruled on March 8, 1971, that the Duke Power Company could require—as a condition of employment or departmental transfer—a high school diploma or a satisfactory score on an intelligence test. Such conditions did not necessarily violate any CIVIL RIGHTS laws, even when they disproportionately screened out members of a racial group. Any test or qualification, however, had to be related to the ability to do the job applied for. Tests or qualifications could not be used to exclude minorities, even if those tests or qualifications appeared to be neutral.

Grimké, Angelina Weld (February 27, 1880, Boston, Massachusetts—June 10, 1958, New York, New York): Poet, playwright, and educator. A prominent poet of the early twentieth century, Grimké was also America's first known African American female dramatist.

Related to famous nineteenth-century abolitionists, Angelina Emily Weld Grimké was born of an interracial marriage. Her mulatto father was a distinguished lawyer and social activist who served as vice president of the NATIONAL ASSOCIATION FOR THE ADVANCEMENT OF COLORED PEOPLE (NAACP). Grimké was abandoned as a child by her white mother and was raised by her father in a highly intellectual, upper-middle-class environment. She attended prestigious schools and after graduation taught at Dunbar High School in WASHINGTON, D.C., a famous black college preparatory school.

Grimké's highly imagistic lyric poetry often explored the mistreatment of African Americans but focused primarily on love, often from her lesbian point of view. She was frequently anthologized in the 1920's as a prominent poet and was seen as part of the HARLEM RENAISSANCE.

Grimké became more well known after her death for her only play, *Rachel*, whose main character refuses to bear children because of the violent racism in America. Produced by the NAACP in 1916, *Rachel* was initially staged in Washington, D.C., but eventually appeared Off-Broadway. It served as an eloquent protest of the increased LYNCHING of African Americans in the early decades of twentieth-century America and as a response to D. W. Griffith's racist film of 1915, THE BIRTH OF A NATION.

—*Terry Nienhuis*

Grimké, Charlotte Forten (August 17, 1837, Philadelphia, Pennsylvania—July 22, 1914, Washington, D.C.): Educator and activist. An African American woman who pursued education on an equal basis with whites in the years before the CIVIL WAR, Grimké was active in African American rights and abolitionist causes.

Charlotte Forten was born into a prominent black family in PHILADELPHIA, at the center of the ABOLITIONIST MOVEMENT and humanitarian activities. Her father educated her at home rather than send her to segregated schools in Philadelphia. In 1854, at sixteen, she traveled to Salem, MASSACHUSETTS, to continue her education in integrated schools. She became active in Salem and Boston abolitionist groups. An intelligent, serious student, she graduated from the Salem Normal School. In 1856 she was hired by the city of Salem to teach white children in the public schools.

Forten spent the two years from 1862 to 1864 in the South Carolina SEA ISLANDS teaching freed slaves. This experience as a volunteer teacher in the Sea Islands reinforced her belief in the importance of education for African Americans. In 1878 Forten was married to Francis J. Grimké, a minister living in Washington, D.C. The couple actively spoke out against prejudice for the rest of their lives. Charlotte Forten Grimké died in 1914 after a long life of activism in education, abolitionism, and civil rights. *The Journal of Charlotte L. Forten* was published in 1953.

See also: Grimké, Angelina (Emily) Weld.

—*Susan Butterworth*

Grovey v. Townsend: U.S. SUPREME COURT voting rights case of 1935. R. R. Grovey, an African American resident of TEXAS, argued that Albert Townsend, a county clerk, refused to give him an absentee ballot for a DEMOCRATIC PARTY primary election because of his race. The nation's Democratic Party did not forbid membership to African Americans, but the Texas Democratic Party did. Since a Democratic nominee was almost certainly guaranteed to win in a state where the Democratic Party was so dominant, Grovey claimed that he was in effect being denied voting privileges in the general election. Such discrimination was in violation of the United States Constitution's Fourteenth and Fifteenth Amendments.

The U.S. SUPREME COURT ruled unanimously that the Texas Democratic Party was a private, not state, organization that could exclude whomever it wished from membership. However, the GROVEY V. TOWNSEND decision was reversed in 1944, in SMITH V. ALLWRIGHT.

—*Rose Secrest*

See also: Fifteenth Amendment; Fourteenth Amendment.

Guinier, Lani (b. April 19, 1950, New York, New York): Attorney and scholar. The child of an African American father and a white Jewish mother, Carol Lani Guinier was reared in Queens, New York. Her father, whose parents immigrated to Boston from the WEST INDIES, was a warrant officer in an all-black unit in WORLD WAR II; her mother served as a Red Cross volunteer. The couple met when they were stationed in Hawaii. Her father had been a student at Harvard University from 1929 to 1930, but had to drop out because he was denied scholarship aid and prevented from living in student housing because he was black.

In junior high, Lani Guinier attended a magnet school that had a special program for academic achievers. She later recalled that all the school buses were bringing students who lived in segregated areas. In 1967 she graduated third from her high school and received a full-tuition scholarship to Radcliffe College. After receiving her bachelor's degree from Radcliffe in 1971, Guinier applied for admission to Yale Law School. Guinier's interest in law was inspired by African American lawyer Constance Baker MOTLEY, who had helped James MEREDITH gain admission to the University of Mississippi. Guinier was also motivated by a desire for public service and fighting for social justice against racism and discrimination. While attending Yale, she was one of three women in a class taught by a law professor who addressed all students as "gentlemen."

After receiving her law degree from Yale in 1974, Guinier accepted a job as a law clerk for Damon Keith, a black federal judge in DETROIT. In 1977 she was offered a position in WASHINGTON, D.C., as a special assistant to Drew Days, the assistant attorney general for CIVIL RIGHTS at the Justice Department under President Jimmy Carter. After leaving the Justice Department, she worked as a counsel for the NAACP Legal Defense and Education Fund from 1981 through 1987. Next, Guinier was hired in 1988 to serve as a professor at the University of Pennsylvania Law School.

In April of 1993, President Bill Clinton nomi-

Lani Guinier around the time President Bill Clinton withdrew her nomination as assistant attorney general for civil rights. *(AP/Wide World Photos)*

nated Guinier to become his assistant attorney general for civil rights at the Justice Department. At the press conference, Guinier was accompanied by her husband and young son. Heated controversy over her nomination erupted almost immediately. Opponents to her nomination disagreed with her liberal views and characterized her as a "quota queen." Her detractors claimed that law review articles she had written proved that she advocated a series of voting rights reforms designed to increase minority representation in legislatures—reforms which they claimed were antidemocratic in nature.

Although her nomination had been supported by four hundred law professors, including the deans of twelve major law schools, the CLINTON ADMINISTRATION withdrew Guinier's nomination prior to her confirmation hearing before the Senate Judiciary Committee. Guinier was deeply hurt by this decision, believing that her writings had been quoted out of context and that her views had been deliberately misrepresented. She blamed the media for accepting her opponents' characterization of her ideas as radical and divisive.

Despite her grueling experience, Guinier continued to work for equity, social justice, and civil rights. In December of 1993, she traveled to Los Angeles to receive the ACLU's Bill of Rights Award. Her book, *The Tyranny of the Majority: Fundamental Fairness in Representative Democracy*, published in 1994 by the Free Press, received favorable reviews and was described in the *Boston Globe* as "must reading for anyone who cares about race or democracy in America."

Guinn v. United States: U.S. SUPREME COURT case involving voting rights. In 1915 the Court outlawed grandfather clauses, which allowed a person to vote without regard to other qualifications if that person's ancestors had been allowed to vote before the end of SLAVERY. By the time of the case, grandfather clauses still in existence had little practical impact. This was one of the first court cases in which the NATIONAL ASSOCIATION FOR THE ADVANCEMENT OF COLORED PEOPLE (NAACP) participated.

Gullah: CREOLE slave language indigenous to the SEA ISLANDS of SOUTH CAROLINA and GEORGIA; also the name of the people who speak it. The word possibly comes from *ngula*, for "Angola." Gullah is based on pidgin English, with some vocabulary and grammar from several West African languages. Joel Chandler Harris used Gullah as the storyteller's language in his Uncle Remus tales.

In 1996 Ron Daise (arm raised) launched a television show for preschool children called *Gullah Gullah Island*, shot on South Carolina's St. Helena Island. *(AP/Wide World Photos)*

Television and increased social contact have eroded its use, and by the late twentieth century it was becoming rare.

See also: African languages and American English.

Gumbel, Bryant (b. September 29, 1948, New Orleans, Louisiana): Sportscaster, broadcast news reporter, and television personality. Bryant Charles Gumbel gained fame in the early 1980's as the first black cohost of NBC's *Today Show.* Born the second of four children to Richard Dunbar and Rhea Alice LeCesne Gumbel, Bryant grew up in Hyde Park, an integrated collegiate section of Chicago, where his father served as a Cook County probate judge. A devoted fan of the Chicago Cubs and White Sox baseball teams, Gumbel shared a close rela-

tionship with his father and older brother Greg GUMBEL, who also became a television broadcaster, frequently playing pick-up games of baseball when his father was free. The center of Bryant's life was his father, against whom he measured his own successes and failures.

Education

Despite Richard Gumbel's influence, Bryant rejected his father's conservatism and the family pressure to study law. Sure of his goals, he remained true to his ambition to report sports news. An average student, Gumbel attended middle-class Catholic elementary and high schools. Though a staunch liberal, he remained aloof from his generation's antiwar activism and racial strife. He chose instead to concentrate on classes at mostly white Bates College in Lewiston, Maine, from which he graduated in 1970 with a bachelor's degree in Russian history. Ineligible for the draft because of a sports injury to his wrist, he moved to New York and sold paper products. The job proved so stultifying and unfulfilling that Gumbel quit after a year, withdrew from his family, and remained unemployed until he could find a more challenging career. He married former flight attendant and artist June Carlyn Baranco in 1973; the couple had two children, Bradley Christopher and Jillian Beth.

Early Career

Gumbel made his first connection with sportscasting by submitting an article to *Black Sports* magazine. Upon the acceptance of his initial offering, he received a writing contract. For the next two years, he worked in print journalism for the magazine as a writer and editor and developed familiarity and connections with the athletic world. In July, 1972, he advanced to the post of weekend sportscaster for KNBC-TV in Burbank, Califor-

Bryant Gumbel (center) with fellow *Today Show* hosts Jane Pauley and Chris Wallace in 1981. *(AP/Wide World Photos)*

nia, deeply regretting that his father had died the week before his on-screen debut. Within eight months, he had moved to a position as evening news sportscaster. By 1976 he had advanced to the role of sports director.

Gumbel's commentary and interviewing skills improved steadily. He cohosted *Grandstand*, the National Football League live pregame show, for which he had to commute to New York, as well as broadcasts of Olympics specials, college basketball, and major league baseball games. Later, he began working on broadcasts of Super Bowl games, Thanksgiving parades, golf tournaments, and the World Series.

The Today Show

Gumbel's big break came in 1980, when he was selected as a part-time cohost for NBC's *Today Show*. A contract as full-time cohost in 1981 brought him a substantial salary increase. Following the departure of Tom Brokaw, Gumbel's temporary pairing with Jane Pauley had won the support of Steve Friedman, the show's executive producer. Backed by a three-man team of critic Gene Shalit, newsman Chris Wallace, and weatherman Willard Scott, Gumbel evolved a warm, fluid style. To most viewers, his race seemed incidental; they enjoyed his smooth, even-tempered flow of patter with cohost Pauley.

Gumbel worked to improve his news delivery, keeping up to date on current events and studying his competitors, sometimes watching three television screens simultaneously and jotting down notes. In September, 1984, the program broadcast on location from Moscow. *The Today Show*, which had slipped to third place in the ratings, returned to second and then, in 1985, to first via the success of broadcasts from the Papal See in Rome and a rail tour of the American Midwest. Gumbel stayed with *The Today Show* until 1997.

Inaugurating *Main Street*, a monthly afternoon news program, in the fall of 1985, Gum-

bel expanded his audience to teenagers, inquiring into the activities, interests, and problems of youth. He soon netted a new four-year, $1.5-million contract and the anchor post for the 1988 Seoul Olympics. In 1999 Gumbel returned to weekday morning television as anchor of *The Early Show* on CBS.

Honors

Gumbel earned a variety of honors, including Emmy Awards in 1976 and 1977, Golden Mike Awards from the Los Angeles Press Club in 1978 and 1979, a New York City Brotherhood Award, and the Edward R. Murrow Award from the Overseas Press Club in 1988.

—*Mary Ellen Snodgrass*
See also: Television industry.

Suggested Readings:
Blum, David. "Today's Man: Bryant Gumbel's Different Strokes." *New York* (August 4, 1986): 30-37.
Carter, Bill. "Forecast for Today: Cloudy." *The New York Times Magazine* (June 10, 1990): 26.
Fields, Cheryl D. "Out of the Public Eye." Interview. *Black Issues in Higher Education* 12 (August 6, 1998): 18-23.
Harris, Joanne. "Questions, No Doubt: Bryant Gumbel Questions All Comers and Answers All Questions." *American Visions* 7 (October/November, 1992): 22-26.
Hewitt, Hugh. "Porcupine Strikes Back." *National Review* (June 8, 1992): 6.
Reilly, Rick. "The Mourning Anchor." *Sports Illustrated* 69 (September 26, 1988): 74-76, 79-82.
Unger, Arthur. "Bryant Gumbel: No More Mr. Humble." *Television Quarterly* 26 (Summer, 1992): 8-21.

Gumbel, Greg (b. May 3, 1946, New Orleans, Louisiana): Sports broadcaster. Greg and his younger brother, Bryant GUMBEL, grew up in

CHICAGO. After completing high school, Greg chose to attend Loras College, a small liberal arts college in Iowa, where he majored in English. He also competed on the school's baseball team and won honors as the team's most valuable player. After receiving his bachelor's degree in 1967, Gumbel returned to Chicago, where he took jobs as an advertising copywriter and as a sales representative for a hospital supply company. While working in Detroit, he met a young nurse whom he married in 1976.

At the suggestion of his younger brother, who had already established himself as a broadcaster, Greg Gumbel auditioned for a job as a sports anchor for Chicago television station WMAQ in 1973. He was hired and eventually earned two local Emmys for his work. In 1981 Gumbel moved to Connecticut to take a new job as coanchor of ESPN's *SportsCenter*, a cable sports program on which he provided

Greg Gumbel in 1992. *(AP/Wide World Photos)*

two half-hour update reports on sporting events every night. The Madison Square Garden Network hired Gumbel in 1986 to host the Knicks basketball games and Yankees baseball games. He also worked as host of a morning drive-time radio sports show on WFAN, an all-sports station in New York City.

Gumbel began his career at CBS television in October of 1989. The network hired him to work as a play-by-play announcer for its broadcasts of college basketball, NBA, and College World Series games. In 1990 he was promoted to be coanchor of the network's *The NFL Today* program with Terry Bradshaw, the former Pittsburgh Steelers quarterback. Gumbel's polished delivery proved to be a perfect complement to Bradshaw's folksy commentary. After serving as morning anchor covering the 1992 Winter Olympic Games in Albertville, France, Gumbel was tapped to serve as lead anchor of the network's prime time broadcasts of the 1994 Winter Olympic Games in Lillehammer, Norway.

In 1994 CBS had to cancel *The NFL Today* after losing broadcasting rights to the league's football games, and Gumbel lost his coanchor post. Previous years had witnessed the network's loss of lucrative broadcasting rights to air NBA and major league baseball games. These developments, together with the fact that Gumbel's contract with CBS was up for renewal in the fall of 1995, led to speculation that he might negotiate for a position as a sports broadcaster with another network. In 1995 Gumbel signed a contract with NBC television and began anchoring its coverage of major league baseball games, including the World Series.

Gunn, Wendell Wilkie: Political appointee. The founder of Gunn Associates, a financial consulting firm in Stamford, CONNECTICUT, Gunn also served as vice president of Chase Manhattan Bank and was an assistant trea-

Economist Wendell Gunn addressing the platform committee at the Republican National Convention in 1976. *(AP/Wide World Photos)*

surer for the Pepsi Company. His first political appointment came in 1982, when President Ronald Reagan selected him to serve as special assistant to the president on international trade policy. Gunn served in this post until 1984. President George Bush appointed Gunn to serve under Secretary Jack Kemp as chief of staff of the Department of Housing and Urban Development in 1989. Gunn also served as a member of the Economic Policy Task Force for the Joint Center for Political Studies.
See also: Housing and Urban Development, Department of.

Guy, Buddy (b. July 30, 1936, Lettsworth, Louisiana): Guitarist, singer, songwriter, and club owner. At the age of thirteen, George "Buddy" Guy taught himself rudimentary guitar skills by fashioning an instrument from window screen wire and replicating the sounds of his boyhood influences Aaron "T-Bone" WALKER,

B. B. KING, Lightnin' HOPKINS, and Eddie "Guitar Slim" Jones. By September of 1957, Guy was in CHICAGO, ILLINOIS, looking for the opportunity to break into Chicago's music scene. His opportunity came at a local battle of the bands, where he defeated guitarists "Magic" Sam Maghett and Otis Rush. These three musicians would go on to create a definitive electric guitar style in Chicago known as the West Side Sound. This triumph brought Guy instant local acclaim and a recording contract with Cobra Records.

After recording "I Sit and Cry and Sing the Blues" for Cobra, Guy joined the Muddy WATERS Band, Chess Records's biggest selling recording act. Guy would be Chess Records's last BLUES star before the company focused on other musical directions. Guy stayed with Muddy Waters until the late 1950's, when he formed a partnership with the band's harmonica player, Amos "Junior" Wells. This alliance continued in various degrees through the early 1990's.

By the mid-1960's, Guy's innovative and frenetic performance style earned him the respect and admiration of the emerging breed of rock-and-roll "guitar heroes," musicians such as Eric Clapton, Jeff Beck, and Jimi HENDRIX whose speed, stage presence, and ear-splitting decibel levels captivated their audiences. During a performance in the late 1960's, Guy overheard a fan mutter something about his having stolen from Hendrix's repertoire when in fact it was the reverse, a fact that Hendrix himself willingly acknowledged.

Guy rarely recorded in the 1970's and 1980's. He purchased the Checkerboard Lounge in Chicago's South Side in 1972. It became a refuge for local and more visible acts who were in town and looking for a relaxed atmosphere in which to play. He continued to perform throughout North America and in Africa, Europe, and Japan, usually with Junior Wells. A 1974 performance with Wells at the Montreaux Jazz Festival resulted in the critically acclaimed *Drinkin' TNT 'n' Smokin' Dynamite*. The record was produced by Rolling Stone Bill Wyman, who also played bass guitar on the record.

By the end of the 1980's, Guy was being touted as a "new" recording star. In 1989 he opened a new blues club, Buddy Guy's Legends, on Chicago's South Side, and it soon became well known, replacing the old Checkerboard Lounge as a place of refuge for musicians wishing to play in an informal setting. In 1990 Guy was presented with the W. C. Handy Award as entertainer of the year. He was now a highly sought live act, and his recording career resumed with the 1991 Grammy Award-winning *Damn Right I Got the Blues* on the Silvertone label. More albums followed, including *Feels Like Rain* (1993), *Slippin' In* (1994), and *As Good as It Gets* (1998). Guy won three Grammy Awards in the 1990's. He also remained active as a live performer; he was a headlining act at the Long Beach Blues Festival in 1999. In addition, in the 1980's and 1990's he did numerous recordings with other artists, including long-time Guy admirers Eric Clapton and Stevie Ray Vaughan.

See also: Music; Songwriters and composers.

H

Hairstyles: Head hair has always been cherished and protected by people of African ancestry. It is a conduit for both personal expression and social commentary, and considerable effort may go into its aesthetic arrangements. In AFRICA, the arranging and grooming of hair have long been meaningful sociocultural formalities. In some African societies, the manner in which the hair is styled reflects various aspects of community life. Status, age, gender, occupation, ethnic affiliations, motherhood, and bereavement all may mandate certain hairstyles. For centuries in Africa, the braiding, threading, shaving, and cutting of hair were familiar practices.

The texture of African hair—usually thick, tightly coiled and spiraled—permits shapes and designs impossible for hair of a less coarse texture. Various materials such as shells, coins, beads, sisal, and strips of material were used to decorate hairstyles. Enslaved African men and women in North America maintained African traditions in their hairstyling practices as much as they could. They made modifications and adjustments by using berries, herbs, and other natural substances found in their new environment.

Hairstyles During Slavery

Nonetheless, many elaborate African hairstyles were soon lost. They gave way to a lack of time, the demands of enslavement, and a lack of implements such as the indigenous comb with its long, smooth teeth for disentangling the hair. The result was hair that lacked manageability and control. For some, the card used to prepare washed wool from sheep was used as a substitute comb.

The appearance of the hair of runaway slaves often figured prominently in newspaper advertisements for their capture and return. Some runaways were simply described as having "bushy" or "wooly" hair, but some advertisements were more detailed and described a wide variety of hairstyles. For example, the runaway's hairstyle might be described as short or long, shaved at the back or front, bushy on the top, or parted and combed neatly to the sides. This documented range of styles shows the innovativeness of the enslaved African hairstyling practices.

Most slaveholders apparently placed few or no restrictions on the slaves in terms of their hairstyling practices, making this one of the few cultural freedoms the slaves were able to maintain. On Sundays, holidays, and other special occasions—in many cases the only times the slaves had to comb their hair—women would remove the bandannas that covered their heads throughout the week. Under these scarves were such creative styles as wrapping, braiding, threading, and cornrowing, all of which were retained from West African societies.

In the eighteenth century, when wigs became a popular status symbol for European men and Europeans in the colonies, some slave men began styling their hair to resemble these wigs. Again, as noted in newspaper advertisements for their capture and return, some slave men wore hair arrangements that resembled hairpieces that ranged from the toupee to the full wig.

Twentieth-Century Styles

Hairstyling practices of the eighteenth and nineteenth centuries carried over into the twentieth, but new styles also emerged. Madame C. J. WALKER's 1905 invention, the straightening comb, made it possible for black women to "hot press" and straighten their hair. From this straightening step, combined with a curling rod, came styles such as the finger waves and pin curls worn during the time of the HARLEM RENAISSANCE.

Also in the 1920's, men began to wear the bone-straight hairstyle that was achieved by applying a harsh mixture of lye, potatoes, and eggs to the hair; the mixture was called "congalene." This "conk" style made hair more manageable and offered new styling options. Many men, however, continued to process their hair with heavy pomades, tonics, and "grease and water" to achieve comb and brush waves. Tying a rag around the head was a simple way to produce a pressurized wave arrangement.

In the mid-1960's, the black pride movement influenced the hairstyles of both men and women. They began wearing the Afro, a natural hairstyle free of chemicals or heat treatments. The wearer's hair could grow to great heights and lengths. Those who wore this style were proclaiming pride in their AFRICAN HERITAGE. However, by the end of the 1970's, propelled in part by new styles in the black entertainment world, the Jheri curl trend began, and once again processed hairstyles were in vogue. This curl was chemically treated, and each lock of the hair was rolled on perm rods. The result was a head full of tight ringlets that would last indefinitely unless allowed to grow out. Both men and women wore this style, partly because it had great manageability and control.

By the 1990's a great variety of hairstyles were being worn by both genders. They included dreadlocks, permanent waves, cornrows, weaves, braids, wraps, sister curls, Afros, and shaved heads. Lengths ranged from shoulder-length to close-cropped naturals and bouncy African locks. Men and women also expressed themselves through a spectrum of bold and vibrant hair colors.

—*Rosalie Black Kiah*

Suggested Readings:

Boston, Lloyd. *Men of Color: Fashion, History, Fundamentals*. New York: Artisan, 1998.

Sagay, Esi. *African Hairstyles: Styles of Yesterday and Today*. London: Heinemann, 1983.

White, Shane, and Graham White. *Stylin': African American Expressive Culture from Beginnings to the Zoot Suit*. Ithaca, N.Y.: Cornell University Press, 1998.

Haiti: The Republic of Haiti is located on the western tip of the island of Hispaniola, the second largest of the Greater Antilles chain, in the West Indies. Haiti occupies approximately one-third of the island; the DOMINICAN REPUBLIC inhabits the remaining two-thirds. Haiti's population in the late 1990's was estimated to be in excess of 6.8 million. Haiti's population is mostly black, but there is also a socially, politically, and economically powerful mulatto, or mixed-blood, minority.

The Colonial Era

The island of Hispaniola was opened for European exploration by Christopher Columbus in 1492 in the name of the Spanish crown. The Spaniards introduced the first African slaves to the colony in 1502. Haiti eventually became a colony of France under a treaty with Spain in 1697.

Known as Saint Domingue at that time, Haiti was developed by the French into one of the major sugar producers in the Western Hemisphere. The sugar plantation owners became rich through the utilization of African slave labor, because the island's original American Indian population had been devastated by disease and overwork.

The owners regarded their slaves as expendable commodities. Owners exploited them so excessively that the average life span of a worker, once assigned to the fields or the plantation sugar mills, rarely extended beyond five years. A steady flow of replacements had to be brought in from Africa in order to meet the high demand. The French brought an estimated 864,000 African slaves to Saint Domingue in the course of the eighteenth century.

Sexual relations between French masters and their African female slaves introduced a third segment to the population, the mulatto segment. Many mulattoes inherited property from their French forebears, and in many cases they became slaveowners themselves. The French refused to accept the mulatto population as their social and political equals, but the mulattoes regarded themselves as a social and economic class separate from the black slave majority.

In 1791 Toussaint-L'Ouverture (holding book) led the most successful slave rebellion in the history of the Americas and made Haiti independent. *(Library of Congress)*

Independence

A slave named Toussaint-L'Ouverture began a rebellion in 1791, leading the oppressed slave population against French authority. Although generally ill-equipped and often half-starved, the slave army under Toussaint-L'Ouverture's leadership managed to defeat the best European troops sent against them by France, England, and Spain. Although the French captured and imprisoned Toussaint-L'Ouverture, his successor, Jean-Jacques Dessalines, ultimately succeeded in leading the rebel forces to independence in 1804. The newly enfranchised country adopted the island's precolonial name, Haiti, and became the first black republic in the Western Hemisphere.

The Nationalist Period

Throughout the nineteenth century, the citizens of Haiti became the victims of a series of inept, cruel, and venal rulers. The country suffered continuous economic, political, and social disasters. From the economic standpoint, its lucrative sugar trade was destroyed when the French plantation owners fled the island. The black revolutionaries massacred those whites remaining on the Haitian side of Hispaniola.

The historic enmity between the mulatto minority and the black majority remained a constant threat to Haiti's stability. Members of the mulatto faction assassinated the country's first post-independence president, General Dessalines, when they felt that he sought to develop closer links with the black majority.

Politically, no true democratic structure developed during Haiti's formative years. A series of self-styled kings, emperors, and dictators modified the republic's original constitution continuously to suit their own political

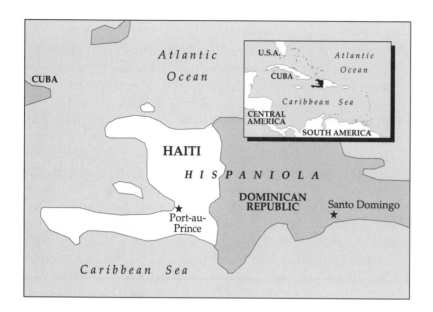

bor on the island, remained volatile. A state of constant warfare existed between the two throughout much of the nineteenth century.

The Twentieth Century

One hundred years after its founding, the Republic of Haiti remained the most backward and poverty-ridden country in the Western Hemisphere. Its rural black majority remained largely illiterate, and the land, stripped of

agendas. These leaders seized and held power by force. They were removed, in turn, by new leaders of the same caliber. Relations between Haiti and the Dominican Republic, its neigh-

its natural forests, had become virtually exhausted by the agricultural techniques practiced by its marginal farmers. A small coterie of largely mulatto upper-class families con-

Haitian emigrants hoping to find a new home in the United States in 1992 are turned back by officials at the U.S. naval base at Guantanamo, Cuba. *(AP/Wide World Photos)*

trolled what little wealth the country produced.

Concerned with the continuing civil disorder in the country and the economic chaos that accompanied it, the United States occupied and began the economic and political administration of Haiti in 1915. For the next nineteen years the United States controlled the country's economy and politics. In the course of its stay, the United States instituted a road-building program and trained a national army. These two processes aided subsequent Haitian administrations to control the countryside after the departure of the U.S. military forces.

Haitian president Jean-Bertrand Aristide addressing the United Nations in October, 1994. *(AP/Wide World Photos)*

François Duvalier, a member of the black majority, succeeded in winning control of the Haitian presidency in 1957. What followed was an oppressive twenty-nine-year dictatorship, first by Duvalier, nicknamed Papa Doc, and then by his son, Jean-Claude Duvalier (Baby Doc). The rule of the Duvaliers reduced the living standards of the country even further. The senior Duvalier severely limited the power of the military, substituting a militia under his personal control, called the Tonton Macoute. Through the Tonton Macoute Duvalier ruthlessly suppressed any opposition. Jean-Claude's excesses led finally to his expulsion and exile in 1986.

During the period of the Duvaliers' rule, particularly in the 1970's and 1980's, thousands of Haitians fled the country by boat. The "boat people," as they were soon called, were fleeing in tiny, fragile craft to escape their homeland's poverty and political oppression. Untold numbers perished at sea in the attempt. At first the United States interdicted these flights and re-turned the escapees to Haitian government control. Subsequently the U.S. government, under pressure, agreed to provide a degree of limited political refugee status on a temporary basis to the Haitian boat people.

A new wave of boat people began fleeing Haiti after democratically elected president Jean-Bertrand Aristide was ousted in 1991. The United States decided to intervene once more in Haiti's domestic affairs. U.S. troops landed at Port-au-Prince in 1994 to support the return to office of Aristide. Aristide in turn supported the popular election of his successor, René Préval, the following year. Although political and economic disorder waned after the country's return to democratic government, by the end of the twentieth century Haiti had made only minor progress in providing a decent standard of living for its inhabitants. Many of its citizens still seek to leave the island to find economic opportunity elsewhere.

—*Carl Henry Marcoux*
See also: Mulattoes; Plantations; Poverty.

Suggested Readings:

Bellegarde-Smith, Patrick. *Haiti: The Breached Citadel*. Boulder, Colo.: Westview Press, 1990.

Cassagnol Chierici, Rose-Marie. *Demele, "Making It": Migration and Adaptation Among Haitian Boat People in the United States*. New York: AMS Press, 1991.

Dupuy, Alex. *Haiti in the New World Order: The Limits of the Democratic Revolution*. Boulder, Colo.: Westview Press, 1997.

Korngold, Ralph. *Citizen Toussaint*. New York: Hill and Wang, 1944.

Stepick, Alex. *Pride Against Prejudice: Haitians in the United States*. Boston: Allyn and Bacon, 1998.

Weinstein, Brian, and Aaron Segal. *Haiti: The Failure of Politics*. New York: Praeger, 1992.

Hale, Clara McBride (April 1, 1905, Philadelphia, Pennsylvania—December 18, 1992, New York, New York): Child-care volunteer. "Mother" Clara McBride Hale established HALE HOUSE, a receiving home for unwanted and drug-dependent infants, as well as those infected with ACQUIRED IMMUNODEFICIENCY SYNDROME (AIDS). She received a commendation on February 5, 1985, from President Ronald Reagan during his state of the union address.

Hale was one of four children who endured POVERTY after their father died, leaving their mother to support them by cooking and taking in lodgers. After graduation from Philadelphia High School, she married Thomas Hale; they had a son and daughter, Nathan and Lorraine, and adopted a second son, Kenneth. The death of her husband in 1932 left her few options. At first, she worked at a theater, scrubbing floors and toilets. Then, because work was keeping her from supervising her family, she chose to board foster children in her Harlem apartment.

Hale retired in 1968. The next year, however, at the insistence of daughter Lorraine, she accepted a cocaine-addicted infant and had soon opened her doors to a stream of needy children. At first, she had no government financial assistance. A public-supported rehabilitation program that separated parent and child for eighteen months, until the mother's addiction was controlled, gave Hale an opportunity to instill self-esteem in children and improve their nutrition, cleanliness, and health habits while keeping family ties intact. In 1971 police and civic authorities, impressed with her results, began supporting her work with local, state, and federal monies. Four years later, Hale House moved to a larger building to offer more play, kitchen, and bed space. Still superintended and cared for by Hale, most of the children thrived and returned to stable homes. Almost none of the children who went through Hale House were put up for adoption.

Although Hale became too infirm to manage the task, the Hale House concept, bolstered by public and private support and managed by Dr. Lorraine Hale, spread to other cities. For her work, Clara Hale received an honorary doctorate from John Jay College of Criminal Justice, recognition from the National Mother's Day Committee, and the Truman Award for Public Service.

Hale House: Treatment center for drug-addicted babies, located in HARLEM, New York. Hale House was started by "Mother" Clara McBride HALE in 1969, after her daughter, Dr. Lorraine Hale, sent an addicted mother—who was wandering the street with her baby—to her for help.

Within three months after receiving this infant, Clara Hale had twenty-two children in her apartment. Later that year, Hale House received its first grant from the federal Office of Economic Opportunity. The Hale House Center for the Promotion of Human Potential was incorporated in 1973 and was licensed by the New York State Department of Social Services and a New York voluntary child-care agency.

The Hale House staff expanded to include child-care workers, a teacher, a social worker, a cook, a house parent, and part-time medical staff. Lorraine Hale, who held a doctoral degree in child development, gradually took over direction of this staff. Hale House had helped a thousand addicted babies ranging in age from two weeks to three years by 1991.

While a child was at the house, its mother was required to attend an eighteen-month rehabilitation program and to visit the child once a week. By 1986 only twelve out of more than five hundred Hale House children had been put up for adoption, and most of the mothers had conquered their addictions. In the late 1980's, addicted babies began to be plagued by two new and fatal problems, crack addiction and ACQUIRED IMMUNODEFICIENCY SYNDROME (AIDS). Hale House also served these babies. Addicted mothers were referred to Hale House by word of mouth as well as by municipal agencies in New York, including the police.

Hale House received government funding and private donations. It received $1.1 million in federal grants to expand in 1986. Musician John Lennon wrote a $10,000 check after visiting the center. After his death, his wife, Yoko Ono, began contributing $20,000 annually. Mother Hale's work received national recognition, and in 1985 President Ronald Reagan called her "an American hero" in his state of the union address.

Haley, Alex (August 11, 1921, Ithaca, New York—February 10, 1992, Seattle, Washington): Writer. The publication of his 688-page *Roots: The Saga of an American Family* (1976)— and the book's quick serialization as an eight-night television special—rocketed author Alex Haley into celebrity status and, as many

see it, represented a unique coming-of-age for African Americans. The February 14, 1977, issue of *Time* magazine, which featured Haley, reported black leader Vernon JORDAN's view that *Roots* was "the single most spectacular educational experience in race relations in America." Both a "literary-television phenomenon" and "sociological event," Haley's *Roots* dramatized the long-suffering adaptability of blacks, affirming for African Americans a new and vital myth of origin—a peculiarly black variant of the American Dream success story, realized through persistent loss and humiliation, strength of personal character, and family continuity. Like Dilsey in William Faulkner's novel *The Sound and the Fury* (1929), Haley's black characters endure and prevail.

The fascinating story of how Haley grew up to write *Roots*, summarized toward the close of the book itself, is tightly linked with the narrative, since *Roots* is a seven-generation saga of one maternal line of Haley's own family, beginning in Africa in the 1750's and ending with Haley's sleuthlike historical research and the writing of the book.

Family History and Biography

Alex Haley was born in Ithaca, New York, where his parents had moved from the South to pursue graduate study—his father in agriculture, his mother in music. Simon Alexander Haley and Bertha George Palmer Haley, Alex's parents, were TENNESSEE natives. Bertha was from Henning, the town where Haley's maternal ancestors had settled after the Civil War. Haley's parents had met at Lane College, a black institution in Jackson, Tennessee.

Haley's maternal great-grandfather, Tom Murray (a slave who used the last name of his NORTH CAROLINA master), had taken a slave named Irene as his spouse and moved to Henning after the Civil War. Tom prospered as a blacksmith. His youngest daughter, Cynthia, was two years old when her family moved.

Cynthia married Will Palmer, who ran a successful lumber company in Henning; their daughter (Alex's mother) Bertha George Palmer was born there in 1895. The Will Palmers eventually owned a ten-room house with music parlor and library; they taught Bertha bookkeeping and imported a teacher forty-eight miles away, from Memphis, for her music lessons. Bertha's marriage to light-skinned, literate Simon Haley from Savannah was a major social affair in Henning, with the Lane College choir and local citizens of both races present.

Thus it happened that Alex Haley—whose mother died in 1931 and whose father moved about with various college teaching jobs—spent his earliest years, and many summers, at his grandparents' comfortable house in Henning, often listening with fascination to the family stories his elder maternal kin told. In brief, as Haley recounts the family narrative in *Roots*, the "furthest back person" was Kunta Kinte, "The African," also called Toby, a young Mandingo abducted by slave traders, imported, and sold to the Waller family in Spotsylvania County, VIRGINIA. There Toby "jumped the broom," marrying Bell, a kitchen servant. (Once caught as a runaway, Toby had had part of his foot chopped off by slave-catchers—who had made him choose between that or castration.) Toby and Bell's bright daughter Kizzy was sold to a North Carolina owner named Lea, by whom Kizzy bore a mulatto son, called Chicken George because he trained gamecocks. George (and Matilda, another slave) had eight children, the fourth being Tom, Alex Haley's great-grandfather. By word of mouth, each of these generations passed down the raw facts of their family's history.

Haley finished high school at fifteen and studied two years at Elizabeth City Teachers College (1937-1939) before joining the U.S. Coast Guard, on the eve of WORLD WAR II, as a mess boy. Haley married Nannie Branch in 1941 (and Juliette Collins in 1964) and fathered three children: Lydia Anna, William Alexander, and Cynthia Gertrude. Thus the family line that had so fascinated young Alex— Kunta Kinte, Kizzy, Chicken George, Tom Murray, Cynthia Palmer, Bertha Haley, then Alex himself—continues.

Early Writing Career

The initial stages of Haley's career quietly set the scene for his later success, since his time with the U.S. Coast Guard (1939-1959) was a period of self-taught apprenticeship. Haley read voraciously and wrote incessantly for eight years before having a single story accepted for publication. After the war, he was rated a journalist in the Coast Guard and published stories occasionally.

A civilian after 1959, Haley settled in NEW YORK CITY's Greenwich Village and tried to support himself by writing. (His Coast Guard pension checks went to his two former wives.) At first, he sold sea narratives to men's magazines and wrote features about adventurous people for *Reader's Digest* (which later helped to subsidize his research and travel, and which published a portion of *Roots* in 1974). In 1962 he started a series of interviews for *Playboy* magazine and in that context met MALCOLM X, the Black Muslim leader; Haley collaborated in writing *The Autobiography of Malcolm X* (1965), a well-received, honest, and probing portrait that demonstrated Haley's stature as a writer. Malcolm X's assassination just after the text was finished punctuated this assignment, gaining considerable attention for the autobiography and thus for Haley.

Haley Seeks His Roots

Soon Haley found evidence in North Carolina census records, housed in the National Archives in Washington, D.C., that his elders' oral accounts had historical authenticity. A London writing assignment led Haley to view the Rosetta Stone in the British Museum, and his seeing the deciphered hieroglyphs on that famous artifact reinforced his passion for unraveling his own family story. From 1965 to 1977, Haley focused on this research. He sought out experts in African dialects; maritime and other historical records in England and the United States; censuses; aging relatives; and eventually an oral historian, or griot, in an African village. Haley's account in *Roots* of this "peak experience," his verification of his own African connection, is moving. While Haley depicts Kunta Kinte as being conscious of Bell's "brown" skin and of his own absolute blackness, Haley records that he felt himself to be notably "brown" among the black African villagers.

Eventually, Haley was able to verify the basic details of his family story—even the SLAVE SHIP's name and date of passage—and to dramatize them in narrative form. At one point, Haley made an ocean voyage on a freighter from Africa to the United States, sleeping stripped to his underwear in the cargo hold in order to help him to imagine Kunta Kinte's ordeal.

Author Alex Haley on the set of the television miniseries *Roots* in 1977. (AP/Wide World Photos)

Publication and Reaction

Though the adequacy of Haley's evidence has been questioned by some, and a small portion of *Roots* has been shown to have been adapted from another printed source, it seems that the book's basic outline is original and can be corroborated. (Haley explained that the accidental borrowing occurred because would-be helpers passed unattributed material on to him.) *Roots*, then, is both a historical and an autobiographical novel—is both "true" and fic-

tional. Haley said that the book is "of necessity a novelized amalgam of what I *know* took place together with what my researching led me to plausibly *feel* took place." In *Roots*, the successive lives of Haley's progenitors take on real dimensions. Despite a happy ending in *Roots*, scenes of Kinte's passage in the slime-filled hold of the slave ship and the depictions of many other cruelties are searingly vivid.

Sales of *Roots* have been in the tens of millions, and 130 million people saw at least part of the miniseries. *Roots* received a special citation from the Pulitzer Prize committee in 1977 and earned Haley hundreds of awards. The book fostered broad interest in genealogy—not just among blacks—even though Haley's circumstances were atypical. Haley acknowledged both the uniqueness and the large applicability of his own story when, toward the end of *Roots*, he expressed in closing "the hope that this story of our people can help to alleviate the legacies of the fact that preponderantly the histories have been written by the winners."

Later Career

Several publicized court cases involving *Roots*, including two alleging plagiarism, helped turn Haley from writing books and toward various promotional projects, including the television sequel *Roots: The Next Generations*, which aired in 1979. Haley left Los ANGELES—where in 1972 he had founded the Kinte Corporation—to settle in Tennessee, on a farm near Knoxville. He continued to write, often on oceangoing vessels, and was much in demand as a speaker, touching audiences with his modesty and warmth. In 1992, on the eve of such an engagement, Haley died of cardiac arrest in Seattle, Washington.

—*Roy Neil Graves*

See also: African heritage; Ancestors; Oral and family history; Slavery.

Suggested Readings:

Fiedler, Leslie A. *The Inadvertent Epic: From Uncle Tom's Cabin to Roots.* New York: Simon & Schuster, 1979.

Haley, Alex. "What Roots Mean to Me." *Reader's Digest* (May, 1977): 73-76.

Harrison, Eric. "Roots of Alex Haley Fame Headed for Auction Block." *Los Angeles Times* (September 27, 1992): A1, A26-A27.

McGuire, Willard, and M. S. Clayton. "Interview with Alex Haley." *Today's Educator* 66 (September, 1977): 45-47.

Massaquoi, Hans J. "Alex Haley: The Man Behind *Roots*." *Ebony* 32 (April, 1977): 33-36.

Moore, Jesse T., Jr. "Alex Haley's *Roots*: Ten Years Later." *The Western Journal of Black Studies* 18 (Summer, 1994): 70-76.

Taylor, Helen. "'The Griot from Tennessee': The Saga of Alex Haley's *Roots*." *Critical Quarterly* 37 (Summer, 1995): 46-62.

Zimmerman, Paul D. "In Search of a Heritage." *Newsweek* (September 27, 1976): 94-96.

Hall, George Cleveland (February 22, 1864, Ypsilanti, Michigan—June 17, 1930, Chicago,

George Cleveland Hall, one of the founders of Provident Hospital. *(National Library of Medicine)*

Illinois): Physician. Hall founded the Cook County Physicians Association in Illinois and helped organize Provident Hospital in CHICAGO in 1890, with Daniel Hale WILLIAMS. He and Williams later had frequent disagreements, but Hall remained connected with the hospital until his death, rising to the position of chief of staff in 1926.

Hall, Katie Beatrice Green (b. April 3, 1938, Mound Bayou, Mississippi): U.S. representative from Indiana. Hall was raised in MISSISSIPPI and was married in 1957. She graduated from Mississippi Valley State University with a bachelor of science degree in 1960. She moved north with her husband and began teaching in public schools in Gary, Indiana, in 1961. During this time, Hall enrolled in graduate school at Indiana University, earning her M.S. degree in 1968.

Hall became involved in local politics in Gary when she worked on the campaigns of Mayor Richard Hatcher in 1967 and 1971. Hall decided to run for political office herself and campaigned for a seat in the Indiana House of Representatives for the Fifth District. She was elected in November of 1973 and served from 1974 until 1976. In 1975 she served as vice chair of the Gary Housing Board Commission and received an outstanding legislator award from the NATIONAL ASSOCIATION FOR THE ADVANCEMENT OF COLORED PEOPLE (NAACP). She ran for state senate from the Third District in 1976 and was elected to a six-year term ending in 1982.

When Congressman Adam Benjamin, Jr., died in 1982, his seat in the House of Representatives became vacant. As the Democratic Party's local chairman, Richard Hatcher selected Hall to run for the remainder of Benjamin's term and for a full term in the next congressional session. Hall defeated her Republican opponent in the election on November 2, 1982. Upon taking office, Hall became the first African American to represent the state of Indiana in the U.S. Congress.

Hall was appointed to serve on the House Committee on the Post Office and Civil Service and the House Committee on Public Works and Transportation. During her term on Capitol Hill, Hall addressed Congress on the subject of protective legislation for the U.S. steel industry and introduced legislation to designate Martin Luther KING, Jr.'s birthday as a national federal holiday. The bill was passed by the House in August of 1983 and was passed by the Senate in October. President Ronald Reagan signed the bill into law in November of 1983. Hall also was the chief sponsor of the King Holiday Commission Law in 1984.

Hall ran for reelection but lost the Democratic nomination in the state primary held in the fall of 1984. She completed her congressio-

nal term at the end of that year and returned to Indiana. In 1985 Hall took the post of city clerk for Gary.

See also: Congress members; Politics and government.

Hall, Prince (c. 1735, Bridgetown, Barbados— December 4, 1807, Boston, Massachusetts): Activist. Hall relocated to Boston in 1765. He became a minister, enlisted in the Revolutionary militia, promoted equal schools for black children, and organized the first group of black masons, African Lodge No. 459, in 1787. He organized other FRATERNAL SOCIETIES, agitated for abolition, and became an early supporter of black colonization to Africa.

Prince Hall surrounded by emblems of Freemasonry. *(Schomburg Center for Research in Black Culture, New York Public Library)*

See also: Abolitionist movement; American Revolution; Colonization movement.

Hamer, Fannie Lou (1917, Sunflower County, Mississippi—March 14, 1977, Montgomery County, Mississippi): CIVIL RIGHTS activist. A courageous and powerful leader, Hamer was a committed force behind the grass-roots organizing of the southern Civil Rights movement of the 1960's. The granddaughter of a slave, Hamer was reared in rural Sunflower County, MISSISSIPPI, one of twenty children born to Jim and Lou Ella Townsend. At six years of age, she was working in the cotton fields, and by age thirteen she could chop and pick as much cotton as a man.

Hamer recognized the difference in status between southern whites and blacks at an early age, but she was taught by her mother to respect herself and her racial identity. A strong belief in Christian values sustained Hamer throughout her life. In the early 1940's, Fannie married Perry Hamer, and the couple later adopted two daughters.

Early Activism
Hamer became involved in the Civil Rights movement after attending a mass meeting in August, 1962, at which the Reverend James BEVEL and James FORMAN, prominent civil rights activists, spoke. Bevel and Forman urged their listeners to register to vote; the talks inspired Hamer and spurred her to become involved in voter-registration efforts.

Hamer's activism caused her many problems; her family was uprooted from their home by an outraged landowner. The family moved, but they continued to experience threats, assaults, and insults from whites who labeled Hamer as "uppity." Undaunted, Hamer continued her work with voter registration, enduring arrests, evictions, and threats.

Upon returning from a workshop in SOUTH CAROLINA in June, 1963, Hamer was con-fronted once again by whites; this time, she was beaten unmercifully and then jailed. Hamer later recalled, "When they finally quit they told me to go to my cell, but I couldn't get up, I couldn't bend my knees." After her release, Hamer was taken to Atlanta for medical treatment, but the beating left her with a noticeable limp.

Creation of the MFDP
Hamer became field secretary for the STUDENT NONVIOLENT COORDINATING COMMITTEE (SNCC) and continued her work in voter registration. She also helped to organize welfare programs. In 1964 Sunflower County had twice as many blacks as whites of voting age, yet blacks made up less than 3 percent of the county's registered VOTERS. The Mississippi DEMOCRATIC PARTY would not help with black voter-registration efforts, so Hamer and others organized the MISSISSIPPI FREEDOM DEMOCRATIC PARTY (MFDP), a political party open to everyone.

The MFDP challenged the all-white Mississippi delegation's credentials at the Democratic National Convention in Atlantic City in 1964, but the MFDP delegation was not seated at the convention. At the 1968 CHICAGO convention, however, Hamer was one of twenty-two African Americans who unseated the white Mississippi delegation; the national Democratic Party pledged never again to seat a racially segregated delegation. During a televised address, Hamer shared her dehumanizing Mississippi story and declared, "This is not Mississippi's problem. It is America's problem." Viewers responded by offering support and money. Demand for Hamer as a speaker increased immediately.

In 1964 Hamer attempted to run for a Mississippi congressional seat, but she was kept off the ballot. The MFDP, in protest, circulated "freedom ballots" to dramatize the level of black disfranchisement. In the MFDP voting, Hamer received more than thirty-three thou-

Fannie Lou Hamer addressing Mississippi Freedom Democratic Party supporters in Washington, D.C., in September, 1965. *(AP/Wide World Photos)*

sand votes; her opponent, Congressmen Jamie Whitten, received fewer than fifty.

Economic Campaigns

Hamer also organized several economic co-operatives. She believed black economic independence would assist in the building of political strength in the African American community. The 670-acre Freedom Farm Co-operative was worked by more than five thousand people who shared the food grown on the farm. The Pig Bank, started with assistance from the NATIONAL COUNCIL OF NEGRO WOMEN, lent pregnant pigs to families who had room to keep them. After delivery, mother pigs were returned to the Pig Bank. Recipient families then gave pregnant pigs to other families. By the third year, after which records were no longer kept, three hundred families had been helped, and the program's net profit was three thousand new pigs.

Hamer was also instrumental in establishing a HEAD START program in Sunflower County and in bringing factory jobs to the area. So that employees could work and not worry about their children, these factory workers were provided on-site day care. Hamer repeatedly stated, "I'm sick and tired of being sick and tired," and her efforts to address social, political, and economic injustices were testimony to the strength of her feelings.

Awards

Hamer was recognized for her tireless efforts with the Voter's Registration and Fight for Freedom Award in 1963, the Noble Example of Womanhood Award and the Mary Church Terrell Award in 1969, and doctoral degrees from Shaw University, Tougaloo College, HOWARD UNIVERSITY, Columbia College in Chicago, and Morehouse College.

—*Emma T. Lucas*

See also: Civil rights and congressional legislation.

Suggested Readings:

Bramlett-Solomon, Sharon. "Civil Rights Vanguard in the Deep South: Newspaper Portrayal of Fannie Lou Hamer, 1964-1977." *Journalism Quarterly* 68 (Autumn, 1991): 515-521.

Davis, Marianna W., ed. *Civil Rights, Politics and Government, Education, Medicine, Science.* Vol. 2 in *Contributions of Black Women to America.* Columbia, S.C.: Kenday Press, 1982.

Hamlet, Janice D. "Fannie Lou Hamer: The Unquenchable Spirit of the Civil Rights Movement." *Journal of Black Studies* 26 (May, 1996): 560-576.

Jordan, June. *Fannie Lou Hamer.* New York: Thomas Y. Crowell, 1972.

Noble, Jeanne L. *Beautiful, Also, Are the Souls of My Black Sisters.* Englewood Cliffs, N.J.: Prentice-Hall, 1978.

Norton, Eleanor H. "Woman Who Changed the South." *Ms.* (July, 1977): 51.

Rubel, David. *Fannie Lou Hamer: From Sharecropping to Politics.* Englewood Cliffs, N.J.: Silver Burdett Press, 1990.

Hamilton, Charles Vernon (b. October 19, 1929, Muskogee, Oklahoma): Author, political scientist, educator, and adviser to civil rights organizations. Hamilton's books include *Black Power: The Politics of Liberation in America* (1967), coauthored with Stokely CARMICHAEL, *The Bench and the Ballot: Southern Federal Judges and Black Votes* (1973), and *Adam Clayton Powell, Jr.: The Political Biography of an American Dilemma* (1991). Hamilton taught at numerous universities and served as chair of the department of political science at Roosevelt University in CHICAGO, as vice president of the American Political Science Association, and as head of New York's Metropolitan Applied Research Center.

Hamilton, Virginia (b. March 13, 1936, Yellow Springs, Ohio): Novelist and children's book author. Virginia Esther Hamilton grew up in Yellow Springs, OHIO, on land that had been in her family since it was settled by her maternal grandfather, Levi Perry, an escaped slave. After completing high school, Hamilton went on to attend Antioch College and Ohio State University. Encouraged to pursue a writing career, she left college and moved to NEW YORK CITY. There, she met and married poet-anthropologist Arnold Adoff, with whom she had two children—Leigh and Levi.

After some fifteen years in New York, Hamilton moved back to Ohio and devoted her full attention to writing. When the manuscript for her first adult novel was rejected, she turned her energies toward writing for children and immediately found her niche. Hamilton's first book, *Zeely* (1967), won the Nancy Block Memorial Award and was cited as a notable children's book for that year by the American Library Association. Many of Hamilton's subsequent works also won prestigious awards and literary honors.

As a writer of works that appeal to adolescent readers, Hamilton helped CHILDREN'S LITERATURE break away from stereotypical depictions of African Americans by consistently portraying them as characters memorable for their intelligence and their ability to rise to challenges. Her works are also known for their richly imaginative plots, settings, and narrative styles. Her work falls into a variety of genres: realistic fiction such as *M. C. Higgins, the Great* (1974) and *The Planet of Junior Brown* (1971); science fiction and fantasy, as in the trilogy *Justice and Her Brothers* (1979), *Dustland* (1980), and *The Gathering* (1981); and mysteries, such as *The House of Dies Drear* (1968).

Hamilton's stories portray strong family ties while often including a child protagonist who is somewhat of a loner. Perhaps Hamilton's most popular novel is *M. C. Higgins, the*

Great, which received critical acclaim and earned distinction as the first book to win the Newbery Medal, the *Boston Globe* Horn Book Award, and the National Book Award. The novel tells the story of a young boy caught between his loyalty to his family and his fear at their seeming lack of concern over a dangerously unstable slag heap that threatens their home and their lives. Here, as in all of her works, Hamilton's black characters are resourceful, courageous, and persevering.

In addition to her interest in portraying African American characters and culture, Hamilton takes a special interest in American Indian culture, as shown in works such as *Arilla Sun Down* (1976). Incorporating elements of FOLKLORE and mythology in many of her works, she published anthologies of African American folktales such as *The People Could Fly* (1985), *In the Beginning* (1988), and *The Dark Way* (1990). *A Ring of Tricksters* (1997) consists of twelve animal trickster tales that show the linkage between African, West Indian, and African American culture.

Among Hamilton's books are biographies aimed at young readers, including works about Paul ROBESON and W. E. B. DU BOIS. In 1995 Hamilton was honored for her work with the Laura Ingalls Wilder Medal from the American Library Association. She also received the 1996 Coretta Scott KING Author Award for her 1995 book *Her Stories: African American Folktales, Fairy Tales, and True Tales*. Hamilton continued writing children's stories in the late 1990's, publishing *Second Cousins* in 1998 and *Bluish* in 1999.

Critics have praised Hamilton's interesting and complex characters. Some have argued that her sophisticated and somewhat experimental narrative styles make her works inaccessible to many young readers, while others counter that her inventiveness invites young readers to expand their imaginations. Regardless, many parents, teachers, and critics agree that Hamilton's large body of work helped push adolescent literature in new and challenging directions.

Hammer (Stanley Kirk Burrell; b. 1963, Oakland, California): RAP singer and dancer. Hammer was the youngest of seven children reared in a three-bedroom apartment in a government-aided building in Oakland. He spent much of his childhood at the Oakland Coliseum trying to catch glimpses of Athletics baseball games. Team owner Charlie Finley noticed him dancing in the parking lot and was so impressed with his demeanor that he offered him a job working as an errand boy in the team clubhouse and traveling on the road with the team as its official bat boy. Burrell was awarded the nickname "Little Hammer" by players who noted his resemblance to the legendary baseball player "Hammerin' Hank" AARON.

After graduating from high school, Hammer attended a local college to earn a degree in communications while trying to pursue his dream of becoming a professional baseball player and earning the chance to try out for the San Francisco Giants. Failing in these endeavors, he joined the U.S. Navy for a three-year enlistment, serving in CALIFORNIA and completing a six-month tour in Japan. After leaving the navy, Hammer organized a gospel rap duo called the Holy Ghost Boys and tried to interest record producers in signing the group. Although he was unsuccessful in this venture, Hammer convinced Oakland A's players Mike Davis and Dwayne Murphy to invest $40,000 in start-up capital and cosign a $125,000 bank loan to enable him to start his own record production company.

Hammer named the company Bust It Records and recorded his first single, "Ring 'Em," which he promoted and distributed himself. After releasing his second single, "Let's Get Started," Hammer worked with musician and producer Felton Pilate of the group Con Funk Shun to produce his first album, *Feel My Power* (1987). The record sold sixty thousand copies. An executive from Capitol Records saw Hammer at an Oakland music club and arranged for him to meet other Capitol executives in LOS ANGELES. In 1988 Hammer signed a multi-album contract under the name "M.C. Hammer" and received an advance of $750,000.

Capitol recouped its advance quickly by releasing a revised edition of M.C. Hammer's first album, newly titled *Let's Get It Started* (1988), which sold more than 1.5 million copies. Hammer's next single, "U Can't Touch This," contained a central musical hook that was sampled from Rick James's 1981 funk hit "Superfreak." James filed a lawsuit against Hammer over alleged infringement on his copyright that was settled out of court; James received cowriting credit. The single had sold more than five million copies by the end of 1990 and was adopted by the Detroit Pistons as its theme song during its 1989-1990 National Basketball Association championship season. His second album with Capitol, *Please Hammer Don't Hurt 'Em* (1990), earned Hammer three Grammy Awards in 1990 and had sold more than ten million copies by 1991.

Hammer helped revolutionize rap music by shifting the emphasis from verbal to visual effects with a stage show that eventually comprised fifteen dancers, twelve backup singers, seven musicians, and two deejays. With numerous commercial endorsements, his own Saturday morning cartoon series (*Hammerman*), and a $10-million joint-venture agreement with Capitol Records, Hammer became one of the most financially successful rap artists.

His third album with Capitol, *Too Legit to Quit*, was released in 1991 after he dropped "M.C." from his stage name. The album sold quite respectably, but sales disappointed executives at Capitol considering the huge media campaign that had promoted it and Hammer. Hammer and Capitol parted ways.

Hammer's 1994 album on Giant Records, *The Funky Headhunter*, saw him adopting a gangsta rap persona and turning his back on the relatively clean-cut image he had previously maintained. The album sold less than his previous efforts. Within two years he had left Giant. In early 1996 he and his wife filed for bankruptcy, having spent millions of dollars in only a few years.

Hampton, Fred (1948, Chicago, Illinois—December 4, 1969, Chicago, Illinois): Political activist. The chairman of the BLACK PANTHER PARTY in Illinois from November, 1968, to December, 1969, and a respected community organizer in CHICAGO, Fred Hampton was credited with helping to quell gang violence and forge a grass-roots coalition consisting of members of the white, African American, and Puerto Rican underclasses, groups historically at odds with one another. Hampton was shot to death by Chicago police in a predawn raid on a Black Panther apartment.

Youth, High School, and the NAACP
Fred Hampton grew up in Maywood, Illinois, a west Chicago suburb. In high school, he was an outstanding student, star athlete, and winner of a Junior Achievement Award. Upon graduation from high school in 1966, he entered Triton Junior College in River Grove, Illinois, as a prelaw student. He also became president of the Youth Council of the West Suburban Branch of the NATIONAL ASSOCIATION FOR THE ADVANCEMENT OF COLORED PEOPLE (NAACP) in Maywood. As youth director, Hampton built a comparatively large, racially integrated, and well-organized youth group of some five hundred members. Committed to nonviolent social change, Hampton led a drive for the establishment of neighborhood recreational facilities and improved schooling for Maywood's African American youth.

Fred Hampton was leader of the Illinois branch of the Black Panther Party until he was killed by police in late 1969. *(National Archives)*

The Black Panthers

Concurrent with Hampton's organizing efforts in Maywood on behalf of the NAACP was the national emergence of a militant African American political organization, the Black Panther Party for Self-Defense. Founded in OAKLAND, CALIFORNIA, in October, 1966, by Merritt College students Huey P. NEWTON and Bobby SEALE, the BLACK PANTHER PARTY (BPP) combined Marxist-Leninist ideology with the black liberation teachings of Frantz Fanon and MALCOLM X. The party advocated a ten-point "platform and program" that included such tenets as African American exemption from military service, political self-determination, full employment, decent housing and better schools, the retrying of all African American convicts by juries of their peers, and an end to white economic exploitation and police brutality.

Attracted to the Panther program, Hampton joined the party and moved to downtown Chicago, where he organized the Illinois chapter of the BPP in November of 1968. Over the next year, Hampton became an increasingly influential and militant leader. As he had already demonstrated in Maywood, Hampton possessed impressive organizational skills. He also understood that GHETTO life would remain desolate as long as it was marked by constant warfare among the various ethnic and racial groups that constituted the urban poor. Accordingly, in the early months of 1969, Hampton worked to form a "RAINBOW COALITION" by radicalizing Chicago's rival street gangs and conciliating them with one another. After numerous meetings with members of such groups as the Black Disciples and the Blackstone Rangers (African American gangs), the Latin Kings and the Young Lords (of mostly Puerto Rican extraction), and the Young Patriots (a North Side gang of white youths from Appalachia), Hampton was able to call a press conference in May to announce a truce among the warring groups and declare that "we're all one army."

A less dramatic but equally important aspect of the Black Panther Party's activities in Chicago (and nationally) was an emphasis on community services. Under Hampton's leadership, a free medical clinic was established, as well as an outlet of the Panthers' breakfast-for-children program, which won strong community support for the party by providing free breakfasts to African American schoolchildren in dozens of American cities.

Panther Relations with the SDS

Hampton also sought alliances with white radicals, especially members of Students for a Democratic Society (SDS), a revolutionary leftist group opposed not only to the VIETNAM WAR but also to the capitalist system in general. In a speech in April, 1969, Hampton noted that the Panther ten-point program was being changed because "we used the word 'white' when we should have used the word 'capitalist.'" Relations between the Chicago Panthers and the SDS were, however, rocky. When it held its annual convention at the Chicago Coliseum in mid-June, 1969, the SDS split into two ideologically opposed factions, Progressive Labor (PL) and the Third Worlders, or Weathermen.

Allied with the Panthers, the Weathermen expelled PL from the SDS and adopted a more desperate militancy, which it acted out on Chicago streets in early October by initiating violent clashes with police. These skirmishes, which came to be known as the "Days of Rage," were publicly denounced by Hampton as an "adventuristic" and politically self-defeating tactic. (Taunted by SDS leader Mark Rudd regarding the Panthers' unwillingness to join the fight, an angry Hampton knocked Rudd to the ground with a punch in the face.) As Hampton's fiery speeches made clear, he was not opposed to violence in self-defense, but he did object to gratuitous violence that worked against the larger goal, which was to form common cause with as many groups as possible.

The Panthers Under Siege
At its inception, the Black Panther Party defined itself in defiant—some would say threatening—terms: as an armed paramilitary organization with revolutionary aims. Hampton and other Chicago Panthers were openly and bitterly hostile to the (mostly white) police, whom they saw as agents of racial and class oppression. Likewise, the city youth gangs the Panthers allied themselves with had always had poor relations with the police, as did Chicago's African American community as a whole.

For their part, Mayor Richard J. Daley and Cook County State's Attorney Edward V. Hanrahan chose to characterize Hampton's Panther-led youth coalition in the worst possible light: not as a legitimate, albeit radical, political alliance but as nothing more than an alarming increase in gang criminality. With Daley's support, Hanrahan mounted an escalating campaign of harassment (including surveillance, arrests, and raids) against the Chicago Panthers and their allies under the rubric of an announced "War on Gangs." What resulted was a year of violence bordering on anarchy. In 1969 alone, eleven black youths from Chicago's South Side were killed in separate clashes with police. In that same year, a dozen Black Panthers and several policemen were either killed or wounded in shoot-outs, more than one hundred Panthers were arrested, and the Panther party headquarters at 2337 West Monroe Street was raided by police and FEDERAL BUREAU OF INVESTIGATION (FBI) agents on four separate occasions.

The Killing of Fred Hampton
The last of these raids, on Thursday, December 4, 1969, took the life of Fred Hampton. The raid began at about 4:45 A.M., when fourteen heavily armed police officers attached to the state's attorney's office arrived at the first floor of 2337 West Monroe to conduct a search for illegal weapons. According to the police version of events, as soon as they knocked at the door, the officers were shot at from within the apartment. Ten minutes of furious gunfire ensued, killing the twenty-one-year-old Hampton and twenty-two-year-old Mark Clark, a Panther leader from Peoria, Illinois.

Four other Chicago Panthers were seriously wounded: eighteen-year-old Ronald "Doc" Satchel was shot five times; seventeen-year-old Verlina Brewer was shot twice; Blair Anderson, eighteen, was shot three times; and Brenda Harris, nineteen, was shot twice. None of the Chicago policemen was shot, but two sustained minor injuries. In the aftermath, the state attorney's office insisted that the raid had been conducted properly and that the shooting had been started by the Panthers; however, a special commission of inquiry chaired by Roy WILKINS and Ramsey Clark investigated the incident and drew some disturbing conclusions. Extensive ballistic tests proved conclusively that there had been no shoot-out. Virtually all the more than one hundred recovered machine-gun and pistol slugs were traced to police weapons; only a single shot could be attributed to the Panthers. Furthermore, new evidence disclosed in a late 1970's civil suit brought by the raid's survivors revealed that Fred Hampton had been drugged with a large dose of sedatives by FBI informant William O'Neal the night before the raid. O'Neal had also provided police with a floor plan of the Panther apartment. Hampton, who never awoke during the shooting, died in bed from four gunshot wounds, two to the head, fired either through his bedroom wall or from within his room. At the very least, the lethal raid had been ill-conceived and carried out with astonishing recklessness; many critics accused the police of carrying out a "death-squad"-style assassination.

Whatever the exact truth about Fred Hampton's killing, his stature as a rising leader in the African American community was clearly attested by his funeral, which was attended by more than five thousand mourners. Eulogies were delivered by Ralph ABERNATHY, Martin Luther KING, Jr.'s successor as head of the SOUTHERN CHRISTIAN LEADERSHIP CONFERENCE (SCLC), and by Jesse JACKSON, who would popularize Hampton's rainbow coalition dream in the 1980's.

—Robert Niemi

Suggested Readings:

Cockburn, Alexander. "The Fate of the Panthers." *The Nation* (July 2, 1990): 6.

Newton, Michael. *Bitter Grain: Huey Newton and the Black Panther Party*. Los Angeles: Holloway House, 1991.

"Slain Panther Fred Hampton Honored by City of Chicago." *Jet* (December 10, 1990): 9.

When One of Us Falls. Chicago: Artists United, 1970.

Hampton, Lionel (b. April 12, 1913, Louisville, Kentucky): JAZZ musician. Hampton gained renown as a jazz vibraphonist. His first musical instrument was the snare drum, which he played as a schoolboy, and it was in marching bands that he began his musical life.

Years later, while playing in a band led by Les Hite, a group that for a time was fronted by Louis ARMSTRONG, Hampton began experimenting with the vibraphone, which is an amplified xylophone. He first recorded it in 1930, on "Memories of You," with Armstrong. Bandleader Benny Goodman hired Hampton in 1936, and he became one of the mainstays of

Vibraphonist Lionel Hampton performing at a jazz festival in New York's Carnegie Hall in 1989. *(AP/Wide World Photos)*

the Goodman organization, playing not only in the band but also with its various small combos, especially the Benny Goodman Quartet. After several years with Goodman, he formed his own band in 1941 and continued to lead it despite the changing taste in popular music, which soon began to focus more on smaller combos than on big bands.

During the 1960's, Hampton successfully toured with his band and was enthusiastically received in Europe and in Israel. In 1963 the band toured Japan, the Philippines, and Formosa, but the realities of the time determined Hampton's decision to disband the big band in 1965 and form a sextet, the Jazz Inner Circle. That group was composed of a trumpet, two saxophones, drums, and Hampton's vibraphones. This group was well received and played major jazz clubs throughout the

United States. Hampton continued to record and to appear at jazz festivals and other special events, in addition to his club dates. Hampton is best known for his use of the vibraphone as an effective instrument of jazz and for placing it securely and solidly with the other percussion instruments of the jazz ensemble. His recording of "Flying Home" (1942) remains a classic of the big band jazz era.

Hampton Institute: HISTORICALLY BLACK COLLEGE in Hampton, VIRGINIA. In 1868 General Samuel Armstrong bought the site of what had been the Butler School and established Hampton Institute. The school emphasized industrial skills that would help freedmen find work in the post-Reconstruction South. Booker T. WASHINGTON was a student at the institute and took some of its philosophy with him to establish TUSKEGEE INSTITUTE. Washington was among the many poor students attracted to Hampton by its programs and tuition-free education.

In 1962 Hampton president Jerome Holland launched a drive to raise $17 million for the institution. *(AP/Wide World Photos)*

Hancock, Herbie (Herbert Jeffrey; b. April 12, 1940, Chicago, Illinois): JAZZ pianist, composer, and fusion keyboardist. Hancock made his musical debut at the age of eleven, playing the first movement of a Wolfgang Mozart piano concerto with the Chicago Symphony Orchestra in a young people's concert. He played jazz, while still in high school, with a group he had formed. He became a regular performer in CHICAGO jazz clubs, playing with such greats as saxophonist Coleman HAWKINS and trumpeter Donald Byrd. He graduated in 1960 from Grinnell College, where he studied music and engineering. He moved to NEW YORK CITY, where he led his own group and began recording his own compositions. His first album, *Takin' Off*, was released on Blue Note in 1962. "Watermelon Man" (1963), a gospel-inspired tune, became an immediate hit. Another Hancock classic is the often-recorded "Maiden Voyage," from his 1965 album of the same name.

During the mid-1960's, in addition to his own work, Hancock played with the legendary Miles DAVIS quintet. The quintet specialized in a blend of blues and hard bop and in cultivating an interaction among members of the combo that relied on rhythmic and harmonic innovation. The classic 1960's Davis quintet was composed of Davis, Hancock, Wayne SHORTER, Ron Carter, and Tony Williams. Hancock continued playing with Davis as Davis pioneered fusion in the late 1960's; along with other keyboardists, he played electric piano on Davis's *Bitches Brew* (1969).

Hancock formed the Herbie Hancock sextet in 1969 to explore new textures and incorporate more electronics, including synthesizers, into his music. Some jazz critics and aficionados objected to what they considered Hancock's emphasis on electronic instruments and gimmickry at the expense of essential jazz elements, but Hancock followed his own musical instincts.

In 1973 he formed the four-member Headhunters group, which combined elements of jazz, rock, and African music with electronic instruments and gadgets. The Headhunters was one of the seminal fusion bands of the 1970's—all of which owed a debt to Davis's experiments in the late 1960's. The song "Chameleon," on the 1973 *Headhunters* album, based on a repeating synthesizer and bass pattern, became one of the best-known fusion pieces of the era.

From the late 1970's on, Hancock both pursued electronic-based music and performed and recorded straight-ahead jazz, as on the 1977 *V.S.O.P. Quintet* album. The V.S.O.P. quintet's personnel was essentially the Davis quintet of 1965 with Freddie Hubbard instead of Davis on trumpet. In 1983 Hancock's decidedly nonjazz album *Future Shock* included the Grammy Award-winning dance hit "Rockit." Among Hancock's releases in the 1990's were *The New Standard* (1996) and *Gershwin's World* (1998).

In the 1980's Hancock also wrote a number of film scores, winning an Academy Award for his jazz-oriented score for the film *'Round Midnight* (1986). As a composer intrigued by technological experimentation who made a number of forays into commercial genres of music such as disco, it is not surprising that Hancock's jazz origins are sometimes obscured. Yet echoes of jazz can almost always be heard even in his pop recordings and film sound tracks.

Handy, W. C. (November 16, 1873, Florence, Alabama—March 28, 1958, New York, New York): Composer. William Christopher Handy is widely considered the "father of the BLUES" because of his pioneering role in making accessible the folk blues of African Americans. He was encouraged by his parents, who had been slaves, to play sacred music. He was forbidden secular music, but he was allowed to study organ and even received some training in music theory. While in high school, he defied his parents and joined a local brass band, playing cornet, and sang with church groups as well as minstrel troups. He became an itinerant musician when he was eighteen, quickly earning a reputation as an outstanding trumpet player. He toured with his own bands, playing ragtime and MINSTREL MUSIC.

Handy and another musician, Harry Pace, created a music publishing company in 1914. The company, which was located in MEMPHIS, TENNESSEE, began issuing Handy's own compositions. With the publication of "St. Louis Blues" in 1914, Handy gained widespread rec-

W. C. Handy, "Father" of the St. Louis Blues, in 1949. *(AP/Wide World Photos)*

Hansberry, Lorraine (May 19, 1930, Chicago, Illinois—January 12, 1965, New York, New York): Playwright. Although the work of black playwrights had previously been produced in the American THEATER, the modern black American theater, according to most experts, began with the 1959 Broadway production of Lorraine Hansberry's *A Raisin in the Sun*, the first play by a black playwright to win the distinguished New York Drama Critics Circle Award. Yet the early promise of this young black female playwright, established by her brilliant first play, remained unfulfilled by the time of her untimely death at the age of thirty-four.

ognition. His songs introduced folk blues, a type of blues distinct from the more familiar spirituals and work songs. Many of his songs were later recorded by his Memphis group.

The publishing company moved to NEW YORK CITY, where it led the field in introducing the music of African American songwriters to the public. In addition to promoting their music through publishing, Handy frequently sponsored concerts, such as one in 1928 in New York's Carnegie Hall in which he presented a cross section of African American music, from work songs to sophisticated orchestral compositions.

Despite an accident in 1943 that left him blind, Handy never stopped his efforts on behalf of the music of his people. In addition to his active participation in promotion, he engaged in important research on African American music. He published *Negro Authors and Composers of the United States* (1935) and *Unsung Americans Sung* (1944), along with books of music and *Father of the Blues: An Autobiography* (1941). Nat "King" COLE portrayed Handy in the film *St. Louis Blues* (1958).

Background

Lorraine Hansberry was one of four children born to Carl Augustus and Nannie Perry Hansberry. Lorraine's parents, both of whom came from well-educated southern families, met in CHICAGO, where Carl Hansberry displayed his gift for finance, opening his own bank and making shrewd real-estate investments. Lorraine grew up in an affluent home, surrounded by the privileges of wealth, a strong family unit, and a sense of dignity, pride, and self-worth. One significant episode of her childhood occurred when her father bought a home in an all-white neighborhood; white neighbors protested against the presence of the black family, an event that likely provided the germ for one of the conflicts in *A Raisin in the Sun*. In high school, Hansberry excelled in such subjects as English and history and displayed a propensity for literature by immersing herself in reading and writing free verse; she also won the school's literary prize by writing a story about football, even though she knew little about the game. The Hansberry home was often visited by such distinguished guests as W. E. B. Du Bois, Langston Hughes, Duke Ellington, Paul Robeson, and William Leo Hansberry, her uncle, a noted scholar of African history at Howard University.

Education and Early Writing Career

After her graduation from high school in 1948, Hansberry attended the University of Wisconsin for two years. She studied art, English, and stage design at Wisconsin before moving to New York City, where she attended the New School for Social Research. She also worked for Robeson's *Freedom* magazine, becoming associate editor in 1952, and became involved in a number of causes that championed black rights. For one year, she studied with Du Bois at the Jefferson School of Social Science in New York and gained a greater awareness and understanding of African culture. During her five-year tenure with *Freedom*, she wrote at least twenty-two articles dealing with Africa, women, and social issues; she also wrote several reviews, and the experience aided her intellectual growth and planted the seeds for many ideas that came to fruition in her later creative work.

Playwright

In 1953 Hansberry married Robert Nemiroff, whom she had met on a picket line. The following year, she wrote a dramatic script, "Pulse of the Peoples: A Cultural Salute to Paul Robeson," for a Harlem rally. In 1956 she began work on *A Raisin in the Sun*, which dramatizes the experiences of a poor black family living in a Chicago ghetto. After trial performances in New Haven, Philadelphia, and Chicago, *A Raisin in the Sun* opened in New York on March 11, 1959, on Broadway. The production at the Barrymore Theatre, which was directed by Lloyd Richards and starred Sidney Poitier, Diana Sands, Ruby Dee, and Claudia

McNeil, was a huge success. When Hansberry received the New York Drama Critics Circle Award, she became, at the age of twenty-nine, the youngest playwright, the fifth woman, and the first black to receive the honor; her play was selected over other plays by Tennessee Williams, Eugene O'Neill, and Archibald MacLeish. When *A Raisin in the Sun* was made into a film, it won the Cannes Film Festival Award in 1961.

During the few remaining years of her life, Lorraine Hansberry began a number of projects, not all of which reached publication or production. She wrote a script for the NBC television network, *The Drinking Gourd*, which was never produced. She also completed in 1962 a script entitled *What Use Are Flowers?* and rewrote it as *Les Blancs* for the stage. Other

Playwright Lorraine Hansberry in 1959. *(Library of Congress)*

works remained unfinished, such as her novel *All the Dark and Beautiful Warriors*, a number of short stories from her earlier years of writing, and a dramatic work about TOUSSAINT-L'OUVERTURE.

Hansberry's last complete stage work was *The Sign in Sidney Brustein's Window*, which she began, finished, and attended rehearsals of while battling cancer that had been detected in early 1963. A rambling, impressionistic play revolving around a Greenwich Village intellectual and his role in a local political campaign, *The Sign in Sidney Brustein's Window* opened on Broadway on October 15, 1964, at the Longacre Theatre; the production starred Gabriel Dell, Ben Aliza, Rita Moreno, and Alice Ghostley. After an unenthusiastic critical reception, many important persons in theater and film came to the aid of the play, and an advertisement in *The New York Times* urging the public to see it was signed by such luminaries as James BALDWIN, Sammy DAVIS, Jr., Ossie DAVIS, Ruby Dee, Alan Alda, Anne Bancroft, Mel Brooks, and Shelley Winters.

Lorraine Hansberry died on January 12, 1965; her funeral was attended by more than six hundred admirers, including Paul Robeson, who sang, and MALCOLM X. At the ceremony, a message was read from Martin Luther KING, Jr. Hansberry was buried in Bethel Cemetery at Croton-on-Hudson, New York.

Posthumous Works

As Hansberry's literary executor, Robert Nemiroff assembled and edited from her unpublished papers *To Be Young, Gifted, and Black* and produced it at the Cherry Lane Theatre in New York in 1969; the play toured nationally from 1970 to 1972. Nemiroff also expanded the work into a full-length biography with the same title. *Les Blancs* was presented on Broadway in 1970, and in 1972, Nemiroff edited and published *Les Blancs: The Collected Last Plays of Lorraine Hansberry*.

—*Tony J. Stafford*

Suggested Readings:

Carter, Steven R. *Hansberry's Drama: Commitment amid Complexity*. Urbana: University of Illinois Press, 1991.

Cheney, Anne. *Lorraine Hansberry*. Boston: Twayne, 1984.

Cherry, Gwendolyn. *Portraits in Color*. New York: Pageant Press, 1962.

Davis, Arthur P. *From the Dark Tower*. Washington, D.C.: Howard University Press, 1974.

Gavin, Christy. *African American Women Playwrights: A Research Guide*. New York: Garland, 1999.

Keppel, Ben. *The Work of Democracy: Ralph Bunche, Kenneth B. Clark, Lorraine Hansberry, and the Cultural Politics of Race*. Cambridge, Mass.: Harvard University Press, 1995.

Leeson, Richard M. *Lorraine Hansberry: A Research and Production Sourcebook*. Westport, Conn.: Greenwood Press, 1997.

Nemiroff, Robert. *Portrait of a Play*. New York: New American Library, 1966.

_____. *To Be Young, Gifted, and Black*. Englewood Cliffs, N.J.: Prentice-Hall, 1969.

Toppin, Edgar A. *A Biographical History of Blacks in America Since 1528*. New York: McKay, 1971.

Harding, Vincent (b. July 25, 1931, New York, New York): Historian, clergyman, and theologian. Harding was educated at City College in New York and received his B.A. in 1952. He eventually received an M.S. from Columbia University in 1953 before going to study at the University of Chicago, where he earned an M.A. in 1956 and a Ph.D. in 1965, both in history.

During the late 1950's and early 1960's, Harding and his wife, Rosemarie Freeney Harding, were extremely active in the CIVIL RIGHTS movement. They were key coworkers with Martin Luther KING, Jr., and worked throughout the South. Harding also worked as a lay pastor in the Seventh-day Adventist

Vincent Harding in 1969. *(AP/Wide World Photos)*

and Mennonite Churches. From 1965 to 1969, he was chair of sociology and history at SPELMAN COLLEGE. He left that position to become the director of the Institute of the Black World at the Martin Luther King Memorial Center in ATLANTA, GEORGIA. In 1981 Harding became professor of religion and social transformation at the Iliff School of Theology, part of the University of Denver. He also continued his involvement with the King Center and in 1981 began serving as chair of its board.

Harding is known as an outstanding historian of African American life. His numerous books include *The Other American Revolution* (1980), *There Is a River: The Black Struggle for Freedom in America* (1981), and *Hope and History: Why We Must Share the Story of the Movement* (1990). Harding's work as a historian is tied intimately to his experiences in the Civil Rights movement. He asserts that the United States has never come to terms fully with the implications of that revolution. As a political and social commentator, Harding always advocated the serious consideration of race as a factor in American life. He was especially well known for his work as chair of the *Black Heritage* series for public television. He also served as senior adviser to *Eyes on the Prize: America's Civil Rights Years*, another public television endeavor. With his wife, Harding created a series of workshops on the relationship between spirituality and social responsibility.

Hare, Nathan (b. April 9, 1934, Slick, Oklahoma): Scholar and writer. Nathan Hare became well known as an articulate champion of African American rights and as a major leader of the BLACK STUDIES movement. Hare's controversial views have sparked much debate, and he has been viewed by many as a stormy petrel. In the 1960's, Hare was a controversial faculty member at HOWARD UNIVERSITY and at San Francisco State College. Departing from both universities, Hare began publication of *The Black Scholar*, a journal of black studies and research. Using the forums of the journal, several books, and articles in the news media, Hare devoted the 1970's and 1980's to developing the sociological and ethical concepts he believed to be most relevant to the needs of blacks. Among his many goals was finding the solutions to black social problems; Hare proposed that cures for such ills can be best accomplished by a coming together of blacks engineered by a black middle class cleansed of materialism and a desire for white approval. He viewed "true" black scholars as essential leaders in such efforts.

Early Life and Education
Nathan Hare was the son of a sharecropper, Seddie H. Hare, and Tishia (Davis) Hare. Hare's serious academic career began with study at Langston University, a black college in OKLAHOMA. In 1954 Hare received the first

of his several university degrees, a bachelor of arts degree in education, from Langston University. Next, he obtained a master of arts in 1957 and a doctorate in 1962 in sociology from the University of Chicago. During his graduate school years, Hare married Julie (Reed) Hare, a public-relations specialist.

Academic Career

In 1961 Hare began a promising academic career at Howard University in WASHINGTON, D.C., as an instructor in sociology. In 1964 Hare was promoted to the rank of assistant professor of sociology. In 1967, however, he

Nathan Hare in early 1969, during the midst of his troubles at San Francisco State College. *(AP/Wide World Photos)*

left Howard after disputes over his controversial views about the draft and the VIETNAM WAR and his public criticism of the university administration. In 1968 Hare moved to San Francisco State College, where he chaired the school's innovative black studies department. Once again at loggerheads with a university administration, Hare ended his affiliation with San Francisco State in 1969.

Remaining in San Francisco, Hare went back to school, earned a doctorate in psychology (1975) at the California School of Professional Psychology, and began publishing *The Black Scholar*. Hare developed many interests; in 1977 he began a private psychology practice, and in 1982 he assumed the presidency and board chairmanship of the Black Think Tank. Hare won public acclaim, honors, and memberships in several learned societies for his endeavors. He was granted the "Black Is Beautiful" citation (1968), the 1983 National Award of the National Council on Black Studies, and memberships in the American Sociological Association and the American Psychological Association.

Hare became a prolific writer on black social issues. His books include *The Endangered Black Family: Coping with the Unisexualization and Coming Extinction of the Black Race* (1984) and *Bringing the Black Boy to Manhood: The Passage* (1987); his credits also include writing for such magazines and professional journals as *Crime and Delinquency*, EBONY, the *Journal of Black Education*, *Liberator*, *Newsweek*, *Phylon*, *Ramparts*, *Saturday Review*, *Social Forces*, *The Black Law Journal*, THE NEGRO HISTORY BULLETIN, *The Saturday Evening Post*, and *U.S. News and World Report*.

Hare's work emphasizes the need for blacks everywhere to recognize the power of traditional black ideas and mores. It is essential, according to Hare, for black scholars to rethink European concepts of social and moral issues and to replace them with new solutions based on the black ethos.

Critique of the Black Middle Class

In an essay in *Black Writers of America: A Comprehensive Anthology* (1972), edited by Richard Barksdale and Kenneth Kinnamon, Hare comments that the genuine intellectual possesses the desire to tell the truth and the courage to do so. Hare is especially critical of the members of the black middle class, whom he refers to as "black Anglo-Saxons." He feels that many such blacks have shed black values and mores and replaced them with values assimilated from a white culture that has become "increasingly corrupt and bloody, with no clear future."

Hare states that, once free of its "unbridled pursuit of materialism and the all-engulfing frenzy for White approval and acceptance," the black middle class will become able to solve the problems that plague blacks and lead them to a better life. The problems that Hare sees as solvable by an adequately enlightened black middle class include racial violence, juvenile delinquency, and poor school performance by black students. The solution of these problems, he claims, will require the leadership of black intellectuals who will "demolish the antisocial attitudes of Ivory-Towerism."

Hare claimed that the American black middle class is in a precarious and ambiguous position; members of the black middle class, he says, are characterized by the public as pretentious, conspicuous consumers and, at the same time, are viewed as black on the surface and white inside. Hare also stated that such blacks, though aware of their African lineage, often seem to be "looked down on, even by themselves, for this lineage."

He also takes black nationalists to task for "seeking safety in the faraway past." Hare suggests that the black middle class do what they "know has to be done" about black problems: "Come together, return to our own people, live with them, learn from the wisdom of a long-suffering and creative race."

—*Sanford S. Singer*

See also: Class structure; Intellectuals and scholars.

Suggested Readings:

Barksdale, Richard, and Kenneth Kinnamon, eds. *Black Writers of America: A Comprehensive Anthology.* New York: Macmillan, 1972.

Cruse, Harold. *The Crisis of the Black Intellectual.* New York: Quill, 1984.

Ford, Nick A. *Black Studies: Threat or Challenge?* Port Washington, N.Y.: Kennikat Press, 1973.

Hare, Nathan. "Is the Black Middle Class Blowing It? . . . Yes!" *Ebony* (August, 1987) 85-86.

Hare, Nathan, and Julia Hare. *The Hare Plan to Overhaul the Public Schools and Educate Every Black Man, Woman, and Child.* San Francisco, Calif.: The Black Think Tank, 1991.

Sammons, Vivian O. *Blacks in Science and Medicine.* New York: Hemisphere, 1990.

Harlem: Community in the Manhattan borough of NEW YORK CITY, on the northern end of Manhattan Island. Harlem is the largest, most compact African American community in the United States. A small group of African Americans settled there around 1900. The area started to become a black enclave between 1905 and 1920, as whites moved out and poor African Americans moved in. By 1920 more than one-quarter million black people lived in Harlem.

Harlem came to represent both the best and the worst of the United States. All manner of social ills were caused by POVERTY, overcrowding, and crime. The district, however, saw a flowering of African American culture, especially LITERATURE, beginning in the 1920's.

This development, first known as the New Negro Movement, is more commonly called the HARLEM RENAISSANCE. The renaissance involved a change in the nature of art, so that instead of imitating white artists, African Americans explored their own lives and culture, establishing racial pride in the process. The Great Depression led to dispersion of Harlem's artists, ending the renaissance period.

The area, which has ill-defined borders, began deteriorating further in its physical structures. As the costs of rehabilitation and complying with city codes increased, buildings were abandoned and rental values fell. This led to a cycle of falling property values and declining economic characteristics. In the 1970's, private community organizations and New York City's administration began taking measures to arrest the cycle, including providing public housing, community-controlled schools, and better medical facilities.

Harlem is often used as a synonym for New York City's African American population. This is inappropriate, both because the Afri-can American population has spread to other parts of the city—most notably Brooklyn—and because other minority groups have moved into the Harlem district.

Harlem Globetrotters: Professional exhibition BASKETBALL team. Their games mix skillful and spectacular basketball with comic and clownish antics. Some individual members of the team have been dubbed as the "World's Greatest Dribbler" and the "Clown Prince of Basketball."

The team was formed in 1927 in CHICAGO, ILLINOIS, by the sports promoter and tailor Abe Saperstein, when he took over the management of a team known as the Savoy Big Five. His new team lacked a hometown base and went on playing tours with Saperstein carrying the entire team in his car. Because of these continuous tours and the desire to give spectators a feeling that the team had been around for a long time, Saperstein renamed the team the Harlem Globetrotters.

The physical deterioration of Harlem is evident in this view of 117th Street in 1957. *(AP/Wide World Photos)*

The team originally played serious basketball against local teams. Later, team members began introducing elements of slapstick comedy, while still playing against opponents who meant to win. Sometimes, the comedy was an attempt to calm hostile local fans who wanted their teams to win, and to avoid embarrassing those teams with overwhelming defeats. The Globetrotters began touring with their own opposing team, and games became a competition between those straight men, the butt of the humor, and the Globetrotters, who

Meadowlark Lemon (left) and Freddie Neal demonstrate their ballhandling skills in downtown Chicago in 1967. *(AP/ Wide World Photos)*

flawlessly executed their jokes and play and were destined to win. Even the game officials were not immune to the pranks of the players.

The Globetrotters have traveled to many countries and to every continent to play their unique brand of basketball. Basketball stars such as Lynette Woodard and Wilt CHAMBERLAIN have played for the team, as well as more comedic players such as Meadowlark Lemon and Reece "Goose" Tatum. The team has had several white players, but its composition has always been predominantly African American.

Harlem Renaissance: The Harlem Renaissance of the 1920's was a blossoming of African American LITERATURE, MUSIC, entertainment, and VISUAL ARTS. It was also an era in which a number of social and political organizations were formed in HARLEM, New York, in an effort to improve the circumstances of African Americans.

As the largest metropolis of black life in the urban North, Harlem was one of the focal points of black social, political, and cultural activities. As a result of demographic shifts in NEW YORK CITY, Harlem became the mecca of black culture; it attracted black creative artists and intellectuals from other areas of the United States and the WEST INDIES. For the most part, literary artists have been recognized as the most prominent exponents of black culture during the Harlem Renaissance. They voiced the concerns of the "New Negro," including increased racial consciousness, social protest, and recognition of an AFRICAN HERITAGE. The cultural developments of the Harlem Renaissance were paralleled by similar movements in PHILADELPHIA, WASHINGTON, D.C., and other cities; the Harlem Renaissance thus symbolized the broader upsurge of black consciousness in the United States.

Various social factors led to the rise of Harlem as a cultural center: the migration of African Americans from the rural South to the urban North in the opening decades of the twentieth century, growing political protest, and an increase in the number of educated African Americans. The popularity of black creative expression in the arts coupled with the performance opportunities Harlem offered in its theaters, ballrooms, and nightclubs to make Harlem a center of the PERFORMING ARTS. A wide variety of black men and women contributed to the Harlem Renaissance as political leaders, entrepreneurs, and creative artists.

Social Background
Originally populated by white residents, at the beginning of the twentieth-century Harlem gradually became a community with a

predominantly African American population as a result of fluctuations in the local rental market. A large number of housing developments had been constructed in Harlem during the early 1900's in expectation of an influx of white residents from other areas of New York City. By the second decade of the 1900's, this influx did not materialize, and realtors began renting to various classes of African Americans, who represented a population on the rise.

One of the important black real-estate speculators of the early 1900's was Philip A. Payton, Jr., whose Afro-American Realty Company was responsible for a large influx of blacks into Harlem. Many blacks residing in areas of downtown Manhattan took advantage of the improved housing in Harlem. Among the first African Americans to come to Harlem after World War I were prosperous members of the middle class who resided in the "Striver's Row" area. Concurrently, the white population of Harlem was decreasing.

By 1919 black Harlem, the largest African American community in the country, was geographically defined by the Harlem River on the east, Eighth Avenue on the west, 125th Street on the south, and 145th Street on the north. By the end of the 1920's, the affluent Sugar Hill district, extending to the 155th Street area, was also populated by people of African descent. The majority of black people in Harlem, however, resided in less-affluent neighborhoods.

The Harlem community became the center for scores of fraternal organizations and social clubs and for black churches, such as the ABYSSINIAN BAPTIST CHURCH led by Adam Clayton POWELL, Sr. Harlem also developed entrepreneurs and supporters of the arts such as A'Lelia Walker, the daughter of Madame C. J. WALKER, who had become a millionaire through her production of beauty products for black women. Casper Holstein, whose profits were gained through gambling and real estate,

was another influential Harlemite who supported literary artists.

Political Activities

With the end of World War I and the return of black soldiers from Europe, political awareness was on the increase in Harlem, fueled by the continued lynching and racial persecution of African Americans. In the early 1920's, "race leaders" came to the foreground and developed journals to express their political positions. Asa Philip RANDOLPH, organizer of the BROTHERHOOD OF SLEEPING CAR PORTERS, Marcus GARVEY, the Jamaican-born founder of the UNIVERSAL NEGRO IMPROVEMENT ASSOCIATION (UNIA), and W. E. B. DU BOIS, the Harvard-trained founder of the NATIONAL ASSOCIATION FOR THE ADVANCEMENT OF COLORED PEOPLE (NAACP), represented the diversity of political organizations in Harlem.

Randolph, along with Chandler Owen, had founded *The Messenger*, a socialist journal that advocated the unity of black workers. Garvey, who had arrived in the United States in 1916, promoted BLACK NATIONALISM through his magazine THE NEGRO WORLD and sought to unify all people of African descent. Du Bois's THE CRISIS promoted the philosophy of integration, and Charles S. JOHNSON's *Opportunity*, sponsored by the NATIONAL URBAN LEAGUE, encouraged literary activities.

These organizations promoted differing strategies for black ascendancy and were often rivals for black constituencies. At the same time, black newspapers such as THE NEW YORK AGE and the AMSTERDAM NEWS published articles relevant to the Harlem community.

Literature

In the 1920's, Harlem also became a focal point for the literary activities of black writers, many of whom migrated to Harlem to further their activities as poets, novelists, playwrights, or journalists. Writers of the Harlem Renaissance can be grouped into two categories: old-guard writers, such as James Weldon JOHNSON and Du Bois, and a prominent younger literary movement that included poets Langston HUGHES, Countée CULLEN; and Claude MCKAY; novelist Jessie Redmon FAUSET; and folklorist Zora Neale HURSTON. Other notable Harlem Renaissance writers were Arna BONTEMPS, Sterling BROWN, Rudolph FISHER, Nella LARSEN, George SCHUYLER, Wallace THURMAN, Jean TOOMER, Eric WALROND, and poets Gwendolyn Bennett, Helene Johnson, and Georgia JOHNSON. Georgia Johnson's Washington, D.C., home was often a gathering place for Harlem Renaissance writers, as were A'Lelia Walker's "Dark Tower" in Harlem and the Civic Club in downtown Manhattan.

The growth of Harlem Renaissance literature was assisted by key publications and journals such as *The Crisis, Opportunity, The Messenger, The Liberator,* and *Survey Graphic,* the March, 1925, edition of which was entitled "Harlem: Mecca of the New Negro." The short-lived *Fire!!,* a journal launched by Richard Bruce Nugent and others, was the voice of the younger writers and artists. In 1925 Alain LOCKE, a HOWARD UNIVERSITY professor of philosophy, published *The New Negro: An Interpretation,* which examined black achievement in the arts. Harlem literary artists were aided by white patrons such as Carl Van Vechten, Charlotte Osgood Mason, Joel Spingarn, and Julius Rosenwald. In addition, bibliophile Arthur SCHOMBURG's collection of

Painter Palmer Hayden's *Baptizin' Day. (National Archives)*

materials related to black culture, housed at the 135th Street branch of the New York Public Library, provided a base for scholarly research.

Publishing opportunities existed through the publishing houses of Alfred A. Knopf, Albert Boni, and others seeking black writers during the period when "Negro" writing was in vogue. Poetry collections were among the first works to be published. James Weldon Johnson's *The Book of American Negro Poetry* (1922) anthologized poets of the earlier generation. Claude McKay's *Harlem Shadows* (1922), Countée Cullen's *Color* (1925), and Langston Hughes's *The Weary Blues* (1926), which demonstrated Hughes's blues poetry, were significant poetic works. Jean Toomer's *Cane* (1923), an experimental poetic prose work, received substantial critical attention. Jessie Fauset's *There Is Confusion* (1924), the first published Harlem Renaissance novel by a black woman, investigated the theme of "color," as did Rudolph Fisher's novel *The Walls of Jericho* (1928).

Music, Entertainment, and the Performing Arts
Harlem also became a center for musical entertainment. Whites ventured from downtown to Harlem's numerous uptown nightclubs, ballrooms, and theaters. The COTTON CLUB, Barron's, and SMALLS' PARADISE were among the more prominent Harlem nightclubs; other night spots included the famous APOLLO THEATER as well as the SAVOY BALLROOM, the Renaissance Casino, the Rockland Palace, and the Lincoln and Lafayette Theaters.

Jazz was performed by numerous ensembles, including such artists as Fats WALLER, Mamie SMITH, Fletcher Henderson, Louis ARMSTRONG, and Duke ELLINGTON. Black musical artists such as Roland HAYES and Paul ROBESON performed in the European classical tradition. Noble Sissle and Eubie BLAKE were notables on the musical stage, as were Fredi

Sculptor Meta Vaux Fuller's *Dark Hero*. (National Archives)

WASHINGTON, Josephine BAKER, and Florence MILLS. Blues singer Bessie SMITH was also active in Harlem during the 1920's.

The Visual Arts
Contributors to the visual arts of the Harlem Renaissance included painters Aaron DOUGLAS, Palmer HAYDEN, William H. JOHNSON, and Archibald MOTLEY and sculptors Richmond BARTHÉ, Meta Warrick FULLER, and Augusta SAVAGE. These artists incorporated black motifs and images in their works. In photography, James VAN DER ZEE was the best-known recorder of Harlem life. Like their contemporaries in literature and the performing arts, the visual artists of the Harlem Renaissance were expressive of the social and cultural developments of the era.

—*Joseph McLaren*
See also: Schomburg Center for Research in Black Culture.

Suggested Readings:

Bloom, Harold, ed. *Black American Poets and Dramatists of the Harlem Renaissance.* New York: Chelsea House, 1995.

Coleman, Leon. *Carl Van Vechten and the Harlem Renaissance: A Critical Assessment.* New York: Garland, 1998.

Hutchinson, George. *The Harlem Renaissance in Black and White.* Cambridge, Mass.: The Belknap Press of Harvard University Press, 1995.

Kramer, Victor A., and Robert A. Russ, eds. *Harlem Renaissance Re-examined.* Rev. ed. Troy, N.Y.: Whitson, 1997.

Lewis, David L. *When Harlem Was in Vogue.* New York: Alfred A. Knopf, 1981.

Locke, Alain, ed. *The New Negro: An Interpretation.* New York: A. and C. Boni, 1925. Reprint. New York: Atheneum, 1968.

Rodgers, Marie E. *The Harlem Renaissance: An Annotated Reference Guide for Student Research.* Englewood, Colo.: Libraries Unlimited, 1998.

Wall, Cheryl A. *Women of the Harlem Renaissance.* Bloomington: Indiana University Press, 1995.

Wintz, Cary D., ed. *Black Writers Interpret the Harlem Renaissance.* New York: Garland, 1996.

_____. *The Critics and the Harlem Renaissance.* New York: Garland, 1996.

_____. *The Emergence of the Harlem Renaissance.* New York: Garland, 1996.

Harlem Rens: Professional BASKETBALL club, formally known as the Harlem Renaissance. An avid basketball fan, Harlemite Robert J. Douglas was distressed by the decline of competitive amateur play in the early 1920's and thought a professional team might capture fans' interest. Appointing himself team manager, he organized the Rens in October of 1923. The team name is a product of circumstance: Needing a home court, Douglas approached the management of the newly built Renaissance Casino and offered to incorporate "Renaissance" into the team name in exchange for the use of floor space.

For seventeen years, the Renaissance players treated fans in NEW YORK CITY and on the road as far west as WYOMING to their playing skills, winning 1,588 games and losing 239. In 1939 the team won 112 games and lost only 7, clinching the world's professional title and a $1,000 purse on March 28 in CHICAGO.

Harlem riots: Extensive rioting occurred in the HARLEM district of NEW YORK CITY in 1935, 1943, and 1964. More than any other black community, Harlem has symbolized both the potential and the agony of the great black northward migration of the early twentieth

Harlem's 1935 riot left hundreds of stores wrecked. *(AP/Wide World Photos)*

century. Harlem is the most widely publicized black community in the United States, both for its artistic and social achievements and for the overwhelming poverty which increasingly afflicted residents throughout the twentieth century.

In both the 1935 and 1943 Harlem riots, African Americans destroyed property and looted buildings. The first major riot occurred at the height of the Depression, in 1935, when hundreds of thousands of African Americans across the country could not find work. Living conditions were so poor that life had become a battle for survival. In contrast, the 1943 riot grew out of a climate of white racial intolerance. Black soldiers returning from WORLD WAR II were subjected to racial insults on numerous occasions. The precipitating event for the 1943 riot was the shooting of a black soldier in a Harlem hotel lobby by a white police officer.

The 1964 Harlem riot was a protest triggered by discrimination against African Americans. In the months prior to the riot, a sense of collective injustice had grown. Rent strikes, rat protests, and subway violence preceded the collective event. The precipitating incident occurred when a white off-duty police officer shot and killed a black teenager in a white New York district called Yorkville. Disturbances in Yorkville were calmed easily, but violence erupted when news of the incident spread to Harlem. The Harlem riot of 1964 lasted for one week and resulted in one death and 141 serious injuries. Paralleling the riots of 1935 and 1943, looting and property damage were primary responses of rioters.

See also: Race riots; Racial discrimination.

Harlem Six: Defendants in a murder case. The Harlem Six were a group of male African American youngsters who were indicted for the knife-slaying of Margit Sugar during a robbery attempt on April 29, 1964, in HARLEM,

New York. Frank, the victim's husband, was also seriously injured during the robbery of the couple's used-clothing store. The youngsters, ranging in age from seventeen to nineteen, were Wallace Baker, William Craig, Daniel Hamm, Ronald Felder, Robert Rice, and Walter Thomas.

The genesis of this case was a seemingly unrelated melee known as the "fruit stand incident" that occurred on April 17, 1964. A group of adolescents, running down Lenox Avenue in Harlem, tipped over a bushel of fruit at a fruit stand. As several of them stopped to pick up the fruit and others tossed the fruit around, the alarmed fruit stand owner called the police. The police came, with guns drawn and nightsticks raised, and began to beat the children. Alarmed passersby, Hamm and Baker in particular, rushed to the children's defense and were themselves beaten. On April 29, following the Margit Sugar murder, Hamm, Baker, and several of their friends were part of a police roundup of black men. They subsequently were indicted for the murder.

The controversy and hysteria surrounding the case were engendered in part by the media. The media alleged that the youngsters, by now dubbed the Harlem Six, were members of the Blood Brothers, an antiwhite hate group that had targeted for annihilation not only the Sugars but also the police and other whites. Supporters of the youngsters, including the Charter Group for the Pledge of Conscience, the Harlem Youth Federation, the Harlem Progressive Labor Movement, and the NATIONAL ASSOCIATION FOR THE ADVANCEMENT OF COLORED PEOPLE (NAACP), demanded that Junius Griffin, the feature writer for *The New York Times* who had written several articles on the Blood Brothers, produce evidence of these allegations. Griffin subsequently was fired when he could not offer any documentary evidence to substantiate the gang's existence. Additional support for the youngsters came from a book, *The Torture of Mothers* (1965), written by Truman Nelson. It gave an account of the events from the youngsters' and their parents' point of view. Unable to find a publisher, Nelson published the book on his own with Garrison Press and it circulated in literary circles.

The mainstay of District Attorney Frank S. Hogan's case was the chief prosecution witness, Robert Barnes, Jr. He claimed to have been a member of the "Blood Brothers" and to have planned the Sugar murder, but he could not be present at the trial. Primarily on the basis of Barnes's testimony, the Harlem Six were convicted of conspiracy in 1965 at their first trial. The verdict subsequently was overturned on appeal because of constitutional violations. Separate trials were then ordered for two of the defendants, Robert Rice and Daniel Hamm. In 1970 Rice was convicted of the actual slaying of Sugar and was sentenced to forty years to life. Hamm pleaded guilty to manslaughter and was sentenced to fifteen to thirty-five years. He became eligible for parole in 1973. The remaining members, then called the Harlem Four, went through second and third trials, both of which ended in hung juries. The third trial ended in January, 1972, with the jury voting seven to five for acquittal. After serving eight years in prison, the Harlem Four were released on bail while District Attorney Hogan considered asking for yet another trial.

In July, 1972, with a fourth trial imminent, Barnes recanted his testimony in a thirty-eight-page affidavit, stating that he had fabricated his story under police intimidation. Defense attorneys William Kunstler and Lewis Steele believed that there was no longer a need for a fourth trial, since much of the prosecution's case hinged upon Barnes's testimony. On April 4, 1973, the Harlem Four pleaded guilty to manslaughter in return for suspended sentences. In an unusual move, New York State supreme court justice Jacob Grumet granted a certificate of relief from disability for the four men that restored their right to vote, hold public employment, and have driver's licenses, in effect restoring their rights of citizenship.

Harney, Ben (Benjamin Robertson; March 1, 1871, Middleboro, Kentucky—March 1, 1938, Philadelphia, Pennsylvania): RAGTIME pianist. Harney, who was often believed to be white, is credited with introducing ragtime to New York, where he arrived in 1896. His popularity in vaudeville theater and elsewhere encouraged imitation and the promotion of ragtime contests, which Harney often won.

Harper, Frances E. W. (September 24, 1825, Baltimore, Maryland—February 22, 1911, Philadelphia, Pennsylvania): Lecturer and poet. Considered by many to be the leading African American poet of her day, Frances Ellen Watkins Harper was a powerful lecturer, a committed activist, and a literary stylist.

Throughout her long life, Frances Harper spoke out and worked against SLAVERY and then inequality. She did this not only from the speaker's platform but also through her contributions to the literary genres of poetry, the short story, and the novel.

Born to free parents but orphaned at the age of three, Frances Watkins was educated in her uncle's school for blacks. She worked as a domestic, then as a teacher before actively becoming involved in the ABOLITIONIST MOVEMENT in the 1850's. In 1860 she married Fenton Harper, a widowed farmer in OHIO, and settled down with him, caring for his children and bearing a daughter. After his death in 1864 she resumed lecturing and writing full time for the rest of her life.

Prior to the CIVIL WAR, Harper wrote poetry that attacked slavery; following the war, its scope broadened to include antilynching statements, temperance, women's rights,

Christianity, black history, and patriotism. She wrote in the formal meter and sentimental style popular in the nineteenth century, and she sometimes wrote DIALECT POETRY. Her 1859 story "The Two Offers" is thought to be the first short story by a black person to have been published in the United States. Her novel *Iola Leroy* (1892) celebrates the endurance and significance of the black family and deals with such issues as white discrimination, women's social roles, and community involvement.

—*Scot M. Guenter*

See also: Literature.

Harper, Michael S. (b. March 18, 1938, Brooklyn, New York): Poet and educator. Michael Steven Harper is known as a distinguished professor and a noted poet. He was selected as the first poet laureate of the state of RHODE ISLAND.

Harper began serving as a professor of English at Brown University in 1970, and begin-

Poet Michael S. Harper. *(© Roy Lewis Archives)*

ning in 1990 he held the honor of the University Professor at Brown. Between 1988 and 1993, he was the poet laureate of Rhode Island. Harper's books of poetry have earned prestigious awards. Both *Dear John, Dear Coltrane* (1970) and *Images of Kin: New and Selected Poems* (1977) won the Melville-Cane Award from the Poetry Society of America. *History in Your Heartbeat* (1971) won the Black Academy of Arts and Letters Award for poetry. Harper edited the *Collected Poems* of Sterling A. BROWN, which was selected for the National Poetry Series in 1979. In 1990 Harper won the Robert Hayden Memorial Poetry Award for his body of work.

Harper developed an aspiration for learning and writing early in his life. He earned degrees from California State University, Hayward (1963), and Brown University (1972). In addition to his professorship at Brown, Harper took posts as a visiting professor at Harvard University (1974-1975, 1977), Yale University (1976), New York University (1991-1992), and other institutions. In 1991 he was selected as a visiting scholar for Phi Beta Kappa, visiting nine different campuses. Harper was also coeditor of *Chant of Saints* (1979), an influential anthology of African American art, writing, and scholarship.

—*Alvin K. Benson*

See also: Literature.

Harpers Ferry: Site of an abolitionist raid that took place on October 16-18, 1859. Harpers Ferry at that time was a town in western VIRGINIA. (A few years later, not wanting to secede during the CIVIL WAR, the western part of Virginia broke away and became the new state of WEST VIRGINIA.)

Harpers Ferry housed a federal arsenal that was chosen by radical abolitionist John BROWN as the starting place for a slave insurrection. African Americans Osborne Anderson, John Copeland, Shields Green, Sherrard

The African American participants in John Brown's raid on Harpers Ferry: Osborne Anderson, Dangerfield Newby, John Copeland, Sherrard Leary, and Shield Green. *(Association for the Study of African-American Life and History)*

Leary, and Dangerfield Newby fought alongside Brown's thirteen white men during his raid on Harpers Ferry. The raid failed in its unrealistic attempt to spark a widespread slave rebellion. Brown was captured and was executed shortly after the incident ended.

See also: Abolitionist movement; Slave resistance.

Harper v. Virginia State Board of Elections: U.S. SUPREME COURT case in 1966 dealing with equal protection of the law. *Harper v. Virginia State Board of Elections* involved Virginia residents who argued that a state poll tax was unconstitutional. The Supreme Court held that a state poll tax, or any fee, limits citizens' right to vote and therefore violates the equal protection clause of the FOURTEENTH AMENDMENT.

The Twenty-fourth Amendment (1964) to the U.S. Constitution banned the use of poll taxes in national elections. African Americans still were being denied the right to vote, however, a situation dramatized by the 1965 march from Selma to Montgomery, ALABAMA, led by Martin Luther KING, Jr., that inspired the passage of the VOTING RIGHTS ACT OF 1965.

In *Harper v. Virginia State Board of Elections* the Court declared that no "invidious discrimination" may be drawn in establishing voter qualifications and that restrictions based on wealth are comparable to discrimination based on race, creed, or color. The franchise—the right to vote—is a fundamental right and liberty, preservative of all others.

—*Gil Richard Musolf*

See also: Selma to Montgomery march.

Harriet Tubman home: Estate located at 180 South Street in Auburn, New York, that was used as a home for the aged by Harriet Tubman. A powerful force for liberation as a conductor on the UNDERGROUND RAILROAD, Tubman had completed five years of successful journeys by 1857 and brought her aging parents to freedom. Finding the Canadian winter too harsh for them, Tubman negotiated with abolitionist William H. Seward for a piece of property in Auburn and moved her parents there. In the winter of 1858-1859, she visited BOSTON to solicit help with her payments on the property and is said to have met with John BROWN, Frederick DOUGLASS, William Lloyd GARRISON, and other prominent abolitionists.

On March 18, 1869, Tubman married Nelson Davis. The couple lived in the clapboard house until Davis built a brick house for them on the neighboring property. That same year, Sarah

President Bill Clinton, Hillary Clinton, the Reverend Paul G. Carter, and Christian Carter at the Harriet Tubman Home in September, 1999. *(AP/ Wide World Photos)*

H. Bradford published *Scenes in the Life of Harriet Tubman* and gave $1,200 from the sale of the book to Tubman. Tubman used this money to pay off her property debts. Throughout her life, she maintained the property as a home for the aged and never turned anyone away. Having exhausted the limited resources of her federal pension for service during the Civil War, Tubman relied on neighbors to help establish the house as the Harriet Tubman Home for Aged and Indigent Negroes in 1908. In her will, recorded June 11, 1903, she bequeathed the building to the AFRICAN METHODIST EPISCOPAL ZION CHURCH. Although Tubman had not used the home as her permanent residence, the church created a small museum within the home. The bed in which Tubman died in 1913 and a few of her household items were moved to the home for public viewing. *See also:* Abolitionist movement.

Harris, Barbara (b. 1951, Philadelphia, Pennsylvania): EPISCOPALIAN cleric. In 1989 Harris became the first female bishop of the Episco-

pal Church in the United States. Her ordination was approved on January 24, and she was consecrated in February. Her ordination was a break with twenty centuries of tradition, during which only men were chosen for the highest position in the church. Harris became an assistant bishop in the diocese of BOSTON, MASSACHUSETTS.

Harris had struggled with her decision to be ordained, and finally did so in 1975. She was ordained a deacon in 1979 and a priest in 1980. Her elevation to the status of bishop is especially surprising considering the fact that she had no formal seminary training and did not possess a college degree. Her appointment as bishop was controversial within the church.

Harris was involved in helping others even as a youth. She marched in Selma, ALABAMA, for CIVIL RIGHTS and registered VOTERS in MISSISSIPPI in the 1960's. She joined the Church of the Advocate in the late 1960's. Her experience with the church in the soup kitchens of Philadelphia and as a prison chaplain convinced her to enter the ministry.

As an Episcopal priest, Harris was outspoken on behalf of racial justice and prisoners' rights. As the executive director of the Episcopal Church Publishing Company, she wrote occasional articles challenging the idea that women should not be bishops. After becoming a bishop, Harris was involved in pastoral outreach programs, ministering to hospitals, prisons, people with ACQUIRED IMMUNODEFICIENCY SYNDROME (AIDS), and women in crisis. She continued to support gay rights and to criticize the Episcopal Church as being male-dominated and racist.
See also: Religion.

Harris, Bernard (b. October 13, 1927, New York, New York): Electrical engineer and educator. Harris was president of his own electrical engineering company, Harris Scientific Services, which he founded in 1979.

Harris earned impeccable academic credentials. He received a bachelor's degree in electrical engineering from Cooper Union College in 1949 before going on to graduate work in engineering at Columbia University, where he received a master's degree in 1951 and a Ph.D. in 1961. He later earned an M.B.A. degree from Pace University.

Harris's professional record is equally impressive. Before launching his own electrical engineering company, Harris served as a design engineer at the RCA (Radio Corporation of America) Laboratory from 1951 to 1954, as a systems research scientist at New York University from 1954 to 1963, and as a member of the technical and managerial staff at Sperry Rand Corporation from 1963 to 1965. He went on to serve as an oceanographic research scientist at the Hudson Laboratory of Columbia University from 1965 to 1968 and worked as the chief microwave engineer at Polarad Electronics Corporation in 1968. From 1968 until he founded his own company in 1979, Harris served as the vice president of Ocean and Atmospheric Science, Inc.

Harris also held a number of teaching positions while pursuing his professional career as an engineer. These positions included serving as an adjunct associate professor of electrical engineering at New York University, Pratt Institute, and Manhattan College from 1960 to 1970, and as an associate professor of electrical engineering at Manhattan College from 1979 through the 1990's.

Harris became a member of a number of professional societies, including the Acoustic Society of America, the Institute of Electrical and Electronics Engineers, the Operations Research Society of America, the American Association for the Advancement of Science, the American Society of Engineering Education, and the Sigma Xi honorary scientific society.

Harris's major research interest involved applications of atmospheric and oceanographic acoustics to such diverse fields as noise pollution and Navy oceanography. His work concentrated on ways noise can be controlled—by making the source of the noise quieter, by blocking the passage of noise from one space to another, and by absorbing noise energy.
See also: Engineers.

Harris, James A. (b. August 25, 1926, Des Moines, Iowa): Association executive. Harris was named president of the National Education Association (NEA) in 1974, a post he held into the 1990's. He had previously gained considerable experience in education, in roles ranging from elementary school teacher to university instructor.
See also: Education.

Harris, Middleton A. "Spike" (January 22, 1908, New York, New York—1977): Historian. Harris used his undergraduate degree in sociology from HOWARD UNIVERSITY as a social worker and parole officer. Personal interest led him to begin an investigation into his own origins and African American history in general. He collected copies of various government documents and other artifacts, some of which eventually went to the collections of the SCHOMBURG CENTER FOR RESEARCH IN BLACK CULTURE in New York City. He also served as president of Negro History Associates and worked on several books.
See also: Historiography.

Harris, Patricia Roberts (May 31, 1924, Mattoon, Illinois—March 23, 1985, Washington, D.C): Government official. Harris attended elementary school in CHICAGO. Her father worked as a railroad dining car waiter, and her mother taught school. Harris obtained her undergraduate education at HOWARD UNIVERSITY, graduating summa cum laude in 1945. Between 1946 and 1949, she worked for the Young Women's Christian Association in Chicago as she did postgraduate studies at the University of Chicago. She later moved to WASHINGTON, D.C., and served as executive director for Delta Sigma Theta, a public service organization, after completing postgraduate work at American University. In 1960 she graduated first in her class from George Washington University Law School.

She joined the Howard University Law School faculty, eventually becoming dean of

In early 2000 the U.S. Postal Service honored Patricia Roberts Harris on a postage stamp. *(Arkent Archive)*

the school of law. She increasingly became interested in the DEMOCRATIC PARTY. In the John F. KENNEDY ADMINISTRATION, she served as cochair of the National Women's Committee on CIVIL RIGHTS and later was named to the Commission on the Status of Puerto Rico. She seconded Lyndon B. Johnson's nomination at the 1964 Democratic National Convention and continued a life of service with the Democratic Party when she served in the Johnson administration as ambassador to Luxembourg. She was the nation's first female African American ambassador.

In 1969 Harris resigned, after only one month of service as dean of Howard University Law School. She protested that Howard had been too compliant in response to student demands. By 1970 she had become a partner in a prominent Washington law firm. She later served on the boards of IBM, Scott Paper, and Chase Manhattan Bank.

In December, 1976, President-elect Jimmy Carter appointed Harris as secretary of the Department of Housing and Urban Development, another first for a black woman. On July 20, 1979, Harris moved within the CARTER ADMINISTRATION to the post of secretary of Health, Education, and Welfare, later renamed the Department of Health and Human Services. After President Ronald Reagan took office in 1981, Harris ran unsuccessfully for MAYOR of the District of Columbia.

See also: Diplomats; Housing and Urban Development, Department of; Politics and government.

Harrison, Richard B. (September 28, 1864, London, Ontario, Canada—March 14, 1935, New York, New York): Shakespearean reader, elocutionist, and actor. The son of fugitive slaves from the United States, Richard B. Harrison was self-educated. In 1923 he was asked to organize a drama school at the Agricultural and Technological College in Greensboro,

Actor Richard B. Harrison in 1935. *(AP/Wide World Photos)*

NORTH CAROLINA. Harrison, in 1931, was given a Spingarn Medal for his portrayal of "De Lawd" in the all-black musical *The Green Pastures* (1930).

Hastie, William Henry (November 17, 1904, Knoxville, Tennessee—April 14, 1976, East Norriton, Pennsylvania): The first African American federal JUDGE, Hastie received his appointment in 1949. He held his post on the Third Circuit Court of Appeals until his retirement in 1971. He had previously served as governor of the Virgin Islands from 1946 to 1949.

Hastings, Alcee Lamar (b. September 5, 1936, Altamonte Springs, Florida): Attorney, JUDGE, and FLORIDA congressman. After receiving his law degree from Florida A&M University in 1963, Hastings was an attorney in private practice until 1977. From 1977 to 1979, he was a circuit court judge in Broward County, Florida. His next judicial position was as a U.S. District Court Judge from 1979 to 1989. To honor his achievements, the city of Daytona Beach proclaimed December 14, 1980, as Judge Alcee Hastings Day. Hastings received the Citizen of the Year Award from the Zeta Phi Beta fraternity in 1978 and the Freedom Award from the NATIONAL ASSOCIATION FOR THE ADVANCEMENT OF COLORED PEOPLE (NAACP).

Hastings began serving in the U.S. House of Representatives in 1993, representing Florida's Twenty-third Congressional District. He was reelected in 1994, 1996, and 1998.
See also: Congress members; Politics and government.

Hatcher, Andrew T. (b. June, 1923, Princeton, New Jersey): Journalist, businessman, and po-

Andrew T. Hatcher, the first African American appointee of John F. Kennedy's administration. *(Library of Congress)*

1149

litical appointee. Hatcher was educated at Springfield College and served in the Army for three years during WORLD WAR II, attaining the rank of second lieutenant. After his discharge, Hatcher became a journalist with the *San Francisco Sun-Reporter* and attended Golden Gate Law School from 1952 to 1954. As a reward for his staunch political support, President John F. Kennedy named Hatcher his associate press secretary in 1960, making Hatcher the first major African American appointee of Kennedy's New Frontier program. Hatcher resigned his post after Kennedy's assassination in 1963 and took an executive post with a NEW JERSEY brewery company. He served as director of communications for the New York State Assembly from 1974 to 1975 and was named vice president of International Sydney S. Baron and Co. in 1976.

Hatcher, Richard Gordon (b. July 10, 1933, Michigan City, Indiana): Politician. Richard Hatcher was one of thirteen children born to Carlton and Katherine Hatcher. The elder Hatchers had moved to Indiana from Macon, GEORGIA, in 1921 to flee the racial oppression of the South and to provide a better life for their growing family. The economic conditions of their new home were not greatly improved, but the Hatchers were hardworking and able to sustain their close-knit family.

Two incidents marred Richard's early life. The first occurred before he entered school; an injury sustained while Richard was throwing rocks with a friend resulted in the loss of his left eye. Later, his mother died of breast cancer when Richard was just thirteen.

Education

Because of Richard's sight disability, the Hatchers, especially the boy's mother, wanted their youngest son to have a college education. At one point, Richard's older sister Gladys was a secretary for Michigan City, Indiana's

only African American attorney, and the boy was very impressed with the man's lifestyle. Richard wanted to be a lawyer; his parents, however, wanted him to be a doctor.

After grade school, Hatcher entered Elston High School. African American students, including Hatcher, were expected to take vocational courses. Hatcher's father fought the administrators, and they finally let the young man take a commercial course, but Hatcher took few of the classes necessary to prepare him for college.

In the fall of 1952, Hatcher entered Indiana University on a partial athletic scholarship. Though the scholarship covered his tuition and books, he still had to work to pay for room, board, and incidentals. The young man was poorly prepared for a college curriculum and had to make up the deficiencies. He was even forced to quit the school's football team in order to concentrate on his studies.

Hatcher made the dean's list his sophomore and junior years and earned straight A's in his last year. With a major in government and minor in economics, Hatcher received a B.S. degree from Indiana University in 1956. He entered Valparaiso Law School the following fall. While attending school, he worked nights as a psychiatric aide at a nearby hospital. He graduated from Valparaiso Law School in 1959 and soon afterward became a law clerk for attorney Henry Walker in East Chicago, Indiana, earning about seventy-five dollars a month.

Legal Career

Working for Walker allowed Hatcher to learn the practical side of the law. He passed the Indiana bar in September, 1959, and Walker began to assign him cases that required court appearances.

His first major case involved an African American teenager who had been accused by a white woman in MISSISSIPPI of making an obscene suggestion. The teenager fled north and was arrested in Gary, Indiana. Knowing that extradition would mean certain death for the youth, Hatcher successfully argued the boy's case in front of the governor of Indiana, and he was released.

The case brought attorney Hatcher local fame. His picture appeared on the front page of the CHICAGO DEFENDER, and Lake County, Indiana, prosecutor Floyd Vance offered him a part-time job as a deputy prosecutor in the county's criminal court at $5,000 per year. For a few months in 1961, Hatcher also maintained a law practice in Michigan City, but faced with clients who were unable or unwilling to pay him, he closed the office.

Early Political Career

Hatcher's father had been active for years in the politics of Michigan City. Hatcher had often worked side by side with his father, performing such chores as driving voters to the polls. From his father, Hatcher had learned the political process and the subtleties of politics.

While still a law student in 1958, at the encouragement of his father, Hatcher ran unsuccessfully in the DEMOCRATIC PARTY primary for election as Michigan City justice of the peace. Five years later, Hatcher was ready to reenter the political arena. By then, the young lawyer was living in Gary, an industrial town on Lake Michigan built early in the twentieth century by the U.S. Steel corporation to supply housing for workers.

By 1963 Hatcher was a member of a group of young African American men called Muigwithania (an African word meaning "we are together") who wanted an end to the vice in Gary and the corruption in city government, and who called for the inclusion of African American people in the town's politics.

Initially, the group wanted Hatcher to run for election as a state representative, but Hatcher had his eye on a councilman-at-large seat on the Gary city council. He resigned his post as deputy prosecutor, joined the juvenile court staff in Gary, and moved his law practice to the Gary office of group member Jackie Shropshire. In the spring primary, he received more votes than any councilman-at-large in Gary's history, receiving 99 percent of the African American vote.

An activist before his election, Hatcher continued to push for social reforms once on the city council. With Hatcher as the prime mover of a fair-housing law, the city council passed the nation's strongest open-occupancy act in 1965. With Hatcher's help, Gary's fire department and the staffs and wards of the city's two major hospitals were integrated. In 1965 Hatcher became the youngest council member to become council president.

Campaigning for Mayor

The following year, African American politicos in Gary prepared for the 1967 mayoral race, with Councilman Hatcher in mind to run for mayor. In January, 1967, Hatcher announced his candidacy for MAYOR. Soon he had a falling out with his friend Dozier Allen, who believed that because Hatcher was from Michigan City he was an outsider and should not run for mayor of Gary. Then came bribery offers to induce Hatcher to withdraw. Hatcher, however, was in the race to the finish.

In the Democratic primary, Hatcher was running against the incumbent mayor, A. Martin Katz, who had failed to carry a single white precinct in his 1963 win. Needing the African American vote, Katz hired Lake County Coroner A. S. Williams, an African American, to be his campaign manager, and Chuck Stone, a former aide to Congressman Adam Clayton POWELL, Jr., to be his speech writer.

Despite all efforts by the Lake County Democratic political machine, and contrary to the predictions of the media, African American voters rallied behind Hatcher, giving him 27,272 votes to Katz's 17,190, with 13,133 going to segregationist businessman Bernard Konrady.

Initially, Lake County Democratic Party Chairman John Krupa announced his endorsement of Hatcher in the general election, but with strings attached. In truth, Krupa wanted Hatcher to allow him to select the new police chief, controller, and several other key city officers. Hatcher refused to bow to Krupa's demands, and the fight was on. Krupa even removed 5,286 names—most of them African American—from the voter-registration rolls, adding the names of some three thousand whites he claimed were new registrants.

Hatcher countered by filing a federal lawsuit, charging Krupa and the county Democratic organization with violations of the VOTING RIGHTS ACT OF 1965. Hearings indicated irregularities involving more than ten thousand voters, yet thirteen hours before the polls were to open, a court ordered only about a thousand false names off the rolls.

Notwithstanding rampant voter fraud on election day, Hatcher emerged victorious, winning with 39,812 votes to 37,947 for his opponent. On that same day, Carl STOKES was elected the first African American mayor of Cleveland, OHIO; since Stokes took office first, Hatcher was the second African American to become mayor of a major American city.

Achievements in Office

Hatcher served as mayor of Gary for twenty years. During his first three terms, he had a positive effect on the city, using revenue sharing and block grants to build housing, streets, miles of sewer lines, and even a new complex in downtown Gary called the Genesis Convention Center.

After Ronald Reagan became president in 1981, revenue sharing was eliminated, block grants were given to the states instead of the cities, and Gary faltered. No longer able to rely on federal funds, and with a declining economy hurt by the country's increased reliance on Japanese steel, Hatcher was faced with even greater challenges.

Like other cities, Gary was besieged with a crack cocaine epidemic, crime, homelessness, and other social ills. Without the means to correct these problems, Hatcher fell victim to voter anger and apathy. Thus, in his fifth reelection bid, Hatcher was beaten by the Lake County Democratic machine's candidate, Thomas D. Barnes, in the Democratic primary in the spring of 1987.

After his defeat, Hatcher moved into academia. He assumed the Harold Washington Chair at Roosevelt University in Chicago lecturing, remaining active in politics, and continuing to live in Gary with his wife and three daughters.

—*Philip G. Smith*

See also: Politics and government; Reagan administration.

Suggested Readings:

Catlin, Robert A. *Racial Politics and Urban Planning: Gary, Indiana, 1980-1989.* Lexington : University Press of Kentucky, 1993.

Drotning, Phillip T., and Wesley W. South. *Up from the Ghetto.* New York: Cowles Book Company, 1970.

Franklin, John Hope, and Alfred A. Moss, Jr. *From Slavery to Freedom: A History of African Americans.* 7th ed. New York: Alfred A. Knopf, 1994.

Landess, Thomas H., and Richard M. Quinn. *Jesse Jackson and the Politics of Race.* Ottawa, Ill.: Jameson Books, 1985.

Nelson, William E. *Black Politics in Gary: Problems and Prospects.* Washington, D.C.: Joint Center for Political Studies, 1972.

Poinsett, Alex. *Black Power: Gary Style.* Chicago: Johnson, 1970.

Reynolds, Barbara A. *Jesse Jackson: The Man, the Movement, the Myth.* Chicago: Nelson-Hall, 1975.

Hate crime: Criminal acts that violate the victims' CIVIL RIGHTS and are motivated by hostility to the victim's race, religion, creed, national origin, sexual orientation, or gender. Although the existence of crime stemming from prejudice is not new, the term "hate crime" is of fairly recent usage. A person may become the victim of a hate crime for many different reasons. Historically, and through the late twentieth century, African Americans have been the group most frequently targeted for acts motivated by racial hostility in the United States.

Funeral of fourteen-year-old Carol Robertson, one of four girls killed by a bomb while attending Sunday school in Birmingham, Alabama, in 1963; the incident was perhaps the most notorious heinous hate crime of the Civil Rights movement era. *(Library of Congress)*

Historical Background

In the broadest sense, it could be argued that the institution of SLAVERY itself and the violence that sustained it were examples of racially based hate crimes. Other types of hate crime—LYNCHING, cross burnings, kidnappings, rapes, and CHURCH BURNINGS—not only injured individuals but also reflected a desire to intimidate an entire race of people. Shortly after the CIVIL WAR, Congress moved to address such types of racial violence. It passed federal legislation designed to curb the activities of the KU KLUX KLAN and other vigilante groups. Although the Civil Rights Act of 1866 and the Enforcement Act of 1870 were intended to protect blacks from the deprivation of "security of person and property . . . by reason of color or race," the acts were enforced only rarely, and the courts interpreted their scope very narrowly. The laws were ineffective.

During the 1960's, as the Civil Rights movement threatened to change the institu-

tions of white supremacy, especially in the South, cross burnings and arson against black churches again became weapons in the racial struggle. Other churches and synagogues that supported integration or that had multiracial congregations were also targets. Among the most notorious attacks during the period was the bombing of the 16th Street Baptist Church in BIRMINGHAM, ALABAMA, where four little girls were killed.

Hate Crime Legislation

More recent legislative efforts to address bias-motivated crimes date from 1990. Advocates of hate crime legislation have advanced several arguments in support of such laws. As hate crimes not only affect individuals but also represent an offense to an entire group of people, the state has a compelling interest in protecting the community from those acts. Hate crimes breed suspicion and fear; they polarize citizens and increase tension. Moreover, they frequently lead to retaliatory violence. Laws written to identify hate-motivated violence and to punish it more severely send a message that the community will not tolerate the behavior. Legislation also reassures the targets of hate crimes that their rights are being protected.

Opponents of laws against bias-motivated crimes typically raise the issue of free speech and expression and charge that under such legislation people could be punished for their beliefs. Legislatures and the courts have attempted to fashion laws that protect free speech but penalize criminal behavior driven by prejudice.

Congress passed the Hate Crime Statistics Act in 1990. It required the U.S. Department of Justice to collect and publish statistical information on crimes of murder, rape, assault, and arson motivated by prejudice against the victim's race, ethnicity, religion or sexual orientation. The attorney general, the legislation held, would define whether a specific crime contained elements of bias. The collection of data was intended to identify patterns of hate crime in order to allocate resources to combat it. The act was set to expire after five years, and it was reauthorized in 1995.

The Juvenile Justice and Delinquency Pre-

Hate Crime Statistics, 1997

	Number of Incidents	Number of Offenses	Number of Victims	Number of Known Offenders
Single-bias Incidents				
Race:	**4,710**	**5,898**	**6,084**	**5,444**
Antiwhite	993	1,267	1,293	1,520
Antiblack	3,120	3,838	3,951	3,301
Anti-American Indian/Alaskan Native	36	44	46	45
Anti-Asian/Pacific Islander	347	437	466	351
Anti-multiracial group	214	312	328	227
Ethnicity/national origin:	**836**	**1,083**	**1,132**	**906**
Anti-Hispanic	491	636	649	614
Anti-other ethnicity/national origin	345	447	483	292
Religion:	**1,385**	**1,483**	**1,586**	**792**
Anti-Jewish	1,087	1,159	1,247	598
Anti-Catholic	31	32	32	16
Anti-Protestant	53	59	61	19
Anti-Islamic	28	31	32	22
Anti-other religious group	159	173	184	120
Anti-multireligious group	24	26	27	11
Anti-atheism/agnosticism/etc.	3	3	3	6
Sexual orientation:	**1,102**	**1,375**	**1,401**	**1,315**
Antimale homosexual	760	912	927	1,032
Antifemale homosexual	188	229	236	158
Antihomosexual	133	210	214	103
Antiheterosexual	12	14	14	14
Antibisexual	9	10	10	8
Multiple-bias incidents	**4**	**10**	**40**	**3**
Total	**8,049**	**9,861**	**10,255**	**8,474**

Source: U.S. Department of Justice, *Uniform Crime Reports.*

vention Act of 1992 provided for the study of hate crimes committed by juveniles, and it included money for prevention programs. It required every state to include a plan for fighting hate crimes in its juvenile justice program. The 1994 Violent Crime Control and Law Enforcement Act included a provision to increase the penalty for violent crimes defined by the Justice Department as hate crimes. Such offenses would have their sentences increased by one-third.

In 1996, in response to arsons that had destroyed sixty-six churches, some of them African American, during the previous eighteen months, Congress passed the Church Arson Prevention Act. The law provided that people who "burn, desecrate, or otherwise damage religious property" could be tried in federal court. It doubled the prison sentence from ten years to twenty years for vandalizing religious property because of the race, color, or ethnicity of those associated with the church. It also provided compensation for victims of such arson.

In addition to hate crime legislation at the federal level, more than three-fourths of the states and the District of Columbia passed laws with a similar purpose. Many of the laws focus on physical injury or threats motivated by a specific bias. They may either define such acts as criminal in themselves or enhance the penalties for crimes motivated by prejudice. For example, such laws consider bias as an aggravating factor in an assault, making it a more serious crime. Many states have statutes that require tracking and reporting of hate crimes by local law enforcement agencies, and some allow victims to sue for monetary damages. Furthermore, many states have older laws on the books that prohibit the wearing of masks or hoods, the interruption of religious meetings or desecration of religious buildings, or the placing of signs, symbols, or burning crosses. It was a cross-burning law that led the U.S. SUPREME COURT to review a hate crimes statute in the 1992 case *R.A.V. v. St. Paul*.

R.A.V. v. St. Paul.

In 1990 a group of teenagers including Robert A. Viktora (called R.A.V. in court proceedings because of his status as a juvenile) were charged with burning a homemade cross in the front yard of Russ and Laura Jones, an African American couple who had recently moved into a predominantly white neighborhood in St. Paul, MINNESOTA. They were convicted under a St. Paul law prohibiting bias-motivated disorderly conduct. When Viktora appealed his case, the Supreme Court found the St. Paul law against cross burning to be unconstitutional. However, the members of the Court were divided with respect to their reasoning.

The majority of five justices found that the law singled out certain kinds of expression— racial, religious, or sexual insults—on the basis of content. The law prohibited the expression of particular disfavored points of view, they said, and thus violated the First Amendment. The remaining four justices also found the law unconstitutional, but on the grounds that it criminalized both "fighting words" and speech that was offensive but did not provoke violence. Fighting words are generally not considered to be protected by the First Amendment; the term includes "conduct which itself inflicts injury or tends to incite immediate violence."

The *R.A.V.* case illustrated the basic disagreement over much hate crime legislation. Is even offensive speech and expression protected by the Constitution, or do some forms of expression cross the line into acts that inflict damage? The case left many states and localities in doubt about the constitutionality of their hate crime laws. In 1993, in *Wisconsin v. Mitchell*, the Supreme Court upheld a WISCONSIN law that provided enhanced penalties for crimes if the victim is "intentionally selected" on the basis of "race, color, religion, disability, sexual orientation, national origin, or ancestry." Ironically, in that case the defendant was black, while the victim was white.

When white-hooded members of the Ku Klux Klan marched through Jasper, Texas, in June, 1998, after an African American man had been dragged to death behind a pickup truck driven by white racists, heavily armed members of the "New Black Panthers" staged a counter demonstration. *(AP/Wide World Photos)*

According to the FEDERAL BUREAU OF INVESTIGATION (FBI), 7,947 hate crimes were reported in 1995. Of those, 60 percent were motivated by race. Two-thirds of those, 2,988 crimes, were committed against African Americans. For such statistics, the FBI relies on the voluntary submission of data from local law enforcement agencies, many of which do not supply information. Some experts believe that the number of hate crimes is much higher—some have estimated as much as five times higher—than is reported to the FBI.

Several particularly notorious crimes brought the issue of bias-motivated violence to public attention in the late 1990's. The brutal torture and murder of James Byrd, an African American, in Jasper, TEXAS, by men who held white supremacist views led to calls for hate crime prosecutions. Likewise, the murder in WYOMING of Matthew Shepherd, primarily because of his sexual orientation, resulted in support for the expansion of hate crime laws to include the protection of gay men and lesbians. In general, hate crime laws, enhanced penalties, and public outcry against bias-motivated violence have resulted in greater recognition of hate crime and in a stronger response from the criminal justice system.

—*Mary Welek Atwell*

See also: Church burnings; Crime and the criminal justice system; Racial violence and hatred.

Suggested Readings:

Haiman, Franklyn S. *"Speech Acts" and the First Amendment*. Carbondale: Southern Illinois University, 1993.

Herek, Gregory M., and Kevin T. Berrill, eds. *Hate Crimes*. Newbury Park, Calif.: Sage Publications, 1992.

Jacobs, James B., and Kimberly Potter. *Hate Crimes: Criminal Law and Identity Politics*. New York: Oxford University Press, 1998.

Jenness, Valerie, and Kendal Broad. *Hate Crimes: New Social Movements and the Politics of Violence*. New York: Aldine de Gruyter, 1997.

Winters, Paul A., ed. *Hate Crimes*. San Diego, Calif.: Greenhaven, 1996.

Hate speech: Term broadly defined as an abusive, insulting, intimidating, or harassing expression or an expression that may incite someone to violence, hatred, or discrimination based on race, ethnicity, religion, or sexual orientation. Hate speech has been called by many courts the "hardest free speech question," involving as it does individual freedom, multiculturalism, and equality issues.

Hate speech is widespread in the United States, but it has special meaning for the African American community because it is so deeply tied to questions of racism and CIVIL RIGHTS. The establishment of the American Civil Liberties Union (ACLU) in 1920, in response to the suppression of dissent during WORLD WAR I, set the stage for the earliest hate speech controversy. When Roman Catholics and Jews united in an attempt to suppress expressions of hate such as KU KLUX KLAN parades and automobile magnate Henry Ford's anti-Semitic newspaper, the ACLU came forward to defend bigots and their First Amendment rights, or rights to freedom of speech and press.

The ACLU argued that every view, no matter how ignorant or harmful it may be regarded, has a legal and constitutional right to be heard. Entitling racist speech to First Amendment protection was a position the ACLU was to defend repeatedly throughout the twentieth century, particularly during the turbulent 1960's, when civil rights issues were confronted head-on by African American activists. The ACLU and NATIONAL ASSOCIATION FOR THE ADVANCEMENT OF COLORED PEOPLE (NAACP), organizations which originally had clashed over First Amendment issues, became allies in the protection of free speech in mid-century.

The U.S. SUPREME COURT made a series of important decisions that interpreted and reinterpreted constitutional rights to free speech. Early interpretations of the First Amendment permitted the suppression of offensive forms of expression under the "bad tendency test." In other words, anything that might have the "tendency" to cause social harm could be restricted. The Supreme Court's position on the First Amendment gave permission for local officials routinely to ban speakers and activities by groups they did not like. The constitution's commitment to free speech, including the protection of hate speech, was reaffirmed in the last half of the twentieth century. The lessons of the Civil Rights movement were that racial minorities and other oppressed

groups were best protected through the broadest, most content-neutral protection of speech. The courts and the major civil rights groups, including the NAACP, embraced that principle, leaving the restriction of hate speech without an advocate.

The 1980's and 1990's saw a new storm of controversy over hate speech that centered on campus speech codes. Many American colleges and universities adopted student conduct codes restricting offensive speech; this strong support for punishing offensive speech was unprecedented and probably in response to a shocking resurgence of racism, particularly against African Americans. The new legal arguments in support of hate speech drew on the FOURTEENTH AMENDMENT. Drawing an analogy to sexual harassment on the job, advocates of campus speech codes argued that hate speech created a hostile environment that infringed on the constitutionally mandated right to equal access to education. Campus speech codes touched off a national debate on the First Amendment and racism. The debate was resolved, at least for a time, by the federal courts, which struck down speech codes in the early 1990's.

—*Linda Kearns Bannister*
See also: Racial discrimination; Racial prejudice; Racial violence and hatred.

Suggested Readings:

Marcus, Lawrence R. *Fighting Words: The Politics of Hateful Speech*. Westport, Conn.: Praeger, 1996.

Walker, Samuel. *Hate Speech: The History of an American Controversy*. Lincoln: University of Nebraska Press, 1994.

Hathaway, Donny (October 1, 1945, Chicago, Illinois—January 13, 1979, New York, New York): Singer, pianist, composer-arranger, and record producer. A driving force in the music field during the 1970's, Hathaway began per-

Singer-songwriter Donny Hathaway died from a fall from a thirteenth-story hotel room in New York. *(AP/Wide World Photos)*

brought more attention to his first release. His 1972 album, *Live*, did even better on the charts, earning gold-record status. Hathaway recorded a single with Roberta Flack, "Where Is the Love," in 1972, and in a *Billboard* survey that year was ranked ninth among top album male vocalists. He released a top-selling single in 1973, "Love, Love, Love." The album *Extension of a Man* also made the charts.

See also: Songwriters and composers.

Havens, Richie (Richard Pierce; b. January 21, 1941, Brooklyn, New York): Folk singer and self-taught guitarist known for his distinctive, husky voice and strongly rhythmic guitar strumming style. Havens began singing as a boy in church choirs and gospel groups. He began his professional career in about 1962, singing in coffeehouses and folk clubs in and around NEW YORK CITY; he became a well-known performer in the New York folk scene

forming as a child in CHICAGO's black churches and was inclined to enter the ministry. He earned a fine arts scholarship to HOWARD UNIVERSITY and began to perform to make ends meet, eventually choosing a career in MUSIC over becoming a minister. He worked as an arranger throughout the 1960's and did session work in studios along the East Coast, rapidly establishing himself as a strong asset to recordings.

Hathaway began to produce and expanded this talent in the 1970's, working with such acts as Curtis MAYFIELD and the Impressions, Roberta FLACK, Jerry Butler, the Staple Singers, Carla Thomas, and Woody Herman. He signed a contract with Atlantic Records in 1970 and released his first album that year, titled *Everything Is Everything*. His second album made a greater impact. Released in 1971, *Donny Hathaway* won great media acclaim and

Richie Havens in 1980. *(AP/Wide World Photos)*

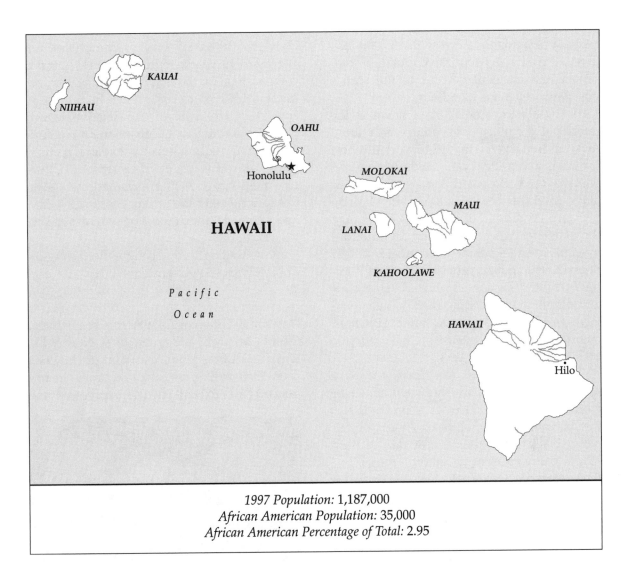

HAWAII

KAUAI

NIIHAU

OAHU

Honolulu

MOLOKAI

MAUI

LANAI

KAHOOLAWE

Pacific

Ocean

HAWAII

Hilo

1997 Population: 1,187,000
African American Population: 35,000
African American Percentage of Total: 2.95

of the early 1960's. Havens made his recording debut in 1965 and thereafter recorded regularly as a soloist and with other performers.

His most critically acclaimed album was *Mixed Bag* (1967). The song "Follow" from that album was later featured in the 1978 film *Coming Home*. He played at a number of folk and pop festivals in the 1960's, including the 1966 Newport Folk Festival and the Isle of Wight Festival (1969). Havens is notably featured in the *Woodstock* concert film and album (1969), singing a partially improvised song entitled "Freedom."

He went on to tour internationally and per-

form on a number of television shows. His biggest hit came in 1971, with his version of "Here Comes the Sun," a George Harrison-penned Beatles song. Havens continued performing through the 1980's and 1990's, including a performance at a twenty-fifth anniversary Woodstock concert in 1994, and his singing was heard in television commercials in the 1980's and 1990's.

Hawaii: In 1997 Hawaii had about 35,000 African American residents, most of whom lived on the island of Oahu, which contains the state capital of Honolulu, a city with 835,000 residents. The African American population comprised just under 3 percent of the state's population of about 1.2 million.

A few blacks came as freed slaves in the middle of the nineteenth century, and about two hundred arrived in 1901 to work on short contracts in the sugar cane fields. Native Hawaiians used the word *popolos* to describe blacks, and the word is still used in common parlance. At the end of the twentieth century, three distinct African American communities lived in Hawaii—military personnel and their dependents; civilian professionals and families of military personnel who have stayed after completing or retiring from military service; and college students, some of whom have been recruited because of their academic abilities or athletic prowess.

Statistically, African Americans occupy a socioeconomic position between those of whites and East Asians on one hand and Native Hawaiians and Southeast Asians on the other. Blacks have the highest rate of high school completion of all ethnic groups, but their income levels are below average, primarily because of the comparatively low pay of the many residents in the armed services.

The relatively higher status of African Americans in Hawaii than on the U.S. mainland is a reflection of a lower degree of discrimination in Hawaii. Indeed, a number of African Americans have risen to prominence despite the small black population in the state. The first superintendent of public schools in Hawaii is thought to have been African American. Since statehood, African Americans have been elected to the Honolulu City Council and to the Hawaii Board of Education.

—*Michael Haas*

Hawkins, Augustus Freeman (b. August 31, 1907, Shreveport, Louisiana): Longest-serving African American legislator in U.S. history.

Hawkins was a CALIFORNIA assemblyman for twenty-eight years, beginning in 1935, and a congressman for the WATTS district of LOS ANGELES from 1963 to 1991, when he retired. A consistent advocate of the disadvantaged, Hawkins wrote major legislation on employment, CIVIL RIGHTS, and EDUCATION, and cowrote the Humphrey-Hawkins Full Employment Act of 1978. He chaired the House Education Committee from 1984 to 1990 and had a considerable impact on federal support for education.

See also: Civil rights and congressional legislation; Politics and government.

Hawkins, Coleman (November 21, 1904, St. Joseph, Missouri—May 19, 1969, New York, New York): JAZZ tenor saxophonist. Hawkins is credited with giving the saxophone its important place in jazz. The full, expressive tone

Coleman Hawkins, the "Daddy" of the tenor sax, at the Newport Jazz Festival in 1963. *(AP/Wide World Photos)*

and "buzzy" sound commonly associated with jazz saxophone was largely invented by Hawkins in the 1920's and 1930's.

Before Hawkins took up the tenor saxophone, it was generally considered a novelty instrument rather than something on which to play serious music. Hawkins began playing saxophone in 1914 at age nine, and he was a professional by the time he was in his teens. In the early 1920's he recorded in the background with blues singer Mamie SMITH. In 1923 he made his first recordings with a group led by Fletcher Henderson, and he continued playing with Henderson until 1934. Both Hawkins and Louis ARMSTRONG were in Henderson's band in the early 1920's, and Hawkins's playing style was influenced by Armstrong as well as by pianist Art TATUM. By the mid-1920's, Hawkins was known as the top tenor player in jazz (in truth there was little competition, as there were not yet many players who excelled on the instrument). His 1939 recording of "Body and Soul," with its relatively long two-chorus sax improvisation, became his most well-known recording.

In the 1940's, after already having had a twenty-year career, Hawkins managed to keep current, encouraging and playing with early BEBOP players such as Dizzy GILLESPIE and Don BYAS. After falling out of fashion in the early 1950's, he enjoyed a renaissance in the late 1950's and early 1960's, and saxophonist Sonny ROLLINS hailed him as a major influence. During this period Hawkins performed regularly with a quintet that included trum-

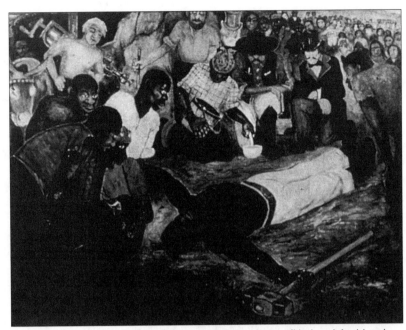

Part of Palmer C. Hayden's series on John Henry. *(National Archives)*

peter Roy ELDRIDGE; they gave a particularly noteworthy performance at the 1957 Newport Jazz Festival. Hawkins continued to perform into the 1960's, although by 1965 he was past his prime.

Hayden, Palmer C. (1893, Wide Water, Virginia—1973): Painter. Palmer was the first recipient of the Harmon Foundation's Gold Medal for distinguished achievement by an African American in the fine arts. He also won the Rockefeller Prize in 1933. Hayden, who studied at Cooper Union, at the Boothbay Colony in MAINE, and with M. Clivett LeFevre in France, combined narrative elements, expressionist techniques, and corollaries to American folklore in his well-known John Henry series of paintings.
See also: Painters and illustrators.

Hayden, Robert (August 4, 1913, Detroit, Michigan—February 25, 1980, Ann Arbor, Michigan): Poet. Robert Earl Hayden is best

Poet Robert Hayden. (© Roy Lewis Archives)

known for his narrative poems and historical themes. Adept at many forms, from the sonnet and ballad to free verse and dialect poetry, Hayden addressed African American issues by placing them in the larger contexts of art and history.

Hayden maintained his ties to his native city throughout his career. He received his B.A. in 1936 from Detroit City College (later Wayne State University) and his M.A. in 1944 from the University of Michigan. He was a professor of English at FISK UNIVERSITY from 1946 to 1969 and at the University of Michigan from 1969 to 1980. From 1976 to 1978, he was the first African American to serve as consultant in poetry at the Library of Congress. He married Erma I. Morris in 1940. They had one child, Maia.

From the publication of his first volume of poetry, *Heart-shape in the Dust* (1940), to *Words in the Mourning Time* (1968) and *American Jour-*

nal (1978), both of which received National Book Award nominations, Hayden made American history emotionally and intellectually accessible. His poems on SLAVERY and the CIVIL WAR won him the Jules and Avery Hopwood Poetry Award in 1938 and 1942. Writing on such topics as slavery, the UNDERGROUND RAILROAD, MALCOLM X, and Martin Luther KING, Jr., Hayden is usually described as a black poet, but he described himself foremost as an American poet. Nevertheless, he researched African American history for the FEDERAL WRITERS' PROJECT in Detroit during the 1930's, and his best poems focus on African American history.

Hayden's poems are intensely emotional, yet carefully wrought. He studied under W. H. Auden at the University of Michigan and wrote much of his own poetry in traditional English forms. Hayden's poetry places the African American experience in all of its contexts, from the cityscapes of his own childhood in Detroit to the historical contexts of the slave trade and ancient Africa. Among the most honored African American poets of his day, Hayden earned worldwide acclaim. In 1966 he won the Grand Prize for Poetry at the Dakar (Senegal) World Festival of Negro Arts. *See also:* Literature.

Hayer, Talmadge (b. c. 1943): Convicted assassin of MALCOLM X. The details of Malcolm X's assassination in 1965 are debated. Eyewitness testimony was conflicting, and Hayer himself changed his story regarding what occurred. Hayer was found guilty on March 11, 1966, and sentenced to life imprisonment on April 14, 1966. Two men convicted of being his accomplices, Norman 3X Butler and Thomas 15X Johnson, also received life sentences.

Malcolm X resigned from the NATION OF ISLAM, or Black Muslims, in 1964 and formed the ORGANIZATION FOR AFRO-AMERICAN UNITY. This led to animosity against Malcolm X by

Nation of Islam Leader Elijah MUHAMMAD. Some accounts describe Hayer as a member of Muhammad's honor guard and as a member of a Nation of Islam chapter in NEWARK, NEW JERSEY. Hayer denied even being a Black Muslim at one time. He did, however, claim to have been offered money to kill Malcolm X. He testified that he refused the money but that the offer prompted him to plan the assassination, which he thought would make him important. He also at one point said that the assassination was in retribution for Malcolm X's attempts to discredit Muhammad.

The most widely accepted account of Malcolm X's assassination on February 21, 1965, in NEW YORK CITY's Audubon Ballroom is as follows. Hayer and another man, identified as Norman 3X Butler, started an argument, drawing guards away from the stage where Malcolm X was standing. Someone detonated a homemade smoke bomb, which later was found to have Hayer's fingerprints on it. During the resulting confusion, a man later identified as Thomas 15X Johnson fired both barrels of a sawed-off shotgun at Malcolm X. Hayer and another gunman then went to the stage and emptied pistols into Malcolm X's body.

Hayer was shot in the thigh while trying to make his escape. He made it down a flight of stairs, reportedly vaulting over another gunman, who was able to blend into the crowd. Members of the crowd caught Hayer, but police protected him from their assaults. Other suspects were not apprehended at the time. Early newspaper accounts reported that police had arrested two suspects, but later accounts described only one arrest. Police sources stated that the two suspects actually were both Hayer, reported by two different officers. Additional confusion came from the fact that police officers took down Hayer's name as Thomas Hagan, misunderstanding him when he told them his name.

This general account of the assassination raised questions in some people's minds. Butler and Johnson were known opponents of Malcolm X, and it seemed unclear how or why security guards let them into the ballroom. According to later testimony by Hayer, they took no part in the assassination. Because they were not arrested at the scene, there was debate concerning whether Butler and Johnson were even there. The judge involved in the case refused to open police files containing notes on interviews with about one hundred eyewitnesses. These facts, combined with the early police reports of a second suspect, who was then discounted, led some to suspect a government cover-up or even government involvement in the assassination.

Hayes, Roland (June 3, 1887, Curryville, Georgia—January 1, 1977, Boston, Massachusetts): Singer and recitalist. Hayes was one of six chil-

Tenor Roland Hayes. *(Associated Publishers, Inc.)*

dren. His father, William Hayes, died in 1898. His mother, Fannie Hayes, had been born a slave. She eventually moved her family to Chattanooga, TENNESSEE, after her husband's death. Hayes studied voice in Chattanooga with Arthur Calhoun and later attended FISK UNIVERSITY. He became a member of the FISK JUBILEE SINGERS, but his membership in the organization, which had no affiliation with the music department at Fisk, resulted in his being dismissed from both the music department and the university.

After spending a brief time in St. Louis, MISSOURI, Hayes left for Boston to rejoin the Fisk Singers. In 1917 he gave his first major recital in BOSTON, handling the ticket sales himself. He was, in 1917, the first black person to give a recital at Boston's Symphony Hall. After touring the United States, Hayes left for Europe to study voice in 1920. London was his first stop, and he sang for Great Britain's King George V in 1921. He then gave recitals and appeared with major orchestras around Europe, performing in Amsterdam, Berlin, London, Paris, and Vienna, among other major cities. By the time he made his official debut at New York City's Carnegie Hall in 1923, he had become an international star.

Although he sang the music of Gabriel Fauré, George Frederick Handel, Wolfgang Mozart, Hector Berlioz, Johann Brahms, Franz Schubert, and Ludwig van Beethoven with skill, he was equally committed to singing spirituals and generally promoting the musical legacy of African Americans. His main contribution to that effort was the production of his own collection of African American spirituals called *My Songs* (1948). He accepted a teaching position at the Boston College of Music in 1950 but continued his extensive recital schedule throughout the 1950's. In 1962 he gave a benefit concert at Carnegie Hall to support HISTORICALLY BLACK COLLEGES. He made his last public appearance in 1973.
See also: Gospel music and spirituals.

Painting of George Edmund Haynes by artist Laura Wheeler Waring. *(National Archives)*

Haynes, George Edmund (May 11, 1880, Pine Bluff, Arkansas—January 8, 1960, Brooklyn, New York): Social activist. Haynes cofounded the Department of Race Relations of the Federal Council of Churches in America, for which he was executive secretary from 1921 to 1947. He held a bachelor's degree from FISK UNIVERSITY and was the first African American to receive a doctorate from Columbia University. His studies of economics and social science sensitized him to the problems of those who migrated from the South to the North in the early twentieth century. His concern led him to assist in the founding of the NATIONAL URBAN LEAGUE (originally called the National League on Urban Conditions Among Negroes) in 1910. He served as executive secretary until 1918, when he became a special assistant to the secretary of labor.
See also: Great Migration.

Haynes, Lemuel (July 8, 1753, West Hartford, Connecticut—September 28, 1833, Granville, New York): CONNECTICUT preacher and AMERICAN REVOLUTION war soldier. Haynes was one of three black soldiers to participate in the first major offensive against the British, the taking of Fort Ticonderoga, New York, on May 10, 1775. He had also served at Lexington, Massachusetts, in the war's first battle. After the war, he became a pastor in the Congregational Church and was probably the first African American to preach to a white congregation on a regular basis. He was also the first African American to receive a degree from an American college, an honorary M.A. from Middlebury College in 1804.

Head Start: Educational program for disadvantaged young students. The Head Start project began in 1965 as part of President Lyndon B. Johnson's WAR ON POVERTY program. It was a federally funded eight-week summer early-intervention program that accommodated 550,000 children from low-income families. Its purpose was to help disadvantaged preschool-aged children to overcome educational roadblocks.

The program grew out of research suggesting that low-income children had difficulties adjusting to formal EDUCATION because of a lack of intellectual stimulation and emotional bonds in their early family life. Designed to compensate for these deficiencies, the pro-

Pre-kindergartners in a Head Start program at Clark Atlanta University in 1995. *(AP/Wide World Photos)*

gram, primarily aimed at preschoolers, reflected the era's optimism that educational intervention could combat the effects of POVERTY and counteract the well-documented relationship between low achievement and low socioeconomic status. By 1972 most programs were running year-round and had been expanded to include handicapped children. More than 450,000 preschool children were being served yearly, in programs in all fifty states and in the U.S. territories. Many facilities doubled as day-care centers.

Because of structural and academic deficiencies, the early program received much criticism and negative publicity. Head Start was therefore modified in 1975, and performance standards were established for its four core components: education, health, parental involvement, and social services. In the realm of education, intellectual, social, and emotional development were to be fostered. Teachers were to be bilingual when necessary and were expected to receive training in early childhood education. Programs were to be individualized to match local ethnic and cultural characteristics, and teacher/student ratios were to be kept low. Health goals stated that children should be provided with medical, dental, nutritional, and mental health care. Parents were encouraged to take a positive and active role in their children's education and to volunteer time. They could serve on policy committees and were given preferential treatment for employment in nonprofessional Head Start positions. Head Start was also instrumental in helping parents who did not graduate from high school to complete their high school education, after which some went on to college.

After these changes, Head Start's efficacy became evident. Research demonstrated that children enrolled in Head Start programs scored higher on tests and achieved higher educational success rates than similar children who did not attend a Head Start center. The ef-

fect was especially noticeable in the area of reading and math scores among nonwhite students. Research has also shown that African American students who attended a Head Start program when young do well on standardized college entrance exams.

Beginning in 1981, Head Start received money through block grants. In other words, funding to maintain the program was given to states from the federal government, in lump sums. The money then could be used according to each state's discretion to maintain a variety of educational programs, not only Head Start. For this reason, Head Start worked to document and publicize its positive effects in low-income communities.

By 1991 Head Start had helped more than eleven million poor children, including many African Americans and recent immigrants, to receive a better education. Congressional appropriations for the approximately thirteen hundred Head Start centers was about $1.4 billion in 1990, with another 20 percent in funding coming from communities. By 1993 Head Start had established operations in nearly thirteen thousand facilities, including schools, community centers, churches, public housing facilities, and government buildings.

As part of the 1994-1995 federal budget, President Bill Clinton requested an increase in spending for educational programs, specifically a boost of $700 million in Head Start's budget. The total amount for which Head Start was approved in 1994-1995 was $4 billion. As part of the program's funding increase and reauthorization, Congress listed a number of requests. The program was to tighten its procedures and prove that it was operating efficiently; it was also to provide extended school hours, programs that would be open all day and all year long, and services for children under the age of three. In addition, with more funding, Head Start was expected to begin new schools in impoverished communities.

—*Updated by Kimberly Battle-Walters*

Health: The modern American health-care system evolved from a series of programs and interventions improvised during the nineteenth and early twentieth centuries. These activities ranged from the development of hospitals, almshouses, and dispensaries for the poor who were sick to experiments in immunization and water purification. Originally, private physicians were the primary source of medical care for the U.S. population. Physicians' services were provided either in a patient's home or in almshouses and public dispensaries, depending on whether the patient was wealthy or poor.

The almshouses built by local governments, voluntary hospitals built by charitable organizations, and public dispensaries were the principal sources of medical care for the poor. Voluntary hospitals cared only for those who were classified as the "worthy poor," leaving the "unworthy poor," along with the incurable and the chronically ill, to rely on almshouses for their care. This excluded the able-bodied poor, typically adult men. People of some religious and ethnic groups also were barred from voluntary hospitals, leading to the development of religious and ethnic hospitals and reliance on public hospitals to serve those who were refused at other sites. Before the introduction of anesthesia in 1846 and antisepsis (sterilization) around 1900, hospitals were avoided as a matter of choice. Before anesthesia, surgery was a matter of brutal, painful work. Furthermore, infections would spread across hospital wards, increasing the patients' risk of acquiring new diseases. The use of antisepsis and anesthesia made the hospital a more appealing setting for the middle and upper classes.

Availability of Medical Care
Before the passage of the CIVIL RIGHTS Act of 1964, there was persistent racial and economic discrimination in health care. In the South, "SEPARATE BUT EQUAL" clauses were used to bar the admission of African Americans to hospitals. The costs of medical care also placed hospital services out of the reach of many African Americans. Until the introduction of the first major private health insurance program at Baylor University's hospital in 1929 (the forerunner of the Blue Cross-Blue Shield health insurance plans), the ability to obtain health care was based solely on one's ability to

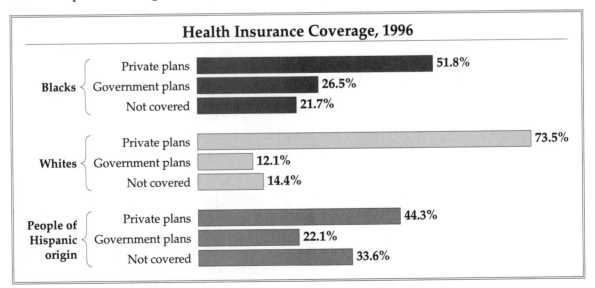

Health Insurance Coverage, 1996

Blacks	Private plans	51.8%
	Government plans	26.5%
	Not covered	21.7%
Whites	Private plans	73.5%
	Government plans	12.1%
	Not covered	14.4%
People of Hispanic origin	Private plans	44.3%
	Government plans	22.1%
	Not covered	33.6%

Source: U.S. Bureau of the Census.
Note: Government health coverage includes Medicaid, Medicare, and military plans.

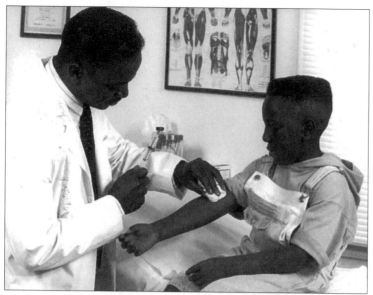

By the end of the twentieth century, control of infectious diseases centered on immunization and preventive measures. *(Tom McCarthy/Unicorn Stock Photos)*

pay for services before treatment. Those unable to pay for medical care were subject to either the public hospital system or the charitable whims of voluntary or church organizations.

In 1933 the committee on the costs of medical care reported that the percentage of individuals who obtained no medical care in 1933 was greater the lower the family income, ranging from slightly less than 14 percent for those in families with annual incomes of $10,000 or more to nearly 50 percent for those families with incomes less than $1,200. The committee concluded that although African American families were not systematically studied, it could be safely assumed that they were receiving less medical care than were white Americans because of their lower incomes. In 1939, 93 percent of African Americans were "poor," compared with 65 percent of white Americans.

Private health insurance went a considerable way toward solving the problem of the affordability of medical care by spreading the risk of the costs of illness across a large base of

people. Although the introduction of private insurance during the GREAT DEPRESSION went a long way toward solving the problem of the affordability of medical services, few insurance plans existed until after 1945. After WORLD WAR II, the number of private health insurance plans increased as the number of unions grew. Unions pressed for health insurance as a fringe benefit of employment. The percentage of privately insured Americans rose to 73 percent by 1953, but the private insurance option tended to underserve African Americans because they were disproportionately employed in industries without insurance coverage or with higher turnovers in employment.

In an effort both to counter the restrictions in access to hospital care put in place by the public and voluntary hospital system and to increase the number of hospital beds available, the federal government passed the Hospital Survey and Construction Act of 1946 (the Hill-Burton Act). This act provided funds for the construction of additional hospital beds in areas with shortages. In exchange for these funds, hospitals were expected to provide charity care to needy patients. A separate but equal clause for some facilities in the South continued to sanction racial segregation.

Health Care System After 1954
Following the U.S. Supreme Court's BROWN V. BOARD OF EDUCATION decision in 1954, which declared segregation in public schools unconstitutional, organizations such as the Medical Committee on Human Rights, the NATIONAL MEDICAL ASSOCIATION, and the Student National Medical Association intensified their ef-

forts to desegregate health facilities. They also lobbied for better health insurance and for increasing the number of minority HEALTH CARE PROFESSIONALS in the United States.

These efforts led to the implementation of several programs to both increase the number of minority health care providers and serve a greater proportion of disadvantaged Americans. The most direct federal support for medical education began with the Health Professions Educational Assistance (HPEA) Act of 1963 and continued with subsequent acts such as those providing for neighborhood health centers, community mental health centers, and the National Health Service Corps (NHSC). After implementing the HPEA Act, the federal government discovered that although it could increase the number of minority and female providers through the use of AFFIRMATIVE ACTION programs, it was not able to redistribute large numbers of them to areas with the greatest need. Through the National Health Service Corps, the government sought not only to finance the training of women and minority physicians but also to target where they would serve upon completion of their medical training.

While the HPEA and NHSC acts focused on the training of individuals, the neighborhood health center program focused on building or leasing centers in urban and rural areas that needed primary health services. These health centers were developed to increase the chance that minorities and the poor would see a physician. Community mental health centers also evolved to ensure that more African Americans would gain access to medical care. The original premise behind the community mental health movement, however, was different from that behind neighborhood health centers.

Neighborhood health centers emphasized access to medical care, using a model that focused on analyzing the determinants of illness and disease on the part of the patient. The

community mental health movement sought to develop centers that would try to improve the health of African Americans via social change. The movement's goal was to provide therapeutic counseling as well as to fight POVERTY, racism, and discrimination. Because of conflicts regarding the overall mission of the community mental health center movement, the centers did not move past the provision of therapeutic services.

Aside from the training of minority health professionals and the development of community health centers, the most significant series of events that helped African Americans in their quest to obtain equal access to medical care was the passage of the Civil Rights Act in 1964 and Medicare and Medicaid legislation

The federal Health Professions Educational Assistance Act of 1963 was designed, in part, to increase the numbers of female and minority physicians. *(Jeff Greenberg/Unicorn Stock Photos)*

in 1965. Title VI of the Civil Rights Act prohibited racial discrimination in any institution receiving federal funds, thus giving hospitals a powerful incentive to alter their practices. Hospitals receiving federal funds were forbidden to deny admission to patients, to subject patients to separate treatments, or to deny admitting privileges to medical personnel solely on the basis of race. Access to health care was further increased when litigation in the 1960's explicitly defined the obligation of hospitals using federally provided construction funds to meet their "free care" requirements and to serve those unable to pay.

The passage of the Medicare and Medicaid programs was particularly helpful to African Americans because of their concentration among the groups who were eligible for the Medicaid program. One of the outcomes of the passage of the Medicare and Medicaid programs was the improvement in the health of older African Americans. The life expectancy of African Americans increased as a result of the increased access to physician care as well as access to nursing home services.

Statisticians have estimated that between 1900 and 1996, the expected remaining years of life at the age of sixty-five increased from 11.5 to 15.8 for white men, from 10.4 to 13.9 for African American men, from 12.8 to 19.0 for white women, and from 11.4 to 17.2 for African American women. Some of these increases in longevity have been attributed to increased access to medical care.

Following 1965, efforts continued within medical schools to improve the recruitment and retention of African American students. It was already known that a disproportionate number of minority health professionals were trained in medical schools associated with HISTORICALLY BLACK COLLEGES. Between 1920 and 1968, MEHARRY MEDICAL SCHOOL and HOWARD UNIVERSITY MEDICAL SCHOOL graduated the majority of the African American physicians in the United States. As late as

1967, 83 percent of all African American first-year medical students were at Meharry and Howard. By 1974 the figure had fallen to 17 percent.

Following pressure from the National Medical Association and the American Medical Association, American medical schools increased the number of special college courses for African American students, summer programs of special study, and scholarship aid targeted to African American students. Some programs supplemented these efforts with in-school social support systems and training programs in test taking. A 1982 report released by the Graduate Medical National Advisory Committee predicted a surplus of doctors and paved the way to cutbacks in medical training programs, somewhat eroding the progress that had been made in the health professions for minorities.

Although the Medicaid and Medicare programs went a long way toward improving the access to care of African Americans, there were still gaps in the insurance coverage of African Americans. In 1996, according to figures of the CENSUS OF THE UNITED STATES, about 51.8 percent of African Americans were covered by some form of private health insurance. Another 26.5 percent had a form of public, or government-supplied, insurance, mostly Medicare or Medicaid. Therefore, 21.7 percent of African Americans were uninsured in 1996.

Mortality from Infectious Illness

Along with being influenced by changes in the delivery of medical services, African Americans were influenced by changes in how diseases were addressed. Americans in general were influenced by public health, medical education, and treatment interventions that shifted the focus on health interventions from eradicating infectious diseases to controlling chronic illness.

During the nineteenth century, industrial, economic, social, technological, and demographic changes reshaped American society. The high birth and mortality rates common to premodern societies began to decline. Mortality rates declined principally because of public health initiatives addressing certain diseases. Americans benefited from earlier experiences in the containment of illness and disease on the European continent. For example, it was discovered that the bubonic plague epidemic in fourteenth-century Europe occurred largely because of poor sanitation and sewage control, combined with dense populations. The health of Americans in general was improved by isolating the ill in hospitals and almshouses. The settlement of Americans in the new territories also helped, because it alleviated overcrowding problems in eastern cities such as Boston, New York, and Philadelphia.

These changes helped to control infectious diseases, but infectious diseases continued to pose the greatest threat to the health of Americans throughout much of the nineteenth century. In many cases, infectious diseases appeared and disappeared without being affected by the therapeutic methods of the medical professions. In other instances, the decline of one disease was accompanied by an increase in the virulence of another.

Malaria subsided in the United States because of the dispersal of the population across the newly developed territories, better sewage removal, and better and cleaner housing. The elimination of cholera came more as a result of understanding the nature of transmission than as a result of medical intervention. The decline in the mortality rates for TUBERCULOSIS came more as a result of environmental changes than as a result of the introduction of a vaccine. The monitoring of dietary intake, cleaner housing, falling population density, and working in safer environments all helped lead to the significant decline in the mortality rates from tuberculosis. The mortality rate from tuberculosis had declined from 369.9 per 100,000 Americans in 1865 to 2.5 per 100,000 in 1970.

The mortality rate from infectious diseases in BALTIMORE (including tuberculosis, diphtheria, measles, scarlet fever, diarrhea, dysentery, and typhoid) declined from 1,267 per 100,000 in 1851 to 357 per 100,000 in 1916. There were significant gains in the control of other infectious diseases, such as the elimination of smallpox, diphtheria, and poliomyelitis. Much of the decline in mortality from infectious disease has been credited to better sanitation, water purification, proper food production and food handling, immunization, and medical therapy. African Americans as a whole have not experienced and benefited from these changes as much as white Americans have.

By the end of the twentieth century, the control of infectious diseases centered on immunization and preventive measures targeted at preschoolers (for diphtheria, tetanus, polio, rubella, and infectious diarrhea) and the elderly (for pneumonia and influenza). Interventions focused on legislation requiring immunization of children before their entry into the school system, eliminating financial barriers to immunization, and expanding the capacity of laboratories to diagnose breakouts of influenza more rapidly. With the control of the transmission of infectious diseases, the emphasis in the reduction of mortality shifted to the reduction of the incidence of chronic diseases.

Infant Mortality
Neonatal (within twenty-eight days of birth) and postneonatal (twenty-nine days after birth up to one year) mortality rates declined steadily for all Americans between 1950 and the 1990's, but African American children continued to face a greater risk of dying within the first year of life than did white Americans. In 1950 27.8 out of each 100,000 African American children died within the first twenty-eight days of life, compared with 19.4 per 100,000 white children. Another 16.1 per 100,000 Afri-

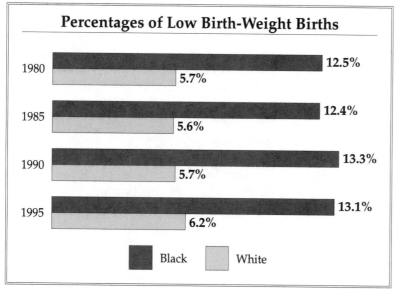

Percentages of Low Birth-Weight Births

1980 — 12.5% (Black), 5.7% (White)
1985 — 12.4% (Black), 5.6% (White)
1990 — 13.3% (Black), 5.7% (White)
1995 — 13.1% (Black), 6.2% (White)

Black ▮ White ▯

Source: Statistical Abstract of the United States, 1998.

can American children died in 1950 between the second month of life and their first birthday, in comparison with 7.4 per 100,000 white children.

By 1990 the rates had declined to 17.7 deaths per 100,000 African American children in their first year, compared with 8.5 per 100,000 white children dying in their first year. In 1996 6.0 white infants per 100,000 births and 14.2 African American infants per 100,000 births died during the first year.

Higher INFANT MORTALITY rates among African Americans have been attributed in part to low birth-weight children. Other conditions that influence infant mortality are poverty, the lack of health insurance (which reduces access to appropriate medical care), poor nutrition, inadequate housing and living conditions, stressful work environments, inadequate support systems, and a lack of adequate transportation to get to needed services.

The problem of low birth weight is particularly prevalent among the children of teenage mothers. In the 1990's, African American women were about twice as likely as white American women to bear children before their eighteenth birthday. In 1996 22.9 percent of births to African American women involved teenage mothers; for white women, the figure was 11.3 percent. In 1995, for women of all ages, 13.1 percent of African American mothers gave birth to low birth-weight children, compared with 6.2 percent for white mothers.

Teenagers are more likely than older women to bear low birth-weight children. These children, in turn, are more likely than other children to die within the first year of life or to have long-term neurological, development, or learning problems. Some of the solutions to the problem of low birth-weight children and infant mortality involve modifying the living conditions and support systems of those at risk for bearing low birth-weight children. Other solutions come via the prevention of TEENAGE PREGNANCY. This could be achieved through preconception counseling and the use of referrals for appropriate services.

Mortality from Chronic Disease

By the close of the twentieth century, the highest rates of mortality in the United States were associated with chronic diseases (CANCER, heart attack, stroke, diabetes) rather than with infectious diseases. At the same time, the U.S. Department of Health and Human Services noted glaring disparities between African and white Americans. African Americans were more likely than white Americans to die from cancer, heart disease, stroke, diabetes, HOMICIDE, and chemical dependency. African Americans were also more likely than white Americans to die from complications associated with ACQUIRED IMMUNODEFICIENCY SYNDROME (AIDS).

Like the trends reflected in the infant mortality data, the mortality data on heart disease, stroke, cancer, diabetes, homicide, and AIDS show disparities between African and white Americans. In 1950 there were 381.1 deaths per 100,000 white men as a result of heart disease, while there were 415.5 for African American men. In 1995 the rates were 297.9 per 100,000 for white men, in contrast to 244.2 per 100,000 for African Americans. In 1950 there were 87 deaths per 100,000 white men as a result of cerebrovascular disease, in comparison with 146.3 deaths per 100,000 African American men. By 1995 the respective rates had fallen to 48.6 and 51.0. In 1950 there were 21.6 deaths per 100,000 white men as a result of respiratory system cancer and 16.9 deaths per 100,000 African American men. By 1988 the rates had increased to 58.0. and 83.4.

African American men consistently suffered higher mortality from homicide. In 1950 there were only 3.9 homicide deaths per 100,000 white men, while there were 51.1 homicide deaths per 100,000 African American men. By 1988 the rates had increased to 7.7 and 58.2; in 1995 they stood at 7.8 and 56.3.

In the case of diabetes, the mortality rate declined for white men while it increased for African American men between 1950 and 1988. In 1950 the mortality rate from diabetes was 11.5 per 100,000 population for both white and African American men. In 1988 it was 9.6 per 100,000 white men in comparison with 19.8 per 100,000 African American men. Finally, in 1988 there were 9.9 deaths per 100,000 white American men as a result of complications associated with AIDS, compared with 31.6 per 100,000 African American men.

Some of the disparities noted between African American and white men can also be found between women. In 1950 there were 223.6 deaths per 100,000 white women as a result of heart disease, while there were 349.5 for African American women. In 1995 the rates were 297.4 and 231.1. In 1950 79.7 deaths per 100,000 white women came as a result of cerebrovascular disease, in comparison with 155.6 deaths per 100,000 African American women. By 1995 the rates were 76.0 and 60.4.

As was true for men, African American women consistently suffered higher rates of mortality from homicide. In 1950 there were only 1.4 homicide deaths per 100,000 white women while there were 11.7 homicide deaths per 100,000 African American women. The rates rose to 2.8 and 12.7, respectively, by 1988; in 1995 they were 2.7 and 11.1.

The mortality rate for diabetes declined far more for white than for African American women between 1950 and 1988. In 1950 16.4 per 100,000 white American women and 22.7 per 100,000 African American women died from diabetes. By 1988 the rate had fallen to 8.0 for white women, in comparison with 22.1 for African American women. Finally, in 1988 there were 0.7 deaths per 100,000 white American women from AIDS-related complications, compared with 6.2 per 100,000 African American women.

Between 1990 and 1997, figures for AIDS cases reported in a given year (including both men and women) fell slightly for white Americans (from 22,267 to 20,188) and rose dramatically for African Americans (from 13,206 to 27,016). The total number of African Americans first reported to have AIDS between 1990 and 1997 was about 229,800.

Explanations for Differences in Mortality
The foregoing statistics reveal that there has been general improvement in the health of both African and white Americans over time, yet at the same time they show that African Americans have always faced a higher risk of dying from certain illnesses than white Americans. The overall mortality from heart disease and stroke improved because of changes in the amount of cholesterol and fats consumed by Americans as well as an increase in the

amount of time Americans devoted to exercise. These rates also improved because Americans received more effective medical therapy for the treatment of HYPERTENSION. The remaining disparities between African and white Americans have been attributed to the fact that African Americans are still less likely than white Americans to be seen by heart specialists, are less likely to undergo heart surgery, and even when they have heart disease of the same severity, are less likely to undergo coronary bypass surgery.

African Americans are believed to be more likely than white Americans to die from cancer as a result of either being particular targets of cigarette and alcohol advertisements or not benefiting from early prevention (as in the case of screening exams such as pap smears or breast exams). ALCOHOLISM is correlated with homicides, cirrhosis of the liver, and cancer of the esophagus. Cigarette smoking is strongly correlated with the incidence of lung cancer.

There are a number of causes for the spread of AIDS and reasons why it afflicts African Americans proportionally more than white Americans. Homosexual men, intravenous drug users, recipients of blood transfusions, those who have had heterosexual contact with infected individuals, and children born to women who are infected are at the greatest risk of AIDS infection. The use of condoms during sex inhibits the transmission of the virus, and the use of sterile needles can help prevent transmission among intravenous drug users.

African Americans are burdened not only by disparities in the acquisition of AIDS but also by differences in treatment patterns once AIDS is acquired. The mean survival time for African Americans diagnosed as having AIDS is significantly less than for white Americans.

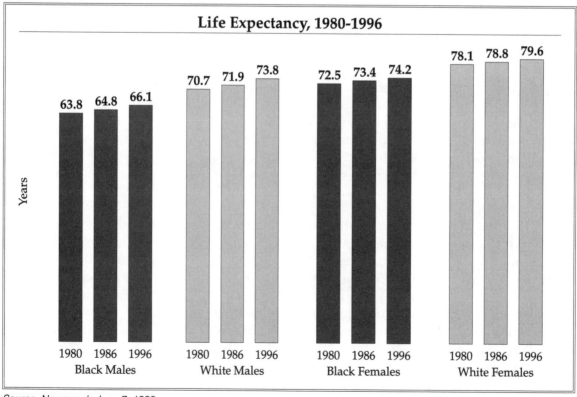

Life Expectancy, 1980-1996

Black Males	White Males	Black Females	White Females
1980: 63.8, 1986: 64.8, 1996: 66.1	1980: 70.7, 1986: 71.9, 1996: 73.8	1980: 72.5, 1986: 73.4, 1996: 74.2	1980: 78.1, 1986: 78.8, 1996: 79.6

Source: Newsweek, June 7, 1999.

Differences in postdiagnosis survival may represent the large number of the African American AIDS cases involving intravenous (IV) drug users and people who have inadequate health insurance. IV drug users are less likely to receive experimental treatments because they are less likely to conform to the regimen of experimental protocol. The uninsured may find the costs of prescribed drugs prohibitive and may be dependent on lower-quality health facilities for their treatment. These problems are compounded by the fact that African Americans have had a weaker support network for dealing with the problem of AIDS. A variety of support services, particularly within the homosexual community, have evolved to deal with AIDS. The African American AIDS population has only weak ties to the gay subculture.

Contemporary Issues and Possible Solutions
African Americans generally are in poorer health than white Americans and are more likely to encounter barriers to medical services. Various interventions have been proposed both to improve the health of African Americans and to improve their access to medical care.

Homicide and intentional injury have been described as problems of interpersonal relations (a psychological problem) and as the deviant behavior of a group (a sociological problem). In either case, the solution proposed was to align the behavior of individuals with the norms of society. Beginning in 1986, after a report by the U.S. Department of Health and Human Services on black and minority health, the model of public health intervention was used as a framework for attempting to reduce the number of homicides. This approach recognized that some of the causes of the problem were related to individual behavior and some were environmental circumstances. Solutions proposed attempting to reduce mortality both by reducing risk on the individual level and by

developing environmental strategies. Some solutions proposed for reducing the number of homicides include behavioral modification interventions for handling anger, community-based programs that call attention to the extent and consequences of violence, legislation regulating the carrying of firearms, improving school programs for conflict resolution, and strengthening state-based programs in violence prevention.

Public health interventions have been proposed to deal not only with homicide but also with other health problems encountered by African Americans. The following interventions have been proposed to reduce the incidence of cancer, heart disease, stroke, and diabetes: increased consumption of fruits and vegetables, reduction in the consumption of saturated fat, reduction of sun exposure, decreasing alcohol and tobacco use, preventive health screening, and exercise. All these changes can be encouraged through public interventions. The reduction of sexual activity among adolescents, the use of condoms, and outreach activities among populations at risk for the human immunodeficiency virus (HIV) are seen as promising interventions for reducing the incidence of AIDS.

Multiple points of intervention in the community have been proposed to implement these initiatives. In some cases, it is believed that nurses, physicians, and other professionals should serve as initiators of patient-education efforts. Voluntary minority lay health workers have been proposed as outreach workers in communities that traditionally do not avail themselves of medical services. Strong community leaders, such as ministers or sports and business leaders, have been considered as other avenues for the dispersal and promotion of health information. It is also believed that to address the health problems in the African American community, models must be developed to increase the flexibility of health service delivery, facilitate

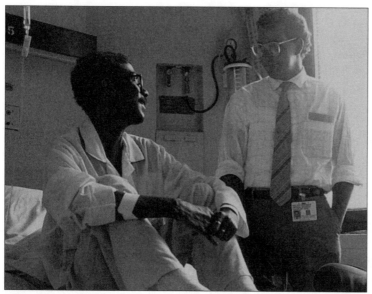

The average African American tends to use fewer professional medical services than does the average white American. *(Alan Reininger/ Unicorn Stock Photos)*

access to health services by minority populations, and improve efficiency of service and payment systems. This may require more flexible hours of service, use of mobile health units, and development of alternate payment strategies for the uninsured and underinsured.

One of the primary reasons for focusing on the issue of access to care is the link between access and health. Poverty and a lack of insurance often translate into delaying the use of preventive medical services. At the same time, the cost of care serves as a barrier to obtaining medical services. Data on access to care indicate that although there has been an improvement in the percentage of African Americans who receive medical services, there are still gaps between African and white Americans.

In 1970 70 percent of whites and 58 percent of nonwhites in the United States made at least one ambulatory visit to a physician during the year. During the same year, whites made an average of 4.1 ambulatory visits to a physician, in comparison with 3.6 visits for nonwhites. In 1989 77.8 percent of white Ameri-

cans made at least one ambulatory visit to a physician, compared with 76.3 percent of African Americans. During the same year, whites made an average of 5.6 visits to a physician, in comparison with 4.7 visits by African Americans. In 1995 the average numbers of visits were 6.1 for whites and 5.2 for African Americans.

Differences in the use of services between African and white Americans have been attributed to the problems of a lack of insurance, lack of available providers, inconvenient services, and cultural barriers to care.

There has been a considerable focus on the lack of African American access to medical services, but the problem of a lack of access to dental care is even more acute. Dental care typically is not covered by private insurance, and public insurance is extremely limited. The problem of access to dental services is progressive in nature, in that problems overlooked among children tend to worsen as the children grow older. The 1979-1980 national dental caries (dental decay) prevalence survey reported that 5.3 percent of white male children (ages five to seventeen) had some missing teeth and 14.3 percent had decayed teeth, while 16.1 percent of the nonwhite children had missing teeth and 37.1 percent had decayed teeth. During the same year, 6.1 percent of white female children had missing teeth and 13.1 percent had decayed teeth, while 15.2 percent of nonwhite female children had missing teeth and 31.5 percent had decayed teeth. Improvements in the dental status of children could be achieved through increased use of fluorides in drinking water, dental sealants and toothpaste, health education efforts, and more frequent visits to dentists.

A variety of proposals for expanding health insurance for the uninsured and underinsured have been proposed. These options range from insurance plans that expand the number of employed individuals who are insured to expanding coverage for poor Americans who are uninsured. It has been noted that an employment-based proposal for expanding health insurance to the uninsured (such as mandating insurance coverage for workers) would insure fewer uninsured African Americans than would an income-based strategy (such as expanding Medicaid), because a large proportion of uninsured African Americans are also unemployed. An employment-based strategy would help a greater proportion of uninsured Hispanic Americans, however, because a greater proportion of uninsured Hispanics are in the labor force.

—*Llewellyn Cornelius*
See also: Environmental hazards and discrimination; Medicine; Sickle-cell anemia.

Suggested Readings:

Alcena, Valiere. *The Status of Health of Blacks in the United States of America: A Prescription for Improvement.* Dubuque, Iowa: Kendall/Hunt, 1992.

Braithwaite, Ronald L., and Sandra E. Taylor, eds. *Health Issues in the Black Community.* San Francisco: Jossey-Bass, 1992.

Crute, Sheree, ed. *Health and Healing for African-Americans: Straight Talk and Tips from More than 150 Black Doctors on Our Top Health Concerns.* Emmaus, Pa.: Rodale Press, 1997.

Gamble, Vanessa N. *Making a Place for Ourselves: The Black Hospital Movement, 1920-1945.* New York: Oxford University Press, 1995.

Livingston, Ivor L., ed. *Handbook of Black American Health: The Mosaic of Conditions, Issues, Policies, and Prospects.* Westport, Conn.: Greenwood Press, 1994.

Neighbors, Harold W., and James S. Kackson, eds. *Mental Health in Black America.* Thousand Oaks, Calif.: Sage Publications, 1996.

Rice, Mitchell F., and Woodrow Jones. *Public Policy and the Black Hospital: From Slavery to Segregation to Integration.* Westport, Conn.: Greenwood Press, 1994.

Secundy, Marian G., and Lois L. Nixon, eds. *Trials, Tribulations, and Celebrations: African American Perspectives on Health, Illness, Aging, and Loss.* Yarmouth, Maine: Intercultural Press, 1992.

Semmes, Clovis E. *Racism, Health, and Postindustrialism: A Theory of African American Health.* Westport, Conn.: Praeger, 1996.

Starling, Kelly. "The Ten Biggest Killers of Blacks." *Ebony* (March, 1998): 124-127.

Sylvester, Judith L. *Directing Health Messages Toward African Americans: Attitudes Toward Health Care and the Mass Media.* New York: Garland, 1998.

Health care professionals: The history of African Americans as health care professionals began in the colonial era. In 1667 Lucas Santonee was called the first trained physician in New Amsterdam—the Dutch settlement on Manhattan Island that would be renamed NEW YORK CITY by the English. About half a century later, in 1706, Onesimus introduced inoculation against smallpox to the American colonies. He revealed the practice to his master, Cotton Mather, the Massachusetts Puritan clergyman, and Mather promoted the procedure during an epidemic in 1721. Highly controversial for many years, this inoculation was not generally accepted until about 1777.

Soon after the birth of the United States, James Durham (or Derham) was recognized as a physician, although he never obtained a medical license. Born a slave in PHILADELPHIA, Durham had been owned by several physicians who taught him to read and write. The last of these was a Scottish physician in NEW ORLEANS, LOUISIANA, who trained him to perform many medical services in 1773. Ten years later, Durham bought his freedom and returned to Philadelphia for a time before going back to New Orleans. He had a flourishing practice there until 1801, when the city council restricted him because he was unlicensed.

The Nineteenth Century

During the 1800's, a number of other African Americans gained distinction. James McCune SMITH obtained his M.D. degree from the AFRICAN FREE SCHOOL in New York City in 1847. Not recognized by the white medical establishment and not allowed to attend white schools, he was unable to pursue further medical education in the United States. Smith went to Scotland, where he earned recognized degrees in medicine, enabling him to return to New York and begin a successful practice.

The first black to graduate from an American medical school (Rush Medical College in CHICAGO) was David J. Peck in 1847. A freeborn Virginian, Alexander Thomas AUGUSTA, became the first black surgeon in the U.S. Army, in 1863. The first black woman to receive a medical degree was Rebecca Lee CRUMPLER, who graduated from the New England Female Medical College in Boston in 1864 after completing a seventeen-week course. The first African American nurse to earn a diploma from an American school, the New England Hospital for Women and Children, was Mary Elizabeth Mahoney, in 1879.

In 1893 Dr. Daniel Hale WILLIAMS performed the world's first successful open heart surgery at Provident Hospital in Chicago, a hospital he had founded. "Dr. Dan" was also the first black physician invited to become a charter member of the American College of Surgeons (1913). The first black surgeon-in-chief to become a hospital administrator was Charles Burleigh Purvis, in 1881.

The Early Twentieth Century

These early successes were by no means the norm. Indeed, it would be a long, uphill climb for African Americans to become widely accepted among health care professionals in the United States. During the period roughly between the 1920's and 1960's, referred to by some historians of black history as the "old" middle-class period, black professionals faced severe restrictions. Chief among them were lack of opportunity for acquiring a professional education and a lack of funds for attaining an education even if one were available. There were also prejudices against black health care workers among educated blacks.

In 1920, nationally, only 1.5 percent of all black workers were professionals—those in health care professions were even fewer—

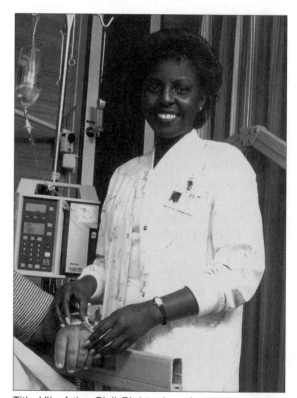

Title VII of the Civil Rights Act of 1964 broadened educational opportunities for members of minorities and helped give rise to a new generation of health care professionals. *(Tom McCarthy/Unicorn Stock Photos)*

compared with more than 5 percent of whites. In the 1930's, the statistics were similar. There was a significant difference between opportunities in the North and the South. It was reported that sometimes there were more professional blacks in one northern city than in a whole state in the South. Even so, during the 1930's, the majority of African American physicians and nurses were located in the South. There were more black dentists in the North. African American women fared worse than did black men in being able to enter professional positions. In addition to the question of race, being a woman was a serious hurdle to surmount.

An important aspect of the entrance of African Americans into the health care fields is parental or family influence and expectations. A number of black physicians and dentists have indicated that family influence was paramount in steering them into a career in the medical sciences. They were often told that a physician was the only person in the African American community who "amounted to anything." Another bias, for a time, involved the choice to pursue medicine rather than dentistry. Within the black community, dentists had little of the prestige that a medical doctor enjoyed.

The 1960's to the 1990's

Title VII of the CIVIL RIGHTS Act of 1964, together with the economic expansion of the 1960's, accounted for the beginning of a dramatic increase in black upward mobility. A study at the time showed that many students with a positive sense of personal competence along with a positive sense of racial identity intended to pursue graduate professional degrees and aspired to enter job fields that were nontraditional for blacks. It was from this group of young African Americans that a generation of health care professionals would come.

In the early 1990's, the distribution and representation of African Americans in health-

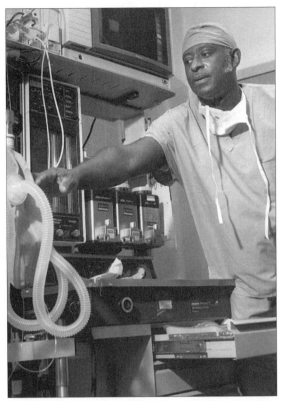

By the 1990's African Americans remained vastly underrepresented in health care fields. *(Hazel Hankin)*

related occupations, as reported by the Bureau of Health Professions, shows the extent of the increase of blacks entering those fields. During the late 1980's, of a total of 15,429 degrees conferred in medicine, 786 went to African Americans, of which 349 were women. In dentistry, 169 African American men and 93 African American women (out of a total of 4,729 graduates) completed dental school training. In optometry, only 8 African American men and 10 African American women graduated out of 1,082. In pharmacy, 75 African American women and 37 African American men out of a total of 861 students earned their degrees. In podiatry, degrees were conferred on 18 men and 15 women among 1,082 graduates. A handful of African Americans also received degrees in veterinary and chiropractic medicine.

In 1984 Alexia Irene Canada became the first black woman neurosurgeon in the United States. Ben CARSON, one of the most celebrated neurosurgeons in the world, had first expressed his desire to become a physician as a child in the late 1950's. He realized that dream in the late 1970's and went on to become the director of pediatric neurosurgery at Johns Hopkins Hospital at age thirty-three. In 1990 Roselyn Payne Epps become the first black woman to serve as president of the American Medical Association.

—*Victoria Price*

See also: Health; Medicine.

Suggested Readings:

Glazer, Penina Migdal, and Miram Slater. *Unequal Colleagues: The Entrance of Women into the Professions, 1890-1986.* New Brunswick, N.J.: Rutgers University Press, 1986.

Landry, Bart. *The New Black Middle Class.* Berkeley: University of California Press, 1987.

Samson, Vivian O. *Blacks in Science and Medicine.* New York: Hemisphere, 1990.

Smith, Jessie Carney. *Black Firsts: Two Thousand Years of Extraordinary Achievement.* Detroit: Gale Research, 1994.

Sokoloff, Natalie J. *Black Women and White Women in the Professions: Occupational Segregation by Race and Gender, 1960-1980.* New York: Routledge, 1992.

Healy, James Augustine (April 6, 1830, Macon, Georgia—August 5, 1900, Portland, Maine): Bishop. In 1854 Healy became the first African American Roman Catholic priest; in 1875 he became the first African American Catholic bishop. Healy was born to an Irish father and a slave mother. Excluded from seminaries in the United States, he studied in Montreal and Paris. As a priest, Healy became the chief administrator of the BOSTON archdiocese and an advocate of the poor. As bishop of Portland, MAINE, he defended Native Americans' rights and served as a consultant to the Bureau of Indian Affairs.

See also: Religion.

Hebrew Israelites: Religious group. The Original Hebrew Israelite Nation, also known as the Black Israelites, claim to be descendants of the ten lost tribes of Israel. By the 1980's, there were thousands of members of the religion. Their religious practices differ from those of Orthodox Jews mainly in that the Black Israelites practice polygyny and do not practice their religion in a synagogue.

The Original Hebrew Israelite Nation was founded in the 1960's by Shaleah Ben-Israel and Ben Ammi Carter in CHICAGO, ILLINOIS, and its affairs are governed by twelve princes, each representing one of the original twelve tribes of Israel. Prince Ashiel Ben-Israel was the most public of the twelve during the 1980's. The group advocates a return to Israel, and by the 1980's, the Black Israelites had founded a small colony there. About two thousand members had emigrated to Israel by 1980.

The Black Israelites are not the only African American Jewish denomination. The first recorded black Jewish congregation in the United States to have a black spiritual leader was the Moorish Zionist Temple, founded in NEW YORK CITY in 1899 and led by Rabbi Leon Reichelieu. The Ethiopian Hebrew Congregation (formally, the Commandment Keepers Congregation of the Living God, or Royal Order of Ethiopian Hebrews, the Sons and Daughters of Culture, Inc.) is one of the largest and is centered in HARLEM, New York. Its first chief rabbi, Wentworth Arthur Matthew, arrived in New York City in 1913 and saw that black people there who had come from the South and from the WEST INDIES were insecure in their new surroundings. He attributed this to the fact that SLAVERY had stripped them of the knowledge of their true identity and

RELIGION. Matthew incorporated his religion in 1930 and taught members that they were Ethiopian Hebrews or Falashas. Some black and other Jews object to the term "falasha," which derives from a term meaning "stranger," as it sets them apart rather than incorporating them into the Jewish community.

There were about one thousand black Jews in Harlem in 1970, and by 1980 there were about forty thousand black Jews (members of Ethiopian Hebrew congregations) across the United States. Many black Jews identify strongly with the nation of Israel. Others stay separated, fearing suspicion and uneasiness if they were to try to enter the predominantly white world of Jewish religion. Many cannot prove their eligibility to be Orthodox Jews to a rabbinical court, even though they have worshiped for years, because eligibility requires one to have a Jewish mother or to be brought into the faith by a properly ordained rabbi. Many of the African American rabbis are self-taught and self-proclaimed, having learned information about the Jewish religion and its practices informally. Most black Jews trace their ancestry to West Africa or to East Africa and link themselves in some way to the Ethiopian Jews who are often referred to as Falashas.

Hector, Edward (c. 1744—1834): AMERICAN REVOLUTION soldier. Hector was mustered into the Patriot army as a volunteer on March 10, 1777. He was in charge of an ammunition wagon at the Battle of Brandywine. Given orders to abandon the wagon and retreat, he refused, gathered firearms left on the battlefield, then managed to take his wagon and horses out of range of the advancing enemy.

Height, Dorothy Irene (b. March 24, 1912, Richmond, Virginia): Administrator. Best known as the fourth president of the NATIONAL COUNCIL OF NEGRO WOMEN, Height had an active career in various WOMEN'S, CIVIL RIGHTS, and community service groups. She attempted to attend Barnard College but was told that she would have to wait at least one term because the school already had two black students. Instead, she attended New York University, where she earned bachelor's and master's degrees. She also studied at the New York School of Social Work.

Height began her civil rights activities during the GREAT DEPRESSION, as an officer of the HARLEM Christian Youth Council. In that position, she worked closely with Congressman Adam Clayton POWELL, Jr. She began a two-

Dorothy Irene Height in early 1998. *(AP/Wide World Photos)*

decade association with the Young Women's Christian Association (YWCA) in 1937, joining the Harlem branch. She later was put in charge of desegregation of the activities for the YWCA. The group professed to be interracial, but there was some segregation. Height also was at one time the YWCA's associate director for leadership training services.

Also during the Depression, Height became interested in the problems of working women and the poor. She urged domestic workers to organize to fight against the less-than-subsistence wages paid to them. She became a NEW YORK CITY welfare department caseworker in 1934 and later served on numerous commissions, including the New York State Social Welfare Board (1958-1968).

Height continued to be interested in and consulted about women's issues. From 1952 to 1955, she was a member of the Defense Advisory Committee on Women in the Services. She also was a visiting professor at the Delhi School of Social Work in New Delhi, India, in the fall of 1952. In 1957 she became the president of the National Council of Negro Women. Previously, she had been on the council's board of directors and had been executive director. She served into the 1990's as president of this civil rights organization with about four million members. Height led the group in making monetary and volunteer time contributions to voter registration and education drives and in giving financial aid from her organization to students who interrupted their studies to work in the Civil Rights movement. The council operated Operation Women Push, a vocational training and business-founding program, in the 1960's, again showing Height's concern with working women.

Height's work has also taken an international scope. In 1960 she visited five African countries to study their women's organizations for the Committee on Correspondence. She also designed a program sponsored by the Agency for International Development and played a major role in the 1974-1975 International Women's Year programs. Height has, in addition, served as a consultant on African affairs to the U.S. secretary of state. Among her many commendations and awards for her work is the Distinguished Service Award (1978) from the NATIONAL NEWSPAPER PUBLISHERS ASSOCIATION (NNPA), a black press organization. She was the first woman to receive this award.

Hemings, Sally (1773-1835): Slave. A biracial house servant, Hemings was the property of Thomas Jefferson and lived most of her adult life at Monticello, Jefferson's plantation near Charlottesville, VIRGINIA.

Hemings's family history and lineal descent remain complex and confused. Her father was apparently John Wayles, Jefferson's father-in-law, so Jefferson's wife, Martha, and Sally were half-sisters. A woman known as Betty, who was a Wayles slave and was the daughter of an English sea captain, was Hemings's mother. With three white grandparents, Hemings was very light-skinned.

Accompanied by brothers John and James, she came to live at Monticello following the death of John Wayles. She gave birth to four children, born from 1798 to 1808. The disputed paternity of these children has intrigued a number of historians. Many interested parties have speculated that Jefferson was the father of one or more of Hemings's offspring. A relationship between Jefferson and Hemings was rumored even during his lifetime; in 1802 a writer in the *Richmond Recorder* claimed that Jefferson kept her as his "concubine." Among Hemings's descendants there has been a long-standing family tradition that they are descendants of Jefferson.

In 1998 the British science journal *Nature* published a DNA study by pathologist Eugene Foster. It indicated strong similarities between the DNA from blood samples of descendants of Jefferson's uncle Field Jefferson and descendants of one of Sally Hemings's children, Eston Hemings, born in 1808. The study found no particular genetic linkage between the Jefferson lineage and any other of Hemings's children. The tests convinced at least one previously skeptical Jefferson scholar, Joseph J. Ellis, that there indeed had been a relationship between Jefferson and Hemings. (Altogether, nineteen male descendants of the Jefferson and Hemings lineages were tested; only men could by used in the test because of the nature of DNA transmission through generations. Thomas Jefferson had no sons, so no direct descendants of his could be tested.) The media quickly spread the story, generally claiming that the tests proved Jefferson's paternity.

The combination of DNA and historical evidence indicates a strong probability that Jefferson was Eston Hemings's father; however, this is not absolutely certain. Three months after the initial publication, *Nature* took a step backward, quoting Foster as noting that the tests, by their nature, could not be conclusive; he said, "We never proved it. We never can. We never will." Jefferson's younger brother Randolph, for example, or one of Randolph's sons, all of whom were sometimes at Monticello, could have been the father.

Moreover, Hemings's children were born at a time when Jefferson was often ill and was between the advanced ages of fifty-five and sixty-five. Jefferson cared deeply about keeping the respect of his daughters and polite society, and he knew that he was under constant surveillance by his bitter enemies, the Federalists. Jefferson himself called the rumors "calumny." Jefferson was also rarely home during the period in question; on the other hand, some historians have noted that, according to available records, Jefferson was always at Monticello eight or nine months before Hemings had a child.

—Frenesi Wheeler

Hendrix, Jimi (November 27, 1942, Seattle, Washington—September 18, 1970, London, England): Guitarist, songwriter, and singer. Jimi Hendrix was born Johnny Allen Hendrix, but his father had him renamed James Marshall Hendrix in 1946. Hendrix's parents, Al and Lucille, separated in 1949 and finally were divorced in December, 1951. Al Hendrix took custody of James (nicknamed "Jimmy") and his younger brother, Leon. Sporadically employed at the time, Al Hendrix had trouble providing for his sons; both frequently stayed with relatives. Sensitive, shy, and mercurial by temperament, Jimmy was dealt a severe blow when his mother died in 1958. In need of an emotional outlet, Hendrix bought a used guitar for five dollars and quickly mastered the basics of the instrument. A year later, in the summer of 1959, he joined a local sextet called the Rocking Kings (later called the Tomcats), bought his first electric guitar that fall, and steadily honed his musical skills by playing at dances in the Seattle, WASHINGTON, area over the next two years.

Legal Troubles and the Military
Hendrix attended Garfield High School in Seattle until the fall of 1960. He quit school without graduating and began to work with his father doing landscape gardening. Six months later, in early May of 1961, he was arrested for using a motor vehicle without permission. He was arrested again three days later for riding in a stolen vehicle. Implicated in a felony, Hendrix was offered two years' probation in lieu of a jail term if he enlisted in the service. He immediately joined the U.S. Army and completed eight weeks of basic training at Fort Ord, CALIFORNIA.

In early November, 1961, Hendrix was assigned to the jump school for the 101st Airborne Division at Fort Campbell, KENTUCKY. Shortly thereafter, he sent home for his electric guitar and joined with fellow paratrooper Billy Cox and others to form a band called the

King Kasuals that played at clubs on base and at nearby Clarksville, TENNESSEE. Hendrix also completed his jump training and was promoted to the rank of private first class, but as his passion for music grew, the regimen of army life lost its attraction. On his twenty-sixth parachute jump (in June, 1962), he broke his ankle and was happy to be discharged from the army on medical grounds.

Journeyman Days

Out of the service by early July, Hendrix settled in Clarksville and waited for Billy Cox's discharge in October. The two then relocated to Nashville and formed a new version of the King Kasuals that toured with the Marvelettes and Curtis MAYFIELD and the Impressions. Restless, Hendrix moved to Vancouver, British Columbia, to live with his grandmother,

Nora. He stayed there, playing in a local band, for only a few months before returning to Nashville in the spring of 1963. The rest of the year was spent with "Gorgeous George" Odell on a series of cross-country package tours that included such RHYTHM-AND-BLUES and SOUL-MUSIC luminaries as Sam COOKE, Jackie WILSON, and the SUPREMES.

Hendrix moved to NEW YORK CITY early in 1964 and almost immediately won first prize at the APOLLO THEATER's amateur night. Yet he remained unemployed until March. He was then hired by the Isley Brothers, with whom he toured North America for the next eight months. He quit the band in October, in Nashville, and rejoined Gorgeous George on tour with Sam COOKE. Left behind in Kansas City, Hendrix found his way to Atlanta, where he met the flamboyant "LITTLE RICHARD"

Jimi Hendrix (center) with drummer Mitch Mitchell and bassist Noel Redding of the Jimi Hendrix Experience. (MCA Records)

Penniman in January, 1965. Hendrix (who now called himself Maurice James) toured with Little Richard for the next six months. He then worked intermittently with Curtis Knight and the Squires until May of 1966. After short stints with bluesman King Curtis and a group called Carl Holmes and the Commanders, Hendrix finally formed his own band, Jimmy James and the Blue Flames, in June of 1966.

The Jimi Hendrix Experience

After four grueling years as an anonymous rhythm-and-blues guitarist, Hendrix happened upon his big break on the evening of July 5, 1966. Playing at the Cafe Wha? in New York City's Greenwich Village, he was discovered by Brian "Chas" Chandler, bass player for the Animals, a popular English rock group. Awed by Hendrix's musicianship, Chandler offered him a management contract and a trip to England to begin a long-delayed assault on pop stardom. Accepting his offer, Hendrix flew to London with Chandler in late September, simplifying the spelling of his first name to "Jimi" on the way for easier audience recognition. Auditions were held, and a rock trio was quickly formed. Called the Jimi Hendrix Experience, the band consisted of Hendrix on lead guitar and Englishmen Noel Redding on bass guitar and John "Mitch" Mitchell on drums.

Chandler and his partner, Mike Jeffery, wasted no time in launching the group. Rehearsals began on October 6, the day Mitchell was hired, and the Jimi Hendrix Experience played its first concert in Evreux, France, just a week later. What followed in the months ahead were numerous recording sessions, scores of concerts, and many television and radio appearances in cities throughout Europe and the United Kingdom. A single, "Hey Joe," was released in mid-December, followed by "Purple Haze," released in March, 1967, and "The Wind Cries Mary," released in early May along with Hendrix's first album, *Are You Experienced?* By dint of his relentless touring, flamboyant style, and dazzling musicianship, Hendrix had become a popular sensation in Europe in a scant six months. The American music industry also took notice; days after the release of the first album, Reprise Records signed a recording contract with the Jimi Hendrix Experience for $120,000.

Monterey and International Celebrity

Firmly established overseas, the Jimi Hendrix Experience was invited to debut in the United States on the last day of the Monterey International Pop Festival (June 16-18, 1967). The historic festival featured many of the top-name acts in pop music, including the Grateful Dead, the Mamas and the Papas, the Byrds, Simon and Garfunkel, the Jefferson Airplane, Janis Joplin, Otis REDDING, Eric Burdon and the Animals, and the Who, but Hendrix's swaggering, joyfully exuberant performance, climaxed by his setting his guitar on fire, was generally regarded as the high point of the festival and ensured his popular success in America.

Hendrix returned to England in late August after an ill-conceived and quickly aborted tour with the Monkees, an American band contrived in Hollywood to imitate the Beatles. He then started a European tour just before the American release of *Are You Experienced?*, and the remainder of the year was taken up with a constant succession of tour dates in England and on the Continent. (Hendrix's managers collected a percentage of his earnings; they therefore had every incentive to book him as often as possible.) A second album, *Axis: Bold as Love*, was released in early December to popular and critical acclaim. On January 2, 1968, Hendrix was named top musician in a *Melody Maker* poll.

Now a bona fide superstar, Hendrix appeared to be on top of the world. In reality, he was beginning to crack under the severe strain of phenomenal success, overwork, and a burgeoning drug and alcohol habit. He finally exploded on January 4, destroying his hotel room in Göteborg, Sweden, in a fit of drunken rage. The warning sign went unheeded, however, and the relentless routine continued; a four-month-long American tour that began in February was followed by tours of Europe and England and a return trip to the United States. A third album, *Electric Ladyland*, recorded in the spring and released in October of 1968, was a huge success; a single from it, Hendrix's version of Bob Dylan's "All Along the Watchtower," was a top-twenty hit.

The Last Years

At the peak of his career, Hendrix was subject to growing artistic frustrations, which he salved with ever more extravagant drug use. Typecast by both public and media as "the wild man of pop," Hendrix felt increasingly constrained by his garish image—and by his management, which worked him hard and wanted him to forsake musical innovation in favor of the "acid rock" formula that had made him famous. There were tensions between Hendrix, Mitchell, and Redding as well that finally caused the Jimi Hendrix Experience to dissolve, more or less permanently, at the end of 1968. Chas Chandler also quit, selling his management interest to Mike Jeffery for $300,000.

To add to Hendrix's troubles, the New York recording studio he was having built, Electric Ladyland, ran massively over budget. Furthermore, he was successfully sued by Curtis Knight's manager, Ed Chalpin, with whom he had signed a contract in 1965. Worse still, on May 3, 1969, Hendrix was arrested for possession of heroin by Canadian customs officials in Toronto. (He was eventually acquitted.) Though increasingly troubled, Hendrix did manage important triumphs: a historic performance of "The Star-Spangled Banner" at the Woodstock Festival on August 17, 1969, and a brilliant 1969-1970 New Year's Eve con-

Jimi Hendrix is remembered as the most influential rock guitarist of his era. *(MCA Records)*

cert with a newly formed group, the Band of Gypsys.

Jimi Hendrix died in London on September 18, 1970, from a barbiturate overdose. He continues to be widely revered as the most talented, innovative, and influential rock guitarist of the 1960's.

—*Robert Niemi*

See also: Blues; Music.

Suggested Readings:

Henderson, David. *Jimi Hendrix: Voodoo Child of the Aquarian Age*. Garden City, N.Y.: Doubleday, 1978.

_____. *'Scuse Me While I Kiss the Sky: The Life of Jimi Hendrix*. Rev. ed. New York: Bantam Books, 1981.

Hendrix, Jimi. *Jimi Hendrix: In His Own Words*. Edited by Tony Brown. New York: Omnibus Press, 1994.

Hopkins, Jerry. *The Jimi Hendrix Experience*. New York: Arcade, 1996.

Mitchell, Mitch, and John Platt. *The Hendrix Experience.* New York: Da Capo Press, 1998.

Murray, Charles S. *Crosstown Traffic: Jimi Hendrix and the Post-war Rock 'n' Roll Revolution.* New York: St. Martin's Press, 1989.

Potash, Chris, ed. *The Jimi Hendrix Companion: Three Decades of Commentary.* New York: Schirmer Books, 1996.

Redding, Noel, and Carol Appleby. *Are You Experienced?: The Inside Story of the Jimi Hendrix Experience.* New York: Da Capo Press, 1996.

Shapiro, Harry, and Caesar Glebbeek. *Electric Gypsy: Jimi Hendrix.* New York: St. Martin's Press, 1991.

Willix, Mary. *Jimi Hendrix: Voices from Home.* San Diego, Calif.: Creative Forces, 1995.

Henson, Josiah (June 15, 1789, Port Tobacco, Maryland—1883?, Dresden, Ontario, Can-

Famous as a fugitive slave during his time, Josiah Henson has been called the model for the title character in Uncle Tom's Cabin; however, Harriet Beecher Stowe's Uncle Tom was never a fugitive. *(Library of Congress)*

ada): Escaped slave. Henson, with his wife and four children, escaped across the Ohio River and fled to Canada in 1830. His autobiography, *The Life of Josiah Henson, Formerly a Slave, Now an Inhabitant of Canada, as Narrated by Himself* (1849), underwent several revisions, including *Truth Is Stranger than Fiction: Father Henson's Story of His Own Life* (1858). Henson became one of the most celebrated of the fugitive slaves when he was identified as Harriet Beecher Stowe's model for the title character in UNCLE TOM'S CABIN (1852). Historians continue to dispute whether he was, in fact, the model.

Henson, Matthew Alexander (August 8, 1866, Charles County, Maryland—March 9, 1955, New York, New York): Explorer. Orphaned at age eight, Henson went to live with an uncle in WASHINGTON, D.C., where he attended public school. At age twelve, he joined the crew of a merchant vessel and spent the next several years at sea. He was working at an F. W. Stinemetz & Sons store in 1887 when Robert E. Peary entered as a customer. Peary convinced Henson to join his surveying expedition in Nicaragua, the beginning of a twenty-three-year association that culminated in their arrival at the North Pole on April 6, 1909.

Henson and Peary made eight Arctic voyages, and Henson became an indispensable part of Peary's team. Henson was the only one to learn the Inuit language, and he was skilled in building boats, repairing sledges, hunting, driving a dog team, and building igloos. Although Peary sent back the rest of his support team as it neared the North Pole, he kept Henson with him. Henson, the only American on the North Pole expedition, planted the U.S. flag and was the first person actually to reach the pole.

Arctic explorer Matthew Henson. *(Library of Congress)*

After retiring from Peary's group, Henson had difficulty finding employment. He worked first as a parking attendant and later as a messenger for the U.S. Customs Bureau in NEW YORK CITY. Henson published his autobiography, *A Negro Explorer at the North Pole*, in 1912. He was elected an honorary member of the Explorers Club in 1937, the first African American to be so recognized. He received a silver medal from the U.S. Navy and honorary M.S. degrees from HOWARD UNIVERSITY and Morgan State College (Baltimore). A bronze plaque in his honor was erected in the MARYLAND State House, the first time an African American has been so honored in the South.

Henson was married to Eva Helen Flint from April, 1891, to 1897, and to Lucy Jane Ross from September 7, 1907, until his death. Henson claimed no children from these marriages. Anaukaq, an Inuit, believes that he was the son of Henson, who was known as Mahri-

Pahluk ("Matthew the Kind One"), conceived while Henson was living with his mother, Akatingwah, in 1902 in Greenland.

Henson was buried in Woodlawn Cemetery in the Bronx, New York. He was reinterred on April 6, 1988, in Arlington National Cemetery, where Peary was buried earlier.

See also: Exploration of North America.

Herndon, Alonzo F. (June 26, 1858, Walton County, Georgia—July 21, 1927, Atlanta, Georgia): Businessman. Herndon's business activities began with barbering. Later, he was engaged in real estate development and insurance, earning a fortune with the Atlanta Life Insurance Company, founded in 1905. That company was one of the largest owned by an African American in the United States. Herndon's son, Norris, established the Alonzo F. and Norris B. Herndon Foundation to extend Herndon's philanthropic activities.

See also: Business and commerce; Life insurance companies.

Herskovits, Melville J. (September 10, 1895, Bellefontaine, Ohio—February 25, 1963, Evanston, Illinois): Anthropologist. The founder of scientific African American studies and the first Africanist in the United States, Melville Jean Herskovits has had a lasting impact on the study of African and African American cultures.

Herskovits devoted his career to countering misconceptions about race. His contributions range from music and art to economics, psychology, theoretical formulations, and the practical application of anthropology to daily life. His work showed the transmission of culture from AFRICA to the Americas and overturned the myth, widely accepted at the time, that African Americans had no past.

Born to Jewish European parents, Herskovits spent his early childhood in El Paso, TEXAS. After his mother's death, Herskovits's family moved to Erie, PENNSYLVANIA, when he was ten years old. In 1915 Herskovits matriculated at the University of Cincinnati, followed by a stint at the Hebrew Union College, where he studied theology. Briefly serving in the Medical Corps during WORLD WAR I, Herskovits graduated from the University of Chicago with a degree in history in 1920.

It was not until his graduate studies at Columbia University that Herskovits began to pursue anthropology as a career. At Columbia he had as a mentor the anthropological luminary Franz Boas. He also developed intellectual exchanges and friendships with the noted sociologist Thorstein Veblen and with anthropologists Margaret Mead, Ruth Benedict, and Elsie Clews Parsons.

Between 1924 and 1927, Herskovits lectured at Columbia, after which he taught briefly at HOWARD UNIVERSITY, a black university in WASHINGTON, D.C. His friendships among the Howard faculty included relationships with such highly esteemed African American intellectuals as Alain LOCKE, E. Franklin FRAZIER, Ralph BUNCHE, and Sterling BROWN.

Herskovits spent the majority of his academic career at Northwestern University, where he taught from 1927 until his death in 1963. Though the university had at that time no department of anthropology, Herskovits managed to become the only anthropologist in the department of sociology. It was largely through his efforts that Northwestern eventually established the Department of Anthropology and the university's Interdisciplinary Program of African Studies. In 1961 Herskovits was appointed to the first chair of African studies in the United States.

Herskovits's career led him to field research throughout Africa and the African diaspora. His subjects of study included among other things, Haitian VOODOO, Dahomean religious practices, and the amalgamation of races in the United States. Among his numerous publications are his classic books *The Myth of the Negro Past* (1941), *The New World Negro: Selected Papers in Afroamerican Studies* (1966), and the posthumously published *Cultural Relativism* (1973).

Within his vast body of work, the most famous of Herskovits's theses was the argument that African Americans had maintained certain cultural forms, such as linguistic structures, FOLKLORE, and religious practices, as well as music and dance, that originated in Af-

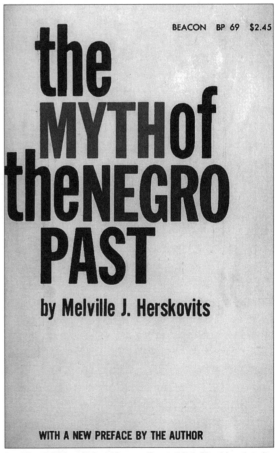

In *The Myth of the Negro Past*, Melville Herskovits demonstrated ways in which West African culture still influenced African American life. *(Arkent Archive)*

rica. Even more controversially, he proposed that some of these Africanisms had become a part of white culture. Herskovits observed that the transmission of African cultural traits was more evident in countries such as Brazil and HAITI than in the United States because of a lesser degree of racial isolation and a lower black-to-white ratio in the United States. In opposition to many of the hierarchical cultural assumptions of his day, Herskovits also advanced the notion of cultural relativism—the idea that no culture possesses an objective set of "correct" values.

—*Elizabeth R. Moore*

See also: African cultural transformations; African languages and American English; African music and dance; Black studies; Diaspora, African.

Suggested Readings:

Harris, Marvin. *The Rise of Anthropological Theory.* New York: Columbia University, 1968.

Hays, H. R. *From Ape to Angel: An Informal History of Social Anthropology.* New York: Alfred A. Knopf, 1958.

Herskovitz, Melville. *The American Negro.* Reprint. Westport, Conn.: Greenwood Press, 1985.

_____. *The Myth of the Negro Past.* Reprint. Boston: Beacon Press, 1990.

Simpson, George Eaton. *Melville J. Herskovits.* New York: Columbia University Press, 1973.

Higginbotham, A. Leon, Jr. (February 25, 1928, Trenton, New Jersey—December 14, 1998, Boston, Massachusetts): Government official. Higginbotham earned his LL.B. from Yale University in 1952. He became the first African American trustee of Yale in 1969. He was appointed to the Federal Trade Commission in 1962. On October 13, 1977, President Jimmy Carter appointed Higginbotham as a circuit judge on the U.S. Court of Appeals.

Higginbotham wrote *The Colonial Period* (1978), the first volume in *In the Matter of Color: Race and the American Legal Process.* The book has received several national citations.

See also: Judges.

Higgins, Chester A., Sr. (May 10, 1917, Chicago, Illinois—May 25, 2000, Washington, D.C.): Journalist and political appointee. Higgins served in the U.S. Army during WORLD WAR II. After his discharge, he attended Kentucky State College from 1946 to 1947 and Louisville Municipal College between 1948 and 1950. He became a reporter and feature writer for the *Louisville Defender* newspaper and for EBONY and *Tan* magazines before being named associate editor of JET magazine in 1959. Higgins also was a pioneering educator who taught a course in black journalism at Malcolm X College from 1971 to 1972.

Higgins left his position at *Jet* in 1972, when he became general assistant to Benjamin HOOKS, the first African American commissioner of the Federal Communications Agency. In 1977 Higgins was appointed by President Jimmy Carter to serve as assistant chief of public affairs for media relations for the Office of the Secretary of the Army. After leaving this post in 1981, Higgins became communications consultant for the NATIONAL ASSOCIATION FOR THE ADVANCEMENT OF COLORED PEOPLE (NAACP), holding this position until 1983. He also served as editor-in-chief of THE CRISIS, the organization's official magazine publication.

Higgins served as a communications consultant for various organizations in the 1980's. In 1984 Higgins took the post of communications specialist with the University of the District of Columbia. He then became a volunteer communications consultant for the National Urban Coalition in 1986. He served as director of communications for the National Caucus and Center on Black Aged, Inc., and as news

Author Chester A. Higgins, Sr. *(© Roy Lewis Archives)*

editor and assistant director of the NATIONAL NEWSPAPER PUBLISHERS ASSOCIATION (NNPA) between 1987 and 1989. In 1990 he became communications consultant and editor for the National Organization of Black Law Enforcement Officials.

See also: Black press.

Higher education: African Americans do not question the value of EDUCATION. A higher education is often the key to a job, career advancement, and economic success. For many college-age African Americans, the pursuit of advanced schooling still represents a difficult challenge despite the changes ushered in by the CIVIL RIGHTS movement of the 1960's.

Historical Background
Just prior to the conclusion of the CIVIL WAR in 1865, Congress created the Bureau of Refugees,

Freedmen, and Abandoned Lands, better known as the FREEDMEN'S BUREAU. One of the bureau's most significant contributions to the welfare of newly freed blacks was the creation of hundreds of freedmen's schools in the South, most of which were supported through the efforts of various churches and charitable organizations. These efforts in the area of elementary education prompted the establishment of a system of colleges that would provide blacks with access to the benefits of higher education and would train those with talent to become teachers, doctors, lawyers, and ministers. Schools such as FISK UNIVERSITY, HOWARD UNIVERSITY, Morehouse College, and Talladega College were founded in the late 1860's to provide the kinds of educational opportunities in the South that had been extended by a few northern institutions of higher learning such as OBERLIN COLLEGE in Ohio and LINCOLN UNIVERSITY in Pennsylvania.

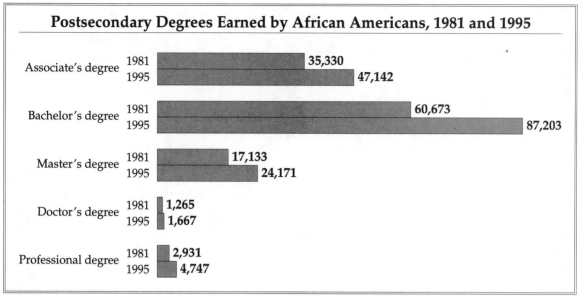

Postsecondary Degrees Earned by African Americans, 1981 and 1995

Associate's degree	1981	35,330
	1995	47,142
Bachelor's degree	1981	60,673
	1995	87,203
Master's degree	1981	17,133
	1995	24,171
Doctor's degree	1981	1,265
	1995	1,667
Professional degree	1981	2,931
	1995	4,747

Source: U.S. National Center for Education Statistics.
Note: Data do not include some institutions that do not report a "field of study" and are therefore a slight undercount of degrees awarded.

In 1823 Alexander Twilight became the first African American to earn a college degree when he graduated from Vermont's Middlebury College, which had earlier awarded an honorary degree to Lemuel Haynes. *(AP/Wide World Photos)*

Early Education and High School Completion
Success in higher education is contingent upon adequate early educational preparation. Instilling in children at an early age the value of an education is critical in order for them to associate early education with achievement in coming years. Black children must see the need to enter the educational pipeline early and stay in it in order to meet college and university admissions criteria.

The gap between the high-school completion rate of African Americans and whites between the ages of eighteen and twenty-four narrowed substantially between 1985 and 1998, as the percentage of blacks completing SECONDARY EDUCATION increased at twice the white completion rate. Nevertheless, the high-school dropout problem remained a particular source of concern to African Americans; for the 1985-1986 school year alone, an average of 3,789 U.S. teenagers dropped out of school each day, and a disproportionately high percentage of such dropouts were black. Although the overall percentage of high-school dropouts fell significantly between 1975 and

1996 (from 27.3 percent to 16 percent), reductions in the annual dropout rate during this period declined more gradually (from 8.7 percent to 6.3 percent).

College Enrollment

Many African Americans can afford college only with the assistance of grants and loans because of the steep, and rising, costs of a college education. In 1990 race-based scholarships used to ensure racial diversity on college campuses were briefly deemed to be violations of the Civil Rights Act of 1964. Actions by the U.S. Department of Education, however, allowed racially based scholarships to continue provided such scholarships were funded by private donations.

In 1996 31.3 percent of all African Americans between the ages of eighteen and twenty-one were enrolled in college, compared with 45.3 percent of white Americans of the same ages. Although the enrollment rate of blacks increased from 1975 to 1996, the percentage of increase for blacks (6.4 percent) was substantially less than the increase for whites (10.7 percent). In order for the college-attendance rate of young black men to increase, experts believe that socialization of this group must begin as early as elementary school, when children are introduced to the values, expectations, and standards that can keep them focused on a good education as a reachable goal.

In 1996 an estimated 1.5 million African Americans were enrolled in U.S. institutions of higher education. During this same period, the nation's HISTORICALLY BLACK COLLEGES and universities experienced a significant increase in the number of African American stu-

During the 1990's only 30 percent of all African American students who entered four-year colleges and universities eventually graduated, compared to 55 percent of white students. *(Hazel Hankin)*

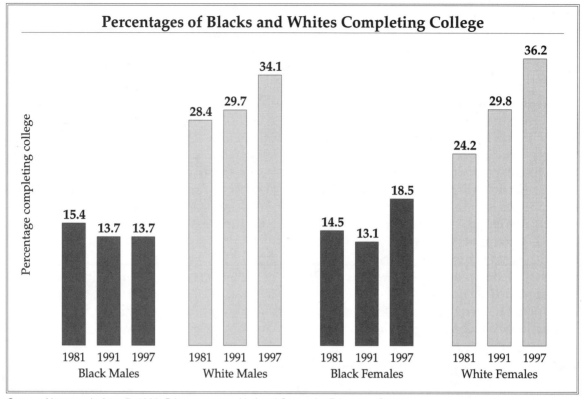

Percentages of Blacks and Whites Completing College

Percentage completing college

15.4	13.7	13.7	28.4	29.7	34.1	14.5	13.1	18.5	24.2	29.8	36.2
1981	1991	1997	1981	1991	1997	1981	1991	1997	1981	1991	1997
Black Males			White Males			Black Females			White Females		

Source: Newsweek, June 7, 1999. Primary source, National Center for Education Statistics.
Note: Percentages represent 25-to-29-year-olds who completed four or more years of college.

dents. Between 1987 and 1989, African American enrollment in black colleges rose 9.9 percent, while other institutions experienced a 3.5 percent gain in black enrollment. In 1988 19 percent of all African American college students attended historically black schools. The overall number of blacks enrolling in historically black schools actually declined during the 1980's (from 215,958 in 1980 to 208,682 in 1990) but had rebounded to 223,498 by 1996, indicating a modest resurgence of interest in black colleges among young African Americans.

Improving Graduation Rates
Statistically, African Americans who attend college stay in school at much lower rates than students of other ethnic groups. College students' persistence is influenced by a variety of factors, including college aspirations, socio-economic status, availability of financial support, academic preparedness, attitude, motivation, institutional selectivity and environment, campus climate, faculty involvement with students, and academic and personal counseling. Many black students who have the ability, motivation, and academic preparation to succeed in college encounter stressful environments—even racist environments—that cause them to leave school before graduation.

Statistics from the early 1990's indicate that 70 percent of all African Americans enrolled in four-year colleges and universities dropped out before graduation, compared with 45 percent of whites. A variety of explanations have been advanced to explain the highly unequal educational achievement of black Americans compared with white Americans. Some explanations cite historical factors such as the legacy of SLAVERY, segregation, and long-standing lack of economic opportunity. Others focus more upon environmental factors such as family instability, drug-infested communities, and other POVERTY-related social problems as responsible for low educational achievement. Some analysts have blamed African American culture for not fostering values critical to school achievement. Nevertheless, these explanations cannot fully account for the high dropout rate among black college students whose Scholastic Aptitude Test (SAT) scores indicate that their preparation for college studies is well above average.

One clue to the relatively high failure rate of such students may lie in the development of peer pressure that classifies academic success as "selling out" to white mainstream society. Some leading black sociologists and educators believe that this alienation is part of a pattern in which black students, categorized as minority students at risk for academic failure, become fearful of confirming their supposed educational inferiority. As a result, these students become coolly disinterested in academic performance, choosing to transfer their attention to other areas of achievement in order to shore up their flagging self-esteem.

Solutions
Several solutions have been advanced to address the problem of helping black youths succeed in higher education. At predominantly white colleges, African American faculty members are often few in comparison to the black student population. Because black PROFESSORS serve as positive role models and provide a needed base of support as mentors and advisers, they have been more vigorously recruited by some predominantly white colleges. Other schools have focused their attention on the creation of accelerated programs that inspire black students to overcome deficits in their education by pooling their skills in a cooperative learning environment and reas-

suring them as to their academic potential to attack challenging work. Regardless of the types of methods proposed for encouraging black success in higher education, colleges and universities are generally more aware than in the past of the particular challenges facing black students and are trying to work with them to help them succeed.

—*Emma T. Lucas*
—*Updated by Michael H. Burchett*
See also: Intellectuals and scholars; Intelligence and achievement testing.

Suggested Readings:

Allen, Walter R., Edgar G. Epps, and Nesha Z. Haniff, eds. *College in Black and White.* Albany: State University of New York Press, 1991.

Bullock, Henry A. *A History of Negro Education in the South.* Cambridge, Mass.: Harvard University Press, 1967.

Committee on the Status of Black Americans, Panel on Education. "The Schooling of Black Americans." In *A Common Destiny: Blacks and American Society*, edited by Gerald D. Jaynes and Robin M. Williams. Washington, D.C.: National Academy Press, 1989.

Moskowitz, Milton. "The Best Business Schools for Blacks." *Business and Society Review* (Winter, 1994): 43-52.

"One-Third of a Nation: A Report of the Commission on Minority Participation in Education and American Life." Washington, D.C.: American Council on Education, 1988.

Richardson, Richard C., and Louis W. Bender. *Fostering Minority Success and Achievement in Higher Education.* San Francisco: Jossey-Bass, 1987.

Hill, Anita Faye (b. July 30, 1956, Lone Tree, Oklahoma): Attorney, law professor, and government appointee. The youngest of thirteen children born to a devout BAPTIST family, Hill attended the local high school in nearby Mor-

Anita Hill testifying during the Clarence Thomas hearings. *(AP/Wide World Photos)*

ris and graduated as class valedictorian. She graduated with honors in 1977 with a B.A. degree in psychology from Oklahoma State University, and then attended Yale Law School, where she graduated with honors in 1980. After passing the bar examination, she went into private practice as an attorney in WASHINGTON, D.C., for one year before being hired to serve under Clarence THOMAS as special counsel at the Department of Education's Office of CIVIL RIGHTS, a position she held from 1981 to 1982. When Thomas was appointed by President Ronald Reagan to serve as chairman of the EQUAL EMPLOYMENT OPPORTUNITY COMMISSION (EEOC) in 1982, Hill took a post as special assistant to Thomas. She left the EEOC in 1983 to accept a teaching position on the faculty of Oral Roberts University in Oklahoma. She left Oral Roberts in 1988 to take a post as a law professor at the University of Oklahoma, where she specialized in commercial and contract law.

In 1991 Hill came under intense national scrutiny during the Senate hearings on Clarence Thomas's appointment to the U.S. SUPREME COURT. Before the final confirmation vote was taken, a confidential FEDERAL BUREAU OF INVESTIGATION (FBI) report containing Hill's allegations of sexual misconduct and harassment against Thomas was leaked to the press. The Senate panel reconvened the hearings in order to investigate Hill's charges, and she appeared before the panel to testify to the incidents which she claimed had occurred during her employment as Thomas's assistant. While Hill's testimony was very convincing, Thomas continued to deny her charges and public opinion was split regarding who was telling the truth. The Senate committee was ultimately unable to determine the validity of the charges and voted to recommend Thomas's confirmation. The full Senate confirmed Thomas's nomination by a vote of 52 to 48 on October 15, 1991.

In the aftermath of the hearings, Hill was bombarded with offers to make public appearances addressing the topic of sexual harassment. Horrified by Hill's treatment by the all-male Senate panel, many women pointed to Hill as a rallying symbol in their efforts to support female candidates for national and local offices in the 1992 political elections.

Hill, Bertha "Chippie" (March 15, 1905, Charleston, South Carolina—May 7, 1950, New York, New York): Singer. Hill first came to prominence as a dancer in popular singer Ethel WATERS's show before touring as a vocalist with blues artist Ma RAINEY. She performed with artists such as Louis ARMSTRONG and Thomas DORSEY. She retired in the early 1930's but was rediscovered in 1946. She appeared at the Blue Note Club and at Carnegie Hall in the later phase of her career.
See also: Blues; Music.